IMPOSING THEIR WILL

MCGILL-QUEEN'S STUDIES IN ETHNIC HISTORY
SERIES ONE: DONALD HARMAN AKENSON, EDITOR

1 Irish Migrants in the Canadas
   A New Approach
   Bruce S. Elliott
   (Second edition, 2004)

2 Critical Years in Immigration
   Canada and Australia Compared
   Freda Hawkins
   (Second edition, 1991)

3 Italians in Toronto
   Development of a National
   Identity, 1875–1935
   John E. Zucchi

4 Linguistics and Poetics of Latvian
   Folk Songs
   Essays in Honour of the Sesqui-
   centennial of the Birth of Kr.
   Barons
   Vaira Vikis-Freibergs

5 Johan Schroder's Travels in
   Canada, 1863
   Orm Overland

6 Class, Ethnicity, and Social
   Inequality
   Christopher McAll

7 The Victorian Interpretation of
   Racial Conflict
   The Maori, the British, and the
   New Zealand Wars
   James Belich

8 White Canada Forever
   Popular Attitudes and Public
   Policy toward Orientals in
   British Columbia
   W. Peter Ward
   (Third edition, 2002)

9 The People of Glengarry
   Highlanders in Transition,
   1745–1820
   Marianne McLean

10 Vancouver's Chinatown
   Racial Discourse in Canada,
   1875–1980
   Kay J. Anderson

11 Best Left as Indians
   Native-White Relations in the
   Yukon Territory, 1840–1973
   Ken Coates

12 Such Hardworking People
   Italian Immigrants in Postwar
   Toronto
   Franca Iacovetta

13 The Little Slaves of the Harp
   Italian Child Street Musicians in
   Nineteenth-Century Paris,
   London, and New York
   John E. Zucchi

14 The Light of Nature and the Law
   of God
   Antislavery in Ontario, 1833–1877
   Allen P. Stouffer

15 Drum Songs
   Glimpses of Dene History
   Kerry Abel

16 Louis Rosenberg
   Canada's Jews
   (Reprint of 1939 original)
   Edited by Morton Weinfeld

17 A New Lease on Life
   Landlords, Tenants, and Immi-
   grants in Ireland and Canada
   Catharine Anne Wilson

18 In Search of Paradise
   The Odyssey of an Italian Family
   Susan Gabori

19 Ethnicity in the Mainstream
   Three Studies of English
   Canadian Culture in Ontario
   Pauline Greenhill

20 Patriots and Proletarians
   The Politicization of Hungarian
   Immigrants in Canada, 1923–1939
   Carmela Patrias

21 The Four Quarters of the Night
   The Life-Journey of an Emigrant
   Sikh
   *Tara Singh Bains and Hugh
   Johnston*

22 Cultural Power, Resistance, and
   Pluralism
   Colonial Guyana, 1838–1900
   Brian L. Moore

23 Search Out the Land
   The Jews and the Growth of
   Equality in British Colonial
   America, 1740–1867
   *Sheldon J. Godfrey and
   Judith C. Godfrey*

24 The Development of Elites in
   Acadian New Brunswick, 1861–
   1881
   Sheila M. Andrew

25 Journey to Vaja
   Reconstructing the World of a
   Hungarian-Jewish Family
   Elaine Kalman Naves

SERIES TWO: JOHN ZUCCHI, EDITOR

1 Inside Ethnic Families
  Three Generations of Portuguese-
  Canadians
  Edite Noivo

2 A House of Words
  Jewish Writing, Identity, and
  Memory
  Norman Ravvin

3 Oatmeal and the Catechism
  Scottish Gaelic Settlers in Quebec
  Margaret Bennett

4 With Scarcely a Ripple
  Anglo-Canadian Migration into
  the United States and Western
  Canada, 1880–1920
  Randy William Widdis

5 Creating Societies
  Immigrant Lives in Canada
  Dirk Hoerder

6 Social Discredit
  Anti-Semitism, Social Credit, and
  the Jewish Response
  Janine Stingel

7 Coalescence of Styles
  The Ethnic Heritage of St John
  River Valley Regional Furniture,
  1763–1851
  Jane L. Cook

8 Brigh an Orain / A Story in Every
  Song
  The Songs and Tales of Lauchie
  MacLellan
  Translated and edited by John Shaw

9 Demography, State and Society
  Irish Migration to Britain,
  1921–1971
  Enda Delaney

10 The West Indians of Costa Rica
   Race, Class, and the Integration of
   an Ethnic Minority
   Ronald N. Harpelle

11 Canada and the Ukrainian Question, 1939–1945
   Bohdan S. Kordan

12 Tortillas and Tomatoes
   Transmigrant Mexican Harvesters
   in Canada
   Tanya Basok

13 Old and New World Highland Bagpiping
John G. Gibson

14 Nationalism from the Margins
The Negotiation of Nationalism and Ethnic Identities among Italian Immigrants in Alberta and British Columbia
Patricia Wood

15 Colonization and Community
The Vancouver Island Coalfield and the Making of the British Columbia Working Class
John Douglas Belshaw

16 Enemy Aliens, Prisoners of War
Internment in Canada during the Great War
Bohdan S. Kordan

17 Like Our Mountains
A History of Armenians in Canada
Isabel Kaprielian-Churchill

18 Exiles and Islanders
The Irish Settlers of Prince Edward Island
Brendan O'Grady

19 Ethnic Relations in Canada
Institutional Dynamics
Raymond Breton
Edited by Jeffrey G. Reitz

20 A Kingdom of the Mind
The Scots' Impact on the Development of Canada
Edited by Peter Rider and Heather McNabb

21 Vikings to U-Boats
The German Experience in Newfoundland and Labrador
Gerhard P. Bassler

22 Being Arab
Ethnic and Religious Identity Building among Second Generation Youth in Montreal
Paul Eid

23 From Peasants to Labourers
Ukrainian and Belarusan Immigration from the Russian Empire to Canada
Vadim Kukushkin

24 Emigrant Worlds and Transatlantic Communities
Migration to Upper Canada in the First Half of the Nineteenth Century
Elizabeth Jane Errington

25 Jerusalem on the Amur
Birobidzhan and the Canadian Jewish Communist Movement, 1924–1951
Henry Felix Srebrnik

26 Irish Nationalism in Canada
Edited by David A. Wilson

27 Managing the Canadian Mosaic in Wartime
Shaping Citizenship Policy, 1939–1945
Ivana Caccia

28 Jewish Roots, Canadian Soil
Yiddish Culture in Montreal, 1905–1945
Rebecca Margolis

29 Imposing Their Will
An Organizational History of Jewish Toronto, 1933–1948
Jack Lipinsky

Imposing Their Will

An Organizational History of Jewish Toronto, 1933–1948

JACK LIPINSKY

McGill-Queen's University Press
Montreal & Kingston · London · Ithaca

© McGill-Queen's University Press 2011
ISBN 978-0-7735-3845-0

Legal deposit second quarter 2011
Bibliothèque nationale du Québec

Printed in Canada on acid-free paper that is 100% ancient forest free (100% post-consumer recycled), processed chlorine free.

This book has been published with the help of a grant from the Canadian Federation for the Humanities and Social Sciences, through the Aid to Scholarly Publications Programme, using funds provided by the Social Sciences and Humanities Research Council of Canada.

McGill-Queen's University Press acknowledges the support of the Canada Council for the Arts for our publishing program. We also acknowledge the financial support of the Government of Canada through the Canada Book Fund for our publishing activities.

Library and Archives Canada Cataloguing in Publication

Lipinsky, Jack, 1957–
    Imposing their will : an organizational history of Jewish Toronto, 1933-1948 / Jack Lipinsky.

(McGill-Queen's studies in ethnic history, series two ; 29)
Includes bibliographical references and index.
ISBN 978-0-7735-3845-0

    1. Jews – Ontario – Toronto – Charities – History – 20th century. 2. Jews – Ontario – Toronto – Identity.
3. Jews – Ontario – Toronto – Social conditions – 20th century. 4. Jews – Ontario – Toronto – History – 20th century. I. Title. II. Series: McGill-Queen's studies in ethnic history. Series 2 ; 29

HV3193.C3L56 2011   361.7089'9240713541   C2011-900762-2

This book was typeset by True to Type in 10.5/13 Sabon

For Barbara

"All depends upon the woman"
Bereishit Rabbah 17:7

Contents

Abbreviations for Names of Organizations   xi
Acknowledgments   xv
Introduction   xix

1 The Road to Community: Toronto Jewry before 1933   3
2 Fragile Signs of Unity: 1933   33
3 The Federation of Jewish Philanthropies: Professionalization from Within, until 1934   59
4 The Toronto Jewish Immigrant Aid Society: "Long Distance" Professionalization, to 1937   79
5 Two Steps Forward and One Step Back: The Canadian Jewish Congress in Toronto, 1934–37   109
6 A Foundation of Unity: The Toronto Hebrew Free School and the Rise of the United Jewish Welfare Fund, 1933–39   153
7 Institutional and Communal Consolidation, 1938–43   177
8 "O Brave New World"? The Imposition of Will, 1943–48   209

Conclusion: Entering the Mainstream   269

Glossary of Individuals   285
Notes   289
Bibliography   337
Index   349

Abbreviations for Names of Organizations

ADL	Anti-Defamation League
AJC	American Jewish Congress
BJE	Board of Jewish Education
CAS	Children's Aid Society
CCF	Cooperative Commonwealth Federation
Central Division	Canadian Jewish Congress, Central Division, Toronto
CFC	Canadian Fur Commission
CJC	Canadian Jewish Congress
CJCR	Canadian Committee for Jewish Refugees
COGC	Canadian Overseas Garment Committee
COJFWF	Council of Jewish Federations and Welfare Funds
COJW	Council of Jewish Women
Congress	Canadian Jewish Congress, Montreal
COS	Charity Organization Society
FCS	Federation for Community Service
FEPA	Fair Employment Practices Act
FJP	Federation of Jewish Philanthropies
FWB	Family Welfare Bureau
ILGWU	International Ladies' Garment Workers Union

IRO	International Refugee Organization
JCB	Jewish Children's Bureau
JCCA	Jewish Centre for Educational and Cultural Activities
JCH	Jewish Childrens' Home of Toronto
JDC	Joint Distribution Committee
JECIT	Jewish Educational and Community Institute of Toronto
JFCS	Jewish Family and Child Services
JFWB	Jewish Family Welfare Bureau
JIAS	Jewish Immigrant Aid Society
JLC	Jewish Labour Committee
JPRC	Joint Public Relations Committee of Canadian Jewish Congress and B'nai Brith
JVS	Jewish Vocational Service
NWA	Neighbourhood Workers' Association
OJA	Ontario Jewish Archives
ORT	People's Organization for Rehabilitation through Training
THBA	Toronto Hebrew Benevolent Association
TZC	Toronto Zionist Council
UCC	United Community Chest
UJRA	United Jewish Relief Agencies of Canada
UJRWRA	United Jewish Refugee and War Relief Agencies
UJRWRA-JDC	United Jewish Refugee & War Relief Agencies Joint Distribution Committee
UJWF	United Jewish Welfare Fund of Toronto, 1937–76
UNRRA	United Nationals Relief and Rehabilitation Association
UPA	United Palestine Appeal

USNA	United Service for New Americans
UWF	United Welfare Fund
YMHA	Young Men's Hebrew Association
YWHA	Young Women's Hebrew Association
ZOC	Zionist Organization of Canada

Acknowledgments

The road to completing this work was almost as long and tortuous as the story of the "imposers of will" this narrative chronicles. This book had its genesis as a doctoral thesis under the supervision of the late and lamented Robert F. Harney, who lived only long enough to read and approve of what is now chapter 2. Bob was a key figure in making Canadian ethnic history an area of serious academic study. His keen wit, generosity of spirit, and humour are alive in my memory. I deeply regret his being unable to read these words, for much of my initial inspiration came from him.

After Bob's untimely passing, I continued my thesis without a supervisor. All but one chapter was completed when my wife, Barbara, became pregnant, and we agreed that I should go to work. I put the thesis on hold and joined the staff of the United Synagogue Day School, now Robbins Hebrew Academy, where I have taught ever since. The thesis sat on old computer disks, seemingly relegated to those things in life that just never get done. As our family grew apace with my teaching career, the disks gathered dust, and I had little time for nostalgia or resentment.

Barbara would have none of this. She pressed me to take a sabbatical, insisting that the family could survive on less but that I would die embittered if I did not complete what I had set out to do so long ago. But technology had taken its toll. The original disks were now unreadable in their "ancient" format; I was about to become a victim of the central subject of my research – change. But here the hand of God – or Fate, depending on your point of view – suddenly appeared. One of my friends, computer engineer Ilia Kaufman, heard my story, took the disks home, and returned the next day with an IBM-readable copy. Heartened, I searched for a supervisor. Once again, Heaven smiled. Professor Janice Stein, whom I knew as a parent and friend rather than as the noted academic she is, introduced me to Hesh Troper, but only on condition that I promised to finish the thesis. Hesh proved a wonderful mentor, ever generous with his time, hospitality, advice, and humour. He sat me down in his kitchen, proceeded to edit my manuscript mercilessly, and sent me off to update my secondary sources. Hesh was a tough master, who taught me to write crisply and clearly, and demanded that I ask and answer difficult questions. This work is all the better for it. Janice, to make sure that her advice was taken, joined the dissertation committee and reworked her busy schedule to attend my oral defence. Her smile and the tears in Hesh's eyes when he announced, "you did it," after an eighteen-year hiatus testified to their friendship and belief in me.

This work is based on an exhaustive analysis of archival material in Toronto, Montreal, and Ottawa. Archivists are the unsung heroes of historical scholarship. I must note the generous assistance of Lawrence Tapper of the Public Archives/Library and Archives of Canada, Gordon Kaufman of the Toronto Jewish Immigrant Aid Society, and Judy Nefsky of the Canadian Jewish Congress Archives in Montreal. I also must thank Ellen Scheinberg of the Ontario Jewish Archives for her assistance with some very specific requests on very short timelines. But most of all, I must thank her predecessor, Dr Stephen Speisman. Steve was my mentor, friend, and inspiration, and the catalyst for my involvement in Canadian Jewish history. I had the great fortune of knowing him in a number of roles. His exciting stories of Toronto Jewish life captivated me when I was seventeen, and he renewed his connection with me when I worked for him in the OJA. He read an early draft of my thesis and incisively analysed and critiqued it. Steve was a true historian of Toronto, who shared his passion for our city with enthusiasm. He taught me so much about Jewish life in Toronto. His passing has left a deep void.

The task of turning a doctoral thesis into a book is gruelling, even more so when summers offer the only time for working. In response to comments from anonymous outside reviewers, the original thesis has been greatly expanded with the addition of an introduction, introductory chapter, and conclusion. The other chapters have been completely rewritten and the research made current. All this would never have been done without Jerry Tulchinsky's help. Frankly, "thanks" is an inadequate word to express how I feel about him. Long before we met in person, he agreed to help me. He buoyed my often flagging spirits with a note, phone call, or email. He suggested more appropriate phrases and made vital suggestions about where to add narrative and especially on how tell the story in engaging prose. All this while writing his own *Canada's Jews,* and with never a hint of being busy when I phoned. Jerry epitomizes the intellectual generosity that marked the scholars who trained me – I only hope it survives the bombardments of undergraduate email.

I must also thank my old PhD seminar colleague John Zucchi, now at McGill, for referring this book to McGill-Queen's University Press and for his patience with my slow, albeit steady progress. I have nothing but heartfelt appreciation for Jon Crago, who explained the myriad details of academic publishing, and for all the other patient, friendly, and helpful staff of McGill-Queen's University Press. I am now grateful to the anonymous reviewers who compelled me to confront inadequate assumptions and refine my research; they reminded me of the vital role of humility in furthering scholarship. Special thanks to my editor, Jane McWhinney, whose eagle eye and nimble phraseology have helped my narrative unravel more smoothly.

I must also thank some generous friends of my work, who believed in me from the beginning. Jay Hennick and Michael Benjamin are two special people, who first crossed my path professionally and then became supporters. Many thanks for your enduring patience and belief in me, which spans almost a decade. Thanks as well to Brendan Caldwell, ever a sage advisor and dear friend in ways too numerous to list here. And special thanks are due to Jules Kronis, not only my lawyer, but a friend and brilliant raconteur of a stream of incredible anecdotes about Toronto Jewish history. He has backed this project from the beginning. It was Jules who arranged for his beloved Junction Shul to assist in my work. I thank the Junction Shul and its president, Edwin Goldstein, for making this possible. Finally, I must thank the Social Science and Humanities Research Council of Canada for the generous grant that made this book possible. I hope the wait was worth it. Of course, I take ownership of any errors and omissions.

Last and most important are my family. My children's births may have caused me to leave academe, but they also compelled me to not give it up. Baruch, who loves Canadian history and government documents; Yoelit, an accomplished writer and reader, and keen critic of literature, who helped organize the index; and Yehezkel, who enjoys history but will probably become a fundraiser, branding guru, and cantor, and who provided encouragement by asking me after every bookstore trip – and there were many – "Why aren't you published yet?" Now I am – and it is partially your fault. Thank you.

As for my mentor, friend, confidante, and fellow researcher in Montreal, my wonderful wife, Barbara, what is there to say? I thank God every day for you. This book exists because you believed in me more than I believed in myself. Hence my dedication. And to my beloved parents, Bernard and Sally Lipinsky, and parents-in-law, Elaine and Jack Geller, all of blessed memory, who participated in and reminisced about Jewish history on both sides of the Atlantic, look down from Heaven and smile – for I am telling a story you were part of.

28 Kislev 5771, 4th Day of Chanuka
5 December 2010
Toronto, Ontario

Introduction

Four men argued loudly, their voices drowning out the sobbing of the Glass family. The only silent person in the room was at their feet. Joseph Glass, wrapped in burial shrouds and *tallit* (prayer shawl), lay on a bed of fresh straw with a candle burning at his head. The red-faced men represented the different organizations to which Joseph had belonged, and each demanded that Joseph be buried in his respective organization's cemetery. Finally, Joseph's widow, Esther, put an end to their arguments by insisting that he be interred in the Lambton Hill cemetery of Beth Jacob Synagogue, which he had helped found a decade earlier.

The funeral procession left the little house on Baldwin Street, passed the open doors of the synagogue a block away, and proceeded on a lengthy ride to the cemetery on Royal York Road. What a sad contrast to the family's first visit there seven years earlier in 1924, when the Glass family and synagogue celebrated the dedication of the newly purchased cemetery with a huge picnic on the grounds. There was much to celebrate: the cemetery was on high ground with good drainage; graves would be accessible to loved ones year round; monuments to mark the departed could be erected with confidence. The picnickers were celebrating both Beth Jacob's institutional achievement and the steps taken to preserve their traditions in a new country. This was a celebration of the perpetuation of Jewish life in a new land.[1]

The Beth Jacob congregants were celebrating – and in a sense Joseph Glass was a victim of – what sociologists call "ethnic completeness," a term coined by Raymond Breton in a seminal 1964 article. Using a host of evidence, Breton observed that an ethnic group's ability to withstand the assimilative forces of a host society is proportional to its ability to provide educational, workplace, religious, and cultural services to its members. Put simply, if immigrant Jews wished to retain their identity they would have to provide kosher butchers, synagogues, social clubs, theatres, hospitals, and other institutions that would help maintain their identity in an environment that preached Angloconformity.

Many sociologists have applied Breton's research, but there is no literature on the mechanism of institutional completeness. How did the vast maze of Toronto Jewish institutions arise and what were the political, economic, and social forces that shaped Toronto Jewry's highly developed index of organizational completeness? This book traces these forces, which peaked in the tumultuous years between 1933 and 1948. It will also grapple with issues of Jewish identity in Toronto and how this identity changed and developed over these years. A great deal of this story has never been told before. It is the narrative of how a tough-minded group of young women and men changed the institutional face of Toronto Jewry between 1933 and 1948, and in the process laid the foundation for today's well-organized community.

Pathologists say dead men tell tales. So do musty old files. Institutional history gives us fascinating glimpses of personal relationships, conflicting loyalties, and the complexities of communal life. Poring through the often passionate correspondence between lay and professional members of Toronto's early Jewish organizations fleshed out the persona behind the serious faces in old photographs. The faces slowly took on personalities. I was struck by the cacophony of voices and the sharp contrasts between flashes of insight and intense parochial pettiness and rivalry. But best of all was the name dropping, and the discovery of correspondence delineating a delicate web of organizational geography among a relatively small group of people in Montreal and Toronto, all passionately concerned with organizing Canadian Jewish life. As I followed each link, I was led to new archival collections in Ottawa, Montreal, and Toronto. All were full of the same names – often in different organizations. Imagine my excitement when I found that some of these men and women were still alive and were willing to be interviewed.

One of the most interesting of these protagonists was Martin Cohn, in some ways the hero of this study. I had interviewed a number of his contemporaries, but the former executive director of the Federation of Jewish Philanthropies (FJP) had refused interview requests. I felt so frustrated because his persona shone through an extensive correspondence. Cohn exemplified the "progressive wedge" of the figures reshaping communal organizations. In my efforts to understand him, I had browsed through old social work studies that he might have read which are still on the shelves in Toronto's Robarts Library. I was stunned to find a heavily annotated book, still complete with library card – and the last signature, from 1935, was Cohn's! Now truly desperate, I sent him an early draft of the chapter on his organization. To my utter surprise it was returned by priority post within a week, also heavily annotated with that now familiar writing, with a note that read: "Did you look over my shoulder? Coming to Toronto in two weeks. Call me." I did, and over the next two hours travelled back decades to the world that had engendered the files I read.

The following pages describe the vision that drove Cohn and his contemporaries to rationalize, redefine, and impose order on their community. To help give the reader the flavour of what they wanted to change, I first offer a brief history of the community until 1933. Succeeding chapters then carry the narrative forward, with a cast of memorable characters and often-competing organizations each claiming a constituency. Mutual fund offerings warn that "past behaviour is no predictor of future performance"; accordingly, I have consciously made every effort not to tell the story as the members of the "progressive wedge" who imposed their will perceived it. After all, history only seems inexorable in hindsight. To accomplish this task, I have employed and integrated techniques from social historians, the sociology of ethnicity, and organizational behaviour. I have consciously shied away from ideological interpretations of history, especially those of Marxist and Socialist historians. Toronto Jews were politicized and very conversant with various streams of political and Zionist ideology. It would be foolishly ironic for me to impose an ideological construct on a group who themselves sought to impose new methodologies of community organization on an often unwilling community. Far better to elucidate their mindsets than to impose mine; occasionally I have subtly editorialized in the narrative. I have tried to capture the uncertainty of those who imposed change – their vision was steadfast, but the roadblocks were many and success was far from assured. Pressures abounded, both external and internal: the Depression, the

Second World War, and the Holocaust, as well as organizational turf wars and intra-ethnic tensions. Those who sought to impose their will and vision on the community ran a veritable obstacle course to achieve success. This is their story.

A word about terminology. I have borrowed the term "Uptowners" to talk about those who sought to rationalize communal organization. It is vital to note that this designation does not conform to residential patterns or socioeconomic groupings in the same way as in large American Jewish communities. At least at the beginning, Uptowners were united more by educational background and a desire to impose professionalism than by other factors. As we shall see, the actions of an elite fringe group can have an impact on a much larger polity. I label their opponents "Downtowners" and *"amcha,"* a Yiddish expression meaning "the people who really matter." Downtowners were those who opposed Uptowners' vision at the organizational level; *amcha*, the vast majority of the Jewish community preoccupied with the daily struggle for survival in Depression times played no direct role in the struggle. Yet, as we shall see, *amcha* were very much affected by the outcome of that struggle. And it is precisely this point that makes this study timely: change is always difficult and comes at some expense. What was the human cost of institutional change in the Jewish community? Who bore the brunt of it, and was it necessary? What factors determined the extent of change? How does the Toronto Jewish community's organizational history compare with that of its American peers?

These questions are important beyond the period under study because they explore communal and individual responses to changing and challenging paradigms of religious and cultural values. We face similar issues today. The breathtaking pace of technological change in the past twenty years has produced not only an overabundance of information but a huge amount of doubt. Which of the 5 million possible answers elicited by a Google search is the *best* one? This lack of clarity is mirrored in bookshelves and websites devoted to "how to" descriptions written by experts of varying capabilities. In an environment of rapid change, tried and traditional answers seem suddenly irrelevant. For instance, what does it mean to be "Jewish" in the Internet age? With more answers and options available than ever before, an unprecedentedly broad debate has arisen about membership in the Jewish community.

The Toronto Jewish polity faced similar issues of change between 1933 and 1948. Certainly the pace of technological change was slower, but in early twentieth-century Toronto competing answers to what "being Jewish" meant were rapidly emerging. Succeeding decades and events increased the relevance of this question. The cataclysmic events of 1933 through 1948 compelled Canadian Jews to confront the issue of Jewish individual and communal identity as never before. In short, what did it mean to be a Canadian Jew between 1933 and 1948? The search to answer this still relevant question lies at the heart of this narrative of communal organizational change. Some of the answers proposed by the architects of community are still instructive now.

Organizational history is instructive because Jews are joiners. Then and now, a listing of individual Toronto Jews' organizational affiliations provides a roadmap of their core beliefs about Jewish identity. Their affiliations speak louder than words. So it was at the beginning of the twentieth century. Downtowners fresh off the boat were often found in *landsmanschaften* (immigrant benevolent societies), synagogues, or societies whose names eponymously reflected their origins – Anshei Staszow, Anshei Minsk – names of Eastern Europe on the streetscape of the New World. Organizationally and emotionally, Downtowners still had one foot and a great deal of emotional investment in *"der alte heim,"* their place of origin in Europe. Toronto was full of synagogues, some in houses, some in rented rooms, some in converted churches, others in dedicated buildings. Their sheer variety and abundance attested to the fact that even Downtowners who believed in the importance of prayer often disagreed on its order or its pronunciation. Immigrants who worshipped ideology rather than religion had a host of options: Zionist organizations – Poalei Zion of the Left and Right stripe – Mizrachi, and General Zionists. There were union locals that attracted Yiddish speakers, and some for English speakers. Unions themselves espoused various political credos – anarchist, Socialist, and Communist – and they spent almost as much time fighting each other as they did employers. Downtowners were cash poor and ideologically rich.

But beyond the time they gave to these organizations, *amcha*, the new immigrants who swelled the ranks of Toronto Jewry in the early twentieth century, had no chance to participate in communal governance. They may have read some articles in the Yiddish papers, but the daily grind of working long days and feeding large families precluded their participation beyond the level of the synagogues, union locals, or the clubs outlined above. Perhaps they could steal moments to write to relatives left behind in Europe, and sometimes could send money or tickets (after fevered saving of every spare nickel and dime) to bring more family to Toronto. Always, knowing how dangerous European conditions were, they had to endure the inevitable tension of the waiting period between letters: was everyone all right?

When everyone wasn't "all right," *amcha* turned to a time-honoured and European-based solution: *tzedakah* – traditional charitable societies that did not cast judgment on a person's reason for needing funds, but merely extended them in accordance with law, custom, and tradition. There were societies that provided gowns for indigent brides, Sabbath and Holy Day food for the poor, and Jewish education for orphans. The assumption that a community must take care of its own had been deeply ingrained in organized Jewish society for centuries. Belief in this value transcended religiosity – it was one of the few defining features of "Jewish behaviour" that the *amcha* community could agree on.

Differing ideologies of how to discharge this obligation, as I will document in detail, go a long way toward explaining the deep cleavages between *amcha* and Uptowners in Toronto. Unlike their New York counterparts, Toronto's Uptowners and Downtowners were separated more by ideology than by place of origin or economic status. The supposed power of the "German Jews" in Toronto was mythical, based on the *amcha* epithet *"Daitche shul"* ("German synagogue"), which was hurled at Holy Blossom Synagogue, Toronto's oldest. Truth be told, a significant community of German Jews never existed in Toronto. Most of the founders of Holy Blossom were British or American, and the synagogue readily admitted rich immigrants who wanted to mark their passage to the Uptown ranks by joining. This practice occurred well before Holy Blossom became a Reform Congregation. Immigrants who became members of Holy Blossom were indicating that they were comfortable with less traditional religious practices – that they were more acculturated religiously (and probably socially as well). This is but one example that underscores a crucial reality: the key differences between Toronto Downtowners and Uptowners lay in the latter's length of residence in Canada and the fact that many of them were university-educated.

A university degree was the culmination of an education that ensured that immigrants would blend into a host society. The Ontario public education system of the time unabashedly sought to assimilate immigrants; no Downtowner could avoid contact with non-Jewish culture. Even the most observant Downtowners experienced some measure of acculturation, even if they resisted assimilation. Unlike Eastern Europe, Toronto had no separate Jewish school system that would isolate observant Jews from the general populace even if they wanted it. Despite its name, however, the Toronto District School Board was solidly Christian. Even if Jewish students succeeded in gaining exemption from saying the Lord's Prayer, they certainly were compelled to learn a great deal about Christmas, Easter, and many other Christian events both from their peers and their teachers. Downtown parents felt uncomfortable about the religious component, but they fervently advocated for their children's success in school. The knowledge children gained was deemed vital to their advancement – the pinnacle of which was university graduation. Downtown parents also supported the public schools' ardently Anglophile culture. Journalist Larry Zolf, for instance, recalled that his father, a lifelong Socialist, wrapped him in a *kipa*, shirt, and shorts all decorated with the Union Jack. One person I interviewed recalled his immigrant parents decorating their living room with a British flag, which they hung outside at every opportunity. This and other anecdotal evidence indicates that Zolf was but one example of a widely observed trend. Canadian Jewry learned to love all things British – at a time when Canadian identity was deeply bound to imperialism and love of Empire. Jews were proudly patriotic.

Jewish students who continued on to university learned about anti-Semitism through the limitations it imposed upon them. Certainly they experienced racism and quotas and discriminatory treatment. They fought against this through organizations and as individuals. But they also learned a deep respect for "British fair play" and sought to find a middle ground between their sense of being more Canadian than their parents and the fact of their being less Canadian than their Gentile classmates. As we shall see, their mediating efforts led them to propose solutions for Jewish communal issues that would bridge the gap between the two worlds they inhabited. The unique experience of this Jewish generation, the first to attend Western university, would shape their vision of community.

The key changes these young men and women wished for were in turn inspired by their university experience: they sought professionalization of their communal polity at all levels. This trend corresponded to the spirit of Progressivism that abounded at universities in this era. Professional schools were established, professions that had existed for many years suddenly required formal credentials for membership, and universities designed courses for new professions such as social work. This process required further delineation in terms of subject matter, accreditation, and supervision. As we shall see, their educational experience and the ethos of the times encouraged these young Jewish graduates to apply this Progressivist agenda to rationalizing Toronto's Jewish communal polity.

This organizational impulse set the stage for an attempted imposition of will lasting twenty years. The paradigms of proposed change were much more complex than simply replacing *tzedakah* with professional fundraising. Proper implementation of communal rationalization would require nothing short of a re-ordering of communal priorities, a reshaping of traditional thinking, and – by extension – a redefinition of the balance of organizational power at the communal and national levels. This sometimes bitter imposition of will provoked an often-unpredicted ripple effect that compelled Toronto's Jewish polity to question many assumptions, destroy once-venerated institutions, and create new solutions in a search for a new communal order made all the more challenging by exceedingly tempestuous times.

Every movement has its heroes, and we find some here. That's good, because Canadian Jewish history is very short on heroes. As we shall see, heroism is not limited to battlefield heroics during wartime, and Martin Cohn is a hero of this story in many ways. He was in one of the first graduating classes of the University of Toronto's School of Social Work, and did his training in the schoolyards of Kensington with the Jewish Boys' Club. He rescued the failing Federation of Jewish Philanthropies, the Uptowners' omnibus communal fundraising agency, from the Depression with a relentless search for pragmatic solutions to the problem of rising demand for social services and falling campaign revenues. Best of all, after engineering the federation's survival, he left at the height of his success to try new challenges in Chicago.

Cohn and his colleagues were agents of change, but not everyone was as effective as Cohn. In the course of this study, we shall meet some of his contemporaries, many of whom were not very enamoured of change. We will encounter leaders who had different visions of change or of which institution or profession was best equipped to mediate the changes necessary for Canadian Jewish survival. All these men and women believed passionately in their respective solution for Jewish communal survival and amelioration. Their passion led to argument, to pettiness, to personal rivalry, and to errors of judgment that bruised the egos of participants and turned some away from engagement in communal affairs.

It is precisely this passion for change and rationalization – and the attendant debate over what being a Canadian Jew meant – that makes this study vitally interesting. Challenge and change are the handmaids of progress; between 1933 and 1948 they catalyzed personal and communal self-definition among Toronto's Jewry. The unprecedented succession of the Depression, rising anti-Semitism, the Holocaust, and Israel's rebirth compelled these young Uptowners to impose their vision in a high-stakes atmosphere where they believed there was little time for persuasion. Surely questions can be raised about their methods. The tensions of the time certainly added edge to their solutions.

Thankfully, Toronto – indeed Canadian – Jewry no longer faces the constellation of pressures described in this study. However, the question of "Jewish continuity" is still vital, an iteration of the "what-is-a-Canadian-Jew" question faced by Uptowners and Downtowners alike. A close study of this era will be rewarding both for its own sake and also for fostering continued engagement with questions of Jewish and ethnic self-definition and group survival in a multicultural society still seeking to define what it means to be Canadian. Jews have ever looked to the past to provide lessons for the present and future – so does this study.

IMPOSING THEIR WILL

I

The Road to Community: Toronto Jewry before 1933

Although Jews had been living in Canada since the mid-eighteenth century, it took them a century to form any organized presence in Toronto. This is not surprising. Toronto is far inland from the Atlantic and even farther from the point at which the great water highway of the St Lawrence empties into Lake Ontario. The Jewish presence in Canada flowed along this path. Jews settled in Halifax at its founding in 1749, but most of them left within a decade. More permanent Jewish communities developed in Quebec and Montreal after the British conquest. Montreal's first synagogue was established in 1768; however, Quebec City's Jewish population did not require a permanent synagogue until the 1850s. Many other Quebec Jews were scattered in smaller communities like Trois-Rivières. But no permanent Jewish community took root west of Montreal until well into the nineteenth century.[1]

Indeed, there was no organized settlement in this vast hinterland until after the *Constitutional Act* of 1791 had divided the former French colony of Quebec into Lower Canada (Quebec) and Upper Canada (Ontario). Between 1791 and the onset of the War of 1812, settlers trickled in and settlements were built, along the shores of the St Lawrence, Lake Ontario, and the Detroit River. Jews were among them. Most were merchants, many of whom played a role in the fur trade, either purchasing furs themselves or supplying the needs of the traders who ventured far into the Western wilderness. Although Jews were officially barred from owning land, British authorities increasingly used a variety of methods to circumvent the rule requiring Jews to take the Oath of Loyalty "on the true faith of a Christian." Individual Jews lived in Cornwall as early as 1790 and in Windsor by 1814.[2]

But the formation of a community would have to await the expansion of Upper Canada itself, a slow process. Lower Canada was far more populous and would remain so for many years. Ice on lakes Erie and Ontario, and on the St Lawrence barred passage to the Atlantic between November and April, and rushing rapids impeded progress upriver during the shipping season. Many contemporary British and Canadian observers lamented this situation. But in reality, albeit recognized only in hindsight, the colony enjoyed steady growth. Settlements advanced inland as forests were cut down to make room for fields, rudimentary roads were built, and regular stagecoach service linked developing settlements. Eventually, canals offered further interior access, and the postal service expanded, gradually becoming more predictable. Increased immigration in the 1840s and 1850s further extended farmland, moved the frontier significantly inland, and catalyzed a boom in secondary industry. Though most immigrants were farmers, a significant number became urban dwellers as the rise of industry provided employment opportunities. The railway boom of the 1850s established London, Hamilton, and especially Toronto, from which railroad lines "radiated to west, north, and east," making the city the commercial capital of Canada West.[3]

Considering its earlier history, Toronto's rise to prominence was certainly not a foregone conclusion. The city, first called York, was founded in 1791 by John Graves Simcoe, the first lieutenant governor of Upper Canada, and was intended as a centre for Loyalist settlers who had fled the American Revolution. Although Simcoe established York as the capital of the new colony, it grew very slowly. Its brief occupation and destruction by American invaders during the War of 1812 forced its inhabitants to begin afresh. They proved equal to the task. By 1817 York had become a banking centre and its harbour attracted an increasing number of steamers and schooners, ships laden with wheat and lumber bound for Great Britain, which had arrived filled with British manufactured and specialty items. The incoming goods were eagerly consumed by the wealthy families locally known as the "Family Compact," who controlled the colonial government and owned a great deal of land. By 1834 the city fathers decided that, despite the city's infamously muddy streets and many ramshackle buildings, York's status as the colonial capital and its population of 9,000 merited incorporation as the City of Toronto.[4]

Jews, among others, took notice of Toronto's widening hinterland, growing population, and consequent prosperity. While most Jews preferred the more populous and prosperous United States, a number, mostly from England and Germany, began to choose this city. The 1831 census records 103 Jews in Upper Canada, but there is no way of determining how many of them lived in Toronto. It is certain that by 1849 there were at least thirty-five Jews in Toronto, almost all of whom were merchants from Britain or Germany who had set up enterprises, mostly dealing in jewellery or fancy goods. They came with sufficient capital to rent stores on major business streets. But these were difficult times and many were soon forced to move on, daunted by debt or by one of the frequent economic downturns that wracked the colony's economy. Many of those who were successful assimilated, often marrying into the upper stratum of society. At times, distinctions between Jews and Christians were blurred. A case in point is the story of George Benjamin, who arrived in Canada around 1833 with his young wife and infant son. He became the editor of the Belleville *Intelligencer* and in 1857 Canada's first Jewish Member of Parliament. Although Benjamin was proud of his faith and followed Jewish custom by entering the names of his children in his family *siddur* (prayer book), he certainly was not a practising Jew. He founded the Orange Lodge in Belleville and between 1846 and 1853 had become the Grand Master of the Orange Order of British North America, even though this necessitated leading prayers that ended with the words "through Jesus Christ our Lord." Benjamin's children were all baptized, but he and his wife only received baptism shortly before his death.[5]

Many Ontario Jews retained their faith, but few were observant. Only one Toronto Jew in the 1840s closed his store on Saturday, the prime business day of the week. Judah Joseph had arrived in Toronto in 1843 after failing as a lawyer and merchant in Cincinnati. In Toronto he prospered as an optician and stockbroker until his death in 1857. He was well regarded by credit agencies, contemporaries, and customers. In 1849 Joseph, together with Abraham Nordheimer, a German immigrant who was a piano teacher of note and had begun manufacturing pianos, purchased land for a Jewish cemetery on what is now Pape Avenue. Jewish law held that the purchase of a cemetery had precedence over building a synagogue. By 1850 the cemetery was in use, but there was still no need for a synagogue.[6]

The railway boom of the 1850s catapulted Toronto into permanent pre-eminence in Canada West. The city was blessed by the confluence of three major railways, with a fine harbour that attracted a steadily expanding maritime trade with both the United States and Britain, and its population grew by leaps and bounds. By 1851 it had reached 31,000, an increase of almost 50 percent in a decade. The next decade would see a further increase to 45,000. Jewish immigration followed suit. By 1856 there were at least a hundred Jews in Toronto. Unlike their predecessors, a significant number of the newer immigrants were observant. By 1853 they had arranged for a *shochet* (a man trained in the ritual slaughter of animals according to Jewish law) to come to Toronto to provide *kosher* meat. In 1856 this group organized Toronto's first synagogue, the Toronto Hebrew Congregation, which held High Holy Day services above a drug store at Yonge and Richmond streets, using a Torah (scroll of the Five Books of Moses) borrowed from Montreal's Spanish and Portuguese Synagogue. But internal relations between this wave of newcomers and the older Jewish community were strained. Those who arrived in the 1840s, such as the Nordheimers, Judah Joseph, and the Rossin brothers, who would later build Toronto's first luxury hotel, owned their own houses and places of business, and they mingled easily with non-Jewish society indeed, Samuel Nordheimer (Abraham's younger brother) became an Anglican upon his 1874 marriage to Edith Louisa Boulton, daughter of one of the colony's most illustrious families. (He built Glen Edyth, one of the city's premier mansions, and remained a pillar of Toronto society until his death in 1912.) But the newcomers of the 1850s were more observant, insular, and less willing to put down roots. They continued to rent, rather than own, their residences and places of business even after they had become prosperous and well established.[7]

The two factions squared off over control of the cemetery. "Not one founding member of the synagogue," observed historian Stephen Speisman, "had been living in Toronto in 1849," when the cemetery plot had been purchased. The earlier arrivals wished to remain aloof. The Nordheimers and Rossins ignored both mailed and personal entreaties for funds for a new congregation, The Sons of Israel. Others offered funds for renting and equipping a place of worship, but still declined membership. It has been suggested that both social distance and the strictness of the second congregation's rules played a role in this dissension. Members could be fined for non-attendance at meetings, for smoking during prayers, and the like. It took three years and the intervention of a mediator to convince the two sides to agree that some cemetery plots would be reserved for families of original members and that the new synagogue, would manage the entire site. These tensions were harbingers of a pattern that would re-emerge even more divisively in the 1890s as Toronto's Jewry multiplied and diversified in response to immigration from Eastern Europe.[8]

In the 1870s Toronto's Jewish ranks were swelled by American Jews fleeing the economic downturn dubbed the Panic of 1873. By 1875 there were about 350 Jews in Toronto. Most were affiliated with the united synagogue, which had formally assumed its present name of Holy Blossom. By 1876 it had outgrown its original home and moved into new premises on fashionable Richmond Street. Christians underwrote over one-quarter of the building fund – a sign of the esteem in which the Jewish community was held. This respect was confirmed by the extensive coverage the synagogue dedication received in the Toronto press. While the synagogue retained Orthodox rituals, the winds of change were already blowing. First, the building committee had chosen a prominent "establishment" architectural firm to design the synagogue. Furthermore, an organ and female singers were used at the dedication ceremony, and women had already complained about the height of the barrier separating the sexes. Holy Blossom also attracted Jews who lived in the small communities around Toronto. Membership provided much-coveted access to cheaper and better cuts of kosher meat, rudimentary Jewish education, cemetery access, and of course, religious services. These services were very much in the English mode. There was no trained rabbi or cantor, however; the *shochet* often had to lead religious services and teach. By the late 1870s life was relatively good. The growing Jewish community was increasingly accepted by its non-Jewish neighbours, and generally prospered.[9]

The relative lack of anti-Semitism meant that Jews could partake of social life beyond the synagogue. Certainly many businessmen did socialize with their non-Jewish contemporaries in the course of business. But socializing outside business hours may not have been as reciprocal. Even though anti-Semitism was not active, a considerable body of opinion still saw Jews as aliens. Many people still remembered when Jews had been barred from commissions and government appointments (let alone from assuming their seats in legislatures to which they were elected) because they could not swear the requisite Oath of Abjuration "on the true faith of a Christian." This legal impediment had only been removed by the *Declaratory Act* of 1832, and only then could Jews in Canada West hold government commissions and become Members of Parliament. The subsequent process of removing the Oath of Abjuration and secularizing the language of the State Oaths that replaced it was only completed in 1858, at which point Jews could finally become Ministers of the Crown and enter Cabinet.[10]

It is not surprising that lingering suspicions and recently removed legal impediments combined with Jewish religious and cultural ties to limit Jewish socialization. Indeed, male Jewish social life in Toronto outside of Holy Blossom centred largely on two clubs: the B'nai Brith lodge, the first of its order in Canada, and the Toronto chapter of another American Jewish society, the Kesher shel Barzel (Chain of Steel). The presence in Toronto of two branches of American Jewish fraternal organizations paralleled their growth in North America. This was the golden age of fraternal societies in Europe and North America. They were often ethnically or religiously based. Their members enjoyed the social aspects of membership, such as parading in uniform, initiation rituals, and the medical care and death benefits they provided. In some ethnic communities, they helped immigrants make the transition to a new society.[11]

While both B'nai Brith and Kesher shel Barzel filled important social needs, they also encouraged philanthropy. This was a core value of traditional Jewish practice known as *tzedakah*, from the Hebrew word for "justice." This name reflected traditional Judaism's belief that helping the poor was a divine imperative rooted in social justice. Rather than blame the poor for their poverty, Jewish tradition taught that it was essential to assist them in re-establishing themselves to the point where they could help others. Indeed, even the poorest of the poor were still expected to give *tzedakah*. Impelled by this belief, Jewish communities over the centuries developed a host of communal and private societies that provided care for the sick, dresses for poor brides, supervision and education for the orphaned, burial for paupers, and religious necessities for the impoverished. As we shall see,

Jews were ready and willing to transplant these societies to North America. Their attitude toward benevolence contrasted starkly with societal perceptions in Britain and North America. Victorians regarded philanthropy with suspicion. It was widely believed that "success could be obtained by all who lived respectfully and worked hard" and therefore, as the *Globe* argued in 1874, that "promiscuous alms-giving" would only deter the poor from seeking gainful employment.[12]

The early growth of Toronto's Jewish population and the local economy's zigzagging between boom and bust obviated the need for communal philanthropy. By 1868 women in Holy Blossom had formed a fraternal and charitable society, the Toronto Ladies' Hebrew Sick and Benevolent Society. The society offered a host of services ... free loans, as well as aid for Jewish orphans, transients in need of railway tickets, and the Jewish unemployed. Renamed the Ladies' Montefiore Hebrew Benevolent Society in 1870, the society carried on the work performed by similar societies in European Jewish communities. Holy Blossom's men were quick to follow suit. In 1877 a "charitable society for the relief of their coreligionists" was founded, which within a decade became the all-male Toronto Hebrew Benevolent Association (THBA). By the 1880s, both societies were donating funds beyond the Jewish community as well: to the Hospital for Sick Children, the Infants' Home, and the Childrens' Aid Society. By 1890 the city of Toronto recognized the effectiveness of the THBA's work with the Jewish unemployed by allocating municipal grants to partially subsidize their efforts.[13]

While on the surface Jewish philanthropy in Toronto followed the customs of parallel European Jewish organizations, some crucial departures from tradition were evident. Women's active participation in philanthropy, and the societies' involvement in supporting institutions outside the Jewish community indicated that, by the 1870s, Toronto Jewry were influenced by the British and American currents that swirled through early social welfare work in Ontario. Their donations to municipal charitable causes reflected the positive relations between Jews and other citizens and a desire for social acceptance and advancement in the wider Toronto community. In this, Toronto Jews were quite successful. The fact that they spoke English, were familiar with American and British customs, and had emigrated for economic reasons allowed for their general acceptance "by the middle class, if not the elite, of Christian society."[14]

Donations to non-Jewish causes were a manifestation of a yearning for acculturation to Canadian values. Toronto's Jewish fraternal organizations held their gala balls, complete with debutantes, in prestigious locations and urged mothers to send their children to dancing classes at St George's Hall. Since the great majority of the Jewish community of Toronto were affiliated with Holy Blossom, it is not surprising that the synagogue mirrored the communal desire for acculturation. As we have seen, an organ and female singers provided music at the dedication of the Richmond Street building, though not during prayer services. While the synagogue was nominally Orthodox, its minutes were in English from the beginning, little Hebrew was inscribed on cemetery tombstones, and an annual Thanksgiving Day service was initiated in 1893 at the governor general's request. The children of Holy Blossomites attended public schools and went to religious school on Sunday, and many enjoyed friendships with non-Jewish children. Of course, these efforts did not result in full cultural acceptance. By the turn of the century, despite considerable evidence of official acceptance into the community, Jews continued to be excluded from the private sphere. Only a very small number of Holy Blossom members belonged to non-Jewish social clubs and were social guests at non-Jewish homes.[15]

Given Toronto's cosmopolitan backdrop, it is certain that the Holy Blossomites were well aware of non-Jewish developments in philanthropy. Their deep-rooted Jewish tradition of *tzedakah*, coupled with their realization that philanthropy both permitted them to show that they cared about Canadian society and served as an entry-point for social acceptance, ensured that philanthropy would receive close attention. And there were many developments to attend to. Toronto's location would make it a testing ground for both British and American models of philanthropic organization, some of which would be modified to meet the unique needs of Jewish communities. It is thus worthwhile to outline briefly some salient developments in British and American social welfare organization.

By the 1850s Britain had survived the most severe social and economic dislocations caused by the Industrial Revolution and entered a prosperous era known as the "Age of Equipoise." This was a time in which certain middle-class values became the public norm – the value of work and thrift, hatred of vice (especially drunkenness and prostitution), and the primacy of a moral and upright family life. To be sure, "the respectability of the Victorians was a hypocritical façade ... Nevertheless, it did produce a growing sensitivity to suffering [and] a concern for others." But, given the power of *laissez-faire* economics in this age, how was this concern to be actualized? Who would care for the suffering masses? The almost unanimous response was "self-help," a doctrine based on the belief that, "given initiative and industry all things are possible" and the supposition that an individual's position in life reflected his or her efforts. By the 1870s the doctrine that people could climb the social ladder by practising the virtues of work and thrift had spread from the middle class to those above and below. Many members of the middle and working classes saw fraternal societies as the best method to "raise themselves," as their terminology indicated. Mutual benefit societies, which dispensed help to members who were ill, called this a "benefit" rather than "charity," and "relief" was termed a "right of membership." Consequently, membership in British fraternal societies increased from 600,000 in 1793 to over 4 million in 1877. By far the majority of these members were participants in mutual benefit or insurance societies, who fervently hoped that the benefits of membership would help them avoid the "ultimate disgrace" of a pauper's funeral.[16]

Britain exported fraternalism and its inherent values to America well before the Revolution. The Freemasons came to America in 1733, less than two decades after being founded in Manchester. The Order's prestige was enhanced by the participation of Revolutionary heroes such as John Hancock, George Washington, and Paul Revere, and its membership rocketed from 3,000 in 1830 to 465,000 by 1877. Other societies experienced similar gains; by 1875 over 5 million Americans were members.[17]

The golden age of fraternalism between 1870 and 1914 also benefited from a lack of state intervention in social services. Governments in Britain, the United States, and Canada all believed that "indoor relief" (as represented in almshouses, poorhouses, or "Houses of Industry," as they were euphemistically called) was a great evil that only bred dependence. Governments generally provided only for the insane, the incurable (a field often shared with private charities), Magdalen Homes for "fallen women" and their children, and those deemed "the undeserving poor" because they were dependent on charity and thus irredeemable. The majority of the working poor were left to fend for themselves. Many, if not most, joined fraternal societies and emulated the middle-class value of self-help, using the benefits paid by the societies to avoid loss of income through illness and the ignominy of a pauper's funeral.[18]

But these valiant efforts at self-help were not enough to halt the spread of poverty in the 1870s, especially in Britain where the Panic of 1873 introduced two decades of economic stagnation. Although the American economy recovered more quickly, poverty became an issue in both countries. *Laissez-faire* government social policies, and the resultant minimal government intervention in the social welfare of the working poor, left plenty of room for philanthropy. The upper and middle classes were quick to respond, with "a torrent of charity raining down upon the poor" from many private individuals and charity societies. A prominent historian of social welfare accounts for this by citing: "a fear of social revolution, a humanitarian concern for suffering, a satisfaction of some psychological or social need and a desire to improve the moral tone of the recipient." The poor hated what social historian David Beito has labelled "hierarchical relief" for its bureaucratic rules and formality, the superior social class and income of the donors, and the attitude of *noblesse oblige* with which they dispensed funds. The poor preferred a form of informal self-help that Beito calls "reciprocal relief," which varied with the circumstances of the impoverished. It often took the form of neighbourhood associations for watching children so that some mothers could work or voluntary associations to teach literacy.[19]

While *tzedakah* had the characteristics of both hierarchical and reciprocal relief, its psychology had become far closer to the latter. Certainly traditional *tzedakah* never involved a sense of *noblesse oblige* – Rabbinic law viewed this attitude with extreme disfavour. But Toronto's Jews, as we have seen, had already held charity balls and were more Victorian than Jewish when it came to philanthropy. As long as the community was still small and relatively homogenous, this seeming discrepancy was not an issue. But as the rising tide of Russian immigration reached Toronto in the 1880s and especially in the 1890s, different attitudes about philanthropy would be at the cutting edge of considerable discord between the Holy Blossomites of the old community and the still-newer immigrants. The Holy Blossomites, armed with economic clout, social prestige, and Victorian attitudes, were not shy about foisting their values on the immigrants.

It took a while for the presence of the late-century new arrivals from Eastern Europe to be felt. The 534 Jews recorded in 1881 were a scant increase over the previous decade, but by 1891 the Jewish population had almost tripled to 1,425, a number that further increased to 3,090 a decade later. While it is undeniable that most Russian immigrants preferred *"der goldene medine"* (the golden land) of the United States, those who came to Toronto proved sufficiently numerous to challenge Holy Blossomites' philanthropic paradigms.[20]

These immigrants gravitated into peddling and rag-picking, while their multi-generation households crowded into ramshackle apartments. Although the influx of Eastern European Jews between 1881 and 1900 was gradual in comparison to the American experience, it nonetheless, as Stephen Speisman has shown in his history of Toronto Jews, contributed to a "more ambivalent public attitude towards the Jewish population." Media criticism of the Jewish immigrants replaced the sympathy their plight in Russia had previously evoked. Many Toronto politicians joined the media in denouncing the "slumlike" conditions of St John's Ward where the immigrants settled, and many specifically noted that Jews formed a considerable part of the problem.[21]

The Holy Blossomites were not pleased; general disapproval of the immigrants threatened their hard-won position and status. They responded to the Eastern European influx by dispensing relief and encouraging acculturation. Both proved inadequate. Attempts to dispense relief were soon overwhelmed by the increasing number and the utter destitution of the new arrivals. It was bad enough that some of the new arrivals needed municipal relief. To make matters worse, the Ladies' Montefiore Society's Victorian approach to philanthropy met with predictable resistance. Not only did few, if any, Montefiore members speak Yiddish, but their overwhelming sense of social superiority and *noblesse oblige* raised the hackles of immigrants who were culturally primed to reject hierarchical relief. The destitute immigrants came from a society that dispensed *tzedakah* according to the Deuteronomic injunction, "You shall surely open your hand to your destitute brother." They expected a helping hand and the empathy of their fellow Jews rather than invasive questions about their economic status and lectures on self-improvement. Nor did they expect stereotyping. But they received all three. From the immigrants' perspective, Montefiore members oozed arrogance and acculturation, could not speak their own language, and made groundless assumptions. In one case, the Montefiore invited a prospective member, an Eastern European woman of means, to a meeting. When she arrived, the member in charge of the meeting assumed that the invitee was a charity case and directed her to sit with other relief cases at the back of the room until she was called. The prospective member left and never returned.[22]

The *Jewish Times*, organ of the acculturated Jews of Toronto and Montreal, dispensed advice to new and old communities alike. Ironically, the newcomers couldn't read the English-language articles that lamented their image and suggested that they improve themselves. Peddlers were blamed for their unkempt appearance, and for the "grotesque figure [the peddler] is making in Gentile neighbourhoods in the city." Indeed, they were seen as "a sore that is troubling the healthy growth and development of the Jews of Toronto." Philanthropic ladies were urged to direct immigrants "into less degrading occupations" to maintain their hard-won status.[23]

This proved easier said than done. Between 1901 and 1911 Eastern European Jews flooded the old community, almost sextupling the Jewish population. By 1911 there were more than 18,000 Jews in Toronto. The new immigrants quickly established a rich network of synagogues and fraternal organizations of all political stripes, most of which like their counterparts in the United States and Great Britain, were mutual benefit societies. Some were friendly societies. Some were politically based, like the Jewish National Workers' Society and the Workmens' Circle, which also supplied life insurance and disability benefits. A few were *landsmanschaften*, mutual benefit societies made up of people from the same European town or province. Roughly 50 percent of Toronto Jews between the ages of twenty and forty-five belonged to these societies to ensure that they were provided with medical services, and unemployment and disability insurance. Pride of Israel, the largest of these societies, took the extra step of endowing a bed in Toronto General Hospital to guarantee its members access to the best medical care. Many societies employed a "lodge doctor," often a newly graduated practitioner, who served the medical needs of the society's members for a fixed annual sum. The availability of a lodge doctor often increased society membership. This emphasis on medical care was one of the unique features of Toronto's Jewish mutual benefit societies. Jewish hospitalization rates were between five and six times greater than those of non-Jews in comparable societies, but the Jewish mortality rate was far lower. But the key difference was Jewish mutual benefit societies' ownership of 40 percent of cemetery land, which allowed them to keep burial costs down. These differences were expensive – the average Jewish mutual benefit society member's dues were double those of his non-Jewish counterparts.[24]

Many mutual benefit society members were also supporters of particular clothing unions, which served the political, fraternal, and economic needs of the many Toronto Jews working in the "schmatta trade," – the clothing industry centred largely on bustling Spadina Avenue. Even though the tailoring trade would eventually be perceived as a "Jewish industry" by Jews and non-Jews alike, Jews began entering the industry in significant numbers just before the turn of the century. These immigrant Jews often held less-skilled jobs than experienced non-Jewish journeymen tailors and were often shunned as a result. This ethnic and experiential gap gave rise to Jewish union locals and non-Jewish locals. The coincidence of impoverished Polish Jewish immigration and the economic downturn of 1907 to 1908 further exacerbated union concerns about "cheap labour."

The rise of unions was a response to what was known as "sweated labour." Mackenzie King's 1897 investigation had revealed children working eighteen-hour days in ill-lit and worse-ventilated "sweat shops," being paid pennies per garment produced. Young girls suffered permanent injuries from the repetitive strain of the work and the poor ventilation. Many sweatshop "bosses" were immigrants themselves, who believed two or three sewing machines and a few *landsleit* workers mapped out the fastest road to success. The relationship between sweatshop bosses and workers was a mixed bag. In some cases the bonds of familiarity and similar levels of religiosity made for quite harmonious relationships – some sweatshops, for example, halted work so the boss and workers could pray *mincha* (the afternoon prayer) together. But in most cases, the brutal combination of long hours, poor conditions, and piecework at poor pay led to militancy and a desire to organize. Sexual harassment and favouritism were also serious issues among union workers. "Female workers who went out with the foremen got the best jobs," observed one. Unfortunately, the male-dominated unions did little for women, who received less strike pay; and issues of sexual harassment were often not dealt with.

Nonetheless, women remained a key and often militant group in Jewish union locals.

Even larger establishments with conditions superior to those of sweatshops were not immune to worker demands and unionization. The watershed strike against the Eaton Company in March 1912 began when the company decided to cut labour costs by firing its female finishers (who "finished" off the garment by sewing in the lining) and instructing the male tailors (who were members of the International Ladies' Garment Workers Union [ILGWU] even though Eaton's was not a "union shop") to assume this work without extra pay. When the sixty-five cloak-makers, all of whom were Jewish, refused, they were physically expelled from the plant. In response, over a thousand workers – mostly Jewish – employed in other sections of the vast Eaton factories downed their tools and declared a solidarity strike. Ruth Frager, in her study of Jewish workers' activism, thus observed that when the strike began male and female self-interests coincided. The large number of Jewish strikers made the strike a communal event, and the fame of Eaton's ensured that the strike remained front-page news for its sixteen-week duration. While the workers ultimately suffered an ignominious defeat, it is more important to note that the strike served as a leading indicator of key Jewish communal fault lines and alliances, which would further coalesce to control communal development over the next few decades.

Downtown Jews demonstrated solidarity with the strikers by boycotting Eaton's and turning to its archrival, Simpsons. This was an important demonstration of women's economic power – since they did the shopping. Two decades later, women would assume a parallel role in the boycott against Nazi goods. Another factor of key importance was the extent of institutional support for the strikers. Downtown Jewry's *landsmanschaften* and mutual benefit societies donated money, while the Associated Hebrew Charities provided food. The failure of the strike also played a role in catalyzing increasingly militant unionism after the First World War. Most significantly, the forces that pressed for an end to the strike on terms less than favourable to the workers, or intervened on the side of management, came from Uptowners' Holy Blossom and Goel Tzedec (established in 1883). Although Jacob Cohen of Holy Blossom, the first Jewish magistrate in Toronto, tried to play a mediatory role, he was distrusted and in his later career was perceived as anti-worker. Goel Tzedec's Rabbi Jacobs had preached a number of anti-union sermons a few years previously and thus it took a while for workers to perceive him as a fair mediator. He failed to persuade the Eaton's strikers to return to their jobs. In future labour wars, he reverted to the more traditional European role of rabbinic mediator, and represented both management and workers. But tellingly, not only did many manufacturers join Holy Blossom, but Signmund Lubelsky, an Eaton's manager, was an important member of the congregation. By the end of the strike, Downtown Jewish workers were convinced that Goel Tzedec and Holy Blossom represented cultural, religious, and economic forces antithetical to and disrespectful of their needs. It is not surprising that Downtown fraternal organizations proliferated.[25]

Despite the fact that the camaraderie and financial support provided by various forms of fraternal organization gave some assurance of support in times of illness or death, day-to-day life in the early decades of the twentieth century was still a struggle for most Toronto Jews. Contrary to their belief, and the subsequent myth, peddlers, tailors, and rag-pickers enjoyed limited upward mobility. For many Jews, especially those who had lived middle-class existences in Russia, the filthy streets and overcrowded apartments of "the Ward," oft-condemned by the Department of Health, bore no resemblance to the fabled *goldene medine*. Indeed, some areas of the Ward made immigrants nostalgic for the Pale. When one mother who arrived with her family in 1912 to join her seventee-year-old son "first saw the shabby house that would become her new home, she cried out '*Feh!* The pig sties in Konstantinov are nicer than this! This is why we gave up our house and everything we had? Tell me my son, is this the *gan aiden* [Garden of Eden] you wrote me about?'" Despite considerable anecdotal evidence that extended families and neighbours provided reciprocal support networks that helped ease daily life, the harsh combination of long workdays and the pressures of coping with new careers, languages, and cultures in cramped conditions took its toll. Allan Grossman, in a passage from *Growing Up Jewish*, puts it well: "It seems that the struggle for existence engaged our attention so much that we missed a great deal. There was a lot of bickering over such matters as who was paying what into the house and whether one was being treated better than another ... Father must have been disappointed by the lack of zeal some of us showed for his strictly Orthodox faith. Perhaps the spiritual separation of immigrant parents from their children is part of the price of migration."[26]

The pace of Jewish immigration reached flood proportions between 1900 and 1914. By now the immigrant community constituted a majority on many streets in the Ward. Some streetscapes became a recreation of European *shtetlach* – Yiddish signs abounded, street vendors' goods lined the sidewalks, and the air crackled with the cacophony of squawking chickens awaiting the Sabbath soup pot. Intellectuals from various ideological factions excitedly expounded their causes in Yiddish at ice cream parlours on Agnes Street (later Dundas) and Chestnut Street in the heart of the Ward. But these intellectual activities were temporary diversions from the difficulty of the conditions immigrants faced. During the recession of 1905–07, many had survived only with the help of their immigrant peers. A number of workers and craftsmen established a soup kitchen. Individuals too embarrassed to come in person were given lunch boxes that they could eat privately. The kitchen operated sporadically until 1909.

The soup kitchen was typical of the new immigrants' wide-ranging efforts to build their own social, cultural, and religious institutions without reference to the established Holy Blossom community. A Mrs Lewis had begun these efforts in 1893 with an *ad hoc* weekly collection system for penurious families. By 1899 she had spearheaded the formal conversion of this group into the Hebrew Ladies' Aid Society, which eschewed the Montefiore group's insulting interview techniques in favour of the more traditional approach of dispensing aid up to two dollars without any discussion even to strangers. As the society grew, its services became more sophisticated. It supplied cooking utensils, coal, and funds for shopping. It found dowries for poor brides and arranged long-term convalescent care in private homes. Other immigrant organizations, both formal and informal, operated alongside the Hebrew Ladies' Society. Collectively they assumed functions that were formerly the responsibility of communal *tzedakah* enterprises in Europe, and dispensed assistance in the traditional manner that respected recipients' dignity while serving them in their native Yiddish. The repeated refusal of the Hebrew Ladies' Society to merge with the Montefiore group reflected the Holy Blossomites' failure to impose their will on the more recent immigrant community. The sheer numbers of newcomers joined forces with linguistic, cultural, and social barriers to keep the old community's acculturationist ethic at bay for the present.[27] The rift between the two communities was such that the *Jewish Times* and its readers spouted ceaseless jeremiads against peddlers and Jews who acted "too Jewish," barely noticing the richly varied Jewish community coming into existence in their own ranks between 1890 and 1914.

This new "community of joiners," requiring institutions to meet its cultural, social, economic, and religious needs, soon developed a diversity of ethnic synagogues, burgeoning friendly and mutual benefit societies, and a host of political and cultural parties, clubs, and societies that ran the gamut from the Zionist Orthodoxy of Mizrachi to the proletarian socialism of the Workmen's Circle. The majority of these institutions, and the population they served, were found in the area bounded by Queen, Yonge, Gerrard, and University Avenue. A reporter attending the 1897 dedication of the Holy Blossom's impressive new synagogue on Bond Street was surely quoting some overly optimistic congregants when he proclaimed that the new building was designed to "result in the union of all the Hebrews in the city in one congregation." Indeed, by 1897 there had already been three new synagogues: Goel Tzedec, founded by Lithuanian immigrants in 1883, and two more congregations four years later. By then, Goel Tzedec had purchased a Methodist church on the corner of Elm and University. The prestige of this address, right at the edge of the Ward and not far from Queen's Park, reflected the congregation's quickly developing claims to pre-eminence. By 1910 Goel Tzedec had become the most prestigious of the immigrant synagogues and formed a real alternative to Holy Blossom for the upwardly mobile.[28]

Members of the Holy Blossom congregation equated upward mobility with acculturation. This principle rationalizes their support for public education (provided that it was kept free of religion) and explains why they endorsed Reform educator Edmund Scheuer's "Sabbath School" at Holy Blossom. This school, far more reformist than the congregation's ritual practices, emphasized ethics and text over Bible and Talmud, and championed English prayers, deportment, dress, and citizenship. This emphasis clashed with attitudes toward Jewish education among both the Holy Blossom and immigrant communities. Some members of both communities still believed the traditional curriculum was valuable, but wanted it taught in "pure English and pure Hebrew" rather than Yiddish, their way of thinking reflecting the progressive acculturation of the first immigrant wave. These groups broadly agreed on establishing a Talmud Torah, a communal school that used broadly based communal support to construct a proper school building and hire certified teachers capable of delivering a prescribed curriculum. This idea was first put forth in 1901, with widespread support from Holy Blossom and three major immigrant synagogues. But a series of events such as the death of a key Talmud Torah supporter, a lack of qualified teachers, and widespread opposition to a progressive Zionist and Hebrew-based curriculum among the many new arrivals, postponed the *Talmud Torah*'s opening until 1908. Students attended on Sunday mornings and on Monday through Thursday after public school. Senior students attended between ten and fourteen hours of classes per week. When it finally opened in a house on Simcoe Street, the school quickly gained a reputation for excellence. It became famous for its *Ivrit b'Ivrit* (Hebrew immersion method), the quality of its teachers, and its commitment to good citizenship. By 1911 enrollment was steady at about a hundred, and tuition was commensurate with ability to pay.[29]

The cooperation between Holy Blossom and the major immigrant synagogues marked the beginning of a key new dynamic in the community. The inter-ethnic lines that separated the Holy Blossom congregation from the upwardly mobile among the new immigrants were beginning to blur. Economic status was becoming more important in community allegiance than place of origin. It was no coincidence that Goel Tzedec's increasingly well-to-do members were key supporters of the new school. Its rise and its ideology mirrored theirs. February 1907 saw the dedication of Goel Tzedec's magnificent new building at Agnes (Dundas) and University. Designed to seat 1,200 worshippers, the building was both larger and more splendidly outfitted than Holy Blossom's, and its presence sharply curtailed the movement of successful immigrants to the latter institution. By this time, ironically, most of Holy Blossom's members were themselves post-1881 immigrants. But the broadening of the communal economic and social elite occurred in tandem with an increase in communal poverty. Destitute new Polish and Galician immigrants poured in after 1908. They often espoused different educational ideologies than those motivating the Talmud Torah. Schools that transplanted specific European ideologies were soon formed: the Jewish National Workers' School, the Peretz School, the Workmen's Circle, and the Eitz Chaim. The three former were secularist and reflected the growing number and influence of Yiddishist and Socialist immigrants, while the latter represented the reaction of those on the religious right to the "acculturated" and Zionistic curriculum of the Simcoe Street Talmud Torah.[30]

This increasingly complex web of ethnic service organizations obscured the differences emerging among the immigrants. After thirty years of immigration, a clear hierarchy had formed within the immigrant community, and early and more successful arrivals frequently lorded it over the destitute and *"prosteh greener"* (uncouth newcomers) fresh off the boat. The latter in turn, decried the acculturation of the earlier arrivals (while envying and seeking to emulate their success!) and, depending on their family background, were critical of their relative lack of passion for various flavours of Socialist Jewish politics or Orthodox Judaism.

Fading inter-ethnic differences combined with the unprecedented destitution of the immigrants of 1907–14 to catalyze the possibility of more broadly based relief efforts. Clearly the established communal organizations were too small and uncoordinated to effectively cope with the burgeoning immigrant population. A number of solutions to this type of influx had been tried in England and the United States, and Toronto Jewish communal activists were aware of them. London's charitable organizations had adopted a centralized casework system in 1869 under the auspices of the Charity Organization Society (COS), whose key legacy was a commitment to the development of professional casework. The agencies that joined the COS had merged their relief functions, and a united board was elected. It arranged for all its constituent agencies to send out workers (some paid, others volunteers) to ensure that applicants met the required aid criteria. This measure also eliminated duplication of aid. In typical Victorian fashion, the workers also verified that recipients were still worthy of help. They made every effort, in the best tradition of self-help, to educate these "worthies" and teach them skills that would enable them to become self-supporting. On this last point, the principles of philanthropy and *tzedakah* coincided. This goes far to explain why the COS plan had crossed the Atlantic that same year with the organization of the United Hebrew Charities in Philadelphia, inspiring the founding of the United Hebrew Charities of New York in 1874. Thus the two major centres of American Jewry had adopted the charity organization model even before it was formally applied to non-sectarian (but mostly

Protestant) charities with the formation of the Buffalo Charity Organization Society in 1877. The movement proved popular, and by 1892 agencies modelled on the cos had sprung up in ninety-two American cities. Although they improved the dispensation of communal aid, serious gaps were still evident.[31]

The Toronto experience was a case in point. In January 1912, after two years of pressure from communal activists, eight organizations in the immigrant community joined to the Associated Hebrew Charities, and moved into a large house at 218 Simcoe Street. This cos-type arrangement included Ladies' Maternity Aid, the Free Burial Society, the Jewish Dispensary, a newly founded Orphanage, a Day Nursery (for working mothers), and some smaller organizations. Unparalleled in Canada, this system differed from its American Jewish counterparts in significant ways. Like them, it served as a central organizational and administrative hub to coordinate services and eliminate overlap. However, the societies did not trust each other enough to completely merge; organizational governance was complex and cumbersome. Most significantly, the Montefiore Ladies and the male communal workers of Holy Blossom Jewish Benevolent Society were not part of the picture.[32]

But the economic and social clout of the Holy Blossomites could not be denied for long, and they were among the most knowledgeable of community workers. By early 1913 both the Montefiore Ladies and the Jewish Benevolent Societies had joined the Associated Hebrew Charities. Their entry was predicated on the Associated Hebrew Charities' endorsing a commitment to scientific charity, the insistence that all relief applicants be rigorously screened and that relief disbursements be linked to this assessment. Of course, scientific charity was anathema to the Downtowners, who upheld the traditional value of *tzedakah*. But Holy Blossom's star was in the ascendant, and philanthropy triumphed over *tzedakah*. As the congregation continued to grow, bolstered by status-seeking immigrants who had made good and were moving out of the Ward to newer residential areas to the west. The rest of the immigrant community was increasingly divided between the successful members of Goel Tzedec, many of whom could afford to join Holy Blossom but were uncomfortable with its gradual movement away from Orthodoxy, and others who, whatever their length of residence, still battled to make ends meet. As immigration peaked just before the fateful summer of 1914, it was apparent that the Associated Hebrew Charities was only an interim solution to the challenges of communal philanthropy.³³

A superior model was available south of the border. As noted, one of the key contributions of the COS philosophy was the development of professional casework in Britain and the United States. The National Conference of Social Work was founded in 1873, with the twin aims of dealing with those who had become dependent on philanthropy and educating communal workers to become professional caseworkers. In the 1890s, as social work curricula were developed and taught at American universities, its practitioners would become professionalized. Ultimately, by the early twentieth century, social work was established as a profession – one especially attractive to young women. The American Jewish communal establishment, aware of these trends, was at the forefront of developments. At first blush, it is surprising that the American Jewish experience would inform Toronto Jews, as there were significant differences between the communities. The American Jewish establishment of New York, Chicago, and Philadelphia was composed mostly of German Jews who used their population mass and economic influence to articulate a sense of community that blended their Jewish roots into American ways. By the time the immigrant wave began, a considerable number of these German Jews occupied important positions in American business life. They perceived the post-1881 flood of Eastern Europeans as a threat to the image of the acculturated American Jew that they had crafted and exemplified. But despite their anxiety and hostility to the "influx of debilitated and pauperized Eastern European Jews," they worked tirelessly to help the immigrants. Since a significant number of Holy Blossom members had American connections through family or business, or read the frequent comments of the *Jewish Messenger*, these trends were known in Toronto. But the American Jewish community found the COS concept of limited utility; by 1890 it had proved inadequate. The solution that emerged by 1895 was elegantly simple: form a federation.³⁴

The federation concept took the COS model to its logical conclusion. It required communal social service agencies who already pooled their resources under the COS model to agree to be financed by a single annual campaign conducted by the federation. It was widely believed, and generally proven correct, that a single efficiently conducted campaign raised more than the individual campaigns of each agency. Thus, the federation plan would remove at one stroke the multiple campaigns that both taxed the agencies' personnel resources and alienated wealthy donors offended by "multiple doorknockers" during the campaign seasons before Rosh Hashanah and Passover. But the real goal of federation went beyond the simple rationalization of fundraising. In theory, a federation's constituent agencies were autonomous. But, in order to determine the annual campaign goal, it was necessary first to add up the budgets of all the agencies. In the early federations, agencies were allowed to compute their needs independently, but as demand for social services increased, changes were required. By 1910 a number of large American federations used accountants to vet agency budgets and impose limits on the spending of agencies considered too profligate or inefficient at meeting their mandate. This accounting check ensured that the largest donors, who inevitably controlled a federation board, could and did use their clout to eliminate duplicate campaigning, to streamline budgeting, and, most influential in the long run, to decide which agencies were most deserving of communal funds. The entire system resembled scientifically managed charity rather than *tzedakah*, and was generally regarded with suspicion by immigrant-run agencies and their clients.[35]

To be sure, the federation model pioneered in Boston (1895) and Cincinnati (1896) had heightened the antagonisms between the German American elite and the Eastern Europeans. But the needs of the immigrants were so pressing that self-help and reliance on their own organizations proved insufficient. One major American Jewish community after another began federations, many of which included immigrant-run agencies. As one federation leader remarked: "There can be no place in the vocabulary of federation, once it serves as the articulate will of the entire Jewish community, for such words as German, Russian, Polish, American, Orthodox, Reform, etc. Federation must concern itself with the cross-section needs and desires of the entire Jewish community." These maxims would be sorely tested in Toronto, where immigrants who distrusted scientific charity were eager to maintain control of their institutions and traditional *tzedakah*-based modalities of self-help.[36]

By 1904 seven other major American Jewish communities, including Chicago, Detroit, and Philadelphia, had adopted the federation model. The pace quickened in the next decade when Pittsburgh, Los Angeles, San Francisco, and New York followed suit. It was clear that

Toronto's turn had arrived. By 1916 Toronto's Associated Jewish Charities had reached the limit of its usefulness. Of course Toronto was different from the major American Jewish communities. The divide between Downtown and Uptown communities was neither as deep nor as defined as in America. But, despite promises of non-interference in agency independence, immigrants in Toronto and Toledo alike resented the power and attitude of the wealthy. The Associated Jewish Charities' smaller immigrant-founded agencies remained deeply suspicious of Holy Blossom's Montefiore Ladies and the Jewish Benevolent Societies. These attitudes, compounded by a floodtide of impoverished immigrants arriving in 1913 and the first half of 1914, undermined all efforts at fundraising. By 1916, Montefiore was but a near bankrupt shell.[37]

Even with the Associated Jewish Charities clearly failing, it proved difficult to establish a federation in Toronto. Notably, the three main backers of this plan were familiar with the American Jewish federations and were members of Holy Blossom and Goel Tzedec. They were able to garner the support of Downtowners because the massive disruption of Jewish life in Russian Poland brought about by the Great War catalyzed relief efforts among the Eastern European immigrants. Their zealous desire to assist their *landsleit* would change the topography of Canadian Jewish organizational life both locally and nationally.

The first key person behind the coming of the federation concept was Ida Siegel. She grew up in an immigrant family that had come to Toronto from Pittsburgh, and was familiar with the advantages of federation. Her family was very active in charitable causes, and she had followed their example. By 1916 she was the president of Maternity Aid, then the most prestigious and influential of the immigrant aid societies, which as its name implied, focused on assisting mothers and their new babies with everything they required to thrive. New mothers received milk, linens, medical care, domestic assistance, and luxuries such as fresh fruit. Maternity Aid members served as interpreters for public health nurse visits, and supplied treats to all patients at the Tuberculosis Sanatorium and three major downtown hospitals. Its annual ball, a major fundraiser, was the gala event of the immigrant community. When they amassed a surplus, funds were distributed to other charities.[38]

By the summer of 1916 there was no surplus. Seeing the writing on the wall, Siegel recruited Abraham Cohen, a young lawyer active in Goel Tzedec who had studied American Jewish federations firsthand and was convinced of their merit. But when an initial attempt to form a committee to plan a federation became dormant, Siegel realized that the scheme was doomed without participation from major donors – and this meant Holy Blossom. Fortunately, Siegel had connections. She got in touch with Edmund Scheuer, her former teacher at Holy Blossom Sabbath School, who was widely regarded as "the grand old man" of Toronto Jewry. Since his emigration from Bavaria in 1847, he had played an important role in Hamilton's Reform temple, Anshe Sholom, and had been the key influence in moving Holy Blossom toward formal affiliation with the Reform movement. Scheuer was a successful wholesale jeweller and lived in a magnificent Rosedale mansion. He kept a scrapbook of clippings from American Jewish papers detailing the development of various federations. He was prepared to lend his prestige to support the scheme, but did not want to take an active part in the organization.[39]

Even with the allure of Scheuer's backing, Cohen and Siegel discovered they were not preaching to the converted. It took Siegel's personal friendship with the wife of Jule J. Allen to persuade the wealthy theatre owner and member of both Holy Blossom and Goel Tzedec to join the federation movement. Allen brought energy and a wide range of contacts among the movers and shakers of the old and new communities, and prevailed upon many of his friends to join the cause. In October 1916, with Scheuer's stately Rosedale residence providing the venue, these men (and a couple of women) approved the formation of the Federation of Jewish Philanthropies of Toronto (FJP). Later that month a provisional board, dominated by members of Goel Tzedec and Holy Blossom and their societies, was elected. However, prominent Yiddishists (such as Abraham Rhinewine, editor of the daily *Yiddisher Zhurnal*), secularists, and members of smaller societies were also represented.[40]

The provisional board quickly approved a February 1917 campaign for $30,000, and with Allen setting the pace, large donors contributed over $7,000 before the campaign even opened. Yet, as would often be the case, the veneer of unity was already stretched thin. The womens' societies, immigrant and Montefiore alike, resented their pending loss of independence and did little to further the campaign. To make matters worse, the new FJP constitution banned women, the backbone of traditional *tzedakah* and a key philanthropic force, from participating on the board. When Siegel appealed, she succeeded in wrangling a single seat for women, which ironically went to a member of the Montefiore. The ousting of the federation's key catalyst at the moment of its birth reflected poorly upon the nascent organization's unity. The marginalization of women ignored their key role in *tzedakah* and further alienated the immigrant community.[41]

This was but the beginning of the FJP's difficulties. Its initial campaign was wracked by dissension from the outset—a large number of potential canvassers withdrew because they believed the $30,000 goal too high. Those recruited to replace them only three days before the campaign kick-off understandably lacked training and confidence. The result was disastrous: only $20,000 was raised and naysayers had a field day pointing fingers at the new organization. Their rejoicing proved premature. The FJP board put the best face on the campaign, displaying from the outset what would become a characteristically tenacious commitment to scientific charity. Despite the campaign's failure to meet its goal, they saw some silver linings: Jewish street begging and individual charitable appeals were sharply diminished. This improvement drew more members from the rising middle class to support the FJP. By 1918 the federation was able to use this appeal to the relatively deep-pocketed to meet a campaign target of $50,000. A grant of $1,000 from the City of Toronto served as recognition of its presence. Its immediate survival was now assured.[42]

But the increased support of the wealthy and upwardly mobile epitomized by Holy Blossom and Goel Tzedec was paralleled by the almost wholesale withdrawal of *amcha* from the federation. During the early 1920s, the smaller womens' societies left the federation as the board lowered or eliminated their share of the funds raised, in order to prevent institutional overlap. The FJP board's commitment to scientific charity and organizational rationalization even drove out the Montefiore Ladies by 1924. The hiring of a professional executive director after 1921 was another step in this process. As we shall see, the FJP's annual campaigns would meet with mixed success during the 1920s, but the federation's use of professional social workers in its affiliated organizations, and its commitment to professional standards would crucially impact communal planning.[43]

The federation's institutional influence reflected the increased economic and political clout of the more established immigrants and the growing influence of the new generation of Jewish Canadians. By 1921 25 percent of Toronto's Jews had lived in the city for at least ten years, and they tended to be the most upwardly mobile. The tendency of successful immigrants to affiliate with Holy Blossom and Goel Tzedec synagogues has already been noted. This economic group spearheaded the pre-1914 residential movement westward out of the Ward to Spadina Avenue and as far west as Bathurst Street. Within a decade the majority of Toronto Jews had followed this vanguard, but by then certain "prestigious" streets such as Beverley and Palmerston were already the domain of the up-and-comers. The residential proximity of the Jewish middle class meant increased social interaction of their children at public school and later at the University of Toronto. By 1921 there was a noticeable and steadily growing stream of Jewish university graduates in Toronto, whose education had influenced them to believe that the rational application of expertise could solve most problems. This progressivist predilection attracted them to the federation and its affiliate agencies, where they found ready acceptance at two levels. Those who became lay leaders and donors found scientific charity appealing, while social work graduates became the backbone of the increasingly professionalized staff of the federation and its affiliated agencies. These Jewish practitioners of a new profession were often women who found social work one of the few upwardly mobile careers available.[44]

But what attracted the classes repelled the masses. *Amcha*, ordinary Jews, the vast majority of the community, remained uncomfortable with scientific charity, wanting organizations to have a more democratic bent. For the more ideological among them – and there were many – the federation symbolized "intra-communal elite control" and they wanted no part of it. Rhinewine and other Yiddishists soon left the FJP to throw their energies into the more broadly based Canadian Jewish Congress. As Toronto's Jewish population continued to swell in the 1920s, the growth of a Yiddish sub-culture around Kensington Market and Spadina Avenue continued unimpeded. The Ward had seemingly moved west. Chickens cackled raucously in the packed stalls of Kensington Market. Battles between various sub-ethnic groups (Polish, Galician, Lithuanian Jews) over the kosher status of the chickens multiplied and spawned highly publicized legal battles. Mutual benefit societies continued to flourish and grow, garment workers' unions of various factions appeared and offered members social benefits and cultural activities, new immigrant synagogues continued to appear in housefronts, and older immigrant synagogues moved into better quarters – all without regard to the federation. And, truth be told, most of the newest immigrants didn't need the federation, didn't know it existed, and never used the services of its affiliate agencies. If they lacked membership in a fraternal organization, they could go to the Folks Farein for aid with drug or hospital care, or continue to benefit from reciprocal relief provided by neighbours and *landsleit*. Since they had a strong distaste for scientific charity, the federation claimed neither their hearts nor their pocketbooks.

The near-unanimous support for Zionism among Toronto Jews contrasted with their decidedly mixed reactions to the federation. In contrast with the American experience, where the largely Reform German-Jewish establishment opposed Zionism as unpatriotic, Canadian Zionism enjoyed wide favour, particularly after the Balfour Declaration of 1917. The Federation of Zionist Societies of Canada, led by Clarence de Sola of Montreal's illustrious family, enjoyed widespread support. But as the war drew to a close and discussions surfaced about the role Zionism would play at Versailles, cracks appeared in the Canadian Zionist façade of unity. Downtowners wanted to see a broad-based agenda that would deal with the Palestine question as well as with "poverty in Montreal, starvation in Eastern Europe, civil and political rights for Jewish minorities." But de Sola focused on Palestine. He did not want to see the Zionist agenda "diluted" by other concerns. This single focus contrasted with the attitude of the founders of the American Jewish Committee, who realized that combining an appeal for funds for Palestine with an appeal for stricken European Jewry would elicit immigrant support and eliminate overlapping campaigns. In fact, the success of the American Jewish Congress turned on this appeal to the Eastern European immigrant masses. As we shall see, it would take until 1948 for Canada's Jewish fundraisers to reach a similar conclusion and create a united national fundraising organization.[45]

Even though de Sola did have some allies among Downtowners, divisions over the relative priority of Zionism and other Jewish issues in the postwar world ran deep enough to produce organizational competition. Supporters of de Sola's views formed the elitist Canadian

Jewish Committee, while its opponents formed the Canadian Jewish Alliance. These organizations fought a spirited campaign of words and editorials between 1915 and 1918. At last, with de Sola ailing, the Canadian jewish Committee agreed to discuss the possibility of founding a democratically elected "parliament of Canadian Jewry." This idea, with its appeal to the democratic polity so favoured by the Downtowners, was the brainchild of the remarkable Hannaniah Meir Caiserman of Montreal. Caiserman was one of the key organizers of the Relief Committee for European Jewry, supported by over a hundred immigrant organizations in 1915, and a prominent Labour Zionist. He envisioned a Canadian Jewish Congress that would speak for Canadian Jews on international Jewish issues, deal with the Zionist agenda, and fight for the democratic rights of Jews everywhere. He wanted this organization to be elected, representative, and, above all, democratic. Canada's Yiddish newspapers in Winnipeg, Toronto, and Montreal eagerly took up the call. These issues resonated with Downtown *amcha* – and after many meetings and false starts it appeared that Canadian Jewry was finally on the road toward political unity.[46]

In late 1918 the Zionists, with the far more sympathetic Queen's graduate A.B. Bennett at the helm in de Sola's place, agreed to discuss plans for a Canadian Jewish Congress with its rivals. A series of meetings in Winnipeg, Toronto, and Montreal confirmed the extent of grassroots support and laid the groundwork for the organization of the Canadian Jewish Congress (CJC) and the rules for electing delegates. The elections in March 1919 were marked by an overwhelming voter turnout: 25,000 ballots cast from among a population of 125,000. Jews from tiny hamlets and large cities alike participated. Thus the CJC truly spoke for Canadian Jews.[47]

The CJC's opening convention produced a formidable list of initiatives among its resolutions. There were promises to deal with the role of Palestine, lobby for the Jewish nation to have a place at Versailles, help immigrants by establishing a national Jewish immigrant aid society, educate Canadians about Jews, and battle anti-Semitism. Committees were struck at the national, regional, and local levels, and work began in earnest. These were heady days full of anticipation: Canadian Jewry had spoken as one and created a national organization. The war was over and the League of Nations had been established to preserve world peace and safeguard Jewish rights in the new European nations mandated at Versailles. The Jews of Eastern Europe, stricken by war and pogroms, would be aided in rebuilding their broken communities. Jewish immigration would resume and long-separated families might be reunited. Anti-Semitism would recede amid education and realization of the patriotic efforts of Canadian Jewry in the First World War. The future of Canadian Jewry seemed bright.

These optimistic prognostications proved naive. In less than a year, the CJC was moribund – suddenly abandoned by the Montreal elite that had supported its birth and starved by a lack of funds from Toronto and Winnipeg. Caiserman soldiered on until early 1921 before he threw in the towel – but he did not abandon the dream of a rejuvenated congress. The only offspring of the congress, the Jewish Immigrant Aid Society of Canada (JIAS), was a shadow of its blueprint. National in name only, run on a shoestring, and staffed by volunteers unschooled in the complexities of the Canadian immigration regime, its Toronto office could not compete with the shady lawyers, influence peddlers, and travel agents who obtained permission for the majority of the Jews entering Canada. By 1921 Toronto's Jewish organizational map had largely regressed to the chaos of 1916.[48]

What ultimately emerged as the organized, professionalized, and efficient Toronto Jewish community of 1948 contrasts starkly with that of 1921. One might think that cataclysmic events produced the organizational paradigm shift that took place in those intervening years. However, as the rest of this narrative will show, that is too simple a presumption. The roots of 1948 stretch back to 1921 – but the path to organizational rationalization was not inevitable. Nor did it follow an easily predictable path when it finally took place. In following this trail to its end we will discover a great deal about what differentiates the Toronto Jewish experience from that of Montreal, and investigate the veracity of assumptions commonly held about Canadian and American Jewish history. One thing is certain: unity was imposed on Toronto's *amcha* – haltingly but irresistibly – as a result of many events within and beyond the community. This imposition of will produced both organizational rationalization and a trail of alienation. The challenges of the 1930s and 1940s catalyzed a communal redefinition of Jewish identity as forged in *der alte heim* (the old homeland) and impelled a new consensus on what constituted Canadian Jewish identity in Toronto. By 1948, as we shall see, this process was irresistible and the organizational expression of a new Canadian Jewish identity had matured to the point that the outlines of the organizational structure of twenty-first-century Toronto were clearly visible.

2

Fragile Signs of Unity: 1933

For Toronto's 46,000 Jews, 1933 did not begin auspiciously. Like other Canadians, they had been badly affected by three and a half years of the Depression. Charities were running out of funds and had begun borrowing money against future campaigns in a desperate attempt to assist the unemployed. Violent strife in the Spadina Avenue clothing factories often grabbed headlines and left hundreds without work. Jobs were lost as factories relocated to smaller towns in order to escape the demands of unionized workers. The Bennett government's tough amendments to the *Immigration Act* hobbled Jewish immigration and made family reunification but a dream. While Canadian Jews were incensed at this injustice, they had no power to protest in an organized way, because they had no central body to speak for them.

There had once been such a central body. But the Canadian Jewish Congress, which had been founded in 1919 on a wave of communal enthusiasm, was by 1921 dormant, a victim of tensions between its leaders in Toronto and Montreal, and the apathy of its leadership. This was ironic, notes Gerald Tulchinsky, given that "immigration, the important topic of the time, was so high on [Congress's] agenda." What remained of Congress in 1933, not surprisingly, was the Jewish Immigrant Aid Society of Canada (JIAS). In the 1920s it had reunited families and lobbied the government for the admission of orphans from the Ukraine. But government restrictions on Jewish immigration had an impact on the JIAS, and by the 1930s even its Montreal headquarters were not very busy. In Toronto, it existed in name only.

The Toronto Jewish community was at this time divided along ethnic and economic lines. The English Jews (and a trickle from Germany) who pioneered the community had been submerged by a tide of immigrants. Polish Jews, arriving in two waves, 1896–1913 and 1921–25, now formed the bulk of the community. Intra-ethnic tensions loomed ever larger, especially as some Polish Jews began to prosper and sought to join Holy Blossom Temple, which they called the *Daitche Shule* (the German synagogue) and move into the upscale Forest Hill neighbourhood. Observant Polish Jews were shocked at the bareheaded worshippers and the prominence of the Sunday morning service at Holy Blossom, and felt repelled by the "scientific charity" practised by the Holy Blossom–dominated Federation of Jewish Philanthropies (FJP). While not all the Polish Jews were observant, most preferred to pray in a *shtibel* (tiny synagogue in one room of a house or store) among their former *landsleit* (townsfolk). Those of a more socialist bent found many organizations to serve their needs, the Workmen's Circle and Labour Zionists to name just two. Communists flocked to the United Jewish People's Order or to Communist unions; despite their political and religious differences, they agreed that if they needed charity or were ill, they would rather receive aid in a friendly way. They did not want to be subjected to embarrassing questions from caseworkers affiliated with social work agencies. Instead, they formed sick benefit societies organized with *landsleit*. *Landsmanschaften* (organizations of people from the same town) also filled their social needs and helped them feel less lonely in a strange land.[1]

What Toronto Jewry had in common was that 75 percent of them had been in Canada for less than twenty years. They looked anxiously back at Europe where many family members remained. Polish Jews had never felt secure, and it was common for families to immigrate in stages to Canada. Often a father would come to find work and assess Canadian living conditions. If he was able to earn a living, he would send for the rest of his family, and in the interim would send money home to provide for them. Polish Jews fortunate enough to settle in Canada kept up a constant stream of remittances and correspondence with their relatives. German Jews were more separated from their native land than their Polish co-religionists, for many of them were second-generation immigrants whose parents had come from Germany forty to sixty years earlier. Nonetheless, they still kept in touch with their relatives and friends in Germany and were intensely interested in German political developments.²

Hitler's rise to power on 30 January 1933 galvanized Canadian Jews, including those in Toronto, to begin working together. S.M. Shapiro, editor of the Toronto Yiddish daily newspaper *Yiddisher Zhurnal*, immediately demanded that Canadian Jewry organize itself to fight Hitler, whom he regarded as a threat to all the Jews of Europe. But, even if Toronto Jews were all to agree, how could they unite against Hitler? How would they unify? What strategies would they use? Where would the money come from? Who would their leaders be? Who would be the communal spokespeople (*shtadlanim*) who negotiated with the government?

In Montreal, home to almost 60,000 Jews, Hannaniah Meir Caiserman was asking the same questions – and had asked them for a long time. He had been the key organizer and general secretary of the original Canadian Jewish Congress (CJC or Congress) that had convened in 1919. Caiserman was a leading Labour Zionist and a well-known English and Yiddish journalist. He believed that a renewed CJC would allow all Jews, rich and poor, capitalist and socialist, observant and non-observant, a chance to influence the formation of Canadian Jewish opinion. He had lobbied for the revival of the CJC throughout the 1920s, but his efforts had gone unrewarded.³

But Hitler's ascendancy and the consequent growth in Canadian anti-Semitism stirred Caiserman to try again. More people were now ready to listen to his message. By March 1933 he had formed the Provisional Committee of the CJC and received support from most middle- and working-class Montreal Jews, with the important exception of the Communists. The wealthy Jews of Westmount, most belonging to Orthodox Shaar HaShomayim or the Reform Emanu-El congregations, remained aloof from this Downtown effort. They formed instead the Canadian Jewish Committee, modelled on the elitist American Jewish Committee.⁴

Caiserman approached Philip Mayerovich, secretary of the Canadian Jewish Committee, and proposed that the two organizations unite.

I told them frankly that the Canadian Jewish Committee represents a hundred or a few hundred important Jews. Why not dissolve in the Canadian Jewish Congress and participate in the leading of Canadian Jewry as a whole? Mr. Mayerovitch [sic] and the chairman, Rabbi Abramovitch, asked on what basis and program? Mr. Bobrov and I suggested that the Canadian Jewish Committee select a committee of five, which committee together with our own committee of five are instructed to meet and endeavor to draft the principles of the proposed Congress, and continue to negotiate until a unanimous report can be brought to both parties.[5]

Mayerovich was interested.

After five meetings, the Canadian Jewish Committee and the Provisional Committee of the Canadian Jewish Congress hammered out an agreement. The groups merged in the spring of 1933 under the name of the Canadian Jewish Congress. What made the committees agree to merge? An article in the *Canadian Jewish Chronicle*, the mouthpiece of Montreal's wealthier Jews, explains:

> Circumstances are the tools which force action, and inasmuch as conditions are constantly changing, so do our viewpoints undergo a transformation ... The plight of our brethren in Germany has crystallized Jewish sentiment into one solid unit ... he most complacent among us will admit that this is a time for decisive action ... we must coordinate our forces. We realize the difficulties that such a step would involve. Our communities are scattered far and wide, and the Congress itself might become an arena for impassioned oratory and innocuous resolutions, but ... with the gravity of the situation that confronts us, we could obviate these hardships, and formulate a program by which all the Jews of Canada could be guided.[6]

With Montreal's Jews now cooperating, Caiserman turned his attention to Toronto where, in March of 1933, Rabbi Samuel Sachs, spiritual leader of the Goel Tzedec synagogue on University Avenue, had organized the League for the Defence of Jewish Rights. This league, composed mainly of Goel Tzedec members, was created in response to the helplessness Jews felt as they watched the rise of Hitler. The league was also attempting to deal with a renewed surge of anti-Semitism in Toronto.[7]

Caiserman hoped to integrate the league with his plan for a nation-wide revival of the CJC, to kick-start with a national conference in Ottawa in June. He suggested that the league send five delegates to the Ottawa conference. Caiserman's letter was warmly received.[8] Despite his planning, however, the conference ended up taking place in Toronto. A group of prospective Winnipeg participants could see no point in travelling all the way to Ottawa via Toronto. Why not stop in Toronto and have the conference there? Other considerations factored in as well: Archie Freiman, a prominent Ottawa businessman and Liberal Party supporter, was not enthusiastic about the proposed revitalization of the Congress. Perhaps he viewed it as competition for the Zionist Organization of Canada (ZOC), Canada's only national Jewish organization, of which he was president. Ottawa was Freiman country and Caiserman feared that without his support the conference would stir needless controversy. Furthermore, Shapiro, popular among the Toronto *landsmanschaften*, did not wish to move from his editorial power base. Besides, a Toronto conference would offer some journalistic "scoops."[9]

Caiserman went with the flow. He proposed that the League take responsibility for coordinating the conference in Toronto, which would begin on the night of Saturday 10 June. Sunday would be used for speeches, discussions, and voting for the regional officers of the resuscitated Congress. Caiserman remained in charge of finding speakers and assembling the agenda. The league accepted this proposal and sent Caiserman a list of its delegates: Rabbi Samuel Sachs, Archie B. Bennett, Elias Pullan, J.J. Glass, and Morris Goldstick.[10]

Dissension set in immediately. Not everyone in Toronto was pleased with the choice of delegates. Few doubted that Rabbi Sachs, a pillar of the community, deserved his nomination. Bennett, a veteran of the first Congress, commanded wide respect. Pullan had served Goel Tzedec and the community for many years, nd his experience would be a valuable asset. Glass, a popular alderman, was a leading *shtadlan* (communal spokesperson). But Goldstick lacked their stature. He was a Yiddish journalist whose *Kanada Naies*, a small newspaper sold together with the New York Yiddish dailies, was the only Toronto Yiddish paper besides Shapiro's *Zhurnal*. Here lay the source of the conflict.[11]

Shapiro was utterly devoted to his newspaper. An avowed Yiddishist, he battled the Depression and decreasing readership to keep the *Zhurnal* alive. He could not stomach the presence of any rival, especially a Socialist like Goldstick, in a body that would serve as a spokesagency for the country's Jews.[12]

The beleaguered Caiserman had other fish to fry. He also found it difficult to deal with Rabbi Maurice Eisendrath, chairman of the Canadian Jewish Committee's Toronto chapter. Eisendrath, the charismatic rabbi of Holy Blossom Temple, a brilliant orator respected by the Gentile community, was also known for his aloofness to *amcha*. Caiserman was most anxious to win over Eisendrath to the CJC cause, but Eisendrath was widely disliked by Downtowners. Further, though not a rabid anti-Zionist, he was no friend of Zionism, and was suspicious that the Congress would become a Zionist forum. Even more significant was Eisendrath's fear that the organization would become enmeshed in petty politicking and accomplish little. He thought Canadian Jewry would be better served by continued involvement in *shtadlanut*; polite backroom negotiations with those in positions of influence.[13]

In late May of 1933 Eisendrath left on a three-month mission to assess the situation in Germany, with his support for a renewed Congress still unconfirmed. This indecision forced Caiserman to delay convincing the Toronto Canadian Jewish Committee. He hoped that the support of leaders like Rabbi Harry Stern of Montreal's Temple Emanu-El and Rabbi Abramovitch of Shaar HaShomayim, would be the catalyst that Eisendrath needed.[14]

In fact, Eisendrath remained aware of Toronto events. He heard of rabbis Abramovitch's and Stern's decision to support Congress and decided to give the fledgling organization a chance. Members of Holy Blossom thus attended the June proceedings. For the moment, Toronto Jewry had a common cause, though the bonds were fragile at best.[15]

The fragility of the organization was a measure of its incompleteness. The almost complete absence of organized labour was a striking, but understandable, omission. By the mid-1920s a significant number of Jews had worked in the male and female garment industry, colloquially referred to by its Yiddish name as "the *shmatte* trade." In 1931 almost half the *shmatte* workers in Toronto and more than one-third in Montreal were Jewish. The three unions in the Toronto clothing trade were at their most militant in this period. Between 1931 and 1936 there were fourteen major strikes (three more, if fur workers are included). Many were brutal affairs, with extensive picket line violence. The politics of the different unions matched those of the Downtown community: the Amalgamated and the International Ladies Garment Workers (ILGWU) were socialist, while the Industrial Union of Needle Trades Workers was Communist. The founding of the new Congress coincided with the heightening of tensions between the Communists and non-Communists among the Jewish union members, a trend that would continue until 1945. Communists extolled the virtues of Birobidjan, the Jewish state formed by Stalin, as proof that "the 'Jewish question' was being solved with the building of the Communist state in the Soviet Union." Of course, this was anathema to non-Communists, who saw Zionism as the great hope of the Jewish people and noted that anti-Semitism was still rife in the Soviet Union.

These divisions within organized Jewish labour mirrored those in the community at large and further interfered with Congress goal of being a communal spokesagency. Many of its principal organizers wore multiple hats; Caiserman, a leader of the Labour Zionist movement, for example, was avowedly anti-Communist. In addition, he had been organizer in a major Montreal strike in 1917. Many *machers* (important leaders) whom he tried to attract to the Congress cause were factory owners or manufacturers with a decidedly anti-union stance. On the other hand, they – like Caiserman – were committed Zionists. Later in the decade, a consensus emerged that focused on the community's widely shared Zionist sympathies. This allowed the "mainstream" unions, the Amalgamated and ILGWU, to affiliate with Congress while excluding the Communists. This tactic proved useful as a counterweight to the widely held belief that "most Jews are Communists." But it also previewed the careful path Congress would have to walk to maintain a semblance of unity in its diverse constituency.

Given these formidable intra-ethnic and inter-class tensions, the Toronto conference was an outstanding success in numbers and breadth of representation. Almost five hundred people attended the lavish opening session in the ballroom of the King Edward Hotel on the Saturday evening. By Sunday afternoon, they had drafted and accepted – though not without some acrimony – a platform that was a response to the Nazi threat abroad and to anti-Semitism at home. The draft also reflected a split between Reform congregations in Montreal and Toronto, however. Rabbi Stern was an ardent Zionist, and his supporters had helped draft an article that went against the grain of their more anti-Zionist Toronto Reform colleagues. This article pledged that Congress would "further the development of the Jewish National Home in Palestine." The Toronto Reform representatives were understandably upset and warned there would be little hope of securing Rabbi Eisendrath's support on his return from Germany.[16]

Beyond the Zionist debate, most of the conference agenda was spent organizing a national administration and the elections that would bring it into existence. Canada was divided into three administrative divisions: East, Central, and West. The Eastern Division, headquartered in Montreal, served the Maritimes and Quebec. The Central Division, headquartered in Toronto, administered all of Ontario except for Port Arthur–Fort William. The Western Division, with headquarters in Winnipeg, included the vast territory from Fort William to the Pacific Coast. The divisions were geographically large and administratively unwieldy, yet it was hard to think of a better scheme, given the demographics of Canadian Jewry. While there were Jews sprinkled across Canada, in reality the three divisions were proxies for Montreal, Toronto, and Winnipeg, where over 70 percent of Canada's Jews lived.

It seemed that Jews in smaller cities would likely be less well represented. The original Congress platform had called for one representative for the first 1,500 Jewish inhabitants and an additional representative for each additional 250 inhabitants in all Jewish communities of more than 1,500 Jews. Communities with fewer than 1,500 Jews were entitled to one delegate each. But Simon Belkin, a demographic expert with the Jewish Colonization Association, observed that such an arrangement would severely affect Jews from such cities as Calgary, Edmonton, and Saskatoon, which would be entitled only to a single delegate each. This allocation would fuel Western hostility and was politically impossible.[17]

Belkin proposed that in communities with Jewish populations ranging between 50 and 1,500, one representative be granted for the first 50 residents, and one for each additional 150. On Caiserman's recommendation, the conference accepted this amendment. The solution was imperfect, but it showed an important willingness to maximize the involvement of Canadian Jewry in the revived Congress.[18]

How would these representatives be chosen? There were two ways. The first provided for each Jewish inhabitant over the age of eighteen, who paid the required dues of 10¢, to vote for the delegates of his or her choice "by popular, general, direct, and secret vote." The second, used in Jewish communities of five hundred or more, allowed the local Congress committees to "devise the basis and mode of selecting delegates, having regard to the existing organizations, and to the need of having representation from all elements of the community." This clause was used to bar Communist unions, though not other "Red" affiliates. Organizations who chose this election method were to contribute between $5 and $10 to Congress, but no one ever bothered to calculate whether these contributions would provide sufficient funds. The representatives thus elected in each region would then select fifteen of their number to the provisional dominion executive, the supreme authority of Congress. Caiserman hoped that the elections could take place on 1 October 1933, and that the first session of the renewed CJC would convene on 22 October.[19]

Another item on the agenda of the Toronto conference was an attempt to map out policy for the newly revitalized Congress. A key resolution called on Canadian Jews to raise $15,000 through a National Campaign for the Relief of German Jewry and other agencies: 65% of the funds were to go to the Joint Distribution Committee to help German Jews; 20% to the Jewish Agency for Palestine; 10% to the Jewish Immigrant Aid Society (JIAS); and 5% to the Organization for Rehabilitation through Training (ORT), which ran work-based training programs for Jews throughout Europe.[20]

The rising tide of Canadian anti-Semitism also drew much attention. In Montreal continued bickering over the Montreal Schools Question kept Judaism in the limelight through the 1920s and early 1930s. As the "third solitude" in Quebec society, Jews found themselves unable to fit among either the French or English. They were burdened with higher entrance requirements and with quotas on Jewish university students at all levels. McGill University had instituted an unofficial Jewish quota in 1929. Pierre Anctil has observed that this restriction led to nationalist pressures on Catholic universities to remove their few Jewish attendees. Beyond the university, Quebec Jews were the targets of vicious anti-Semitism. The daily *Le Devoir* showed itself particularly adept at parroting the views of extreme nationalist Lionel Groulx. Its readers were informed that a Jew could be recognized by an "exceedingly long nose [that] gets lost in his beard" or by the fact that Jews smelled of "caviar, garlic, and vodka." *Le Devoir*, paralleling *Der Stuermer* in its medieval anti-Semitism, demanded that Jews be forbidden to change their surnames, to prevent them from disappearing into the population. Groulx and *Le Devoir* also suggested an *"Achat chez nous"* movement to boycott all Jewish businesses. As if this were not enough, Quebec Jews had to contend with "Canadian Fuehrer" Adrian Arcand's activities. From 1929 Arcand's newspapers spewed forth hatred toward Jews and advocated for the purification of the French race. Though many nationalist intellectuals looked down their noses at Arcand's activities, Quebec Jews regarded him with alarm.

In Ontario the situation was "better," but Jews were always made aware of the limits of tolerance. Upwardly mobile Jews found their efforts to move to tony areas such as Forest Hill barred by residential covenants that legally allowed vendors to prohibit home sales to certain ethnic groups. These rules were not struck down until the 1950s. The pervasiveness of social anti-Semitism is illustrated by David Dunkelman, scion of the wealthy owners of Tip Top Tailors. David recalled that even though he and his brother were the only Jews in their schools (Upper Canada College, Jarvis Collegiate, and Northern Vocational School) "as a boy I never encountered any overt anti-Semitism in any school I attended." But he tellingly remembered another incident: "When Mother discovered that the summer resorts around Toronto were turning into exclusive WASP enclaves that were placing restrictions on Jews buying land, another campaign was launched. In those days (even more than now) one of the symbols of social status in Toronto was a summer home and Mother was resolved that Jews were not going be excluded. By way of a Gentile intermediary, she bought one hundred acres of land on Lake Simcoe and built a holiday resort of thirty cottages ... Mother named it Balfour Beach." Indeed the Dunkelmans ensured the land remained part of the Jewish community. In the 1950s the Balfour Beach Association formed Camp Katonim, which continues to serve the Jewish community. One of the streets of the resort is called Dunkelman Drive.

But not everyone had the economic clout, business savvy, and willpower of Mrs Dunkelman. Most Jews found themselves barred from resorts throughout Ontario by "Gentiles only" signs. Ontario resorts advertised this status in the United States. Worse, those who could not afford Muskoka vacations found numerous Toronto beaches and places of popular entertainment sporting the signs as well. This was a new experience in a city where Jews had long known they were outsiders. In 1933 over 80 percent of Torontonians were of British origin, and Jews, who made up more than 7 percent of the population, were the largest minority group. Since most Jews lived in their "own" neighbourhoods, many Torontonians could rightly claim that they had never dealt with Jews. Indeed, as Robert Fulford has argued, Toronto was so much a city of neighbourhoods at this time, that people regarded those who lived outside their neighbourhood as "people from strange lands to which they should only occasionally venture." It was thus understandable (though not excusable) that residents of the east-end community of "the Beach" resented the "invasion" of "their beaches" (located on public parkland) by "outsiders" on weekends. Of course, the Jews were the most noticeable "outsiders," and thus became targets.

The formation of the Balmy Beach Swastika Club in spring 1933 marked a key turning point in Jewish-Christian relations in Toronto. With the support of many local residents, club members beat up, harassed, and chased Jews from the boardwalk along Lake Ontario. This type of organized violence was new, and it had frightening parallels. For many, it marked a sharp and unprecedented contrast to the more systemic anti-Semitism they had until now experienced. After all, xenophobia and exclusion had long been part of the Toronto scene. Jews knew (and the older generation accepted) that they couldn't work in major department stores or banks or in government. They knew about residential covenants. From time to time Jews were beaten up; many could tell stories of being called "kike" or "sheeny" or other epithets, and of fighting for their rights. But Jews being beaten by swastikaed ruffians and a proliferation of "No Dogs or Jews" signs marked an ominous new trend that aped Nazi Germany.

Swastika clubs began to organize in late July 1933, barely a month after the Congress organizing conference and scarcely three weeks after the Congress delegates had left Toronto. Their "official" formation drew the attention of the major Toronto dailies and the *Zhurnal*. The sight of young men strutting up and down the Balmy and Kew Beach boardwalks inspired the *Zhurnal* to advise its readers not be afraid or stand down. Younger Jews, appalled by the unprecedented number of swastikas appearing at Balmy and Kew beaches, took the message to heart. Two major confrontations took place between Jewish youth and Swastika club members, with the police barely averting a riot on both occasions. The tension continued. On 16 August the unfurling of yet another swastika flag and chants of "Heil Hitler" after a baseball game triggered the Christie Pits Riot. The Pit Gang, who were known for harassing Jews, Italians, and other minorities (with some Italian and Ukrainian help), took on the Jewish baseball players, who were reinforced by self-defence activists and other young Jews who dashed out of Spadina clothing factories, improvised weapons in hand, and jumped on trucks that rushed to the Pits. As a Spadina worker recalled: "Some guys ran in and said: 'the goyim are beating up our guys in the Pits.' I grabbed a wrench and ran downstairs. The boss told us to get out and fight. We got to the Pits and I took that wrench and just started whackin." The unprecedented scale of the Riot – it raged for five hours and needed over two hundred police to break up the more than five thousand combatants – both heightened tensions between Christians and Jews and ensured continued interest in the "Congress idea."[21]

Fittingly, Congress's new constitution pledged that the CJC would devote a large part of its time and budget to combatting anti-Semitism. Since many people believed that anti-Semitism could be defeated by education, Congress pledged to create a Press Bureau to supply "the public with exact data and statistics of Jewish contributions, and the Jewish position in the economic, social, and cultural life of Canada...and throughout the world." Public meetings led by prominent individuals in all fields of Canadian life would reaffirm the accuracy of the Press Bureau's statements. Congress was also prepared to pressure federal and provincial governments to enforce existing legislation for "the preservation of the enjoyment of law and order and equal opportunity for all citizens." If this proved insufficient, Congress would advocate for governments to introduce new legislation to protect Jews from anti-Semitism.[22]

Significantly, no budgetary provisions were made for achieving these vital goals. Here was Caiserman's trademark: long on words and ever short of cash. They could only hope that the funds paid by voters and by the organizations that wanted to affiliate with Congress would provide enough money to start the organization operating. The lack of any dedicated additional funds proved a harbinger of future problems.

Many other potential difficulties lurked just beneath the veneer of cooperation. Congress was remarkable for those who were omitted from its proposed "parliament of Canadian Jewry." Unions were conspicuous by their absence. The openly Communist unions had not been invited, while the others were preoccupied with their members out on strike or on strike pay, and preferred to monitor the situation. There was broad agreement on Congress's proposed initiatives – which had been publicized well in advance. Besides, Shapiro's presence guaranteed that union concerns would be represented in the press.

When the delegates dispersed on 11 June, it was time for the real work to begin. Goldstick was elected president of the Provisional Congress Committee. He was joined by Shapiro as vice-president, Fred Catzman as secretary, Bennett as publicity chairman, Sol Gross as chairman of organizations, Pullan as chairman of finance, and Glass as treasurer. The ex-officio members were Nathan Phillips, who had recently been elected alderman; Fred Singer, a prominent lawyer and MPP; and MP Samuel Factor. Though the list looked impressive on paper, the executive was actually weak and unrepresentative of the community. Personality issues were never far from the surface. Shapiro refused to work with his arch-rival Goldstick. Bennett, angered that his friend Shapiro had to play "second fiddle," did little. Pullan and Gross did nothing, knowing they had been deployed to appease Goel Tzedec and the *landsmanschaften* respectively. Glass, who hoped to become an MPP in the next election (he would succeed) and press for civil rights legislation (this would fail), was too busy to help. As post-conference enthusiasm dissipated, little was accomplished.[23]

By default, the work fell to Goldstick, Catzman, and Caiserman. There was a lot to do, but no money. The deep pockets of Holy Blossomites could not be tapped as long as Eisendrath was away. Many of the Toronto Reform leaders were unhappy with Congress's pro-Zionist stance and awaited Eisendrath's advice. This prolonged deferral of support left Congress without representation from an important segment of the community vitally interested in the fate of German Jews and well able to help organize and contribute to the proposed fundraising campaign.[24]

Caiserman was mainly to blame for Congress's empty coffers. Historian Irving Abella has criticized him for being "a hopeless administrator." True, Caiserman had been the secretary of the short-lived Congress of 1920, and his dogged persistence and tireless correspondence had kept the idea of Congress alive in the intervening decade. But a study of this correspondence reveals that Caiserman never understood that money would need to be a vital part of organizational resuscitation. He worried about raising funds only when payrolls could not be met and staff were ready to quit.[25]

With June almost over and Congress quickly going nowhere, Caiserman wrote beseechingly to Bennett, begging him to use his "constructive ... cool, and logical mind" to help activate Congress. He acknowledged Bennett's displeasure with the goings-on at the conference, but implored his help "in the name of our old friendship."[26]

Caiserman's praise of Bennett's intellect was not mere flattery. Bennett had attended Queen's University and studied under the eminent Canadian philosopher John Watson. Economic realities, however, got in the way, and Bennett never got the chance to write his doctoral dissertation. Nevertheless, his intellect remained razor-sharp, and he channelled some of his energy into brilliant and innovative articles in both English and Yiddish. Bennett also had a legendary temper and did not suffer fools gladly, but he was an important player, and Caiserman was a determined and financially desperate man.[27]

Bennett, however, simply ignored Caiserman's entreaties. The summer of 1933 finally passed, with anti-Semitism reaching new heights, and Congress was still doing nothing to get onto the communal radar. Caiserman finally bit the bullet; on 4 September he wrote to Eisendrath, urging him to recognize Congress.[28]

Unbeknownst to Caiserman, Eisendrath had already had a change of heart. The horrors he had seen in Germany and the apparent outbreak of Nazism in Toronto during the summer had convinced him that Canadian Jews had to unite. He signalled his willingness to negotiate by allowing two of his most prominent congregants, Edmund Scheuer and Egmont Frankel, to attend an Emergency Conference for German Jewry on 17 September 1933, and encouraging them to act as chairman and honorary chairman respectively of a community-wide appeal for $15,000 in aid of German Jews. Eisendrath also agreed to speak about his German trip at the meeting kicking off the campaign.[29]

Fragile Signs of Unity: 1933

Eisendrath's newfound support was not without a political edge, the price for helping Congress gain credibility was the placement of influential Holy Blossomites in key positions. This was a pointed reminder to Downtowners that the names of Frankel and Scheuer would fain access to fundraising doors that no Downtown Jew could open.

But Eisendrath had also made concessions. Holy Blossom could certainly have run the entire campaign; four years later, in the worst years of the Depression, the congregation easily raised enough to build a magnificent new temple on Bathurst Street at Ava Road. It was also a great concession for Eisendrath to participate in a campaign that gave 20 percent of the funds collected to Palestine. His association with the Emergency Campaign marked a vital departure and experiment in Toronto Jewish life. Common tragedy forged common bonds.[30]

Like most fundraising campaigns, this one was carefully timed to coincide with the High Holy Days of Rosh Hashanah and Yom Kippur. Fundraisers always counted on the combination of packed synagogues and congregants praying for a good year to create a receptive attitude toward demands for charitable contributions. Mass mailings and information sheets were sent throughout Ontario, urging spiritual leaders to devote their sermons to the plight of German Jews and to encourage their congregants to give generously. After the Holy Days, communities and synagogues who did not respond were canvassed once again by mail. By mid-October, the campaign had almost reached its goal despite the depressed economic conditions. In fact, strapped donors switched their support from the annual Federation of Jewish Philanthropies campaign to the Campaign for German Jewry. This was the first time that donors would support overseas Jewish needs in preference to domestic ones. It would not be the last.[31]

While the campaign chugged along, the organizational framework of the Central Division came into existence. The League for the Defence of Jewish Rights dissolved and became the more broadly based Congress Provisional Committee. This committee united all the Polish synagogues, *landsmanschaften*, Zionists, and fraternal orders behind the Congress concept. Only the Jewish Communists were excluded, as historian Stephen Speisman has pointed out, "not because they declined to join, but because the organizers of the Congress ... felt that their presence would tarnish the reputation of the Congress." Holy Blossom and union locals were still conspicuous by their absence, but the organizers expected that Eisendrath's participation in the Emergency Campaign was a prelude to his full participation and that the unions could yet be persuaded.[32]

But Congress's financial status remained perilous despite the relevance of its campaign issues to the community. Caiserman reminded Catzman, the new secretary of the Provisional Committee, of Toronto's pledge of $25 per month to support Congress's national headquarters in Montreal because "the head office ... is operating as though the entire movement is a Caiserman affair, and not a National movement." Caiserman got his money. But it was all one step forward and two back. In the same letter Caiserman noted that the Western Division needed more time to get organized, and rescheduled the Dominion-wide elections to January 1934. The Toronto Committee agreed. They would need every extra minute.[33]

A bit of forethought – unusual for Caiserman – would have avoided this. It was naïve to attempt organizational work in the High Holy Day season. Rosh Hashanah, Yom Kippur, and Sukkot all followed one another in quick succession in late September and early October. In addition, Congress organizers needed Eisendrath's complete backing. But Eisendrath, one of the greatest orators of his day, was busy preparing his sermons, replete with stories of what he had seen in Germany, and had no time for meetings. By the time Eisendrath came on board, the Holy Days had prevented the Provisional Committee from convening until 19 October. At this meeting, the committee offered to resign to make room for the Reform group to participate in Congress's executive. Toronto Jewry was one step closer to forming a united front.[34]

With elections completed, the long-scheduled Dominion Executive meeting would take place in Montreal on 12 November. It was composed of fifteen members from each region's Provisional Executive plus the members of the National Executive. It would prove largely ceremonial. Caiserman invited Rabbi Sachs, Bennett, Catzman, Ida Siegal (an active participant in Jewish women's causes and organizations), and Shapiro to be the Toronto delegates.[35] They received a royal welcome in Montreal, and the meeting was a success, at least on paper. The Dominion Executive agreed to pay Caiserman $3,600 per year, and budgeted $25,000 for the first year of Congress's operations. Eastern and Central divisions would each contribute 40 percent towards this budget; Western Division would chip in the remainder. The

Dominion Executive set national elections for 31 December and scheduled the First Plenary for 27, 28, and 29 January 1934, in Toronto. The delegates returned home flush with success and eager to begin organizing the election of delegates.[36]

On 17 November Holy Blossom officially agreed to affiliate with Congress. Central Division's Provisional Executive reaffirmed its offer of 19 October and agreed to resign en masse and reorganize to accommodate their new colleagues. With the support of many societies and *landsmanschaften* already assured, the Provisional Executive confidently expected that elections would proceed without incident.[37]

On the evening of 28 November, thirty-five delegates met at the Zionist Institute on Beverley Street. They represented a true cross-section of Toronto Jewry: from large synagogues like Goel Tzedec and Beth Jacob to *shtiblech* such as the Anshei New York; from mutual benefit organizations such as the Mosirer and Kielcer societies; from diverse international organizations such as the B'nai Brith, Labour Zionists, Revisionists, and General Zionists. No members of Holy Blossom were present, though a number of its congregants were on the new executive slate. The unions were still absent, but two seats were reserved to entice them to join the ranks.[38]

While Congress's organizers dallied over details, other groups in the community had already taken the lead in reacting to Hitler's rise. When the Nazis began a boycott of Jewish business, the Jewish Women's League responded by organizing a boycott of German goods. They were inspired by the huge anti-Nazi protest held at Madison Square Garden on 27 March 1933. While 20,000 packed the Garden, 35,000 stood outside listening on loudspeakers as American Jewish Congress president Bernard Deutsch, American Federation of Labor president William Green, Senator Robert F. Wagner, former New York governor Al Smith, and several Christian clergy called for an immediate cessation of the brutal treatment being inflicted on German Jewry and an American boycott of German goods. Parallel events were held in more than seventy other American cities. With Congress still experiencing birth pangs, the Jewish Women's League made the boycott issue their own. There were ample precedents for this, and Toronto Jewish women had been a formidable force in previous economic boycotts, such as the boycott of Eaton's during the garment workers' strike in 1912. In 1924 women had organized a successful kosher meat boycott. This action was repeated in 1933 when over two thousand women won large price concessions within a week by picketing butcher shops, and "snatching packages of meat out of the customers' hands and [throwing] the meat in the mud."

Goldstick recognized the salience of the issue and, hoping to move the Jewish Women's League under the Congress umbrella, let them lead off the meeting with a report on boycott work. The report's highlight was the Robert Simpson Company's written promise to make no further purchases from Germany. In addition, the company promised to allow Jews to compose up to 7.5 percent of its total staff (a figure that matched their proportion of the Toronto population) and Jews would not have to hide their religion to obtain employment. Woolworth's had made a similar commitment. It seemed that the boycott truly had teeth when the league announced that Jewish druggists, doctors, dentists, the clothing industry, and Jewish unions had all agreed to the boycott.[39]

The Nomination Committee reported that a forty-person provisional executive for the Central Division had been chosen and that all the organizations were well represented. But predictably, Downtowners fared poorly while Holy Blossom fared particularly well: Rabbi Eisendrath, Arthur Cohen, and Egmont Frankel were elected. So were Rabbi Sachs, Bennett, Catzman, Shapiro, Oscar Cohen (editor of the *Jewish Standard*), and Goldstick. The community *shtadlanim* could not complain of neglect: Factor, Singer, Glass, and Phillips were all re-elected. There were entrepreneurs as well: David Dunkelman, who owned Tip Top Tailors, and Jule Allen of Premier Operating Company, one of Toronto's largest owners of movie houses. A few representatives of *landsmanschaften* and societies were also elected, but the executive represented the victory of the classes over the masses.[40]

The Provisional Executive held its first meeting on 6 December and elected Frankel as president. The other officers were Bennett, vice-president; Pullan, treasurer; Arthur Brodey and Catzman, secretaries. Goldstick was elected as returning officer for the 31 December election of delegates to the First Plenary. The entire executive save Goldstick belonged to Goel Tzedec or Holy Blossom. Frankel's election was especially revealing of the power of *shtadlanut*; prior to September he had shown no interest in Congress's affairs. He owed his position to the lustre of his name and the size of his chequing account. The Provisional Executive quickly selected fifteen of their number to serve on the dominion executive and then began planning the Plenary.

Congress's constitution allotted forty-eight Plenary delegates to Toronto; forty-six from the city itself and one each from Forest Hill and York. For all of Caiserman's platitudes about Congress being "the Parliament of Canadian Jewry," the last thing most of the executive wanted was a wide open nomination meeting on 31 December. The Nominating Committee was thus instructed to draw up a list of forty-eight recommended nominees for election. Tellingly, motions by Rabbi Sachs, Shapiro, and Goldstick to allow a limited number of freely electable delegates were all defeated.[41]

Goldstick was perturbed by this turn of events. Within three weeks, Holy Blossom's entry changed the organizational balance of Central Division. A loose confederation of the various Downtown elements had morphed into an increasingly formal and elitist organization that threatened to exclude many of the founding societies and *landsmanschaften*. Goldstick suggested a new compromise to Belkin, who was in charge of the elections at the national level: the Executive Committee would choose forty-eight nominees and present them to a special meeting of "the Congress Organization" on 31 December. The executive would then accept nominations from the floor, and then the elections would take place. Belkin was not pleased by the official plans of Central Division's Provisional Executive or by Goldstick's compromise. "May we point out," Belkin wrote to Goldstick, "that it would be preferable that the delegates receive a mandate from the representatives of Jewish organizations in Toronto, which would avoid any complaints and criticism."[42]

Belkin's observation was prescient. As soon as local societies heard of Goldstick's election proposals, many complained. The Revisionists and the Farband (Association) were particularly indignant, and when Goldstick, though personally sympathetic, would do nothing to help them, they wrote to Caiserman. Normally, Caiserman, a lifelong Labour Zionist, would have been a receptive audience. But his ideological commitment to Congress transcended his Socialist feelings and he stood his ground. Better a "Congress of the classes" than no Congress at all. On 30 December, when it seemed obvious that Goldstick was going to proceed with his election plans, dissidents fired off a blunt telegram to Caiserman: "Zionist Socialist movement of Toronto demanded popular elections to the Congress and we were refused by the Officers. We are calling a large conference to protest against the attitude of the Toronto Congress leadership and to urge democratic election. We are supported by many mass and labour organizations. We request that the National Committee instruct the Toronto leaders to grant our just demands otherwise our participation in Congress will have to be withdrawn."[43]

Caiserman refused to yield and informed the dissidents: "It is too late to protest now." Though he acknowledged that the elections were not "popular," they were legal, and "this is the price paid for a united Canadian Jewry behind the Congress." He urged the dissidents not to sabotage the elections but to participate in them: "Let us first build the Congress and later decide popular elections so that later the work done by each will be decided accordingly."[44]

The protest didn't change Caiserman's mind, but it had an unexpectedly powerful effect on the Provisional Executive. Without informing Caiserman, the executive postponed the election until a more equitable election plan could be devised. No minutes of this meeting were taken, but the evidence available indicates that the executive believed the organizations were bluffing until the protest telegram was sent. In the face of protest from such respected Downtown groups as the Farband and Pioneer Women, the executive reconsidered its stance. In the meantime, Caiserman did some soul-searching. His socialist populist heart was upset by "the price paid for a united Canadian Jewry." In a letter to Ezra Chaikes, one of the leaders of the dissidents, Caiserman poured out his heart:

> I want you to understand that the Canadian Jewish plutocracy was none too enthusiastic about the Congress. We had to work hard to convince them because we realized through tragic experience ... that two competing organizations are worse than none at all. We should also recall that right at the beginning, on 10 and 11 June in Toronto, we had to accede to the demands of an election as a basis for unity ... We now can only hope that election results will produce many good opportunities for all. This is *realpolitik*; and no other type of politics will be successful in building a permanent Congress. At this time the plutocrats are the only ones who can supply the money, without which the Congress movement cannot be maintained. In this emergency I ask for your cooperation for a short while. Our Poale Zion movement understood *realpolitik* well, that is why we are well represented in the Congress ... Of course this does not mean that we should stop

demanding democratic elections. We should not just direct our demands at Congress but at all Canadian Jewry. Thus, if we lose, we need only strengthen our propaganda and appeal once more to the broadest constituency of Canadian Jewry, and convince them of the rightness of our demands. In the meantime, we have made every effort in Toronto to secure as our representatives the best and brightest elements of the community. It is no longer a question of class warfare but of class cooperation for all our sakes.[45]

Caiserman was no narrow ideologue. He was willing to concede many cherished beliefs in order to establish Congress's primacy in Canadian Jewish life. Despite his selflessness and vision, and his protestations to the contrary, however, Caiserman did not understand *realpolitik*. His opponents did. Their threatened mass protest might not change the electoral system, but the resultant stain on Congress's unity in the public eye could render it impotent. Ironically, their stand would produce the "peoples' Congress" Caiserman most fervently desired but was incapable of masterminding.

Goldstick used his new mandate to completely reconfigure the electoral method. He allocated delegates to all participating organizations according to the interest groups they represented: Orthodox (8 delegates), Reform (3), Zionist Organization of Canada (5), Zionist Socialist (5), labour unions (4), fraternal and sick benefit societies (8), and social and philanthropic organizations (3). This allocation reasonably reflected the organizational demographics of Toronto Jewry. Thirty-six of the forty-eight Toronto delegates were to be elected in this way; the other members already appointed to the Dominion Executive, were to be acclaimed. Nine of these were already on the Central Division Executive (Frankel, Eisendrath, Bennett, Kaufman, Goldstick, Pullan, William Agranove, Catzman, and Brodey), and the three others chosen – Rabbi Sachs, Shapiro, and Arthur Cohen – were so respected that no one would challenge their right to acclamation. Goldstick was not too concerned about leaving the rest of the executive on their own. Most of them were so active in other organizations that their election was all but assured. Goldstick's masterful compromise was revealed to Caiserman on 8 January and approved by the executive on 14 January, two days before the vote was scheduled.[46]

Voting was orderly and carefully supervised, and representatives were elected by six of the general groups designated. However, serious irregularities were detected in the ballots cast by the Orthodox group. After an investigation, Goldstick concluded that ballots had been stuffed, and five candidates apparently elected lost their places and were replaced by others. But the elections were still seen as a tremendous success; 272 delegates from over 110 organizations had come to vote, and those elected represented a true cross-section of Toronto Jewry.[47]

Now the Central Division Executive could turn its attention to finalizing the details of the First Plenary. The executive had already booked the ballroom of the King Edward Hotel and drawn up a tentative agenda and list of speakers.

On Sunday, 28 January 1934, at 10:30 a.m. Rabbi Sachs opened the Plenary with a moving invocation to the more than 250 delegates and visitors who "taxed the capacity and overflowed into the galleries" of the Crystal Ballroom of the King Edward Hotel. Caiserman followed with a lengthy summary of the accomplishments of Congress since its founding in 1919. He argued that this was not a new Congress, but a resuscitation of the original. Rabbi Sachs then spoke about the reasons behind the revival. He warned that indignation at Hitler's treatment of the Jews was insufficient reason to sustain a national organization. He likened Jewish indignation to a "cloud of steam" that would have no energy unless harnessed. Congress was to be the "machine which the fire of indignation will drive." Dr Samuel Margoshes, the editor of *Der Tog*, the prominent New York Yiddish daily, urged the delegates to look beyond Canada and unite behind Congress in the battle against Hitlerian anti-Semitism throughout the world.[48]

These speeches reflected two very different views of Congress's raison d'être. Though Sachs acknowledged that fear had catalyzed the rebirth of Congress, he urged that the organization channel itself in a far broader context. Congress needed to offer a forum for its various factions to debate issues intelligently and develop rational policies. Above all, it must work proactively and constructively to achieve equality for Canadian Jewry and give voice to community concerns about anti-Semitism. In contrast, Margoshes' speech envisioned an organization whose primary role was to join the fight against Hitlerism, subordinating concerns for parochially domestic Jewish issues to international interests.

Certainly it was tempting to adopt the latter attitude, especially with community feeling whipped up by coverage of German anti-Semitism. But some understood that this approach would have created a Congress that responded to anti-Semitism rather than worked to prevent it. It was just such a tendency to focus on one issue that had been largely responsible for the quick demise of the original Congress in 1919. Indeed, the speeches delivered during the morning session of the Plenary raised fears among some that the revived Congress would meet the same fate as its predecessor.

But a research paper on "Anti-Semitism in Western Canada," presented by Louis Rosenberg, a Regina statistician and economist, dispelled these fears. After an insightful analysis of Nazi propaganda on the Prairies, Rosenberg argued that Canadian Jews had to conduct themselves so as to "make it an impossibility for the searching finger of anti-Semitism to find excuses upon which to erect accusations and charges." All this was standard fare. But when Rosenberg challenged his audience with the statement that, even though anti-Semitism at home and abroad was a vital issue, he would not have them believe for a moment that it was the most important of all, they became most attentive. He brought them to their feet with a prophetic and insightful declaration: "If this organization is to become permanent ... our decisions ... will not only have to be defensive but also constructive."[49]

When the Plenary reconvened the next morning, the delegates were scheduled to formally amend and ratify the constitution adopted in June 1933, and to elect the committees that would carry the burden of Congress's day-to-day work. All went smoothly until the resolution that committed Congress to promoting "the development of the Jewish National Home in Palestine" was reached. Rabbi Eisendrath and his supporters threatened to leave the session unless the wording was amended. In a moving speech Eisendrath declared that this plank violated his principles; he was "a religious Jew and not a racial one." He also reminded delegates that because his stand was well known, the resolution seemed a deliberate attempt to isolate him and his group. The future of an effective Congress depended on what course the Zionist majority pursued.[50]

Henry Rosenberg, president of the Ontario Zionist Region, appealed for a compromise that would preserve the unity of Congress.

Congress amended the resolution to affirm support "for the work of the Jewish Agency in Palestine." By taking a step back from advocating Jewish sovereignty in Palestine, the delegates made it possible for community unity momentarily to triumph over organizational jealousies and ideological pettiness.[51]

That moment passed quickly. Resentment over the compromise soon bubbled to the surface. Not all delegates agreed that this compromise was necessarily a good thing. Local Yiddishists and Socialists dismissed it as a betrayal and a weak-kneed gesture of goodwill to the Uptown Jews represented by Rabbi Eisendrath and his influential congregants. Bennett and Shapiro resigned from the Plenary. The Uptown-dominated *Canadian Jewish Chronicle* discreetly noted that their resignations had been "indirectly" related to the Eisendrath compromise. Many drew the conclusion that the two men were egotists. Certainly Bennett was particularly piqued by the deference shown to Eisendrath. An ardent Zionist and populist, he had little use for the rabbi's apparent lack of Zionist fervour and surfeit of elitism. In Bennett's view, Eisendrath had wormed his way into Congress because Caiserman had abandoned his principles in order to placate the Uptown Jews of Montreal and Toronto. Shapiro, for his part, shared Bennett's Zionism but, while not as traditional as Bennett, found Eisendrath's brand of Reform Judaism too radical for his taste. The newfound prominence of his archrival Goldstick made his participation in Congress even more distasteful. In truth, both Bennett and Shapiro craved the limelight. When they realized they could not have the leverage they desired, they withdrew. To their consternation, Congress did not collapse without them, though their loss was keenly felt.[52]

The Plenary continued, with members quickly building the framework for Congress. Committees were struck to deal with finance, anti-defamation, the *kehilla* (a Hebrew term for "organized Jewish community"), boycotts, legal issues, actions and organizations, and education. The financial structure of Congress was formalized. Each division agreed to pay its share of the national budget on the basis of the figures agreed on at the Dominion Executive in November. To ensure as wide a representation as possible, each division was entitled to elect five additional members to the Dominion Council.

The Plenary closed with a mass meeting at Massey Hall, which was jammed to capacity. After two hours of rousing speeches, the delegates, fatigued but pleased with the proceedings, prepared to return home. The Toronto Jewish press reported favourably on the accomplishments of the Plenary. The *Jewish Standard* noted that "if the Congress had done no more than to establish a general office and empower the General Secretary with a certain amount of authority, the Congress would have justified itself." Shapiro's *Zhurnal* adopted a wait-and-see attitude, but even it was forced to acknowledge Congress because of the newsworthiness of the Plenary.[53]

The approved committee structure indicates that Congress was prepared to respond to Louis Rosenberg's challenge and move beyond merely reacting to anti-Semitism. The Kehilla and Education Committees reflected the importance of focusing on the organization, analysis, and rejuvenation of Jewish life at a community level. The value of social order, efficiency, and accountability was taken seriously. Jewish intellectuals were encouraged to study their respective communities and offer plans to vitalize Jewish life. But all agreed that success would depend on how well Congress could raise the money needed to build a national organization and form a consensus during the economic uncertainty of the Depression and considering the vast range of ideologies within a fractious community.

The initial reaction of most delegates was positive. In his correspondence with Caiserman, Eisendrath was cautiously optimistic. He believed that the revival of Congress was vitally important and that, if carefully orchestrated, the organization could serve as a mouthpiece for Canadian Jewry. He was careful to point to a number of issues that still required resolution. He was especially critical of the Plenary's short duration, which allowed only one real day of work in which to accomplish the monumental task of blueprinting Congress's structure. Even more serious was the petty grubbing for honours which culminated in the Bennett-Shapiro walkout. But to Eisendrath these problems were relatively minor; at the worst they involved a clash of personalities. However, he was not prepared to paper over the discord regarding the Palestine plank of the constitution. This troubled him the most, he wrote, because it contained the seeds of disaster. The Rabbi referred to Zionism as "thinking with the blood," a thought pattern filled with blind insensitivity to the ideas of those who disagreed with it. Such an ideology, argued Eisendrath, was dangerously narrow-minded and should not be allowed to disrupt the unity of Canadian Jewry.[54]

Knowing he had to keep Eisendrath onside, Caiserman, a life-long Zionist, was careful to acknowledge the rabbi's grievance. He observed: "There is no doubt whatsoever that Zionism at the present time is ... a religious obsession of the Jewish masses of the world, Canada included." Tactfully changing the subject, he stressed the positive accomplishments of the Plenary: "We should also accept that it took courage, altruism, understanding and pathos, which has raised the plenum of the Congress to the highest heights to adopt unanimously the compromise that they have adopted. Each time I think of the unforgettable scene, I am overcome with emotion, and I cannot forget that the motion was a splendid compliment paid to your important minority."[55]

In the final analysis both men were correct. Certainly "anti-Semitism united the community politically," but the rebirth of Congress was only possible thanks to compromises between Uptown and Downtown visions of organizational behaviour, and its continued existence would depend on continued goodwill. Even at the outset, some key leaders showed a distinct distrust. For Congress to fulfill the mandate so grandly stated at the Plenary, its leaders would have to maintain a willingness to compromise while raising the organization's profile on the national and community stages. Events would prove this a challenging task.

3

The Federation of Jewish Philanthropies: Professionalization from Within, to 1934

On Sunday mornings the odour of cigar smoke drifted along Beverley Street between College and Dundas. Many neighbourhood houses had been turned into offices for Jewish organizations, and through their open windows came snippets of conversations in Yiddish and accented English. Sunday was the only day when most Toronto Jews were free for leisure and community activity, a day when they could socialize in their clubs, synagogues, and organizations, which ran the gamut from Communism to ultra-Orthodoxy. Each clung jealously to its membership and ideology.

When these organizations mounted their separate annual fundraising campaigns around the time of the High Holy Days, Jewish householders found themselves besieged by collectors. Though charity was regarded as a noble ideal in the Jewish tradition, potential donors, especially the wealthy, were displeased by the disorder of the numerous decentralized appeals. After considerable effort, the Federation of Jewish Philanthropies (FJP) had been organized in 1916, to replace the myriad appeals with one central one. In theory, all these organizations would join the federation and receive allocations from the proceeds of the single campaign.[1]

By 1920 the FJP boasted a wide spectrum of community representation but it had come at the cost of alienating many significant Downtown organizations such as the Folks Farein and other immigrant self-help societies. These groups abhorred the federation's insistence on scientific charity and professionalized accountability in spending. The Progressive-style reforms brought to the federation by its upwardly mobile leaders from Holy Blossom and Goel Tzedec congregations especially angered the women's groups that had traditionally provided the soldiers of Jewish charity work. They had withdrawn from the federation one by one, during the 1920s, and the federation had hired professional administrators to fill the vacuum. But, since most Jews in the community now had "lost their taste for individual philanthropy and preferred to leave everything to Federation," many of the women's organizations had either dissolved or carried on their activities on a greatly reduced scale. Fundraising fell to the wealthy few, who headed up the organization but hired professional administrators for the day-to-day tasks.[2]

The concept of a federation in Toronto was part of a larger movement throughout North American Jewish communities. By 1938 over seventy-five communities in the United States, representing 85 percent of American Jewry, had set up federations. In addition to Toronto, Montreal and Hamilton had joined this trend in the 1920s. It took years for the federation model to be accepted. Its opponents upheld the traditional modality of informal volunteer fundraising and social service delivery. In Toronto, as elsewhere, this difference in approaches led to a clash between two value systems: the Jewish versus the British and North American. The Jewish system stressed charity as an individual responsibility and focused on the ethic of communal service shown by those who served in positions of responsibility. Proponents of this approach later embraced the theory of scientific charity and put their trust in the professionalizing of all aspects of fundraising and disbursement. But the struggle would take three decades to resolve.[3]

In the meantime, the success of FJP campaigns during the relatively prosperous 1920s glossed over these serious issues. The FJP lacked the clout to compel its member agencies to submit budgets to justify their allocation requests. This lack of clout would eventually prove fatal during the Depression, when it became impossible for the federation to fulfill its mandate and become a community planning agency. Even in good times, too much effort was spent on fundraising at the expense of planning.[4]

Though the FJP failed as a planning agency, it had been moderately successful at fundraising during the 1920s. By 1928 it had organized and carried out a successful campaign for over $111,000, almost quadruple what had been raised in the first campaign eleven years earlier. The 1928 campaign was so successful that it generated a $7,000 surplus. The 1929 campaign, most of which was completed before the stock market crash, boasted similar success. Thus, even when the Depression broke, the members of the federation board had reason to believe that it could weather the storm, despite persistent problems of arrears.[5]

As economic conditions worsened, the FJP became increasingly reliant on a small group of relatively affluent Uptown donors.[6] Meanwhile, disaffected donors disproportionately predominated among *amcha*, the more recent immigrants. They, like the agencies they supported, were alienated by the brusque methods the federation used to impose professionalism on its constituent agencies. For Downtown Jews, scientific charity ran counter to the familiar and established principles of *tzedakah* practised in Eastern Europe. Traditional *tzedakah* created a host of voluntary special groups that ensured that the needy were looked after literally from cradle to grave. Communities provided for the education and vocational training of poor boys, while women's *tzedakah* groups supplied brides with used bridal gowns. The poor received food for the Sabbath and Holy Days, while poor but clever students were sponsored so that they could attend advanced Talmudic academies. Those who lacked funds for burial were taken care of by a *chevra kadisha* ("holy society"), which supplied burial garments and a grave. Most important, all this *tzedakah* was undertaken because it was considered a biblical imperative (*mitzvah*) to do so; help was dispensed without lengthy investigation or analysis. Being poor was embarrassing enough – and Jewish law taught that "embarrassment is worse than death."

Scientific charity was therefore perceived as antithetical to *tzedakah*. In addition to necessitating rigorous inquiry into the socio-economic profile of its recipients, it allowed little room for volunteers to exercise their traditional administrative role. The federation often used its control of the purse to drive experienced but unprofessional volunteers from key administrative positions. The long-term effects of this policy proved highly beneficial to the formation of a professional and rationally organized system of Jewish social services in Toronto. But its immediate effect was to produce outrage among displaced volunteers and their constituent organizations. However, while the federation held the purse strings, it held the cards, and the onset of the Depression strengthened its hand. At a time of financial restraint and panic, it was the one organization that had the clout to wring contributions from straitened donors. In 1930 the federation campaign collected $112,000 of its $125,000 goal. With increasing numbers clamouring for relief, however, the $13,000 shortfall wiped out the previous decade's painfully accumulated surplus. It was clear that 1931 would be a critical year for the federation, and much depended on the success of its campaign.[7]

But it was not to be. By 1931 many among the federation's economically comfortable contributors were feeling the pinch of the bad times. The campaign fell $16,000 short of its goal, and the organization faced an accumulated deficit of close to $30,000. Campaign funds could not be used to pay down this debt because they were desperately needed by the agencies trying to deal with the human casualties of Depression. The Executive was forced to weigh alternative options.[8]

To their credit, they allowed neither the mounting deficit nor the constituent agencies' clamouring for cash to undermine their commitment to scientific charity. In March 1932 the executive hired Martin Cohn, a young man who had grown up at Holy Blossom Temple, as the new executive director of the FJP. With a BA from the University of Toronto, some graduate courses in psychology, and most important, some courses in the School of Social Work of the University of Toronto, Cohn represented the native-born generation of Canadian Jews. He already had community experience, having served as executive secretary for the Jewish Boys' Club between 1924 and 1927. A man of "tremendous vitality [and] empathy," Cohn knew that many Jewish working-class parents had little time to supervise their children. With fathers and some mothers working long hours in factories, mothers were often compelled to give most of their attention to their younger children. Thus, noted a contemporary observer, "many of them [the teenagers] were constantly in difficulties either with the law or with their school teachers or among themselves."[9]

The selection of a professional social worker as the executive director of the FJP paralleled a now-established pattern for community organizations across North America. Social work as a professional field had begun to emerge in the 1890s but it took twenty more years to gain recognition at the university level. In 1914 the University of Toronto gave its first courses in what was then known as Social Science, and the first graduating class of 1915 consisted of twelve women. The course took one year to complete, but despite the best efforts of its supporters, there was little market for the graduates. The First World War created demand, and enrolment grew to include 252 part-time students. Many had previously worked in such organizations as the Neighbourhood Workers' Association (NWA) or the Children's Aid Society (CAS) and now sought to upgrade their skills. By 1919 the University of Toronto had formally affiliated with the American Association of Social Work, and in 1920 the university established a permanent Chair of Social Science.[10]

Graduates of social science programs were not universally welcomed back into community organizations. Volunteers who ran agencies often resented being told by young women (and some men) fresh out of university how their organizations should be run. As one editorialist sardonically observed: "In the chair sat Mrs. Sanford the septogenarian [sic] president ... a woman of strong personal charm and strong Christian inspiration. Mrs. Sanford bestows on the office which she graces the finest elements of the Victorian heritage, and a power of judging the thing and the question in its bare essential, away from intrigue, prejudice, or dust cloud of argument. This characteristic is a more valuable possession ... in a day of emphasis on technique and training, than is at first evident to the outsider."[11]

Grassroots mistrust of professionalization put Canadian social workers on the defensive. They also had to deal with fears that university-trained personnel would erode the religious basis and volunteer focus of many charitable organizations. By hiring Cohn, FJP was asserting its place in the vanguard of organizational reform. This was not surprising. Holy Blossom Temple, the source for many of the federation's board members, had been involved with the University of Toronto's School of Social Science since the early 1920s. The Temple's Rabbi Barnett Brickner occasionally lectured at the school, where a scholarship was established in his honour. Thus many federation leaders were receptive to Cohn's aim of applying social work maxims to communal organization. But Cohn first had to resolve two critical problems that threatened the federation's survival: the grim prospect that revenue from the 1932 campaign would drop significantly, and the organization's increasing dependence on municipal grants after 1930 to maintain even a reduced level of service.[12]

The central challenge was organizational. The FJP was only as strong as its constituent organizations. Many of these were already hard-pressed to deal with the devastating effects of the Depression. The Family Welfare Bureau (FWB), the largest of all the agencies, verged on collapse. It was particularly vulnerable because of its "omnibus" mandate – it was responsible for dispensing food, clothes, and shelter. In the relatively good times of the 1920s this had been a convenient arrangement for the FWB, its clientele, and the City of Toronto. Since most Jews refused to eat the food supplied by the House of Industry (the euphemistic name for the Municipal Poorhouse), the city agreed to reimburse the federation for its clients' kosher food expenditures. At the end of each fiscal year, federation and city officials met to negotiate the exact reimbursement due the federation. This agreement remained in force from 1928 until 25 March 1933, and the guaranteed source of funds allowed the FWB to develop a "one stop" relief service that attended to the medical, financial, psychological, and social problems caused by poverty, while leaving the city some measure of control over the Jewish social welfare system. Social worker Bernard Lappin observed that the city grants were "used as a means of demonstrating new possibilities created by such a grant as an additional means of financing agency programs." Civic politicians correctly assumed that Jews preferred to take care of their own. The municipal payment to the federation in lieu of food costs thus helped the Jewish social welfare system to develop while removing some of the casework burden from understaffed municipal agencies.[13]

The City of Toronto invested considerable sums in the social welfare of the Jewish community, despite the community's lack of political clout because the concept of public relief was in its infancy. Its advocates had not yet decided whether to fund traditional religiously and/or ethnically based social welfare agencies, or to establish centralized government-run and staffed agencies as the sole dispensers of social welfare. Throughout the 1920s established private agencies, fearful of public agencies meddling in their affairs, joined forced to defend against the attacks of government encroachment. Public officials were insisting that supervision of private agencies was essential to prevent overlap and ensure that all programs conformed to the social planning priorities of City Hall.[14]

Many American Jewish federation leaders were delighted to download social welfare onto municipal agencies, and the Depression hastened this trend. But Cohn viewed the FWB's dependence on the municipal grant as a threat to the survival of the FJP. It made financial planning problematic, especially as the city became increasingly reluctant to reimburse the federation in full. As far as Cohn was concerned, he was in a "no win" situation: "In the eyes of the [Jewish] community we carried the responsibility for providing adequate relief. We were placed in the position of continually negotiating for special "grants" to pay for what was ... a public responsibility. There was no certainty in the amount of the grants, a large amount of which was negotiated after the expenditures had been made, and the Federation was forced to assume any losses."[15]

Cohn thus found himself trapped between his social work instincts and his role as executive director. His instincts told him that the FJP was acting in an organizationally irrational manner by duplicating services provided by municipal social welfare agencies. On the other hand, its continued survival and legitimacy depended on its ability to provide specialized relief – such as kosher food and the Mount Sinai Hospital Dispensary – to the Jewish community. But costs were rising, and the campaigns raised less and less. After mulling over his strategy, Cohn decided to continue the federation's efforts to professionalize the staff of its constituent agencies. He ordered the FWB to hire only professionally trained case workers or he would withhold the FWB annual municipal grant. This was no idle threat, since the City of Toronto paid the FWB grant to the federation, which in turn disbursed it to the FWB. Much to Cohn's dismay, this decision led to a crisis. In April the entire FWB board resigned in protest.[16]

It would have been easy for Cohn to dissolve the FWB and farm out its kosher food distribution to merchants. But the FJP would not survive for long without its largest agency. Cohn wisely concluded that the federation's survival was paramount, and that it trumped social planning and the imposition of professionalization. Therefore, in May 1932 the federation handpicked a new FWB Board. Eight of the eleven members were appointed directly by the federation Board of Management; the others were chosen by the Folks Farein and the Federation Community Council. The Folks Farein, or Hebrew National Association, was a venerated Downtown organization founded in 1913. Originally designed as a Yiddish social club, it gradually took on a much broader role as Christian missionaries began actively proselytizing among Jews by offering them medical care, English classes, food, and employment aid. In response, the Folks Farein began doing the same, and it continued to supply these services into the 1920s. The appointment of Folks Farein representatives indicated an acceptance of the federation's authority in the area of social welfare from a key Downtown constituency. But the vast majority of core *amcha* institutions such as *landsmanschaften*, mutual benefit societies, and many Jewish union locals still remained apart. This gap would not be addressed fully until after the Second World War.

In keeping with the tenets of scientific charity, Cohn gave the members of the new FWB board a year to familiarize themselves with the agency. Cohn and the Board of Management deliberately chose not to specify the length of the its term. They wanted lay leaders with a passion for professionalization, efficiency, and accountability who were willing to sacrifice a measure of democracy to reach these ends.[17]

Dora Wilensky signed on as FWB executive director in April 1931 to spearhead the professionalization campaign. Like Cohn, she epitomized the university-educated generation seeking jobs in the burgeoning Jewish federation bureaucracy. Her impressive qualifications included a BA in English and History from McMaster University, a teaching certificate, some courses at the School of Social Science of the University of Toronto, and a degree from the prestigious School of Social Science of Northwestern University. She had solid practical experience as a playground supervisor in the early 1920s and in casework with the Jewish Social Services Bureau of Chicago. Wilensky was a feminist and worked using her maiden name. Her husband was the well-known Communist alderman Joseph B. Salsberg, who later became an MPP. Her acceptance on the basis of her credentials alone speaks volumes about Cohn's professionalism.

Wilensky brought many other assets to her job. She shared Cohn's belief that the FWB had to maintain its role as an omnibus agency in the short term. However, her long-term goals differed: she believed public authorities should be in charge of all relief. This assumption of responsibility would allow the FWB to concentrate on developing a caseload grounded in quality rather than quantity, special vocational guidance for the Jewish community, and parent education programs designed exclusively to serve a Jewish clientele. Her vision would prove prophetic, though its fulfilment would take considerable time.[18]

Once Cohn found himself unable to change the basic budgetary structure of the FJP, he turned to organizing as successful a 1932 federation campaign as economic conditions would permit. He brought in a professional campaign manager from New York and prepared donor lists. Given the economic crisis, the campaign proved quite successful, raising just over $82,000, only 8 percent less than in 1931. But measured against the unprecedented demand for funds, the bald truth was that the federation would have to double its debt load just to maintain its level of social service.[19]

But with creditors making anxious noises, Cohn could not go further into debt in order to maximize the availability of social services. He had to balance the budget. Judging that the Depression would be around for some time, he decided to trim funding for the federation's constituent agencies. He also had no choice but to allow the federation to accept increased municipal funding. By 1932, 23 percent of federation funding came through municipal grants – and these monies were insufficient to stave off allocation cuts to all agencies. It was clear that some faced imminent closure if conditions worsened.

To keep track of funds, Cohn ordered a complete review of bookkeeping procedures in all agencies and in the FJP office itself. While many agencies perceived this as an attack on their independence, they had little choice but to comply. Despite these downsizing efforts, the federation's 1932 deficit still topped $5,000. Accumulated debt now exceeded $21,000, and it was clear to Cohn that 1933 would be a year of difficult decisions.[20]

The Jewish social welfare network that had shown such promise in 1929 was in danger of collapse. It was increasingly unable to support itself financially and its services were strained to the point of saturation. The unusually cold winter of 1933 exacerbated conditions. The FWB staggered under the weight of 913 active cases, including 112 new ones. Many of the latter involved skilled workers and the lower middle class who had joined the ranks of the unemployed and, overwhelmed by the sudden downturn in their fortunes, required considerable social work intervention. But the resulting increase in agency casework threatened to engulf Wilensky and her four social workers. At the FWB's overcrowded office, staff members worked late on Thursday evenings and on Sunday mornings without putting a dent into the backlog. No money was available to hire additional staff. Their task was made even more difficult by the fragmented nature of relief services. Some was provided by the provincial government and some municipally. Of course, needy and often desperate clients, some facing immediate eviction for rent arrears, did not care about bureaucratic niceties. Their needs were urgent. Failure to serve them would irreparably damage the credibility of the FWB and the federation.[21]

In addition to struggling with these communal pressures, the FJP had to cope with fundamental changes in government policy catalyzed by the Depression. Provincial and municipal governments hurried to rationalize the public welfare system, and it was unclear how the changes would affect the federation. The Ontario government had established the Department of Public Welfare (DPW) in September 1930. By 1932 it was generally accepted that the Depression was not a passing phenomenon, and a committee was struck to recommend appropriate ways of administering public relief in Ontario. This committee, chaired by MPP Wallace Campbell, issued its report on 28 July 1932, and their recommendations constituted the basis of all provincial public welfare policy for the next decade. The report argued that public works enterprises, traditionally favoured by governments in times of economic depression, were useless. It urged that the provincial Department of Public Welfare dissociate itself from the Department of Public Works and devote itself solely to the administration of public relief. The Campbell committee also set guidelines for the cost of food, shelter, clothing, fuel, and medical services. Since standards for relief were a provincial responsibility, the province would supervise municipal relief workers closely to ensure that standards were maintained. The committee designed all the paperwork needed for direct relief work, and further urged private and public welfare agencies to cooperate in the field of direct relief.[22]

Many of the objectives of Toronto's public relief had anticipated those of the Campbell Report. In November 1930 the Toronto Board of Control instructed the Civic Unemployment Relief Commission to investigate the state of public welfare in the city. In its May 1931 report, the commission strongly urged the establishment of a municipal Department of Public Works "under a powerful Commissioner." It also recommended that the city and provincial Departments of Public Welfare cooperate, and that the House of Industry's investigative staff be fired to eliminate casework overlap. The commission further recommended that the House of Industry be stripped of control over the distribution of Mothers' Allowances and Old Age Pensions. The House of Industry, protective of its autonomy, fought this recommendation, but by June 1932 the report had been implemented.[23]

The municipal authorities now focused on the FJP's mandate by investigating private providers of public relief. This proved helpful to the FWB, as the commission had given the FWB a clean bill of health. It also recommended that the city grant $13,000 to the federation in 1932 to defray FWB expenses. This measure was in line with the new municipal policy of allocating grants to all private charities alleviating economic distress as long as they avoided duplication of municipal services.[24]

Duplication became harder to avoid, however, as the Depression relentlessly continued. On 25 March 1933 the city announced that the DPW had taken over the House of Industry. With indigents now receiving food and fuel municipally, the FWB would be reimbursed only for clothing. This reorganization caused a financial nightmare for Wilensky and Cohn. They knew many Jewish relief recipients would not use non-kosher food, and that many did not want the shame of publically admitting their indigence by using municipal relief. Now the FJP would have to provide the FWB with funds for food and fuel – but there simply was no money. Cohn feared that the federation, now dependent on city funds, would find its 1933 campaign a bust. If so, disaster loomed.[25]

Facing this possibility gave Cohn a renewed impetus to further reduce the number of overlapping programs among FJP's constituent agencies. He was determined to trim spending before preparations for a new campaign began in May 1933, but he faced considerable opposition, some from agencies that had predated the FJP. Each agency jealously guarded its turf – aware that giving ground might jeopardize its existence. More seriously, volunteers who were still running some agencies looked askance at social planning and organizational rationalization. Many were proud of their agency's achievements and had long regarded the FJP with suspicion. If Cohn hoped to rationalize the federation, he would first have to convince these agencies that rationalization was in their best interest.

The Jewish Childrens' Home (JCH) was most strongly opposed to Cohn's strategy. The communal orphanage had been founded in the early years of the century, and by 1910 had occupied the upper floors of the Associated Hebrew Charities Building on Simcoe Street. For the next decade its loyal volunteers fended off the attacks of the Toronto Board of Health, which was unimpressed with the facilities.

But in 1922, with the help of the Maternity Aid Society, the JCH had purchased a large house on Annette Street in the Toronto Junction. As historian Stephen Speisman notes: "The improvement was phenomenal. The number of children who could be accommodated far exceeded the number who needed care. A graduate nurse was appointed superintendent and dispensary facilities were provided. By 1924 the institution was housing sixty-one children and, in recognition of its effectiveness, was receiving both municipal and provincial grants, in addition to its support from the Federation of Jewish Philanthropies."[26]

The improvement was a considerable achievement, accomplished through the hard work of dedicated volunteers – a triumph of the Downtown community. The Maternity Aid Society, which had devoted itself to the care of young mothers and their infant children since 1906, continued its support of the JCH. Maternity Aid had a long history of organizational independence, and had resisted takeover attempts by the Ladies' Montefiore Hebrew Benevolent Society, essentially an arm of Holy Blossom. In 1917 Maternity Aid had affiliated with the FJP, but it separated again in the late 1920s when it felt threatened with a loss of independence. It was financially self-sufficient, thanks to *amcha* support, even as the federation campaign struggled during the 1930s.[27]

The Children's Home seemed to be bargaining from a position of strength. By the late 1920s it had achieved almost complete financial independence by means of an agreement between the Toronto Children's Aid Society and the FJP. The CAS recognized the FJP as its agent in the Jewish community and permitted it to appoint one member to the CAS board. This arrangement meant that Jewish children who were made permanent or temporary wards of the CAS and placed in the JCH had their maintenance paid by the CAS. The only obstacle to complete financial independence for the JCH was the fact that the CAS paid its grant to the federation, rather than directly to the JCH. The federation thus maintained nominal financial control.[28]

The JCH board approved the CAS agreement because it would purportedly save money. This was to prove fatally naïve. All the JCH volunteers cared about, as one put it, were "their children." Each volunteer had a child assigned to her on the particular day she volunteered, and many formed very close attachments with their charges. They brought them gifts, played with them, and kept their pictures at home. This sentimentality did not endear them to the FJP "professionals" or the child welfare authorities. For its part, the CAS disagreed with JCH's emphasis on institutionalization at a time when a new trend toward "placing out" children into foster homes was growing. The JCH further angered the CAS by clearly disregarding provisions of the *Child Protection Act* and allowing parents to visit their children in the JCH and by returning children to their parents once they turned sixteen. By the early 1930s a clash was in the offing.[29]

The FWB Board shared the concerns of the CAS. It accused the Children's Home board of "narrowness of vision" and lack of professional training – considering them the reason for the JCH's lack of interest in developing a foster home program. The JCH board understandably feared that such a program might decrease the number of residents, reduce their grant, and curtail their independence. In 1928 the FWB made a decisive move: it secured control of all admissions to the JCH and set up a "placing out" (foster home) service. The JCH was now in the peculiar situation of controlling its internal administration but not its admissions. It was obvious that this impasse could not last long and that any solution would create intense alienation among the losing stakeholders at a time when the federation could ill afford it.[30]

The JCH problem was just one of the many Cohn faced as he began to plan the 1933 campaign. He could only hope that the appeal would not fall too far short of its $85,000 goal. But the times were not favourable to campaigns – the Depression and the sudden emergence of the Canadian Jewish Congress, and competition from its $15,000 Emergency Relief Campaign for Stricken German Jewry ran stiff interference. This latter campaign was particularly irksome. Not only was it carried out in competition with the federation's campaign, but it was also sponsored by many of Uptown's leading lights. In the end, the Emergency Campaign won out, and its success undermined the federation's campaign, which netted a paltry $56,000.[31]

Few could have blamed the federation had it given up the ghost. But to their credit, Cohn and the Board of Management refused to quit or to yield to blind panic and begin wholesale cutbacks in the federation's level of service. Instead, the board struck a Personnel Committee with broad powers to review the federation's constituent agencies and recommend future policy. Cohn insisted that the FJP set its own financial house in order before demanding the same of its agencies.

The establishment of this committee in late April of 1934 marked a watershed in Toronto Jewish history. It signified the first acceptance of "scientific charity" and its attendant beliefs in communal organization based on the theories of social work and communal planning. Cohn and the FWB board knew this approach flew in the face of traditional *tzedakah*. They didn't care – nor could they afford to. The committee was deliberately kept small to allow it to work as quickly as possible, and perhaps to ensure maximum secrecy. It hoped to use the information it gathered to help prepare the federation's budget, and stated that it was "most important such a study would create a better understanding of the need for trained personnel and the meaning of adequate training." To get the information it needed, the committee designed and distributed a standardized questionnaire to all the constituent agencies, to the federation office, and to Cohn. The responses led to a series of reports that were dissected at Personnel Committee meetings. Each agency was invited to send participant observers when its report was discussed by the committee.[32]

Cohn ensured that each report focused on the professional qualifications of the FJP and agency personnel. He was certain that the communal image of federation staff as "inefficient, lazy, and overpaid" would change once the community learned to appreciate professional standards. Professionalization was certainly required in many agencies; however, it is doubtful whether those outside the federation understood this. For Downtown *amcha*, professionalization implied impersonality, money grubbing, and a lack of devotion to the traditional tenets of *tzedakah*. These attitudes contributed to the often hostile characterizations that Downtowners applied to federation workers.[33]

The Personnel Committee produced a detailed analysis of the FWB, the largest and most professionalized agency, which bore the brunt of the Depression caseload. Wilensky reported seven professionals, four bookkeepers and clerical staff, and forty-nine volunteers associated with the FWB. The professionals were quite well trained by contemporary standards: two had university degrees and diplomas in social work, while two others had university degrees and some social work courses. Nonetheless, reported Wilensky, the agency was being torn apart by the pressures of Depression casework and its omnibus mandate. She envisioned a highly specialized, individual casework–oriented agency, and reiterated her support for municipal control of unemployment relief, which could leave the FWB free to concentrate on "special vocational guidance for youths who [were] now demoralized by the lack of employment and opportunities ... parent-education groups, and adult recreation." Wilensky doubtless hoped these reforms would help debunk the image of the FWB as "serving mostly destitute families" and allow it to become a social worker's "dream agency" with specialized casework, communal social counselling and planning, and high professional standards – the ideal training ground for student social workers.[34]

The report of the Jewish Children's Bureau (JCB) was considerably less optimistic. It complained of the volunteers' role in the orphanage. The JCB, created in 1930 to deal with problem children and unwed mothers, was perceived by Downtown volunteers as an FJP lapdog trying to assert control over the vacuum created when Maternity Aid left the federation. The orphanage volunteers had good reason to be wary of the agency, because the federation had entrusted it with the administering the annual CAS allocation. This gave the JCB control over the orphanage even though, as noted, the orphanage board of directors was allowed to remain. The federation thus hoped to allay Downtown communal suspicions that its *de facto* control over the JCH might soon lead to an outright takeover. But many JCH directors saw the writing on the wall, and by late 1933 all the Downtown directors had resigned.[35]

Conflict quickly erupted. The anger of the orphanage volunteers exacerbated an already tense situation. By early 1934 the official report claimed that "a general dissatisfaction with conditions in the Jewish Children's Home [was] voiced both by agencies outside of Federation and at meetings within the organization."[36] In July, the federation asked the municipal Department of Mental Hygiene to investigate conditions in the JCH. The departmental report found that the superintendent of the home was unqualified for her job because she lacked training in child psychology, social case work, and recreation skills, and recommended that she be removed and retrained.[37]

The JCH volunteers exploded in fury. "Going to the Gentiles!" shrieked an article in the *Yiddisher Zhurnal*. A fundamental Downtown taboo had been broken by the arrogant Uptowners. The volunteers assumed, not without reason, that the recommendations of the muncipal report would lead to a federation takeover of the home. In a way, this clash was a reprise of the bitter battles that Maternity Aid had fought with the Holy Blossom–dominated Ladies' Montefiore almost fifty years earlier. This time, the odds were stacked against the JCH. The CAS also had a long-standing grudge against the orphanage's policies, and the orphanage's supporters were much weakened by the Depression. Most important, the FJP controlled the CAS funding allocation. In short order, the JCH superintendent was deposed via a nine-month "educational sabbatical," and replaced by an "acting superintendent" seconded from the JCB. Volunteers were told they were no longer needed, and were left shattered by this experience. Little was done to win back their support, even though many of these women had been active in community work for twenty-five years or more. In December 1934 the Personnel Committee observed that the former JCH volunteers were still distraught, cound not accept the fact that the home had lost its place in community planning, and were furious at the federation. The Personnel Committee airily decided that all these problems could easily be handled through some simple public relations work and recommended the JCH's closure.[38]

The Personnel Committee justified this administrative buccaneering as yet another necessary step on the road to communal rationalization. They argued that "from the point of view of social policy there is no question as to the advisability of continuing the development of the foster home program ... which would make the use of the Home unnecessary." The bitter volunteers begged to differ. The hurt did not pass. Decades later, one volunteer recalled while sitting in a magnificently appointed penthouse apartment: "Every Tuesday for five years I came and played with her. I gave money to the home and I brought my orphan gifts. I helped make meals and was on the organizing committee. But the professionals – what did they know? They came and they took away my orphan. But I got even. You can imagine that I could well afford to support UJA [the successor organization of the Federation] but whenever they asked, I gave them nothing! They took my orphan!"[39]

Cohn and Wilensky, consistent in advocating proper social work techniques, were unmoved. Cohn, for his part, deplored the JCH as an agency that had outlived its usefulness. "When the need [for an agency] no longer exists – the agency should die. Unfortunately, death for an agency does not always mean extinction; there may still be a continuing of a state of death in life." Cohn took pains to ensure that the JCH would completely disappear. The building was sold, the volunteers were dispersed, and the orphans all placed in foster homes. The FJP consistently defended this decision as one of necessary professionalization. It is difficult not to agree. Most JCH staff were untrained. None of the four caseworkers was a member of the Canadian Association of Social Workers, only two had taken any social work courses, and only one had previous experience in childcare. JCB executive secretary, Anne Gussack, noted that the JCH had "no definite standards of qualifications for professional staff." In addition, no effort was made to establish definite standards for foster homes and institutional care, or to examine the childcare problems of the community, even though these procedures had been recommended as far back as 1921. From a simply professional point of view, the dissolution of the orphanage only added to the FWB's woes: the hard-pressed agency now had to also handle the orphanage casework.[40]

In its last full year of operation, the JCH received $9,110 from the FJP, $13,314 from the Toronto CAS, $4,894 from the city, and $1,643 from the province – a total of $28,961 to maintain a sixty-five-bed institution that served eighty children. However, the hundreds of hours worked by its loyal volunteers had kept the JCH's costs at $0.98 per child per day: one of the lowest among Toronto orphanages despite the extra expense of kosher meat.[41]

The FWB Board of Management ignored these cost efficiencies in its quest to divert more of the rapidly shrinking federation allocations pie to agencies such as the FWB and the JCB, which were amenable to rationalization and professionalization. A study by federation auditors confirmed that a foster home program would be much cheaper, requiring only one full-time worker, lower food costs, and no building expenses. What is more, this move corresponded with an already well-advanced continent-wide trend from orphanages to foster homes.[42]

The FJP succeeded beyond its expectations. In 1937 the JCB's cost of $0.53 per foster child per day represented the lowest cost of any Toronto childcare institution. In addition, foster care increased the number of places available from 65 in 1933 to 111 in 1937. The closing of the orphanage left the federation free to assume its long-sought goal of communal social planning by rationalizing the entire framework of Jewish childcare services. In 1935 the JCB, the FWB, and Big Brother and Sister organizations were consolidated into the Jewish Family Welfare Bureau (JFWB), creating one specialized agency to meet all family needs. Wilensky was delighted by the rapid fulfilment of her vision. The monopoly of the municipal and provincial Departments of Public Welfare over the distribution of unemployment relief (and the increasing tendency of Jews to accept such relief) allowed the JFWB to devote itself exclusively to specialized casework and community planning.[43]

The FJP completely triumphed in the orphanage affair, but its success proved Pyrrhic in some ways. The method of its victory laid the basis for its downfall. Its insistence on imposing the "power of the purse" upon a constituent agency, its callous assumption that it alone knew what was good for the community, and the roughshod way in which it trampled over volunteers' sensitivities and considerable record of communal service proved costly. Throughout its existence, a substantial and vocal minority of Downtown Jews had opposed the federation for its high-handedness, but remained relatively powerless. *Amcha* were equally powerless, but simply ignored the federation. They could only protest by refusing to contribute to the federation campaign. None of this was new.

However, vocal opposition to the FJP now emerged from a rapidly emerging counter-group. These were the young professionals, the university-educated, the first largely Canadian-born post–First World War generation: accountants, lawyers, doctors, and social workers. They believed that the federation would never succeed unless it was able to involve the whole community efficiently in a central fundraising campaign and use its organizational leadership as a springboard to successful community planning. The financial collapse of a key communal school would soon provide them with a platform for their vision.

The FJP seemed unconcerned by the increasingly strident complaints about its methods and continued on its path of agency consolidation. After the takeover of the orphanage, the Personnel Committee turned its attention to the internal dynamics of the federation's constituent agencies. There was a wide disparity in agency salary scales, qualifications, hours worked, vacation time, and time allotted for professional development. The Personnel Committee was anxious to standardize agency-wide conditions of employment, and after considerable negotiation, the agencies all adopted uniform policies on hours of work, vacation time, and professional development. Each set up its own salary scale, however, on the basis of professional qualifications. Cohn modelled the professional criteria on those described by the official handbook of the American Association of Social Workers.

This historic achievement overshadowed the FJP's considerable inadequacies in other areas. By professionalizing its constituent agencies and clearly defining their mandates, the federation ensured the agencies' survival and the perpetuation of community social planning. What followed was the bureaucratization of community leadership as lay leaders increasingly turned to agency social workers for advice in communal affairs. This in turn created a burgeoning "Jewish civil service" made up almost entirely of social workers, the group of professionals that would eventually supervise the community's unsure strides toward unity.[44]

Mandating professional standards proved far easier than solving the FJP's by-now chronic budgetary problems. The 1934 campaign fell 20 percent below its $80,000 goal. This shortfall occurred just as the Depression reached its peak and a resurgence of anti-Semitism in Poland caused many to divert available funds to overseas causes. In addition, as described, the situation in Germany diverted a good deal of the limited Uptown money to the Campaign for the Emergency Relief of Stricken German Jewry just as the "JCH affair" heightened Downtown distrust of the federation. To make matters worse, both the municipal and provincial Departments of Public Welfare now sidestepped the federation by giving grants directly to constituent agencies under the provisions of the *Charitable Institutions Act*. This change allowed the Jewish Old Folks' Home and the JCB to apply for such funds independently and evade federation control. The federation could no longer impose its will by threatening to cut agency allocations.[45]

To the vast majority *of amcha*, traditionalists never fully "re-educated" to appreciate what professionalization had accomplished, the JFP became irrelevant. It was not involved in overseas relief, at a time when Downtown Jews were anxious about their European kin. Furthermore, having no role in the important field of Jewish education, the federation could not intervene when bankruptcy threatened to close the popular Toronto Hebrew Free School, and in fact stood aside while much communal energy was diverted to the eventually successful campaign for its reopening. In fact, many of those who saved the Free School would shortly use their experience to ensure the federation's demise. But for all who had eyes to see, the federation's weakness was already evident.[46]

Without money, a community-wide mandate, or universal community support, Federation of Jewish Philanthropies crumbled. By 1936 it could barely fund its constituent agencies. But, despite its faults and heavy-handed tactics, the federation left the Toronto Jewish community an organizational legacy: "It established the importance of professionalism in Jewish social work, community planning, and fundraising. Federation mediated between the community and the provincial and municipal governments. Above all, the Federation laid the institutional and professional framework for the development of the Toronto Jewish community."[47]

The legacy would very shortly be handed on to those who knew how to build on it and impose their will on those who did not share it. But in the interim, the truth was that in 1936 only the close observer of organizational life would have noted any significant changes. The Canadian Jewish Congress was nationally moribund, though its Toronto branch had at least established a tenuous presence in attempting to raise public consciousness of issues important to the Jewish community. From the *amcha's* perspective, the organizational landscape of 1936 differed little from that of 1933: there were too many meetings and too few mass protests. Canada's gates remained securely bolted against family reunion through immigration. In truth, little tangible progress had been made, as Speisman cogently observed, beyond building a foundation for the future. But the federation's *modus operandi*, especially in the orphanage issue, served notice that the winds of change were blowing. The only question was: could they gain communal ascendancy and if so, how? The answers were not long in coming but the circumstances proved surprising.

4

The Toronto Jewish Immigrant Aid Society: "Long Distance" Professionalization, to 1937

Vital changes were afoot in the organizational behaviour of Toronto Jewry. The tendency toward bureaucratic efficiency and scientific management was on the upswing. But change was imposed in a variety of ways. In the case of the Federation of Jewish Philanthropies, change was driven from within. Executive Director Martin Cohn professionalized the inner working of the federation in accordance with modern management principles. He systematically used self-study methods first to promote and then to impose professional criteria on front-line workers. Once the federation had done this, it used persuasion, the power of the purse, and the placement of university-trained personnel in tune with Cohn's philosophy to professionalize its constituent organizations.

But change could be imposed from outside Toronto as well. This chapter narrates how this process took place at the Toronto branch of the Jewish Immigrant Aid Society (JIAS). Though many scientific managers from within and outside Toronto shared similar goals, there were crucial differences among them which foreshadowed the struggle that would erupt between the Montreal and Toronto Jewish communities for organizational hegemony. The local and national organizations of Canadian Jewry were often proxies in this larger battle. But in order to better understand all this, it is necessary to understand the origins of the JIAS. When the original Canadian Jewish Congress of 1919 had expired not long after its birth, it left Canadian Jewry a vital legacy: the Jewish Immigrant Aid Society (JIAS). In its first five years, the JIAS played a key role in the immigration and resettlement of large numbers of Russian and Romanian Jews. By 1925 the JIAS could claim responsibility for the admission of at least five thousand Jews to Canada.[1]

This mass immigration of Jews was an anomaly in Canadian immigration history. The emphasis in the *Immigration Act* of 1919 on attracting "qualified agriculturists" impeded Jewish immigration, because Canadian immigration officials knew Jews were city dwellers who had no interest in farming. This characteristic made them the least desirable of those officially designated as "non-preferred immigrants." Asians and Blacks, the other members of this immigrant class, "were acceptable as long as they were out of sight." But urbanized Jews competed with British and other desirable immigrants. During the 1920s, a series of Orders-in-Council made it increasingly difficult for "non-preferred immigrants" to enter Canada; PC #185 of 1923 mandating medical inspection by Canadian-authorized doctors at the port of exit proved particularly onerous because not all ports had "Canadian-authorized doctors." Even those who passed these medical tests were frequently detained at their destinations for medical observation. Immigration officials frequently used the infamous "continuous journey" requirement (PC #23-1914), which was originally applied against Asian immigration, to halt prospective Jewish immigrants. One immigrant in 1921, for instance, was detained because he had to wait in Antwerp (after being directed there by the Immigration Department) while the Canadian Embassy checked his paperwork, and therefore did not proceed directly from Rotterdam to Quebec. More than a quarter of the Jewish immigrants arriving in Canada in the summer of 1921 were detained for this reason. However JIAS intervention secured the release of over 85 percent of those detained. But the government wanted narrower gates. Between 31 January 1923, and 7 April 1926, a Jew already in Canada could bring into the country only his wife and unmarried children under eighteen years of age (PC #183-1923). It wasn't until after 1926 that the list was lengthened to include the father, mother, unmarried son and daughter, and unmarried brother and sister of "any person legally admitted previously and resident in Canada."[2]

In 1923 the Immigration Branch introduced the permit system. Without amending the *Immigration Act* itself, the government craftily used Orders-in-Council to create three classes of immigrants. The Preferred Group came from northern and western Europe and the Non-

Preferred Group from the pre-war Austro-Hungarian and Russian empires. The Special Permit Group comprised southern Europeans and Jews, regardless of country of origin. This latter group could enter Canada only if approved by a cabinet Order-in-Council. As historian Harold Troper observed: "Issuing this permit was not the task of immigration officials, nor was the permit issued according to fixed criteria. Rather the permit was issued by cabinet as an act of political patronage. This meant that immigration of anyone in the Special Permit Group ... was now shifted directly into the political arena ... A special permit, dispensed as an act of patronage, was a prize precious few Jews could hope to win."[3]

These regulations combined to severely restrict Jewish immigration into Canada. Some immigrant Jews hoping to bring family into Canada felt compelled to use shady "immigration lawyers" and "ward heelers," many of whom were steamship agents who claimed to have "pull" with the Department of Immigration. Though this was not the first time Jewish "immigration consultants" had preyed on prospective immigrants, the introduction of the permit system made their services more enticing to those hoping to bring over their loved ones. Of course, not all steamship agents were dishonest; many played an important role in Jewish immigration. But in many cases they charged exorbitant fees and did not succeed in obtaining permits. The permit system placed high expectation on Jewish Liberal party supporters and businessmen such as Archie Freiman and Lyon Cohen, or the Jewish MPs Abraham Heaps and Samuel W. Jacobs. It was widely rumoured – and correct – that an application from an in-the-loop travel agent or politically connected lawyer backed by such agents could produce a permit. Nonetheless, permits were rare and Jewish immigration continued to decline.

The mandate of the JIAS was to advocate for greater Jewish immigration and to assist in immigrant reception and settlement. Even as Canada was closing its doors to Jews, the JIAS maintained representatives at most major Canadian ports and in almost every city in which Jews lived. These representatives, mainly volunteers although some were paid, were the front-liners not only of immigrant reception but of negotiations with local Immigration Department authorities. They had a good knowledge of immigration regulations, worked hard to develop working relationships with local Immigration Department officials, and pitched the JIAS to the local Jewish community to raise funds. But despite the presence of important Jewish community leaders on its letterhead, the JIAS was far from being a cohesive national organization. It had a strong presence in Montreal, where its headquarters were located, and enjoyed considerable support in Winnipeg, Ottawa, and Atlantic Canada. But the society was weak in Toronto. This was hard to credit, given the size of the immigrant community and the dire immigration statistics of the first summer of the society's existence. Yet in 1921 it raised only $2,500 in Toronto, but $6,000 in Winnipeg, a community less than half as large.

What happened to Toronto? Simply put, Downtown Jews, the group for which immigration was the most important, lost faith in the Toronto JIAS and very soon abandoned it. Abraham Rhinewine, the well-known editor of the *Yiddisher Zhurnal*, became the Toronto JIAS President in 1920, but left a year later. From his subsequent behaviour, it is clear that he believed that steamship agents and other influence peddlers understood the immigration business better than the JIAS. The vacuum left by his departure was filled by Rabbi Julius Siegel of Goel Tzedec in 1922. He was followed by Holy Blossom's advocate of scientific charity, Rabbi Brickner, who held the position until 1925. The minutes of the JIAS board, which met sporadically despite the influx of immigrants, indicate that Siegel and Brickner were not fully behind the organization. They did little, for example, to set up immigrant reception at Union Station, seeing it as their mandate simply to ensure that arriving immigrants conformed to immigration regulations, avoided becoming "public charges," and were prepared to settle down and Canadianize. These leaders believed that the surge of immigration was temporary and that the JIAS had no responsibility to assist immigrants in finding housing or to lend them money. In fact, the society's official name, the Emergency Jewish Aid Committee, was not changed until June 1924. Worse yet, its mindset outlived its moniker. Dr Abraham Brodey, who succeeded Brickner as president of the newly renamed Jewish Immigrant Aid Society of Ontario, came from a world far removed from the rough and tumble of the JIAS's "Downtown" immigrant clientele. His family was a pillar of the community, and he was a gifted student who had earned an MA before he turned his attention to medicine. After a brilliant record in North American and European medical schools, Brodey became a key member of the Mount Sinai staff and maintained a busy private practice. He first involved himself with the

JIAS because, like others of his class, he saw community voluntarism as a social imperative. He had no immigration experience and believed that, since Jewish immigration was winding down, the Toronto "Emergency Committee" had fulfilled its mandate and would soon "go out of business."[4]

Fortunately, this was not to be. The importance of immigration in the community ensured the continued existence of the Toronto JIAS, and would eventually bring its executive out of their somnolence. After 1925 the government's increasing and incessant use of regulations to control Jewish immigration forced the National JIAS to emphasize lobbying for immigrant admission. The society's national leaders understood that the existing immigration regulations compelled them to actively engage government, and they eventually negotiated an unwritten "quota" of Jewish immigrants. The JIAS proposed that in return for an agreement to a few thousand Jews a year, the society would pre-screen immigration applications and forward only those that complied with the regulations. It was estimated that this commitment would eliminate 75 percent of the applications. The Immigration Branch agreed to the quota thanks to the influence of Liberal MP Sam Jacobs in the King minority government. The precarious position of the Liberal government after the general election of October 1925 offered Jacobs an ideal situation to wield what little power he possessed on behalf of the society. The JIAS collected the $10 application fee, and an additional $25 for all approved applications sent to Ottawa for submission to Cabinet. The results were impressive. Over 70 percent of Jewish immigrants who arrived between 1 April 1925 and 31 March 1926 came under JIAS auspices.[5]

Word travelled quickly in the Montreal Jewish immigrant community, and it soon became common knowledge that the JIAS offered the best chance of obtaining permits. The Montreal office was packed with applicants and the staff were run off their feet, kept busy by a renewal of the quota agreement on slightly more favourable terms. The political uncertainty in Ottawa had caused delays in these negotiations, and the highly charged political atmosphere added to the usual tensions of immigration work. A member of the Montreal JIAS wryly observed: "Sam Jacobs' office is the busiest immigration place in the city." It was a climate ripe for corruption with a great deal of money to be made through illegally selling quota permits to individuals seeking to reunite their families.[6]

A similarly charged atmosphere prevailed on Spadina Avenue. The Toronto JIAS office, a few cramped rooms, became more packed then ever with Jews desperately trying to bring in relatives. Suddenly, the tables were turned. In June 1926, at a secret emergency meeting, the Toronto JIAS executive were told that prominent lawyer Joseph Singer had somehow obtained 300 of the society's 3,000 permits and sold them at prices ranging between $75 and $125. It was rumoured that Singer had used these funds for his unsuccessful bid to become alderman in November 1925. Since the signature of the JIAS national secretary was on the permits, it did not take long for steamship agents to complain that the society was gouging those it was mandated to serve.[7]

Steamship agents, as their name indicates, originally concentrated on issuing boat and train tickets, mostly to immigrants. They received sales commissions and arranged passages for agricultural immigrants. Jews had begun to enter this field in the early twentieth century as Jewish immigration increased. Their role was further enhanced as *landsmanschaften* sought to bring in more *landsleit*, often hiring an agent to facilitate the process. In many cases one family member came first, and sent money to relatives still in the "Old Country." Agents responded to this demand by becoming "remittance agents" as well. The business proved lucrative and further enlarged the circle of prospective clientele, since many remittance customers would use the same agent to arrange their relatives' passage to Canada. As regulations tightened, agents found ways around them. Some would lend money so that clients could meet the "minimum landing" money clause on arrival. The immigrants would later repay the loan with interest. The battle against immigration restriction exerted a unifying force in the community. Agents and clients often became very close, at times acting like extended family. Sometimes the agent was a *landsman*, or a member of the same synagogue. In the early 1920s Jewish shipping agents in Montreal and Toronto cooperated with the JIAS in immigrant resettlement. Some even sat on the Toronto JIAS board.[8]

The partnership seemed likely to continue. The JIAS quota would provide immigrants, and the steamship agents stood ready to provide tickets once permits were issued. Unfortunately, however, the dishonest behaviour of a minority tarnished their collective reputation.

The best-documented case was that of David Gurofsky, who defrauded hundreds of prospective immigrants and did "serious damage to the immigrants' interest and the Jewish community generally" by making key immigration official Frederick C. Blair permanently suspicious of all Jewish steamship agents. The prejudiced Blair concluded that all Jews were untrustworthy and that the Immigration Branch therefore had to exercise extreme caution in matters of Jewish immigration. Blair's views hardened as he rose through the ranks, finally becoming deputy minister in 1936. His colleagues had their own reasons for disliking Jews. Deputy Minister of Immigration W.J. Black, who had held the post until the end of 1923, hated Sam Jacobs for forcing his transfer to the Canadian National Railroad. By 1925 it was clear to Jacobs that the department was increasingly unsympathetic to all appeals, and after the 1926 election, with a Liberal government now firmly in the saddle, the department stiffened its resolve to give the JIAS "no more quotas." To make matters worse, the Immigration Branch discovered how Singer had illegally obtained and resold permits.[9]

The society's credibility was on the line. The Toronto JIAS executive had tried in vain to hush up this messy matter. In an age where washing Jewish dirty linen in public was taboo, news of a *shtadlan* acting no better than Gurofsky would be disastrous. The society trumpeted its superiority over the "fixers" at every opportunity, yet it would seem that its leaders acted no better. The remaining credibility of the JIAS with the Department of Immigration and its status in the Jewish community was threatened. *Zhurnal* editor Abraham Rhinewine theorized that Jacobs had covertly advised Singer to approach acting minister of immigration Charles Stewart to obtain the permits. Other evidence suggests that JIAS national manager Samuel B. Haltrecht had sold some of the 1926 quota's pre-approved permits. Whatever the facts, the Toronto executive were in a conundrum. It was impossible to approach Singer openly and further violate *shtadlanut*, and Jacobs was off in Montreal. The executive could only lamely instruct Brodey to empower a committee "to negotiate an honorable solution with the parties involved, or with the Government if necessary, submitting a further report to this committee."[10]

Of course, the committee never carried out its mandate. It was impossible to investigate Singer's actions without arousing further suspicions. Rhinewine made sure that the matter was never discussed in the *Yiddisher Zhurnal*. It was not prudent to excoriate the leading Jewish solicitor of the day, a man whose brother was chairman of the board of Mount Sinai Hospital. That Brodey worked at Mount Sinai and was a friend of the Singers only added another reason to whitewash the whole affair.

Further immigration restriction added to communal angst and JIAS woes. The promulgation of PC #534 in April 1926 empowered the Department of Immigration to admit only those whose "labour or service is needed in Canada." First-degree relatives were still admissible, but it was easy for the department to keep families separated by excluding some members under the "labour or service provision." With the Singer scandal looming large, the department refused to allocate the JIAS a new quota of immigrants. With no more guaranteed permits, the society would have to fall back on case-by-case pleading, forcing it to compete directly with solicitors and steamship agents for whatever permits the department benevolently chose to bestow. For the embattled Toronto executive (and for their national counterparts) the future looked bleak.[11]

These events would profoundly affect Dr Brodey and the Toronto JIAS for almost a decade. Brodey served as Toronto JIAS president from 1926 to 1940, but his temperament was not ideal for the position. Though highly intelligent and well intentioned, he was not "a man of the people." Dealing with the public, and especially working-class, Yiddish-speaking clients, was not his forte. He was snobbish, stubborn, aloof, unemotional, and often arrogant. He was put off by the personalities and petty rivalries of community politics and could not understand the desperate passions aroused in the battle to obtain permits. The Singer affair struck him very personally. He was friendly with both Singer brothers, and Singer's permit selling outraged Brodey's strong sense of propriety. Why would a person who didn't need the money fall victim to such greed? How could a lawyer so misuse his clients? The fact that there was a political prize to be won, that greed was an unfortunate human predilection, and that Singer's clients were delighted to pay for obtaining rare and precious permits, seems to have completely escaped Brodey.[12]

The imposition of PC #534 struck the final blow, because the discretion it gave the department gave rise to a battle over every permit.

Brodey had no stomach for lobbying. He hated the buzz and clamour of Sunday office hours, and complained: "Too many applicants are lying to obtain permits." Now he reacted predictably: if the department had so much discretion, then lobbying was pointless. Why should he associate himself or the Toronto JIAS with a process so rife with corruption? It seemed far better to avoid the whole unseemly mess and simply do what Ottawa wanted. Family unification applications being the only ones with any hope of success, Brodey limited his immigration work to simply filling in application forms, sending them to Ottawa, and waiting for the department to exercise the discretion it so obviously enjoyed.

Brodey's passive approach explains the descent of the Toronto JIAS into semi-dormancy between 1927 and 1932. On average only five hundred people a year came to the JIAS between 1927 and 1929. This was a mere fraction of the potential Toronto market for immigration aid services. Contrast this with the 2,105 applications in 1936, when a full-service office re-opened despite the Depression and Ottawa's highly restrictive immigration rules![13]

Brodey's arrogance and lack of empathy for the JIAS drove the remaining Downtown Jews from the board. By 1928 none remained. For the next five years, the society was a one-man operation. This did not bother Brodey very much. Indeed, he loftily proclaimed to head office: "On Sunday mornings, the office requires little management. A few people come in to buy remittances. Some have easily answerable questions. A few file forms. These I complete and send to your office. There is little interest here in immigration." The line-ups at shipping agents visible from the society's windows told a different story, of course. But why would Downtown Jews want to come to a cold and unfeeling man who didn't speak Yiddish? Their dissatisfaction with the JIAS was corroborated by a series of articles in Montreal's Yiddish newspaper *Der Kanader Adler* in December 1926. These alleged that during the term of the quota agreement with Ottawa the JIAS had charged excessive fees and showed favouritism in selecting those who were to receive permits.

In truth, the JIAS fee structure was reasonable. Permit applicants were charged $10 as a "membership fee" and a further $25 (or more if they could afford it) if their application was actually forwarded to Ottawa. Certainly some wealthier Toronto applicants were approached for contributions after permits were approved by Ottawa, but there is no documentary evidence that some people were given preference over others.

But word on the street disagreed. The *Adler*'s informant also spoke to Ottawa. On the same day as the *Adler* story broke, Deputy Minister Egan told a JIAS delegation summoned to Ottawa on short notice (Brodey among them) that "the Department was in possession of thousands of complaints from Montreal and Toronto." In his anger, Egan (with Blair present) barely allowed the JIAS delegation any chance to reply. Three days later Egan raised the issues again until Jacobs and Heaps, his fellow MP, finally succeeded in changing the subject. Egan and Blair smelled scandal. For Blair, Jewish impropriety, even if only alleged, justified his mistrust of the JIAS and Jews more generally. The *Adler* revelations brought an end to the unofficial "JIAS quota" on 3 January 1927. The department insisted that henceforth PC #534 would be applied in all Jewish applications. In addition, Egan demanded that the JIAS prove that its membership dues were legitimately derived, and he openly encouraged solicitors and steamship agents to compete with the society despite Blair's acknowledgment that its pre-screening of applicants was useful.[14]

The national office responded by cleaning house. Two employees involved in stealing permits were fired. Organizational renewal began with the appointment of A.J. Paull as executive director in late 1927. Paull exemplified professionalism. He had a degree in social work, was trained in accounting procedures, and brought extensive field experience in Palestine and Europe with the Joint Distribution Committee. He was a manager to the core. Paull's mandate was to re-establish the supremacy of the JIAS in all matters of Jewish immigration. If Ottawa was now only prepared to deal with Jews on a case-by-case basis, then Paull would play the government's game and argue each case on its merits. He also competed directly with lawyers, influence peddlers, and steamship agents. His board gave him the financial backing to "minimize the depredations of middlemen who charged exorbitant sums and were often unable to deliver the permits they promised." By 1930 the Montreal JIAS office was humming once again.[15]

The Toronto office took the opposite course. Brodey browbeat his executive into agreement on a much more low-key approach. He was determined to avoid any repetition of the Singer affair that could taint his personal reputation for probity or offend his sensibility. Downtowners still wanted an office that would actively attempt to obtain permits. However, the combination of the department's restrictive measures and the newly unsavoury reputation of the JIAS compelled them to make common cause with Brodey for the time being. By late 1927 the society's Toronto business had fallen drastically and the board had postponed a membership campaign. Joining the Federation of Jewish Philanthropies in November 1927 was no help; the office's budget was too small to receive an allocation. As it became starved for business, the Downtowners suggested that the office be shut down entirely. The board decided to keep it office open on a part-time basis, which was more than sufficient given the small amount of activity and since, according to board minutes, "it is not clear if the public even knows what JIAS does."[16]

By 1928 the Toronto Downtown Jews no longer used the JIAS. Why waste funds on an organization that had no hope of obtaining permits? The resignations of Rhinewhine and H.M. Kirshenbaum, a *Zhurnal* colleague from the JIAS executive, underscored the society's irrelevance. Their departure left Brodey in charge of an all but moribund organization. The remaining Toronto executive blamed the politics of immigration. But this blame was unfounded. Despite PC #534, lobbying worked. There was more Jewish immigration in 1927 and 1928 than in 1926. In 1928 over 1,400 Jews were admitted through special permits, and an additional 2,000 were admitted under PC #534. According to National Executive Director Paull, it was the Toronto JIAS that had failed to bring in a single immigrant.[17]

Thus, by 1929 the Montreal and Toronto offices of the JIAS were completely at loggerheads over strategy. Though Paull was aware of the situation, the loose structure of the national organization made it impossible for him to exert any control over the Toronto branch. As the Depression worsened, the Federal government moved to restrict eastern European immigration completely. In 1930 an Order-in-Council would allow only immigrants with enough capital to establish and maintain themselves on farms. In 1931 the Bennett government announced further regulations, which almost completely halted what remained of Jewish immigration to Canada, seriously weakened JIAS headquarters in Montreal, and led to an almost complete cessation of immigration activity in Toronto.

To boot, by 1931 the Toronto JIAS was in such serious financial difficulty that it was open for business only on Wednesdays and Sunday mornings. Toronto Jews became increasingly reliant on steamship agents, who offered remittance services to European relatives, prepared permit applications for immigrants, arranged immigrants' tickets, dealt in currency exchange, and sent telegrams to the Old Country. For a fee, they also promised to lobby Ottawa for immigration permits in family reunification cases. Even when permits were almost impossible to obtain, agents such as Harry Dworkin, Joseph Graner, and Anshel Wise flourished through their lucrative remittance and telegram business. These agencies advertised heavily in the Yiddish press and served their customers in Yiddish.[18]

Only the combined visions of JIAS national president, Benjamin Robinson, and executive director Paull prevented the Toronto JIAS from disappearing. Both men believed that national society could not wait passively for immigration to resume. It had to seize the initiative to strengthen the organization in preparation for better times by restoring full service to the Toronto office. In late 1932 Robinson suggested that the Toronto JIAS raise its profile by leaving the offices it shared with other Federation constituent organizations and open a separate, full-time office. Brodey replied that as long as immigration remained low, keeping the Toronto JIAS "as an adjunct to the Federation ... was as good an arrangement as possible."[19]

The JIAS national executive directed Robinson to re-open negotiations in early 1933. Brodey refused to budge. His trump card, which he chose not to reveal, was the society's ownership of $10,000 in municipal bonds. These were the proceeds of funds once paid to ensure that immigrants would not become "public charges." Brodey zealously guarded this hoard – and his independence – while continuing to accept a small monthly subsidy from the almost bankrupt Montreal office. But Paull got wind of the money stash, probably from the disgruntled Rhinewhine, and demanded that Brodey use it to enhance the level of Toronto JIAS services. Brodey rejected this suggestion out of hand while professing to remain open to any other suggestions that the national board might have.[20]

Robinson countered with a different approach. "You will agree with me," he argued, "that Toronto has an appreciable number of first-generation Jews, almost as many ... as Montreal ...Why does Montreal foster an efficient immigrant aid office and why is there not such an office in Toronto?" Robinson suggested that not all Jews could afford to go to steamship agents, and informed Brodey: "We feel that the Jewish Immigrant Aid Society of Canada owes a duty to these individuals to give them at least the same service that we give them in Montreal." He then bluntly pointedly added that the board took the position that "what Montreal can do, Toronto can do."[21]

By now it was eminently clear that the men in Toronto and Montreal had little in common besides their JIAS membership. Each organization had a different vision of the society's mandate and how to promote it. By now, the difference over strategy had been overshadowed by Robinson and Paull's antipathy toward Brodey. Their exchanges grew ever sharper, as Robinson threatened Brodey by revealing the presence of "a group in Toronto that wants an independent JIAS office."[22] If Brodey continued to be unreasonable, then Robinson would have "no other alternative but to give that group the encouragement it deserves." Predictably, Brodey would have none of it, and relations between the two offices became even worse.[23]

Brodey's attitude benefited the steamship agents, politicians, and others who claimed to be able to obtain permits for a price. One contemporary observer asserted that while Brodey was "not being bribed by the agents and their crowd," his *modus operandi* certainly fuelled such rumours. But this "perfect gentleman, incapable of raising his voice, a man from the upper stratum of Toronto Jewish society," didn't care what the street said of him. His attitude toward immigration work and those who needed JIAS assistance remained unchanged.[24]

As European conditions worsened and Canadian immigration restrictions became still more rigid, Brodey continued to hold to the erroneous premise that immigration work was a simple matter of answering "elementary questions," filling out forms, and waiting for Ottawa to act. He could not comprehend what historian Gerald Tulchinsky has aptly called "the landscape of memory," the nostalgia and connection to Europe that the Downtown Jews felt so strongly. Remitting a portion of their meagre wages to *der alter heim* (the old hometown), sending a telegram to Poland to mark a special occasion, or even the simple act of filling out immigration applications offered a glimmer of hope that they might reunite their families. For them immigration was not about filling out forms; it was about retrieving a life and remaining connected with loved ones. It was far worse to not submit an application for a permit than it was to try and fail. But the aloof patrician Brodey continued to distance himself from the very people the JIAS was set up to serve. Despite the rise of Hitler and fresh anti-Semitic outbreaks in Poland, he persisted in believing that "to bring people to our office in order to hear their sad tales regarding relatives in Europe and then tell them we can do nothing is certainly not a pleasing task to us, nor does it help the status of the Society."[25]

Independent opposition to Brodey was rapidly building in Toronto. When Robinson and Paull attended Toronto meetings to revive Congress in June 1933 and the First Plenary in January 1934, they met with a group of young businessmen and professionals, largely drawn from the Goel Tzedec and McCaul Street synagogues, many of whom had worked together previously on the boards of the FJP and Mount Sinai Hospital. They understood popular concerns about immigration because they came from immigrant homes, and voiced complaints that "working-class Jews were paying too much and getting too little" from those who ran the immigration business in Toronto in the absence of competition from the JIAS.[26] What was needed, they claimed, was "a National [JIAS] Board, with officers from the Eastern, Central, and newly created Western Regions. This Board [would] deal with National issues while local Boards would run the local offices and deal with local issues." So far Brodey had succeeded in keeping this group off his board.[27]

But unrest soon burst into the open. On 13 May 1934, a sombre gathering took place in Montreal for the Fourteenth Annual Meeting of the JIAS. It was a time for soul searching. Jewish immigration was at a nadir. Only 599 Jews had come to Canada during the fiscal year ending 31 March 1934, only 2 percent from Germany. Many men in Canada had waited for up to three years to bring fiancées to Canada, only to have their applications denied, despite a slight hope that James G. Macdonald, League of Nations High Commissioner for Refugees, might obtain some concessions on Jewish admissions from Prime Minister Bennett. After the presentation of the report containing these dire statistics, the floor was opened for questions and comments. One of the first to rise to the attack was Samuel Shapiro, Rhinewhine's successor as editor of the Toronto *Yiddisher Zhurnal*, who saw himself as the emissary of Toronto's Downtown Jews. Shapiro personally knew of "difficulties encountered by Toronto

Jews in obtaining their citizen's papers" and of a German Jewish woman vainly searching for relatives. He emphatically concluded that "it was high time that an active Immigrant Aid office be opened in Toronto."[28]

The meeting quickly passed a resolution calling on the newly elected national board of the JIAS to "call a conference in Toronto and to organize an active Immigrant Aid Society office." Robinson and Paull now felt sufficiently empowered to extend Montreal's centralized model into the Toronto JIAS office. But Robinson, ever conscious of the society's weak financial state and determined to alienate as few members as possible, decided to make a final attempt to co-opt Brodey. He sent Brodey an extract of Shapiro's remarks and reminded him that it was his responsibility to open a full-time and "full service" Toronto office.[29]

Brodey, although unhappy with Shapiro's "immature conclusions based on insufficient grounds," did agree to call a board meeting for 20 June. He promised to bring "an open mind to the meeting and permit the establishment of such an office if the Committee may direct." The meeting agreed to strike a sub-committee to investigate the utility of a full-service office. Robinson and Paull dismissed this as yet another delaying tactic, and were surprised when Brodey told them in late August that the Toronto committee was working on the financial arrangements for the new office and, "it may be possible to start an office in Toronto in the near future." Brodey promised to forward more detailed plans within ten days.[30]

But ten days became two months. Robinson, tired of waiting, unleashed Paull, who wasted no time and minced few words. He lashed out at the Toronto staff for their ignorance of Department of Immigration regulations, and for cooperating with steamship agents who "misled, mishandled, and victimized" their customers. By late October, Paull refused to deal with any more Toronto cases, but Brodey remained intractable.[31]

Incensed by Brodey's obstinacy, Paull drafted a brutally frank letter, which Robinson forwarded to Brodey unrevised. Paull charged that Brodey had no appreciation for the ideals of the JIAS; he accomplished little and attracted little business because "with ... an inexperienced girl in the Federation Building meeting our immigrants for about an hour every Sunday morning, you will admit that very little can be accomplished ... I will never agree with you that Toronto is different than Montreal, and that the problems we are called upon to meet in Montreal are non-exist[ent] in Toronto."[32]

Robinson vowed that head office would persist in the request "that an efficient office with a capable man in charge be established in your City," and urged Brodey to "advise us of your favourable decision without undue delay." Paull was even less kind to Freda Berk (the "inexperienced girl" in the federation office) when she wrote for advice on some casework. He castigated her for how little she knew about immigration work. Paull then proceeded to vent his anger on the unfortunate secretary, perhaps hoping that the letter's abusive tone would be communicated to Brodey: "Your Committee during the last four years took the attitude that there was nothing for you to do in Toronto. As a result, hundreds of cases were mishandled by irresponsible agencies with very grave consequences to the people concerned ... The hopelessness which exists ... will continue to exist in Toronto until such time as our Society begins to function in your City. During the years that you have been dormant, Montreal has cleared up most of the cases which are such a serious problem at the present time in your City."[33]

Brodey may have been stubborn, but he also prided himself on being polite and gentlemanly. This sort of correspondence was outside his experience.[34] He knew when he was beaten. He needed Robinson and Paull's support to retain his precious presidency, and realized that the forces arrayed against him would depose him at the next JIAS annual meeting. So he finally swallowed his pride and decided that an active JIAS office in Toronto might not be such a bad thing after all.[35]

On 6 March 1935, Paull came to Toronto to present his plan for a revitalized office. He and Robinson were willing to compromise to get the office open as quickly as possible. They insisted that Toronto contribute $200 per month toward the enterprise during the first six months of its operation. But to mollify Brodey, they promised that Montreal would pay any excess costs and the salary of Paull or any other Montreal employee who helped in the transition. Montreal would also arrange for the leasing of the new premises at the corner of Spadina and College in the heart of the Jewish neighbourhood. "All we ask," wrote Paull to Brodey, "is that you appropriate the sum of $1200 for the first six months."[36]

But Brodey still moved slowly, evidently wary of challenging the effective monopoly that the Toronto steamship agents had carved out. He hated confrontations and would have preferred peaceful coexistence with the agents. In fact, one of these agents was a tenant in the building where the new office was to be located, and he understandably raised a considerable fuss with the landlord about the JIAS intrusion. Feeling snookered, Brodey called an emergency meeting of his board on 17 March to "decide definitely once and for all whether we are to open an office on a full time basis." The board agreed to open the office and appropriate the necessary funds for a six-month trial operation, but only if Paull would send them an official letter confirming the terms of "our mutual responsibilities." They also requested that Paull refrain from competing directly with the steamship agents by not entering the remittance business for at least the first three months, hoping to "avoid undue friction and unnecessary criticism."[37]

This was the last straw. It was obvious to the Montrealers that Brodey cared only about his presidency, so that was all he would be allowed to retain. Robinson, using the authority given him by the national board, took over the Toronto office and made it clear that it would be run as a Montreal subsidiary. This manoeuvre proved to be a watershed event. The Toronto JIAS would remain subservient to Montreal's policy and decision making until the early 1970s.[38]

Robinson then commenced Brodey's long overdue education by reminding him that remittances were very often "a point of contact between an individual desiring immigration aid and our Society." In addition, Montreal needed the small profit it made on remittances to help finance the expenses of fighting for permits. Therefore, the new Toronto office would have to provide this service. Robinson also explained that he objected to steamship agents because their ignorance of immigration regulations often spoiled the chances of potential immigrants. More to the point: "Steamship agents will always criticize us whether we do remittance work or not as our activities in Toronto will deprive them of their many sources of income from all kinds of immigration work."[39]

All that remained was to finalize a site and hire an executive secretary to manage the office. Paull pressured the Dominion Bank into renting space to the JIAS, and the society re-opened its office in the basement of the Dominion Bank building on the southeast corner of College Street and Spadina Avenue. This location was excellent, and considerable walk-in trade could be expected.[40]

For his part, Brodey began actively seeking an executive secretary. In mid-March he had interviewed Maurice A. Solkin, a thirty-five-year-old Romanian Jew who had come to Canada with JIAS help in the 1920s. Brodey was impressed with Solkin's "considerable immigration experience." He had worked for the Joint Distribution Committee in Bucharest and in Toronto for Joseph Graner's steamship agency. At the time of his interview, he was the executive secretary of the Folks Farein, which Graner had helped found in 1914. Solkin wrote impeccable Yiddish and English and was charming and personable. While he could also be very sensitive to criticism and high strung, he was eager to please.[41]

Montreal office manager Samuel Kaplan was to supervise the opening of the office and show Solkin the ropes while securing as much free publicity as possible from Shapiro's *Zhurnal* and bringing the office to the attention of the *landsmanschaften*. Solkin sought to hire a qualified secretary who could also "read a Russian and Polish address ... be able to speak Yiddish ... and be efficient, industrious, and well recommended." Eventually Tobie Taback, a graduate of the Brunswick Avenue Talmud Torah, was hired. It was made clear to Solkin that he and his staff would be "subject to the control and direction of the Executive Director" and that the Toronto office would have "no direct communication with the Government Departments in Ottawa, all such matters to be submitted to the Executive Director."[42]

The first ten days of April 1935 were hectic. Brodey rushed between his practice and the new JIAS office, delivering furniture, supervising carpenters, and begging equipment from friends. Solkin helped as much as possible, but he had to be discreet because he had yet to submit his formal resignation to the Folks Farein. He did find time to interview and hire the office secretary. Brodey and Solkin's hard work paid off.[43]

Arriving in April on an inspection tour, Kaplan immediately contacted Shapiro of the *Zhurnal*, who had rejoined the Toronto JIAS Board, and inserted special advertisements of the JIAS remittance service in the *Zhurnal*. Kaplan spent most of his time setting up a remittance system for the Toronto office. He arranged informal meetings with "those people who have an influence in the Jewish Press and the leaders of the Jewish Societies." On 12 April he held two meetings "with great success," which, he was sure, convinced influential *landsmanschaft* leaders of "the necessity of our office in Toronto."[44]

The results of the first day's business confirmed Kaplan's optimism. No fewer than sixty-two people came to the office, but they came to do business. A jubilant Kaplan reported: "We made out ten applications. Our visitors in the morning brought their friends a few minutes later, and at the same time the majority of them made new appointments for their relatives and friends in the matter of applications, information, etc., at the same time I informed them that we are accepting remittances."[45] To Kaplan's delight, Brodey appeared "in the middle of the rush" and "was surprised to see so many people ... at the first day of our opening."[46]

After a week Kaplan returned to Montreal "well satisfied." With good reason. The JIAS had attracted business, much "by word of mouth," and was ready to do battle with the steamship agencies. Certainly the volume and type of business attracted on opening day supported Paull's contention that there was a need for an independent Toronto JIAS office.

The Toronto office was now in Solkin's hands, and Paull, from his seat in Montreal, was determined to ensure his success. He provided his protégé with letters of introduction to the American Consulate and to those responsible for the Toronto office of the Department of Immigration. In order to maintain Montreal's control and knowledge of Toronto developments, Solkin was required to submit a monthly statistical update to head office.

Within two weeks a delegation of steamship agents appeared at Solkin's office, understandably resentful of the hostile tone of the *Zhurnal* ads. Many agents were honest and boasted strong ties to their customers, and before immigration restriction, some had been quite successful in helping Jews enter Canada. They also offered immigrants banking and remittance services and legal advice in their native Yiddish. The agents argued that their fees were of necessity higher than those of the JIAS – they had families to feed and were not nonprofit agencies. Hoping for a "live and let live" attitude, they sought a truce with the JIAS. They proposed that the society get out of the remittance business, into which, they protested, it had "unfairly" intruded. Most Toronto board members were sympathetic; Solkin needed considerable persuasion to convince the board to refer the matter to Paull.

Solkin was distressed by the board's sympathy for the agents, realizing that the JIAS could only succeed in Toronto if it competed with the agents head-on in all areas of immigration aid. He informed Albert [Anshel] Wise, the head of the agents' delegation, that even though the Toronto board had "gone on record as favouring harmonious collaboration with the local agents and refraining from active advertising of [its] Foreign Remittance services," the final decision was in the hands of "the Head Office in Montreal." Solkin then advised Paull to veto the agents' request, for fear of "creating a dangerous precedent."[47]

Solkin needn't have worried. Paull harboured a long-standing antipathy toward steamship agents and he had a chance to vent it now. He observed that "any compromise with the steamship agents would be fatal to the existence of our Toronto branch." Agents ought to confine themselves to selling steamship and railroad tickets. Paull astutely refrained from officially condemning "trafficking in permits" because the JIAS did "not wish to be accused of preventing the entry of Jews" into Canada. Nonetheless, the ultimate goal was to see the Toronto JIAS take a "larger share" of the immigrant aid market away from the steamship agents. Paull passionately believed that the agents, because they operated for profit, "lived on and off the immigrants." Only the JIAS, he proclaimed, had a "duty to the wanderer, whether he is on our shores, or whether he is coming."[48]

Surely the truth of the matter lay somewhere between the agents' views and Paull's. But Paull's single-minded toughness in defining the JIAS role was crucial to its ultimate success in Toronto. Emboldened by Paull's support, Brodey and Solkin continued to advertise remittances aggressively, and the Toronto office grew quickly, receiving 350 customers in the first two weeks. These numbers had an immediate impact on the immigration marketplace, even though the JIAS had not yet secured any permits. Solkin reported that "traffic in immigration permits had subsided considerably, and the prices ... while still exorbitant, are much lower than they were only two weeks ago." The JIAS office grew busier by the month. Although the agents continued to spread rumours against the society, they steadily lost business.[49]

By the end of 1935, more than fifteen hundred people had used the office's facilities. Solkin accepted all permit applications and forwarded them to Paull in Montreal. To ensure client satisfaction, Paull forwarded them all, and was not surprised when they were routinely rejected by the immigration department. He then used his immigration experience to appeal only those cases that offered a hope of success. Paull and the Immigration Branch had an unspoken understanding: as long as appeals were limited, the department would give JIAS cases the utmost consideration. Herein lay the society's advantage over the agents. Like the quota system, this tacit arrangement put the JIAS in the unenviable position of doing the department's "dirty work." This arrangement dovetailed with the department's own interests in imposing the permit system. But since Canadian Jews lacked political clout, the JIAS was compelled to deal with Immigration authorities "as supplicants requesting favours." At least their methods could claim some success – almost half of the Toronto appeals to the department between April 1935 and August 1939 were awarded permits.[50]

Of course, neither Solkin nor Paull had any illusions about their track record. They knew that ten applications were rejected for every case forwarded to appeal. Certainly many Jews, realizing the poor odds of success, either didn't bother applying or gave up trying. In some tragic cases the JIAS obtained a permit, only to have outside events prevent the immigrant from entering Canada. In January 1936, for instance, a couple began paperwork to adopt their thirteen-year-old Polish nephew. Paull obtained a permit by August, but the department suddenly demanded legal adoption papers and a $300 bond. After six months of frantic saving, the couple sent in the money, but now the department insisted on the boy's parents' legal consent to his adoption. The Second World War broke out before the complex legal requirements were completed, and the boy was swept away in the Holocaust.

Solkin remained undaunted by the demands that derailed most applications – he truly believed "that a single immigration permit" was far more valuable to the office "than all of my propaganda speeches before the various societies put together." He began a more aggressive business policy even though the steamship agents were "yelling murder," and JIAS business continued to increase.[51] Between April and December 1935 the office sent out 165 remittances averaging $12.75 each and 405 parcels of food and clothing to Poland. By 1937 they had sent 1,092 remittances worth an average of $18.14 each. Business peaked during the two weeks before Passover. Staff could barely keep up with the forty extra customers a day coming to purchase remittances.[52]

This successful expansion of the remittance business was largely due to Paull's decision to undercut the agents' commission rates. He was determined that the Toronto office's initial success would continue, and therefore the board authorized funds to ensure its permanence. Solkin also deserves much credit for the office's successful beginning. He was aggressive, had good contacts in the community, and got along very well with Brodey. While Solkin did not come to his position with a strong background in immigration work, he proved to be an apt pupil. He regarded Paull as his master, eagerly went to Montreal for training sessions, was anxious to please, and, as long as it came from Paull, took criticism well. Paull came to respect Solkin's judgment and increased his latitude in handling the Toronto office.[53]

Brodey, on the other hand, was not pleased to have ceded so much control over the Toronto office to Montreal. He kept up a continuous stream of complaints about paying 25 percent of general office expenses and refused to help with Montreal's growing deficit. To make matters worse, Brodey decided to reduce the $200 monthly subsidy to $125. Despite the Toronto office's obvious success, Brodey and the board hedged on continuing the monthly contribution at the end of the six-month term of their agreement with the national JIAS. It was time to step up to the plate, but Brodey remained obstinate.[54]

Paull, inflexible when his control over the Toronto office was challenged, moved quickly to squelch any thoughts of local autonomy. "I want to make it clear once and for all," he angrily wrote to Solkin, "that the entire machinery of the Toronto office is ours." Paull then proceeded to dictate new financial terms to Toronto. But Brodey remained adamant and then turned defiant. In October 1935, just before Paull was to sail on a European fact-finding mission, Brodey proposed to make up the subsidy shortfall by actively ensuring that all clients paid for services rendered and building up society membership.[55]

Paull was furious but, committed to depart within days, left the matter to Robinson. Ever the conciliator, the JIAS national president tried to convince Brodey to maintain the original subsidy, at least until Toronto had paid off the debt incurred in re-opening its office. Brodey refused. Solkin began to assemble a list of businessmen who could be recruited as JIAS members, but Brodey and the board, despite its professed interest in attracting members, offered Solkin no help. Only two of the twenty-three-member executive even bothered to pay their annual dues. When Paull returned in mid-December, he discovered that the Toronto office, even with its increasing traffic, was in danger of financial collapse. Brodey and his board again refused to pay more than $125 a month. Brodey then launched into a lengthy denunciation of all the "unnecessary outlays" that had been incurred "to satisfy Mr. Paull's desires," such as special advertising and competing in the remittances business. Brodey proposed to eliminate these services and return to "serving the community."[56]

Solkin was trapped in the middle of this battle for control. He could ill afford to divert from prioritizing immigration work. In late 1936 the Department of Immigration was reorganized, with JIAS nemesis Blair as its new director. As immigration assumed a more prominent political role, Blair's promotion made it inevitable that immigration requests would continue to be considered on a case-by-case basis.[57] What is more, it was soon apparent that the Liberals had no intention of modifying the severity of the immigration regulations. In early 1936 Paull informed all prospective Jewish immigrants without first-degree relatives in Canada that it was useless to hope for Department of Immigration consideration unless they had at least $5,000 in liquid capital. This severe requirement was made even harder to meet when, in late April, Poland forbade the export of more than $1,000 in foreign currency.[58]

Word quickly spread through the Jewish community that Liberal immigration policy was the harshest to date. In 1935 an average of fifty people per month had come to the JIAS office to apply for the admission of relatives.[59] A year later, this number was halved, even though economic conditions were slowly beginning to improve and more people could afford to act as sponsors. Most people could only remit funds to their relatives rather than apply for their immigration.

The society's monthly remittance business tripled in volume, and the average remittance amount increased.[60]

A tiny trickle of Jews were still arriving, but the JIAS was the source (even by the most generous calculations) for no more than 15 percent of Jewish immigrants into Toronto. The permit process was becoming ever more politicized. Private individuals and steamship agents with political leverage were able to squeeze out a few permits for the lucky – and often wealthy – few. This made it essential for the JIAS to remain active in the remittance business. In 1936 remittances made up 40 percent of the office's business, while immigration applications represented only 14 percent. In 1937 overall business increased by 12 percent while immigration again declined by half.[61]

There is no evidence to suggest that these trends can be explained by immigrants taking advantage of the JIAS's cheaper remittance rates while continuing to give their permit requests to steamship agents. The society's lower rates forced the agents to reduce their prices, but didn't force them out of business. And their rates continued to drop as agents actively competed with the JIAS. This was a gratifying result for the society, but the agents were far from out of business.[62]

Indeed, by late 1936 Paull had to admit: "The agents in Toronto have got such hold on the people that it is difficult to dislodge them." Given this, and observing that Jewish immigration fell from 655 in 1936 to 391 in 1937, JIAS's decline in immigration business probably reflected the communal sense of the futility of even making applications. Of course, steamship agents and influence-peddlers did receive a handful of permits during this period. A desperate few doubtless thought their higher fees correlated to their chance of delivering a permit. Most were disappointed.[63]

The financial crisis at the Toronto JIAS worsened. Immigration was in decline and little time was available for membership drives. In October 1936 Brodey paid his last $125 to Montreal and informed Paull that, from now on, the Toronto office would rely on memberships and income from services for its revenue. This strategy would not prove easy. Solkin's "sporadic" work in a membership drive brought in 106 members between February and June 1936, but they came at a price. It had taken three thousand letters and a thousand distributed annual reports to make these gains. Undaunted, Solkin again hired a collector in late December 1936 and prepared for a second membership drive. This netted a further hundred members but only

60 percent of them actually paid dues. When the collector's salary and commission were taken into account, the membership campaign was a fundraising failure.[64]

However, JIAS immigration business continued to grow, thanks to a new source. In addition to the steadily increasing remittance business came an increase in American visa cases. Many Jews used Canada as a "way station" to the United States. Solkin soon built a close working relationship with the American consul and vice-consul and with the Toronto Immigration office. Thanks to these relationships, the JIAS so dominated the increasingly important American visa business that by early 1937 a larger office and more money were needed. But the Toronto board, still Brodey's mouthpiece, refused to help.[65]

As national executive director, Paull broke all precedent. He conspired with Solkin to take charge of reconstituting the board, and Solkin carefully planned for the annual election of the executive on 16 February 1937. After much arm-twisting, he obtained agreement to run a new executive slate. These were from the group waiting on the sidelines, since it was they who had first complained to Robinson in 1933 and again in 1935. Many wanted the same rationalization of organization and services that had been imposed on the Federation of Jewish Philanthropies. Most prominent among these new men were lawyer Maurice Ezrin, Dr John Atkins, and Ben Forer, a manufacturer active in many communal matters. *Zhurnal* editor Shapiro also agreed to become more active on the board. He was so anxious to improve the Toronto JIAS that he even consented to the presence of his arch-rival Morris Goldstick, publisher of the *Kanada Naies* and brother-in-law of steamship agent Harny Dworkin, on the board.

Faced by this determined group, Brodey finally bowed to reality. In return for retaining the presidency he so craved, he agreed to the reformed slate. Forer assumed the first vice-president's mantle, and the others were elected executive members. Delighted, the Montreal Board gave Solkin a week's salary as a bonus for his excellent work.[66]

With Brodey's control of the board broken, Paull and Robinson moved to ensure that Toronto paid its share of the national JIAS debt. They demanded full control over the Toronto JIAS reserve funds. As noted, these represented the residue of the money first raised in the early 1920s to aid destitute Russian and Romanian immigrants and a fund to ensure that immigrants would not be "public charges." Brodey had used these funds to take care of two patients in mental homes and for the now-discontinued monthly subsidy. This considerable sum now became his best defence against a takeover by head office. But Montreal, now supported by the newly activist Toronto board, was ready to do battle. Robinson informed Brodey, "Toronto has not paid its way nor is it paying its way today." Because of this, said the Montrealer, head office faced a large deficit, and it was only right that Brodey authorize "a substantial contribution" to ameliorate this situation. He then showed the mailed fist inside the velvet glove by claiming that the Toronto board had always believed that this fund belonged to the national organization rather than to Toronto alone. He strongly implied that legal steps would be taken to obtain the money if Brodey balked.[67]

Bereft of board support, and with his presidency up for grabs, Brodey suddenly proved sympathetic and malleable. He professed to be "very pleased" with the work that was being accomplished and observed that Robinson's request was "not a very grave issue." It was simply a matter of deciding whether the payments were to be made "in a large sum or by gradual subvention." Paull had calculated correctly that Brodey preferred his presidency to control over the money. Fearing that something might go wrong at the last moment, Solkin begged Paull and Robinson to attend the 28 February Toronto JIAS general meeting. They did, and the meeting went off without a hitch. Many important community leaders endorsed the JIAS and lauded its fine work. Full of enthusiasm, the newly elected Toronto executive met on 7 March and approved the transfer of the entire Toronto JIAS fund to Montreal. They also decided to relocate their office to the more favourable circumstances of 365 Spadina Avenue. The executive formed Membership, Organization, Publicity, and House committees to take the yoke of organizing membership drives off Solkin's shoulders. A delighted Solkin could now devote himself full-time to office management and service delivery. He was soon able to inform Paull that the chairman of the Membership Committee was "going after the slackers within and without with great zeal."[68]

Paull's hard-nosed professionalism and insistence on centralized authority complemented Solkin's rapidly improving administrative skills and personal charm. They could take credit for shaking Brodey and the Toronto Board from the passivity and parochialism that had long kept the Toronto JIAS from taking its rightful place in immigrant aid. Immigration numbers were still negligible, but now the Toronto organization would be ready to act when the opportunity presented itself. This revitalization of the JIAS brought it more in line with the larger thrust to centralize and professionalize Jewish fundraising and community planning beyond what the FJP had been able to achieve. By the early summer of 1937, negotiations aimed at securing the society's membership in the newly organized United Jewish Welfare Fund (UJWF) were well underway. Both Solkin and Paull were predictably delighted at the prospect of such membership, which promised to ease its financial difficulties and further raise its communal profile. Despite the bleak prospects for European immigration, the future of the Toronto JIAS looked bright.[69]

Solkin and Paull had done gruelling work, but their gains came at a price. The strain had become too much for the Montreal executive director. Working for the JIAS was not an easy job at the best of times. As Paull explained to Solkin, "Between the Jewish public and the gov't officials and consular offices my nerves were going." He hoped that his annual vacation would solve this problem, but when he returned to his desk in mid-September, he wrote: "I found that my nerves didn't steady and my patience, which is so necessary in this type of work, was not what it should be." Paull promptly dictated his letter of resignation and fought off the entreaties of Robinson and the Montreal Board to stay.[70]

On 6 October the Montreal board decided to advertise for a suitable candidate. It did not notify the Toronto board officially, but Paull informed both Solkin and Brodey around mid-October. The Toronto board, now used to working hand in hand with the national office, demanded that Robinson consult with them before hiring Paull's replacement. They also officially recommended Solkin for the position. As Brodey observed: "Mr. Solkin seems a very logical and very desirable person to follow Mr. Paull's footsteps. His thorough knowledge of the work ... makes his promotion highly desirable and certainly preferable to bringing some outsider in." Parochialism had become an organizational artifact.[71]

Robinson welcomed this endorsement. and Paull also lobbied for his protégé. On 11 November the Executive Committee of the Montreal JIAS endorsed Solkin's application and a week later offered him the position of acting executive director. Solkin was deeply honoured.

He accepted, pledging to follow in his mentor's footsteps. At the end of November he left for Montreal, planning to return to Toronto every two to three weeks to keep tabs on the office he had done so much to set up. If all went well during the course of his training in Montreal, he would become executive director on 1 January 1938.[72]

Solkin's departure ended a turbulent period of JIAS history in Toronto. Rapid changes had marked his short tenure. The Jewish public was now far more aware of the society and more willing to use its services. Even sceptics like Brodey now realized that there was a great deal more to immigrant aid than filling out forms and dispensing token information on Sunday mornings. A revitalized Toronto JIAS had won an important share of a highly competitive market and had caused a significant decline in the influence of the steamship agents.[73]

Solkin's appointment and his subsequently successful tenure in Montreal ensured continuity in the daily administration of the national JIAS. Like Paull, Solkin stressed the importance of efficient administration without getting bogged down in needless paperwork. He had a clear vision of JIAS goals and zealously defended its hegemony over Jewish immigrant affairs. This role would be reprised after 1938 when the newly resurgent Canadian Jewish Congress attempted to encroach on the society's domain.

The changes that occurred at the Toronto office of the Jewish Immigrant Aid Society, unlike those that took place in the Federation of Jewish Philanthropies or the United Jewish Welfare Fund, were largely imposed on the Toronto branch by Montreal. It was only as a result of great pressure that the Toronto board shed its narrow parochial vision and adopted an activist stance toward in immigrant aid. Whether the catalyst came from without or within, the result was the same: professionalization and rationalization at any cost. But in the case of the JIAS, control over organizational policy moved away from Toronto to Montreal. The Canadian Jewish Congress would also feature a similar battle for control between Canada's largest Jewish polities. With Solkin's promotion, the Toronto JIAS believed that it had a sympathetic friend in the executive suite. It turned out that Solkin's first loyalty, like that of his mentor Paull, would be to the national organization and head office.

A revitalized, professionally run Toronto JIAS, with its strong leadership cooperating with a well-run head office, was a key achievement for national JIAS. Though it could not affect Canadian immigration policy, efficiently delivered immigration aid would prove crucial as the full tragedy of European Jewry unfolded.

The irony of Montreal's triumph in revitalizing the Toronto JIAS is that Brodey, the epitome of the Uptown Jew, opposed the agenda that his class typically supported. Brodey's institutional loyalty and attitude were more in line with the Downtown volunteers, who had resented the federation's takeover of the Jewish Children's Home. Most Uptowners opposed Brodey's vision and allied themselves with the Montreal JIAS in order to accomplish their mutual agenda. But these two groups would prove uneasy bedfellows. Both agreed that a more active JIAS office would better serve Toronto Jewry. But many of the Toronto Board shared Brodey's resentment at Montreal's imposition of will and had tempered their desire to defer to Paull. Solkin's departure left the Toronto JIAS weaker and increasingly resentful of Montreal's control. As we shall see, this issue would cause difficulties with immigrant absorption for the next decade.

Certainly Solkin, who imposed order on the Toronto JIAS at a distance, agreed with Martin Cohn, who did the same locally, on the importance of running efficient and professional operations easily transparent to management's oversight. But here the two parted ways. Cohn's ultimate goal was to rationalize community-wide social planning and fundraising. But Solkin wanted to ensure that the Montreal JIAS completely controlled the Toronto branch in terms of policy making and planning. Solkin's goal would place the members of the Toronto JIAS board, many of whom had close ties with the young university-educated generation supporting the Federation of Jewish Philanthropies, in a difficult position. They would be torn between their organizational and communal loyalties. In a short while, they would be forced to choose between the two.

This issue rapidly gained traction as the decade drew to a close. Similar strains between Toronto and Montreal were evident in the Canadian Jewish Congress. Once the first flush of organizational enthusiasm had waned, problems surfaced. Hannaniah Caiserman proved a poor administrator and fundraiser, leaving both Congress head office and Central Division chronically short of funds. The bonds of unity, so paper-thin to begin with, were soon ragged and torn. Old tensions re-emerged as various shades of community opinion battled for organizational supremacy, and Caiserman would be unable to halt the squabbling. Given its financial straits and lack of consensus on how to fulfill its high-minded agenda, Congress was irrelevant for many just at a time when Canadian Jewry most needed a voice. Given the brewing tensions, could such unity be achieved? If so, would it come in the national arena or solely at the local level? The events of 1937 would supply some important clues.

5

Two Steps Forward and One Step Back: The Canadian Jewish Congress in Toronto, 1934-37

The narrative of the Montreal JIAS's imposition of will on its Toronto branch is straightforward compared to the first four years of Canadian Jewish Congress history in Toronto. On one level, Congress's history can be seen as a reflection of the splintered communal dynamics of Toronto Jewry; on another, it was a nasty inter-organizational feud triggered by Hannanniah Meir Caiserman's attempts – like those of Maurice Solkin at the JIAS – to impose his will from a distance. Unlike Solkin, Caiserman failed. The reasons for his failure speak volumes about his own management skills and even more about the general lack of interest in the revived Congress. But also Congress's efforts in Toronto to assert its claim to be the "Parliament of Canadian Jewry" would meet with mixed success at best. Toronto Jews paid lip service to communal and national unity, but many conflicting priorities barred the path.

As noted in chapter 2, 1933 had brought the first signs of potential unity to Toronto Jewish communal life. The Canadian Jewish Congress (CJC) had been revitalized. Professionalization was becoming a hallmark of the Federation of Jewish Philanthropies (FJP) and its constituent agencies. As we have seen in the case of the JIAS, with constant pressure from its Montreal headquarters, the Toronto society soon followed suit. The Depression at home and anti-Semitism both at home and in Germany demanded unified responses. But the roadmap toward organizational unity proved elusive. By early February 1934, Congress founders in Toronto were well aware that the time for self-congratulation had passed, as Congress found itself struggling to survive financially and to justify its claim to be the voice of Canadian Jewry.

To survive, Congress needed money, a commodity difficult to come by at the height of the Depression. Sitting in Montreal, Caiserman waited in vain for the central region to remit the 40 percent of the national office budget that it had promised only weeks before at the First Plenary held in January 1933. National office's large expenditures had caused the bank debt to grow rapidly. Finally, Caiserman had to "urgently appeal" to the Toronto executive to send "a few hundred dollars towards our regular expenses." But Toronto was itself just getting organized and was also in serious financial difficulties. Caiserman was left alone to keep his creditors at bay.[1]

This was clearly not the way to run a national organization, but the shortcomings did not end there. Congress's financial woes paralleled its serious administrative and organizational difficulties, which centred on the organization's effort to take control of anti-Nazi boycott work and coordinate an organized response to domestic anti-Semitism. In essence, the CJC wanted to emulate its larger American cousin, the American Jewish Congress, whose anti-Nazi rally at Madison Square Garden and seventy other locations had kindled widespread public interest. Caiserman hoped to move to the next stage and coordinate a boycott of German goods in Canada, correctly perceiving that this strategy would offer instant credibility to the fledgling Congress. Flaunting its mandate as communal spokesagency, Congress tried to bully the Jewish Women's League, then organizing the boycott, and B'nai Brith, coordinators of a sophisticated campaign against anti-Semitism, to work under the Congress banner. Neither organization was prepared to concede turf to an upstart rival, even though lip service to communal unity was *de rigueur*. Indeed, B'nai Brith had specialized in combatting anti-Semitism since the turn of the century. And, since women were the principal shoppers, the Women's League regarded the boycott as one of the few communal causes that fell exclusively within their orbit and jealously guarded their turf.

While close observers might have noticed this resistance building even before the First Plenary convened in late January 1934, the organizational turf wars over boycott work had erupted in late November 1933. At that time Mrs Karlin, secretary of the Jewish Women's League, announced to the Toronto Congress executive that the Robert

Simpson Company, the Toronto-based retailer, had agreed to take strong action against German imports and to hire Jewish staff. Seizing the moment, Caiserman looked to piggyback Congress onto the league's efforts, so as to quickly raise Congress's profile. He wrote to Fred Catzman, secretary of the Toronto Congress executive, asking for copies of the agreement between Simpson's and the Women's League.²

Catzman dutifully asked Karlin to forward a copy of the agreement to him. But when a week went by without the documents arriving, Caiserman impatiently asked Catzman to repeat his request. By 8 January 1934, an exasperated Caiserman begged Catzman to forward the text of the purported agreement, since "our entire success among the employers of the community [was] inspired by the achievements reported." With the First Plenary about to open, Caiserman demanded clarity: "If the facts are right, OK. If there is a measure of misrepresentation, let us know it ... we are entitled to an answer."³

Suspicious, Catzman went to see Mrs L.M. Schwartz, president of the Jewish Women's League, and delivered an ultimatum. If Schwartz did not bring the documents to his office by two p.m. the next day, he would assume that there was no Simpson's agreement. In the end, Congress obtained neither the documentation nor the hoped-for confrontation with the league's leadership. For its part, the league insisted that they had the documents and would withhold them from Congress, which, it contended, had no right to question – let alone oversee – the league's work. This resulting standoff pleased no one and increased factionalism. The league obviously had no intention of allowing Congress to assume control of boycott work, and its subsequent refusal to cooperate with Congress's Boycott Committee gave the lie to Congress's pretensions of community leadership.⁴

A similar situation existed in anti-defamation work. Most Canadian Jews believed that fighting anti-Semitism would be a key raison d'être of Congress. Caiserman knew Congress had to make an immediate impact in this area to establish its credibility, but this field belonged to the formidable and well-established B'nai Brith. This mass-membership organization took a proprietary interest in American anti-defamation work and was considering an expansion of its Anti-Defamation League (ADL) into Canada. This would deal a death blow to Congress's plans.⁵

But Canadian B'nai Brith members (termed "Ben Brits") were torn between organizational loyalty and Canadian nationalism. Although B'nai Brith was an American organization, its Canadian membership had increased during the interwar years. By 1925 there were enough Canadian members to form the Canadian Conference of B'nai Brith, and by the early 1930s the conference demanded that a separate Canadian grand lodge be organized. They were refused, and the loyalists were only spurred to agitate further.[6]

Yet Canadian Ben Brits were proud of the organization's worldwide accomplishments. A good deal of this pride was reserved for the resurgent ADL, which, under the leadership of the dynamic Richard "Dick" Gutstadt, was rapidly developing into a powerful semi-autonomous affiliate of B'nai Brith. "By 1933," noted a well-informed observer, "the ADL became the organization's most important activity." By late 1933 Gutstadt was exploring the possibility of opening an ADL office in Montreal.[7]

Many lodges, especially those in Quebec, clamoured for the organization to spearhead a campaign against the rising tide of Canadian anti-Semitism and Fascism in their communities. In addition, many Ben Brits regarded the ADL approach of eschewing publicity in favour of quiet diplomacy as the most effective way of advancing Jewish rights. According to historian Edward Grusd: "The approach ... to anyone ... who had held up the Jew to ridicule was quiet, private, polite. There were no public demonstrations, pickets, threats, or boycotts, or even public exposure." This low-key approach was widely admired for its success in the United States, and many Canadian Ben Brits were eager to import it.[8]

But at the same time, many influential Ben Brits had conflicted loyalties and supported a coalition with Congress. There was considerable overlap among the senior leaders: Caiserman, Catzman, Joseph I. Oelbaum, Rabbi Eisendrath, and Saul Kaufman were active in both organizations. They recognized that Congress was more representative of the diversity of Canadian Jews than B'nai Brith, and believed that an anti-defamation coalition with Congress would be very much in the interests of Canadian Jewry.[9]

Considerable organizational and methodological forces were arrayed against them. B'nai Brith rightly claimed to be the premier Jewish fraternal organization in North America. Its American leaders (and a considerable number of Canadian Conference members) were understandably wary of lending B'nai Brith's prestigious name to any sort of organizational coalition without receiving due credit. They proposed that Congress defer to B'nai Brith's expertise in anti-defamation work and agree to work under its aegis and direction.[10]

Astute observers noted, however, that the ADL's anti-defamation approach was becoming ineffective against the "New Anti-Semitism" represented by Madison Grant, the Ku Klux Klan, Father Coughlin, and Henry Ford's *Dearborn Independent*. But the ADL steadfastly clung to its long established methods, and their recalcitrance took a toll. In early 1933 B'nai Brith split from the American Jewish Congress (AJC) after the AJC bowed to demands from a largely immigrant constituency and organized public anti-Nazi demonstrations and a Jewish boycott of German goods. Fearful of completely alienating numerous activist first-generation immigrant Jews who had joined its ranks, the ADL slowly began to break from its long-standing tradition of "behind the scenes" anti-defamation work by supporting a non-sectarian boycott of German goods. It hoped the very public nature of the boycott would prevent the Nazis from retaliating against the well-established German B'nai Brith lodges. The league's new approach contrasted sharply with the approach of the elitist American Jewish Committee, which staunchly maintained its aversion to public comment or action of any type that might leave it open to charges of dual allegiance or ethnocentricity. These differing methods contributed to American Jewry's failure to organize a unified response to German anti-Semitism between 1933 and Kristallnacht.[11]

The Depression wreaked havoc on fraternal organizations; memberships lapsed and revenues plummeted. B'nai Brith was not immune to this trend, which heightened its fear of being pushed into the margins of North American Jewish life. The rise of Jewish federations, escalating demands of Jewish educational institutions, and surging interest in overseas relief were further threats. Isaac M. Rubinow, the famous pioneer of social security and ADL director until 1932, observed perceptively: "Jewish community life has become so complex that many of the services B'nai Brith had once rendered were now being conducted locally by all kinds of organizations; that the lodge as a place of social gathering has lost the importance it once had, and that the interest of people in philanthropic institutions was in direct ratio to their geographic closeness."[12]

These developments left the American leadership of B'nai Brith in a difficult position. Its leaders were now inclined to move away from the elitist approach they had once shared with the American Jewish Committee, but remained distrustful of the American Jewish Congress's "mass appeal" anti-defamation methods. Historian Deborah Dash Moore has shown that B'nai Brith used the ADL to attract new members, an observation that explains why Gutstadt was allowed to move the ADL away from B'nai Brith's international headquarters in Washington DC to Chicago, why B'nai Brith permitted separate ADL campaigns, and why the ADL received a whopping 25 percent of B'nai Brith's total budget.[13]

The use of the ADL to spearhead interest in B'nai Brith also explains why American B'nai Brith leaders would not allow Congress into Canadian anti-defamation work. In addition, the Canadian Jewish Congress's name may have evoked parallels with the detested American Jewish Congress. On the eve of the First Plenary, in early January 1934, the national president of B'nai Brith ordered its Canadian Conference not to participate in the Congress movement.[14]

Ben Brit Catzman informed Caiserman of these developments on 16 January. Caiserman, in hopes of conciliation, obtained a resolution at the First Plenary calling on the "Canadian Jewish Congress to invite the cooperation of various B'nai Brith lodges in the Dominion of Canada in dealing with Anti-Defamation work." He followed up by inviting Rubinow to send Caiserman a Canadian lodge membership list to pave the way for cooperation in anti-defamation matters. Rubinow promised to do so, and assured Caiserman that he would be hearing from ADL director Gutstadt shortly.[15]

Caiserman did not hear from Gutstadt, who was busy attempting to marshal support among the members of the Canadian Conference for the proposed Canadian ADL office. It was not to be. The Ben Brits affiliated with Congress had no intention of allowing it to be left out of anti-defamation work. The presence of Rabbi Eisendrath and his cohort of Holy Blossomites allayed Uptown fears of Congress's becoming another Downtown-dominated American Jewish Congress. But, as a counterweight to the Downtowners, Ben Brits wished to ensure that organizational collaboration in anti-defamation work would follow ADL methods. Eisendrath reassured delegates to B'nai Brith's Canadian Conference's biannual meeting on 6 May 1934, in Toronto that: "B'nai Brith had established and pursued a course which other organizations should emulate ... The general cry at the present time was for action, whether it was strategic, tactful, or otherwise and it often resulted in headlines in the newspapers. This B'nai Brith has avoided ... He [Eisendrath] wanted to see B'nai Brith undertake this constructive programme and assured the delegates that if his services or the services of his committee were desired they could feel free to call on them."[16]

Eisendrath's speech won over the delegates, who quickly passed a resolution "that the Conference confer and cooperate with the Canadian Jewish Congress in carrying on ... anti-defamation work." Most delegates hoped that by the time Gutstadt arrived in Montreal on 22 May 1934 all the plans for a CJC–ADL merger would be finalized, and a Canadian ADL office would be opened when sufficient funds had been raised.[17]

This hoped-for dénouement did not take place. The Supreme Lodge executive remained committed to introducing an independent ADL office into Canada and wanted the Canadian Conference to pay for it. What is more, both B'nai Brith and Congress misunderstood each other's intentions and each sought primacy in Canadian anti-defamation work. But in the summer of 1934 Congress's relations with B'nai Brith seemed good, and Caiserman was thus able to turn his attention to Congress's difficulties in Toronto.

The First Plenary's success in attracting media attention, and the praise greeting its inception led many Jews to expect great things. In three months, these lofty expectations turned to ashes. By spending almost all its time building an institutional structure, Congress left little time for creating visible changes in communal life. By April 1934 the frustrated Toronto Jewish press dismissed Congress as a "do nothing organization."[18]

Given the media hype surrounding Congress, Downtowners unrealistically expected the barely organized Congress to instantaneously strike against anti-Semitism at home and abroad and challenge the stringent Canadian immigration laws. Impatient *amcha* dismissed the tedious but necessary task of organizing Congress's infrastructure as nothing more than a series of committee meetings producing mounds of redundant minutes. This pressure for instant results worried many Uptowners. They feared that, under pressure, Congress might leave the path of moderation and turn itself into a vociferous protest group that would paradoxically provoke anti-Semitism. If this happened, they would leave Congress and resurrect the Canadian Jewish Committee, thus jeopardizing the fragile unity that Congress had begun establishing.[19]

Caiserman hoped that Congress's moderate path would unite Canadian Jewry behind its aims and methods. He was disappointed. After the "honeymoon period" was over, the Canadian Jewish press complained about the endless committee meetings that produced no tangible results. S.M. Shapiro, editor of the *Yiddisher Zhurnal*, took special delight in attacking the organization. Even the pro-Congress *Jewish Standard* became impatient. In April 1934 its editor, Oscar Cohen, chastised Congress for its apparent lack of accomplishment. Furious, Caiserman fired back: "I have sent you a report of our doings and hope you will give it the proper publicity and dispel the crazy idea that we are sitting around here." Caiserman refused, despite all evidence to the contrary, to believe that the press accurately reflected *amcha* impatience with the organization. From his perspective, Congress – his Congress – was under attack, and when Congress was threatened, Caiserman became "a man possessed of energy and determination."[20]

He would need it. Congress's *amcha* backbone – the rank and file of many *hilfsverein* (immigrant self-help societies), *landsmanschaften*, and Zionist groups affiliated with Congress were already disenchanted with the perceived lack of progress. Further disappointment was in store. Rather than use its first meeting to approve an action plan, the Toronto Congress executive organized Central Division's committee infrastructure. The executive authorized the formation of the various Congress committees, provided each with a chairman, and suggested the names of appropriate committee members. Egmont Frankel was named Central Division president. Frankel was a prosperous scrap dealer well known to upper-class Toronto society and an Upper Canada College "Old Boy." He was also a prominent member of Holy Blossom. His presence was a guarantee of sorts for the cautious Holy Blossomites that executive policy would not descend to the level of the activist American Jewish Congress–style agenda demanded by Sam Shapiro, Morris Goldstick, and their allies.[21]

The roster of committee chairs underscored Congress's attitude of political moderation. Rabbi Eisendrath, an admirer of the ADL, and a man widely respected also by Christians for his oratorical skills, became chairman of the Public Relations Committee. Saul Kaufman, an English Jew and prominent Ben Brit, assumed control of the Relief Committee, mandated to organize a nationwide fundraising campaign to aid German Jewry. The Boycott Committee, a highly sensitive post, was given to former Toronto alderman John J. Glass, who had just been elected to the Ontario Legislature after campaigning to combat Nazism and discrimination through legislation. The Legal Committee's main task was to try to establish a Jewish Arbitration Court so that Jews could avoid the public court system and not fuel the common assumption that Jews were "litigious." Rabbi Sachs, who had no enemies and no axe to grind, headed the Education and Culture Committee. This left the *amcha* advocates of action in control of two committees that served relatively minor roles. Joseph Graner headed the Kehilla Committee, which hoped to mediate the long simmering Rabbinic wars that had fragmented supervision of kosher meat in Toronto, while Goldstick attempted to *attract amcha* organizations to the Congress banner through the Organizations Committee.[22]

Certainly this was vital work, but the press screamed for action. *Amcha* agreed by voting with their pocketbooks. To make matters worse, the Zionist Organization of Canada (ZOC), resentful of Congress's infringement on its monopoly as a national organization, retaliated by establishing its own Campaign for German Jewry on 8 March. This unprecedented foray into non-Zionist fundraising was designed to stall the nascent Congress movement before it could gain political traction. Even worse, the perception that the ZOC was taking action on a topic with resonance for the *amcha* would further undermine Congress's standing. Most *amcha* were Zionists or Zionist sympathizers and openly distrustful of the compromise that enabled a non-Zionist like Eisendrath and his group to remain in Congress. In sum the ZOC sought to convince observers that it was more suited than its rival to act on behalf of Canadian Jewry.[23]

The ZOC strategy also revealed that organizational jealousy was still a force to be reckoned with in Canadian Jewish life. This was understandable, given the geography of Canada and the fact that Canadian Jews were overwhelmingly composed of first-generation immigrants. But the ZOC's refusal to cooperate with Congress in aid of German Jewry and its use of the plight of German Jews in the name of organizational domination are certainly open to criticism. In Canada, unlike the United States, there was considerable overlap between the membership of the ZOC, B'nai Brith, and Congress, and the anti- and non-Zionist movements had never been strong. Moreover, men such as Eisendrath and Frankel, who were uncomfortable with Zionism, had supported "the work of the Jewish Agency in Palestine" in the interests of Canadian Jewish unity. ZOC president Archie Freiman and its executive director Rabbi Jesse Schwartz advocated unity only on their terms. It was with reason that Frankel complained to Caiserman:

> I noticed ... that the Zionist organization was starting a campaign for German Jewish relief and ... I resented it. If the co-operation that was anticipated were forthcoming, this drive would never have been undertaken ... I was under the impression that inasmuch as the Congress embraced so many Zionists, that the resolution passed would mean that all efforts in this direction would come under the auspices of the Congress. I am not at all surprised at Mr. Freeman's [sic] attitude ... if there was any disruption ... of unity, he played no little part towards that end ... I have long since abandoned the thought of having unity amongst Canadian Jewry, but I did anticipate that there would be a spirit of co-operation particularly for the cause of German Jewish relief.[24]

The ZOC's German Jewish relief campaign reminded Congress loyalists that they could not yet compete organizationally with the longer-established, better-known, and more richly financed ZOC, let alone with B'nai Brith, unless Congress captured the public imagination quickly.[25] But Congress could not hope to show results unless each of its three divisions (Eastern, Central, and Western) was equipped with the minimal bureaucracy required to coordinate committee work. Caiserman acted as permanent secretary of the Eastern Division (and of National Congress). The other divisions needed full-time secretaries, even though they could not be paid decent wages.[26] In March 1934 the Central Division executive hired Alexander Brown, a young, unemployed teacher, as secretary. The Central Division was so bereft of funds that Brown had to accept $10 a week and pay his secretary out of his own pocket.[27]

Brown was immediately overwhelmed. The fault was partly Caiserman's. His ignorance of efficient management procedure and his desire to maintain control of all Congress activity, even at a distance, kept Brown out of the loop. Caiserman even refused to allow Brown to be the policy conduit between himself and the Divisional Executive. Instead, Caiserman maintained an extensive correspondence with the Central Division's committee chairmen and left Brown to schedule meetings, take minutes, and handle routine correspondence. Brown soon discovered that he was unaware of many major policy decisions and had little input into the process.[28]

In spite of the administrative confusion, Central Division continued to attract men of very high calibre. One of the most important recruits was Otto B. Roger, a Shell Oil executive from England who had been dispatched to Canada to take over an important company position. With his English wife, mannerisms, and Reform background, he was quickly admitted to the highest circles of Toronto society. He was an extremely adept negotiator and a man of great dignity, and was admirably suited to assume the chairmanship of Congress's moribund Finance Committee and rescue the division from its chronic lack of funds.[29]

Roger proved an excellent choice. When he took over the committee, it had no budget. Why would anyone support an organization without a track record in the midst of Depression? Besides, how was the committee to organize a campaign when the Congress office did not even have a telephone until mid-May 1934? But, by August, Roger had appointed an entirely new committee and was drawing up careful plans for a well-designed and well-publicized campaign to fill Congress's coffers.[30]

Congress's survival into the summer permitted Roger to initiate his campaign and allowed for the Public Relations and Actions Committees to rack up enough measurable results to pacify some of Congress's all too numerous detractors. Eisendrath's vital Public Relations Committee was a whirlwind of activity. It dispatched numerous "Letters to the Editor" in response to unfriendly newspaper commentary. It shared information and cooperated with the Anti-Defamation Committees of various B'nai Brith lodges throughout Ontario, organized a clipping service to keep abreast of newspaper opinion throughout the province, and set up a committee on Jewish-Gentile relations, which became the forerunner of the Canadian Council of Christians and Jews. Eisendrath barnstormed the province to deal with overt and covert pro-Nazi propaganda. The eloquent rabbi was frequently called on to counter the Nazi claim that the Jews deserved to be persecuted because they had unpatriotically attempted to promote a Communist revolution and had engineered the economic and political collapse of Germany after the First World War.

Nazi propaganda was not the only source of anti-Semitism in Toronto. Toronto, like the rest of Canada, had been rife with anti-Semitism long before Hitler's ascent to power. Restrictive covenants, clubs, beaches, resorts, and restrictions on employment in banking, department stores, and large firms severely affected the lives of Toronto Jews. The public school system was public in name only; it was far from religiously neutral. There was mandatory school prayer, a lowest-common-denominator Protestant curriculum passed as values education, and teachers frequently subjected Jewish pupils to insulting or patronizing remarks. Thus, the community hailed the Public Relations Committee's success in persuading the Ontario government to remove *The Merchant of Venice* from the curriculum in the hope of curtailing the spread of anti-Semitic stereotypes. But the committee promptly shot itself in the foot when its Uptown members showed their own prejudices by suggesting that Downtown Jews refrain from loud behaviour in public places and refer any litigation to Congress's Arbitration Court.[31] Although a*mcha* were pleased that anti-Semitism was finally being challenged, they remained suspicious of Eisendrath, who once wrote: "The right ... to dislike the traits and habits of individual Jews we do not for a moment challenge. But we do respectfully submit that it is woefully inconsistent ... when they [anti-Semites] impute the specific cause of their dislike to a people as a whole." As far as *amcha* were concerned, any admission that a Jew could be disliked was dangerous.

Emphasizing the right of anyone to criticize Jews as individuals while firmly refuting all criticism of Jews as a group may have raised the eyebrows of Downtown Jews, but it followed contemporary anti-defamation tactics. These tactics put great stock in "education," which consisted of distributing pamphlets and articles full of facts about Jewish accomplishments in the world and corrections of common anti-Semitic accusations. The Uptown Canadian Jewish press was filled with Jewish contributions to the common good but often echoed Eisendrath with articles about "internal Jewish behaviour" that urged readers to "know their place." In a revealing story about Jews vacationing on the Toronto Island, the *Jewish Standard* observed: "The Jews confined their dancing to their living quarters and their driving to friendly places. True, some of them, particularly girls, showed a sad lack of racial pride and chanced the verboten areas. These seemed to take a cheap pride in being exceptions until asked to leave. There are Jews like that. But they were mostly proud and well behaved as befits our race in these times."[32]

At first glance, the advice offered may well be attacked as self-hating "Uncle Tomism." Perhaps it was. But Uptowners cautioning Downtowners to be mindful of their place raises the question: what was their place? This was a matter in flux. In some neighbourhoods, such as the Toronto Junction, Jews and Gentiles lived peacefully together and incidents were rare. The small Jewish community in the Toronto Junction area was respected by their neighbours, and the synagogue with its intricate murals was a source of communal pride. The tale was different in many areas of more concentrated Jewish settlement. A careful appraisal of anecdotal history indicates that a constant "turf war" raged between Jews and "Anglos" in neighbourhoods like Spadina, Hillcrest, and Dovercourt from 1920 until 1945. The Christie Pits Riot of August 1933 was simply the largest example of the kind of fighting that continually raged between the "Pit Gang" (and other similar groups) and Toronto's Jewish young men and teenagers. But whatever their pugilistic prowess, even the toughest of Downtown Jews could not deny that restrictive covenants, "Gentiles only" resorts, and prejudicial employment practices severely restricted their residential, social, and occupational mobility. Many Jews were all too aware of these limits: "Housing was clearly restricted ... I knew that the area from Bloor to Queen and from University to Ossington was predominantly Jewish. I vaguely knew that out beyond this area was a vast *terra incognita* inhabited mainly by Gentiles. What happened to Jews who tried to rent or buy in this area I never knew because the idea had certainly not occurred to me."[33]

Some observers have argued that this cloistered response was atypical of its time. They argue that eastern European immigrants responded differently to anti-Semitism that their Canadian-born children. Sociologists Cyril Levitt and William Shaffir suggest that the immigrant generation was less likely to feel victimized by the relatively mild nature of the self-created North American ghetto and remained willingly within its borders. Members of this group hesitated to challenge the restrictions that anti-Semitism imposed. For them, "anti-Jewish sentiment in Toronto was a minor inconvenience" compared to the deadly anti-Semitism of their native Russia and Poland. But their children lacked this external frame of reference. They expected to be free and boldly crossed the lines of demarcation their parents had accepted without challenge. When they encountered anti-Semitism on the baseball diamond, in the schoolyard, at the dance hall and the cottage, they fought back.[34]

It is also possible to understand Eisendrath, the *Standard* article, and the Public Relations Committee's frequent requests that Jews behave in a "less Jewish" manner as reflecting long-standing, class-based fears of more established Jews who did not want to be linked by identification with "lower elements" of the community. Although rising anti-Semitism catalyzed the rebirth of the Canadian Jewish Congress, Congress's response was removed from *amcha* expectations. Toronto's Jewish leaders, drawn from the Uptown elite, approved the ADL-like strategy of educating both non-Jews and their Downtown co-religionists. This paralleled the "Uptown" response of the acculturated German Jews in the United States to the mass influx of the eastern Europeans in the 1880s, and involved overt efforts to Americanize them. In Toronto, the Uptown community was smaller. Consequently, attempts at educating *amcha* were more muted. As early as 1916 the Uptown *Jewish Chronicle* bemoaned the large number of immigrants who became peddlers and upset upper-class Gentiles by constantly selling goods at their door. The paper noted that the peddlers had become "extremely unpopular with the Gentile population, who at best, in Toronto have never shown a friendly disposition to our people." The reporter urged the "leading Jews of Toronto who have the fair name of the Jew at heart" to ensure that new immigrants are diverted into "less degrading occupations." Ironically, the *amcha* targets of this article were unable to read it and were doubtless too occupied with the daily struggle for a living to care about what their social betters thought of them.[35]

Two decades later, similar class divisions left *amcha*, who faced daily anti-Semitism, cold to Congress's suggestions about how they should behave. These attempts at re-education continued until the end of the Second World War. The fact that their efforts bore little fruit did not keep the Uptowners from trying.[36]

Congress's efforts to achieve some sort of legislative response to worsening anti-Semitism were also persistent. The Tory government of Premier George S. Henry (1930–34) lacked any political reason to listen to Congress's concerns about anti-Semitism. The Tories emphasized battling unemployment through massive public works projects, and had reduced other expenses to balance the budget. Besides, few Jews voted Conservative. But when lone Jewish MPP Fred Singer rose in the Legislature to expose systematic discrimination on the part of major insurance companies against Jews and other minorities, he received some press coverage. Remarkably, he was able to obtain amendments to the *Insurance Act* to halt discriminatory practices. However, this achievement marked the limit of Jewish political advocacy. In 1933 anti-Semitism was so blatant that Argue Martin, a non-Jewish Conservative MPP, challenged the Legislature to do something about anti-Jewish signs that "were spreading like weeds" in resort areas. He sponsored a private member's bill designed to ban them. Premier Henry pointedly underscored the government's lack of concern by noting that the bill "required discussion," which, as the *Toronto Star* pointed out, meant "that was about all he thought it deserved." The bill generated laughter from government members as it was referred to committee – and to legislative perdition.[37]

In battling anti-Semitism, Congress leaders found themselves between the proverbial rock and hard place. The powers of the day would not listen to their representatives, while *amcha* demands for marches or demonstrations were anathema to the Uptown controllers of Congress. With no compelling reason to act and no groundswell of voter concern, the government did nothing about discrimination against Jews, Blacks, and Asians in employment, education, and housing. Given these realities, and Jewish community division over how to respond, a feeble and underfinanced Congress saw little point in head-on confrontation with government.[38]

Only Eisendrath seemed undeterred by Jews' lack of political influence and the ineffectiveness of their activism. With his Public Relations Committee organized and set for action, the rabbi prepared to take the offensive and coordinate a boycott of German goods. He invited Caiserman to come and help manage this campaign. With Caiserman's access to Zionists and Yiddishists, Eisendrath hoped to unite the community behind the proposed boycott. He believed a successful campaign would generate wider sympathy for the Jewish cause, woo the disaffected *amcha*, promote a more efficient organization, and help attract the financing needed to carry Central Division through to its proposed fall campaign.

It was fitting for Caiserman to be summoned to Toronto to deal with these Central Division problems, as he was responsible for many of them. Without administrative reform, it would be impossible to rationalize the divisional administration. Quick action was needed. Monthly executive meetings had become little more than forums for lengthy committee reports rather than devoting time to analysis of goals or organizational strategy. The more active committees (Actions, Boycott, Public Relations) met frequently and pursued their own courses of action without executive direction. Weaker committees (Education, Industry, Organizations, Kehilla) languished. By May 1934 organizational disarray had reached the point where Frankel did not even know that Eisendrath had invited Caiserman to come to Toronto, while Caiserman in turn assumed that Eisendrath would have consulted with Frankel before inviting him.[39]

Caiserman arrived on 3 June to attend the first Dominion Executive meeting ever held outside Montreal. He hoped this all-day session, which welcomed delegates from all three Congress divisions, would attract communal attention and make his subsequent work in Toronto easier. Instead, the meeting highlighted the poor organization at both National and Central Division levels. Few elected delegates bothered to attend. In just six months, "Congress euphoria" was dispelled. It was evident that without quality administration and a higher community profile, Congress would again disappear.[40]

Furthermore, the campaign to boycott German goods faced external and internal challenges. The campaign started slowly around a controversy over aims and tactics and the fear that it might alienate non-Jews and hurt German Jewry. Even after these obstacles were overcome and the Actions Committee under Alderman Glass had finally begun the campaign in late April 1934, it stumbled badly. Inadequate research led to a number of manufacturers being falsely accused of importing or using German goods. Their vociferous protests proved embarrassing.[41]

Even worse, Congress lacked control over the boycott. The Jewish Women's League, still stinging from its earlier run-in with Congress, refused to cooperate. But Caiserman wanted the league's support and proposed a simple plan: in return for the appointment of league president Mrs Schwartz to the Actions Committee, the league would merge its work with that of Congress. Caiserman's conciliatory proposal was rewarded when Schwartz planned a large mass meeting of women's organizations on 22 May.⁴² The group agreed to form the Women's Consumer League, which would work under the aegis of the Actions Committee, and agreed to tax themselves to help support the boycott campaign.⁴³

But Schwartz was still angry that her organization's pre-eminence in boycott work had gone unrecognized. It had begun its work before Congress had entered this field, and she felt that it was entitled to a leadership role in the ongoing boycott campaign.⁴⁴ When Schwartz found herself just one of many, she threatened to pull her members out of the united boycott campaign. As usual, Caiserman played the conciliator, offering Schwartz and her allies key positions in the Actions Committee. Schwartz also knew how to play the organizational game and negotiated for maximum advantage.⁴⁵ After wasting almost two valuable weeks, Caiserman convinced Schwartz and the league to cease its boycott work "for the present" and join with Congress.⁴⁶

Somehow Caiserman regarded his eleven-day stay in Toronto as an overall success. He was not perturbed by the fact that he had to convince the Divisional Executive to borrow $1,500 to cover expenses. It escaped him that Central Division's credit was so low that thirteen members of the executive had to sign a promissory note for the money. Perhaps he had to look away – two-thirds of the funds were immediately dispatched to Montreal to buy National Congress three more months of life. This money would allow Caiserman to make a cross-Canada tour which would "finally" – in his estimation – bring financial stability to Congress. All this amounted to organizational life-support. But, as Rogers observed, "the machinery of the Congress had to be kept in motion at all costs so that the Congress would later have a much stronger case to place before the Jewish people of the Dominion."⁴⁷

Indeed Caiserman made Congress's mere survival a virtue: "I have created a substantial Congress consciousness in certain parts of the community ... and I have animated the employees of our office [in Toronto] with a new conception of our work." There were only two office employees at the time. The feelings of Brown's secretary remain unknown, but Brown's views are clear. He believed he had gained nothing from Caiserman's visit, while remaining more of a minute-taker than an executive secretary, and Caiserman continued to bypass him in correspondence with committee chairmen. Nor had Caiserman eased the situation of Congress in Toronto, despite his claims to the contrary. The only place in which he "had created a substantial Congress consciousness" was in the boardroom of the Central Division executive members who dug into their pockets to maintain the Congress dream. His speeches to *landsmanschaften* that had sent delegates to the Plenary only a few months before had little impact. Very few organizations were willing to levy the 25-cent per capita tax on their membership to support the central organization that Congress had urged since its inception. The Central Division had ignored its constituency for too long, and now it ignored Congress.[48]

The truth of the matter was that Congress was a failure in Toronto. In the first half-year of its existence, it was unable to consolidate support from the larger Jewish community. It failed to retain the support of those who had fought to be elected delegates to the First Plenary, and few took it seriously as the voice of Canadian Jewry. Its continued existence, if only by a thread, was a tribute to its supporters' tenacity and dogged perseverance. At the height of the Depression, Congress was not in a position to compete with the Federation of Jewish Philanthropies, the ZOC, the JIAS, and a host of educational, religious, and overseas aid organizations for a rapidly shrinking pool of funds.

Indeed, the history of Central Division between the summer of 1934 and the winter of 1938 simply echoed the division's first six months, albeit with some change in the cast of characters. During this period, Congress had little effect on the organizational life of Toronto Jewry. Despite all its pretensions, as will be seen, it was just another weak organization trying to carve out a constituency amid the fractured politics of Toronto's Jewish organizations. Central Division may have envisioned itself as the political voice of Jewish life in Toronto; but when the community needed a unified fundraising arm, it created the United Jewish Welfare Fund and bypassed Congress. Despite all its efforts, Congress continued to have a far lower communal profile than the federation (or its successor the Welfare Fund) and proved less capable of winning communal financial support than the Brunswick Avenue Talmud Torah, the Mount Sinai Hospital, or the Old Folks' Home. This failure was due to profound divisions over Congress's raison d'être. Caiserman had hoped the CJC would oversee all facets of Toronto Jewish life, but the community regarded Congress as no more than an Uptown self-defence group and thwarted its attempts to claim control of communal life. Moreover, Toronto Jewry was not ready to submit to central authority via Montreal. This unwillingness would prove increasingly significant between 1937 and 1948.⁴⁹

Other important currents also mediated against Congress's efforts at ascendancy. As a new organization, it had difficulty coping with what historian Stephen Speisman has described as "the voluntarism of North American life." Nor could it displace the well-entrenched Downtown support network already erected by *landsmanschaften*, ethnic synagogues, mutual benefit societies, and labour unions. In addition, Congress's gratuitous efforts to impose "Uptown norms" had little resonance for Downtowners, especially in the wake of Hitler's rise to power and the Christie Pits Riot. By 1934, when Congress finally organized a communal reaction, the issue of German Jewry had lost some of its edge. As Naomi Cohen has observed, until the passage of the Nuremberg Laws of 1935, German Jews had suffered little physical harm and their false sense of security undermined the urgency that drove Congress's mandate. By late 1934, Eisendrath bleakly noted that "the German and East European situation was no longer news, [and] that the larger givers were cold on the whole idea." The consequent perception of Congress as non-essential, coupled with a general refusal to recognize it as the voice of a community, stripped it of its sense of purpose, and left it in a "moribund state."⁵⁰

As if to ensure Congress's demise, ZOC president Archie Freiman forced the Toronto section of the ZOC to abandon its plans for conducting a joint ZOC–CJC campaign, and the division's subsequent "mini-campaign" failed. As chairman of the Finance Committee, Roger was particularly angry at this turn of events. He singled out Division President Frankel for "doing nothing useful" and observed to Caiserman: "The campaign did not cover itself with any glory, and you know that psychologically speaking 'nothing succeeds like success'... It seems like an awful pity to allow so much sincere(?) work to go to waste."⁵¹

Dissent from within Congress's ranks paralleled resistance from without. Caiserman's next jolt came from a confidential, seven-page, handwritten missive from Brown, the long-suffering Central Division executive secretary. Stung by Caiserman's comment that the Central Division was working "at an extremely slow tempo," Brown laid out what he saw as reasons for the division's difficulties. The basic problem, he wrote, was that most of the committees were "labouring under a misapprehension ... It is not merely their duty to convene once in two or three weeks, pass a resolution or two, mouth a few pious wishes and let it go at that. To some of them it never occurs that it is necessary also to do some work." Brown added that he and his secretary could not possibly handle all the work of Congress unless each committee chairman pulled his own weight.[52]

More crucially, Brown contended that the time-honoured practice of *shtadlanut*, the use of communal leaders to speak on behalf of the community, was the root cause of these problems. There was certainly merit in this observation. Caiserman deliberately made every effort to recruit high profile and established community members to legitimize Congress in the eyes of non-Jewish political leaders. This often meant that individuals were recruited because of their social rank rather than their abilities. Brown cited the selection of Frankel as president to prove his thesis: "The President is woefully apathetic," his letter complained. "There is lacking enthusiasm and interest – and his disinterestedness would lead one to think that his major reason for accepting the office is that the title 'President, Canadian Jewish Congress,' lends a certain amount of prestige in the business world, and at the golf club."[53]

It was true that Frankel had only been asked to lend his name to the new organization and was promised his duties would not be too onerous. Cognizant of his intended role, he was doing exactly what he had committed to – which wasn't much. And here lay the heart of Brown's critique: the contention that *shtadlanim* like Frankel, who failed to pull their weight on Congress's behalf, were useless. So was Caiserman, who sustained a system that no longer worked. In Brown's opinion, presidents should be leaders. If the Frankels and their ilk did not wish to provide hands-on leadership, they ought to resign. "The situation can certainly be improved," counselled Brown, "by a complete shakeup of the Committees, and an injection of new members who would be willing to work."[54]

Brown did not expect his bluntness to endear him to Caiserman. No matter. He had chosen to write in the hope of saving Central Division and inducing Caiserman to return to Toronto and try once again to rejuvenate it. Certainly the Roger and Brown letters powerfully affected Caiserman. He now had to face the fact that the most effective lay leader of Central Division and its secretary had both, unbeknownst to one other, labelled Frankel as a do-nothing president. A shaken Caiserman quietly informed Roger that he agreed with his views, but National CJC president S.W. Jacobs suggested that Frankel's consent would be needed before Caiserman could make a housecleaning visit to Toronto. Roger was instructed to put the matter on the agenda of the next Divisional Executive meeting.[55]

Caiserman was not ready to abandon *shtadlanut*. It had become a question of seeking new *shtadlanim* with Downtown appeal. Caiserman approached the mercurial, brilliant, and volatile businessman A.B. (Archie) Bennett and *Zhurnal* editor Shapiro, offering vice-presidencies in exchange for their participation. They had rebuffed him the previous year, but the situation was now so desperate that the Congress constitution was amended at 21 October 1934 executive meeting to raise the number of vice-presidents from five to seven to make room for Bennett and Shapiro. Caiserman pleaded with both men to "take their rightful places in our midst." Their egos sufficiently massaged, both assumed their posts and began to attend executive meetings.[56]

Downtowners now held the balance of power in the executive. Frankel was increasingly taken up with his own business, and simply presided over meetings. Leadership and planning came from Eisendrath and Roger, while Brown and Goldstick concentrated on publicizing Congress and keeping the office running. But pettiness did not disappear. Brown and Goldstick were very friendly because Brown had briefly worked for *Kanada Naies*. Of course, this association automatically made Brown *persona non grata* with Shapiro and therefore, by extension, with Bennett. In fact, Bennett was disdainful of most of his colleagues. After all, he held a graduate degree from Queen's University, where he had been invited to write a doctoral dissertation by the brilliant philosopher John Watson. Bennett was the *wunderkind* of his generation, one of the leaders of the first Canadian Jewish generation to attend university in significant numbers. He considered himself to be better qualified than anyone for the divisional presidency and he coveted the position. To reach this goal, he realized that he would have to take over both the office machinery, which Brown controlled, and the Organizations Committee, which was chaired by Goldstick. His ambition set the stage for bitter interpersonal rivalries at a time when the division could ill afford them.[57]

Early in November, the Executive Committee approved final plans for a fundraising campaign that would run from 27 January to 7 February 1935. Significantly, the organizers recognized that if they tried to raise money for Congress alone, they would fail because they lacked broad communal support. Instead, the campaign was billed to gather money for impoverished Jews in Palestine, North Africa, and Europe. The funds would be allocated to such organizations as the Jewish Agency, the Organization for Rehabilitation through Training (ORT), the Joint Distribution Committee (JDC), and HICEM, an amalgamated group involved with Jewish immigration from Europe. Congress would retain 20 percent of the total $30,000 goal for its own operation. The Divisional Executive invited Caiserman to spend a month in Toronto during the campaign to review and report on Central Division's work.[58]

Caiserman arrived just before the opening of the campaign and stayed for three and a half weeks, ample time for him to watch a comedy of errors unfold. The campaign reeked of amateurism and desperation. It was poorly scheduled, beginning scarcely two months after the much more professionally run FJP annual campaign had ended. As if to underscore the federation's insistence on a single unified campaign, most donors refused to contribute, citing overlap with the ZOC campaign. Mr Hyams, the fundraising expert, abandoned ship in mid-campaign to accept the editorship of the *Jewish Standard*. A paltry $9,600 was raised despite a two-week extension. Congress's share was but $1,860. After the division had paid off its $1,500 debt, the total income realized was only $360.[59]

Caiserman may well have envied Hyams. Shaken, he returned to Montreal and immediately drafted a memorandum designed to save an obviously dying division. He admitted that Central Division's Executive Committee was inefficient and recommended the appointment of a Control Committee empowered to dismiss those whose did not attend meetings and co-opt others to fill their places. Substantiating Roger's and Brown's critiques, the memorandum admitted that the committee system was not functioning and *amcha* support was slipping away. Caiserman also agreed that the vice-presidents and committee chairmen had to become more active. Significantly, he did not blame Frankel for the division's shortcomings; he was "a very busy man" and could not be expected "to devote more time than he can." Rapidly backpedalling from his earlier stance despite contrary evidence, Caiserman still wanted Frankel to remain president, in the hopes of retaining his money and perceived influence.

But Frankel wanted out. "Although you are kind enough to indicate that too much should not be expected of the president of the division," wrote Frankel on 22 February, "I feel that the responsibility does lie in that direction. We need a man who is vitally interested in Congress and who can spend a great deal of time in its development. Unfortunately, my time is much too occupied in other ... directions, so, I feel ... that I should resign as President." Caiserman immediately wrote to Eisendrath and Brown encouraging them to dissuade Frankel from resigning.[60]

Revealingly, even Bennett was not prepared to lay all the blame for the division's shortcomings at Frankel's feet. At a stormy meeting of the Divisional Executive on 13 March, Bennett argued that Frankel was the victim of inadequate support from the executive and that his resignation was "symptomatic of the whole situation of Congress in the Central Division." Eisendrath, authorized to speak in Frankel's name, suggested that Frankel might accept an honorary position. The executive stalled for time, setting up a Planning Committee to deal with Frankel's resignation and report on how some of Caiserman's suggestions for improvement might be implemented.[61]

The Planning Committee recommended that Eisendrath approach Frankel and offer him the newly created position of honorary president. Real power was to rest in the hands of an Executive Praesidium composed of rabbis Eisendrath and Sachs. Frankel refused to bite; he wanted out. In response, the Steering Committee went beyond its mandate and reconstituted itself as a self-named Control Committee. The freshly minted committee quickly drew up a plan designed to deal with the organizational shortcomings listed by Caiserman. Events would soon prove that this decision would have far-reaching consequences.[62]

The plan to concentrate administrative and decision-making power in the hands of a few self-appointed individuals paralleled similar developments at the FJP and the Toronto JIAS. It is hard to judge to what extent the formation of the Control Committee was modelled after Martin Cohn's work at the FJP and whether similar centralization at the JIAS also played a role. Certainly some key Control Committee members were aware of these developments. Shapiro was active in the reorganization of the Toronto JIAS, and Eisendrath certainly conversed with a number of his congregants who occupied key lay positions at the FJP. One thing is certain: the members of the Control Committee determined that only radical reorganization would ensure Congress's survival in Toronto. In contrast to Caiserman's emphasis on an open Congress as "a Parliament of Canadian Jewry," the committee intended to rule by fiat, at least until the division's survival was ensured. The fact that Congress's constitution did not even mention their committee was irrelevant to its members. Committee members simply assumed the power and ultimately wielded more *de facto* authority than the Divisional Executive.[63]

These autocratic actions brought the various class and ideological disparities among the division's constituent organizations to a head. A concerned executive member questioned the non-democratic character of the executive, because it "did not touch or represent the masses." Bennett's reply was revealingly blunt: "The Executive and delegate body has the sanction of over 300 electors, who represented 252 Jewish organizations of the city." As usual, vociferous *amcha* had plenty to say about this. Members of labour unions and the Jewish Communists claimed that Congress was too "elitist" and autocratic, and sought to perpetuate the rule of the rich over the toiling Jewish masses. Others, principally Labour Zionists, believed that the executive ought to consult the Congress delegates before any important measures were approved. Still others attacked Congress's refusal to hold elections by popular vote, arguing that Congress's system of proportional representation along religious, Zionist, and fraternal organizations perpetuated the re-election of the same people.[64]

Caiserman's attitude was characteristically pragmatic. He had no intention of listening to "those who scream democracy and let it die." Despite his own ideological predilections, he agreed with the Control Committee that democracy was secondary to survival. It was the "autocrats" who kept Congress alive. When the "democrats" began to contribute, he would be ready to listen to them.[65]

With Frankel now out of the way, who would run the division? Contrary to their detractors' expectations, Bennett and his committee did not monopolize control. Bennett pointed out that the committee "was not sufficiently large or representative enough" and called instead for an open, democratic, but above all, workable governing process. Put simply, it was recommended that the executive meet regularly twice a month and that a Council of Organizations composed of organizational delegates to Congress, set policy, review and approve executive recommendations, and direct executive activity. The executive therefore supervised the day-to-day work of Congress, and the Council of Organizations ensured that the executive acted in the best interests of the *amcha*.[66]

On 11 April, the executive chose Roger as chairman of the board. This was done even though Caiserman had originally promised this position to Bennett as part of the package enticing him onto the executive. Bennett proved magnanimous. He praised Roger as "a man of culture, [who] was not affiliated with any particular group," and pointed out "that Congress was close to his heart." The executive then agreed to appoint the Control Committee to advise the executive, and not become an inner executive. The Control Committee was evenly divided between the two rival groups: Bennett and Shapiro were balanced by Goldstick and Kramer, Eisendrath and Sachs, who worked well together, and Ida Siegal representing all women's groups.[67]

Roger demonstrated brilliant leadership. Under his influence, long-dormant committees began to function again. For the first time since its inception, Central Division's administration was working well. The Public Relations Committee rejuvenated Congress's "Boycott Campaign Against German Goods." Boycott Committee chair John Glass dismissed all committee members who failed to attend meetings and replaced them with representatives of Jewish labour who had agreed to work with Congress against the Nazi threat.[68]

In August the Boycott Committee began a two-pronged campaign. Glass appealed to the Canadian Manufacturers' Association and the government to curtail the flow of German goods into Canada, claiming that they were being dumped on the Canadian market below cost. In October the committee followed up by launching a revived consumer protest campaign designed to encourage Gentiles to join the boycott. The Women's Consumers League was opened up to male and female representatives, especially from Jewish unions, and was renamed the Anti-Nazi Consumer League. The league, operating as a Congress front, sought to popularize the idea "that the fight against Hitlerism was no longer a purely Jewish question, but that Hitlerism represented a threat to all liberal and peaceful people throughout the civilized world." The league got off to a bold start, with Toronto's CCF Mayor, James Simpson, attending its initial meeting. The Trades and

Labour Congress endorsed the boycott and sent a representative as well. The League Against War and Fascism and the CCF also became involved, as did sympathetic church groups. By November, over five thousand Jewish workers had pledged to boycott German goods. Soon such prominent chains as Woolworth's and Aikenhead's came on side. Less spectacular but equally important work was done to convince manufacturers to substitute Canadian, British, or American materials for German goods. Hospitals were informed of substitutes for popular German drugs and surgical equipment. Every effort was made to convince Canadians to "buy British."[69]

Eisendrath's Public Relations Committee also took up its advocacy work with renewed vigour. In association with B'nai Brith, it won some symbolic victories. It was able to prevent a Nazi propaganda film from being shown under the guise of a "travelogue" and planted informants in the Ku Klux Klan and Silver Shirt Organizations to monitor their activities.[70]

The B'nai Brith connection also helped the committee prepare a mailing list of thirty thousand names, and assisted it in paying for a clipping bureau that monitored press opinion across Ontario. Eisendrath was proactive, cultivating media support and trying to shape public opinion through education. The educational campaign now reached beyond the simple refutation of anti-Semitic myths in an effort to convince Canadians that anti-Semitism was an attack not only on Jews, but on the principles of freedom, democracy, and "British fair play." Much to Caiserman's chagrin, Eisendrath cautiously cooperated with the League Against War and Fascism. Eisendrath knew that the league counted many Communists among its members (it was in fact a front for the Communist Party of Canada) but believed that as long as well-known non-Communists remained on the executive, this connection would be a useful.[71]

Impressed by Eisendrath's work, B'nai Brith began to plan a more formal alliance with Congress. In early April 1935, the Eastern Canadian Conference of B'nai Brith asked Richard Gutstadt to set up a Canadian ADL office and invited Congress to participate. At first Caiserman was pleased to cooperate, and both organizations seemed well on their way to building a united approach to anti-defamation. Unfortunately, a major misunderstanding nearly derailed this good will.

The Polish government began to make ominous noises about getting rid of its Jews by "encouraging" mass emigration, and threatened to pass laws that would ban ritual slaughter of meat. Simultaneously a new wave of violence erupted against German Jews. These events gripped Toronto Jewry. Congress suddenly found itself in the communal limelight and under heavy pressure to "do something." As usual, Congress responded with *shtadlanut* rather than demonstrations. A blue-ribbon group of Eastern Division leaders met in Montreal to draft a formal protest to Prime Minister Bennett. Judging that it would be most effective to deliver this memorandum directly, they obtained an appointment for 15 August.[72]

Caiserman decided that each Congress division should send a delegate to this meeting in Ottawa. But Central Division didn't have a quorum at its meeting and Roger made the decision to send ZOC president Freiman, since he lived in Ottawa. Roger also suggested that Caiserman invite B'nai Brith president, Benjamin Goldfield, to join the group. Caiserman invited Goldfield but neglected to provide the exact meeting information, and Goldfield missed meeting the prime minister. This omission ignited the still-smouldering tensions between the two organizations. B'nai Brith accused Congress of acting in bad faith. "The Canadian Jewish Congress thought it fit to handle this matter alone," Goldfield wrote angrily to Caiserman, "but for appearance's sake, sent me an ... invitation to be a party to something in which ... I could not participate." Goldfield then backed the plans to set up an independent Canadian ADL office without Congress participation.[73]

Caiserman did his best to salvage the situation. He succeeded in convincing B'nai Brith's Toronto Lodge, many of whom were members of Central Division, that he had not deliberately tricked Goldfield and truly wanted a unified approach to anti-defamation. Roger, who did most of the actual negotiating with B'nai Brith, achieved an important breakthrough when he was invited to speak at the biannual B'nai Brith conference on 10 November, to which ADL president, Gutstadt, was also invited. It was widely known that Goldfield and the powerful Mount Royal Lodge of Montreal favoured an independent ADL office. Would the Toronto lodge's support for Congress be enough to stop a potentially fatal breach between Congress and B'nai Brith?

Roger made the most of his speaking opportunity. He argued that even though Congress was a young organization, and in many ways administratively inferior to B'nai Brith, it was the only organization authorized to speak for Canadian Jewry as a whole. If B'nai Brith excluded Congress from anti-defamation work, it would turn its back on much of the Jewish community and further fracture Canadian Jewry.

Gutstadt was impressed by Roger's speech and allowed that as long as Congress did not act unilaterally in its anti-defamation work, B'nai Brith would seek to cooperate with it. It took three and a half hours to convince Goldfield and the Montreal Lodge to sign on. The conference finally agreed to form joint community councils of both Congress and B'nai Brith, resolving that "every effort should be made at effective cooperation between the B'nai Brith and the Canadian Jewish Congress in the work of anti-defamation in Canada."[74]

This resolution was a decisive breakthrough in Canadian Jewish communal advocacy. Thereafter, both organizations were committed to joint action, though each still jealously guarded its turf. One point remained unresolved. Caiserman's insistence that all joint anti-defamation work be done under the Congress umbrella understandably irritated B'nai Brith, which had pioneered this work and believed that it had already shown sufficient deference to Congress. But Caiserman insisted and, in February 1938, B'nai Brith capitulated, and the Joint Public Relations Committee (JPRC) came into existence – a committee of Congress in which B'nai Brith was an equal partner. At a stroke, the fledgling Congress legitimized its mandate to represent and defend Canadian Jewry. Membership overlap increased and the influx of Ben Brits was especially beneficial to the Central Division.[75]

How did Congress in its weak condition bring B'nai Brith on side in the very field that the American-based order had long claimed for itself? The penurious state of the Eastern Canadian Conference of B'nai Brith worked in Congress's favour. The organization was weaker in Canada than in the United States. Anti-defamation work was very expensive, and in 1933 the Canadian lodges were strapped for funds. By this time, the CJC had been reorganized, and enthusiasm for organizational cooperation was the order of the day, with Ben Brits Eisendrath, Catzman, and Caiserman also key players who continuously emphasized the importance of unified Canadian anti-defamation work. Many rank-and-file Ontario Ben Brits saw cooperation as serving the interests of both B'nai Brith and the larger Jewish community.[76]

But, as noted, the Ottawa and Quebec lodges favoured an independent ADL office. Quebec Jews, and those in Ottawa where there was a sizable French Canadian population, had observed that they faced more virulent anti-Semitism than Ontario Jews. They did not want to stand idly by while Congress got itself going. B'nai Brith in the United States had a track record in dealing with anti-Semitism and they saw no reason why they should be denied the immediate and effective protection of the well-established ADL.[77]

These arguments took little account of the differences in American and Canadian society and the patterns of anti-Semitism spawned by each. Oscar Cohen, who worked for both Congress and the ADL, believed that "even the most highly seasoned ADL professional would require two years to acclimatize himself to Canadian conditions." Cohen had the advantage of hindsight but his point was sound: anti-Semitism in Quebec was running at floodtide. But in the flush of organizational rationalization most observers ignored the legitimate concerns of Ottawa and Montreal Ben Brits. This lack of understanding previewed larger divisions between Toronto and Montreal Jewry which would colour organizational politics in the next decade and beyond.[78]

Unfortunately for Central Division, its anti-defamation effort was overtaken by events in the summer of 1935 in the wake of a sharp rise in Polish anti-Semitism and the renewed surge of German anti-Semitism that culminated in the Nuremberg Laws. As conditions worsened, an increasingly angry Jewish public demanded not hand-picked delegations quietly talking to unbending politicians, but some form of mass public community protest. Central Division, with its modest, gradualist approach to anti-defamation and the Nazi threat, seemed out of step with *amcha* sentiments, despite two years of reorganization and its affiliation with the ADL.[79]

What is more, the Central Division executive continually echoed the American Jewish Committee by cautioning against any public stand that did not have the support of like-minded Protestants and Catholics. It was better public relations to emphasize the threat that Nazism posed to all religions. Until Christian support for public protest could be assured, *shtadlanut* would suffice. Surely, Congress leadership argued, the coup of obtaining an audience with Prime Minister Bennett should prove to Toronto *amcha* that Congress was making representations on their behalf in the highest quarters.

Not surprisingly, *amcha* completely disagreed. And this time they did something about it. The Arbeiter Ring (Workmen's Circle), a democratic socialist organization unaffiliated with Congress which enjoyed considerable support among many Spadina factory operatives, called a conference of labour and union leaders on 30 July to discuss plans for a public protest. This meeting gave vent to their impatience with Uptown *shtadlanut*. The issues gained traction because most of Toronto's Jews had relatives in Poland or Germany and were seized by a tremendous need to do something – anything – to demonstrate concern for their kin. The dissenters demanded the opportunity to express their feelings publicly and loudly.[80]

Congress's pretensions to power were now exposed. Central Division lacked the political clout to stop the proposed public protest. Nor did it dare incur the wrath of the Arbeiter Ring or risk losing their support. The harsh truth was that Central Division did not command *amcha* loyalty. Two years of effort had gone for nought. "The man on the street," observed Roger, "looks on Congress as a 'super-super organization' that is stealing the prerogatives from existing organizations of their own activities."[81]

Roger attempted damage control; it was of utmost importance that the protest meeting not be perceived as exclusively Jewish. He permitted the League Against War and Fascism to run the public protest because "an entirely Jewish mass meeting ... would have been disastrous," and he secretly allocated $200 to help defer the cost of the public protest. Roger thus ensured that the league served as the firewall behind which "we could shelter ourselves and ... permit our people to let off steam." Caiserman was left on the sidelines to fume and lament that this matter had given him "hours of mental depression."[82]

Caiserman fervently sought to reconfirm the quieter methods of *shtadlanut*, and strengthened Congress's efforts to convince Canadian athletes to boycott the 1936 Berlin Olympics. Congress had begun this work in 1934 when the International Olympic Committee (IOC) ruled that the 1936 games could remain in Germany provided that German Jewish athletes were allowed to qualify for their national team. The Unity and Goodwill Association, which had operated as "the confidential subsidiary of Congress" since 1934, was unable to arouse wide public support for an Olympic boycott. In early 1935 Caiserman asked Eisendrath to take a leading role in the Olympic boycott effort.[83]

The Olympic boycott campaign had begun soon after Hitler became chancellor in January 1933. In 1931 the IOC had awarded both the 1936 Winter and Summer Games to Germany. Germany pledged to show the world "the full reintegration of post-war Germany, no longer a pariah nation, into the world of international sport." When he came to power, Hitler had little interest either in sports or in the Olympic Games. But Propaganda Minister Josef Goebbels realized that the games offered a chance to showcase Nazi achievement. He prevailed upon Hitler to become actively involved in politicizing this event and turning it into a propaganda spectacle. In March 1933 Hitler informed both the president and secretary of the German Olympic Organizing Committee that his government fully supported the games.[84]

For Hitler and his inner circle, Nazi ideology could be well served by co-opting the athletic fraternity. The Nazis were displeased with two key Olympic organizers: Theodor Lewald, president of the Organizing Committee, was the son of a Jewish convert; Carl Diem, the committee's secretary, had a wife of Jewish ancestry and was pilloried in the Nazi press because his German Sport University had a number of Jews on its faculty. Both key officials were permitted to retain their posts in order to placate the IOC and to maintain the pretense of non-interference in the participation of German Jewish athletes in the Games.[85]

Eisendrath became involved at a crucial point. In early 1935 it was evident that American participation would determine the boycott's success. Hitler's sudden occupation of the Rhineland on 7 March just after the close of the Winter Games, led to a sharp increase in pro-boycott sentiments from important government and sports figures in Britain and France. But the British Olympic Committee (BOC) argued that the Rhineland situation made it even more essential that the games be held because they were a symbol of "the ideal of harmony and reconciliation between nations." While the British government remained politically aloof, many MPs voiced the opinion that it was best not to boycott the games and further inflame the unstable European situation.

British Jews were divided on their strategy; especially after 1924 gold medal winner Harold Abrahams argued that "the isolation of Germany would be bad for the world. If the British team went to Berlin, it would be an influence for good." Abrahams' statement carried weight. It persuaded the Socialist National Workers Sports Association to withdraw its motion to boycott the Berlin Games at the British Amateur Athletic Association (BAAA) annual meeting on 22 March. In early May the BAAA voted overwhelmingly (200 to 8) to send the British team.[86]

The French Socialist government of Léon Blum was much more sympathetic to the boycott cause. The re-occupation of the Rhineland and Hitler's militarism threatened France directly, and the memory of the Great War was still very fresh. The powerful French Communist party supported Blum after a mid-1935 change in Comintern strategy allowed the Communists to support Socialist sport organizations in their call for a boycott. But the French Olympic Committee and its Athletic Union desperately wanted French athletes to compete on the world stage. In the end a compromise was reached: the government paid for French athletes to compete in either the Berlin Olympics or the Barcelona Games, organized at the last minute to offer an alternative to the Berlin Olympics.[87]

The American boycott battle was the closest and most vicious of all. Alan Guttman, biographer of the American Athletic Union (AAU), and later IOC head Avery Brundage, argues that the American boycott struggle was crucial and that its outcome determined British and French policy. American groups supporting a boycott included the powerful Catholic Church, Jews, and many blacks. In addition, the AAU was almost evenly divided in its sympathies. A Gallup poll taken in mid-1935 found that 43 percent of Americans supported a boycott. But Brundage, after a deliberately superficial "on site" investigation of Germany in September 1935, convinced the American Olympic Committee to support American participation at Berlin. The normally quiescent AAU refused to assent. A formal vote on American participation was delayed pending further investigation. A furious lobbying campaign began. Brundage lashed out at his opponents, claiming that they were all "Communists and Jews." He ignored the brutal persecution of Jews in Germany and alienated many former friends in his single-minded drive. In the end, "his opponents had the facts, but Brundage had the votes." On 6 December, by a narrow margin, the AAU voted against any further investigation of a boycott and approved AAU participation in Berlin.[88]

While Brundage's vicious lobbying defeated weighty mainstream opposition, in Canada, according to sports historian Bruce Kidd, "the [Olympic boycott] campaign leadership never really broadened beyond the ranks of the Communist party." Eisendrath's task was made doubly difficult. He would have to fight the pro-Berlin sports press and attempt to steer clear of the "Jews are Communists" canard. He was unable to make much headway on either front. Few Canadian sportswriters supported an Olympic boycott. The attitude of *Toronto Star* sports editor Lou Marsh was typical. He informed Eisendrath that "the whole matter is an internal problem that concerns Germany and not ourselves." Ted Reeve, coach of the Queen's University football team and sports columnist of the *Toronto Telegram*, consistently used his column to castigate pro-boycott Jewish and Catholic athletes. Only the *Vancouver Sun* openly supported a boycott.[89]

This atmosphere made it difficult for Eisendrath to carry the boycott message much beyond the Jewish community. The Communist *Daily Worker* pressed hard for a boycott, and some assistance was received from Mayor Simpson, who refused to subsidize any Toronto athletes who went to Berlin. Some prominent liberals also supported the boycott campaign, but for most Torontonians the issue had little resonance. It was soon apparent that Canada would follow British policy on a boycott. Once British participation was assured, the Canadian Olympic Committee fell in line and authorized its athletes to participate in the games. Even with the promulgation of the Nuremberg Laws, it refused to reconsider its decision. Canadian amateur athletic associations supported the Canadian Olympic Committee and rejected continued protests by Jewish groups and organized labour. When the Toronto YMHA refused to pay a percentage of its "Boxing Nights" ticket revenue to support the Canadian Olympic boxing team, it was suspended from competition.[90]

This was especially galling because two Jewish boxers, Sammy Luftspring and "Baby" Yack, had good chances of winning Olympic medals. The Jewish community had followed their careers closely. Their success in the boxing ring was an assertion that Jews could fight back against anti-Semitism in the street and in the ring. Tension in the ring was further increased by what Luftspring called the "casual bigotry" of boxing promoters and sports writers. They routinely linked fighters to their ethnic group or religion. But so did the Jewish community. It was not uncommon for ethnically partisan fans to battle each other in the stands while their champions battled in the ring.[91]

Luftspring was very conscious of this. He didn't mind Marsh calling him "an aggressive little Jew boy." He loved seeing his name in print and was proud to fight with a Star of David on his trunks. In his autobiography, Luftspring recalls that after qualifying for the Olympic team with a second place finish in his weight class at the Canadian Championships, he decided not to go. His parents told him about the persecution of Jews in Germany and expressed fears for his personal safety. He wasn't concerned for his personal safety, but recalled "that there was enough Jew in me that I knew I had to make a protest, and the only protest I could make was to declare my refusal to go to Berlin on political grounds."[92]

Luftspring claims he then convinced "Baby" Yack to join his protest. Together they drafted a letter published on 7 July 1936. They acknowledged that "as Canadian boys, we would be personally safe," but continued "that all true Canadian sportsmen will appreciate that we could have been very low to hurt the feelings of our fellow Jews by going to a land that would exterminate them if they could." Two lesser-known Jewish athletes, boxer Lenny Stein and walker Henry Cleman, wrote similar letters the next week. A few days later Luftspring, Yack, and Stein announced they would attend the Communist-organized International Workers' Games in Barcelona as an alternative to the Berlin games.[93]

Luftspring's memoirs and oral recollections differ from the received historical record in a number of key areas, even though they support it in others. His omissions may reflect the failed memory or the naïveté of a young man preoccupied with making a career in a brutal sport. Luftspring later admitted he had "never been much of a student of politics." But Central Division's leaders were politically aware. The political implications of Canadian Jewish athletes going to Berlin were clearly disastrous. Indeed, the Public Relations Committee had been following Luftspring's career, and that of other Jewish athletes, with interest throughout its unsuccessful Berlin Olympic boycott efforts. The committee hoped that it could at least convince Jewish athletes to boycott the games and discreetly asked Luftspring and Yack what they intended to do.[94]

In early February 1936, FJP executive director Martin Cohn was informed that Luftspring, Yack, and Stein had originally "planned to go through the [Olympic] trials as far as they could, but that if they were selected they would refuse to participate in the Olympics." This was part of a game plan "to get to the top of the amateur ranks and then turn professional." This would have put any communal concerns to rest. But Cohn was later informed that, just before announcing their decision, the men had a change of heart and wanted to go to the Olympics. Cohn was alarmed and called Roger, who agreed that this would be a public relations nightmare. As Cohn understood it, the boxers had to be approached again to find out what their views were. Cohn argued that it was essential to convince them not to go. He believed that Roger and the JPRC could effectively intervene. Roger complied.[95]

To stop Luftspring from going to Berlin, Roger made common cause with the Communists, who wanted athletes to go to Barcelona. He invited Luftspring and Yack to the Congress offices on 4 July 1936 and "prevailed upon [the boxers] to officially renounce the Berlin Games, and instead go to the Barcelona Games." Ideologically, the Division Executive was not happy about the Barcelona Games. But Bennett and Roger knew they had no choice. The athletes deserved something. Ideology would momentarily be ignored – better Barcelona than Berlin. Furthermore, Congress's support for their trip could be explained as a demonstration of Jewish pride, thus denying the local Communists a publicity windfall. An appropriate letter to the Toronto papers was composed at this meeting. It appeared in the *Globe* on 6 July and in the *Star* and *Telegram* the next day. On 9 July Central Division sponsored a community-wide fundraising event and raised about $1,000, more than the estimated $750 the trip to Barcelona would cost.[96]

Congress may have saved face, but in the wider Canadian context the Canadian Jewish athletes' protest was ineffective beyond their community. Hitler took care to ensure that anti-Semitic outbreaks were quelled during the games. Most Canadians, including some Olympians, did not even know that a boycott had been staged.[97]

In the midst of all these activities, Roger tried desperately to organize yet another Central Division fundraising campaign. The coffers of Congress headquarters and Central Division were so depleted that Roger, Bennett, and Eisendrath decided to begin the campaign before the High Holy Days and continue it indefinitely until the goal was reached. They invited 1,100 people to a mass meeting on 22 September. Roger called the meeting a "mixed success": 250 people attended but chose the cheapest form of support – a $2 annual membership – and only $500 was raised. Nonetheless, Congress did acquire quite a few new members, and – more important – Holy Blossom's members, concerned by the "poor response," decided to take a more active role in ensuring the division's fiscal survival.[98]

Roger forwarded $250 to Caiserman and hoped the remaining funds would last until November when the Federation of Jewish Philanthropies' campaign would be over and divisional fundraising could resume. But representations to government and the Olympic boycott campaign were costly. Caiserman noted that existing reserves would "give us another lease [on] life for about three or four weeks." He was forced to stop drawing his own salary to keep headquarters solvent. But he saw one ray of light. Central Division was in the process of moving its headquarters into the Hermant Building on Dundas Square. Percy Hermant, president of Imperial Optical, had donated office space to Congress for its 1934 campaign, and was now persuaded to donate a large suite to the division. The ever-optimistic Caiserman was hopeful that the move to such a "prominent building" would be the beginning of new things for the division.[99]

This hope proved to be mere wishful thinking. Congress still didn't rate with Downtowners. From time to time, as with the Olympic boycott, it became involved in issues that resonated for *amcha*, but its commitment to *shtadlanut*, its aloofness from the labour movement, and its lack of direct involvement in immigrant aid all worked against it. A good number surely suspected not a few Congress leaders of looking down their collective noses at the Downtown community – Roger's "let them blow off a bit a steam" comment being a case in point. Congress's visibility fell to a new low. Yet another financial campaign failed, and embattled Alexander Brown resigned on 23 October 1935. His departure reopened the feud between Shapiro and Goldstick, who also resigned. Central Division's collapse seemed imminent.[100]

Caiserman took Brown's resignation badly. Indeed, the general secretary was an increasingly embittered man in the fall of 1935. He hadn't drawn his salary since September, preferring to allocate precious funds to the cause of Congress. But nothing seemed to help. The Olympic boycott had met a wall of resistance, the Central Division was impotent, negotiations with B'nai Brith were problematic, and anti-Semitism was increasing in Canada and rampant in Germany. It seemed to Caiserman that despite his indomitable will and the help of a few Congress stalwarts, the "Congress idea" was doomed. With the fundraising campaign "drying up" and no hope of "start[ing] up energetically until the middle of November," Caiserman found little solace in Roger's advice to "hold out till then, and we will send you every penny we can spare." This was impossible. Caiserman directed Roger to canvass the small Jewish communities of Ontario for funds to "save the existence of the Congress." This also proved impossible. In late November Roger again told Caiserman to continue waiting until a new campaign was launched in mid-December. But Caiserman was desperate. Congress was dying. He hurried to Toronto on 12 December to assess the situation personally.[101]

All the organizational reforms that looked so good on paper had failed in practice. The Divisional Executive seldom met, leaving matters in the hands of the Control Committee. The division was still in financial difficulty, and only 20 percent of the Jewish organizations in the city paid the promised 25¢ per capita tax to Congress. The boycott of German goods was going nowhere, as Glass, its chairman, reported: "Not only are Jewish merchants handling and assisting in the sale of goods made in Germany, but a considerable number of Jewish housewives buy German goods ... knowing them to be made in Germany ... because the price is cheaper." Extremely concerned, Caiserman went to other Ontario communities and found them ill-informed or lacking interest in Congress's work. They were resentful that the Toronto office appeared to ignore their needs and was interested only in how much money they might supply. He returned to Montreal and prepared for Congress's demise.[102]

If Caiserman had been able to look beyond Congress, he would have observed that Central Division was in far better financial shape than other Jewish communal institutions of the time, including the Mount Sinai Hospital and Brunswick Avenue Talmud Torah, both of which had incurred large debts running into the tens of thousands of dollars. The division had no rent to pay, no mortgage to worry about, and its sole debt was a $1,200 bank loan. This source of funds became Congress's salvation. With no overhead, the trickle of funds from

Toronto and smaller Ontario centres proved sufficient to keep Central Division limping along. With little enthusiasm, Caiserman began to organize the Third Plenary, tentatively scheduled for Ottawa in May. He was "disgusted and heartbroken" by the state of affairs in Toronto and the rest of the division. He confessed, "I more than once contemplated to run away from the work." It was not that easy. There was no running away from a life's work.

A fresh outbreak of anti-Semitism rocked Poland. The Polish government again threatened to halt kosher slaughtering and increase economic sanctions against its already struggling Jewish population. Toronto Jews, mainly Polish immigrants and their children, were convulsed by anger. Bypassing Central Division entirely, twenty-one *landsmanschaften* and Arbeiter Ring branches met on 24 March 1936, and proclaimed themselves the Workers' Conference.[103] The Conference promptly organized a public demonstration against Polish anti-Semitism for 29 March.[104] The speed with which this group convened and their conviction that "Congress has done nothing" indicated that *amcha* anger and power had waxed as Congress's had waned, and would make it much more difficult for Central Division to advocate its usual remedy of cap-in-hand *shtadlanut*.[105]

Unable to break with the past, Caiserman nevertheless pursued his policy of *shtadlanut*. He had already convinced the Eastern and Western Divisions to participate in a delegation of protest to the Polish Consul General in Ottawa, and naïvely expected Central Division to fall into line. Time was tight and tempers were short in Toronto. A blue-ribbon Central Division delegation trotted out the usual line that Polish Jewry had asked world Jewry not to interfere, for fear of "impugning their patriotism" and that a relief campaign would be a far better use of *amcha* passions. This time they were stonewalled as Workers' Conference representatives forcefully argued that conditions in Poland were worsening daily and demanded divisional support for their protest. They threatened to boycott the upcoming Central Division elections if help was not forthcoming.[106]

Amcha assertiveness had its effect. The ensuing divisional executive meeting hosted a passionate debate between the advocates of *shtadlanut* and public protest. For the first time, everyone agreed that the situation in Poland was so bad that they had nothing to lose by protest. But, asked Eisendrath, what did Congress and Toronto Jewry stand to gain? "Toronto Jewish opinion," he argued, "[did] not necessarily comprise Toronto public opinion, let alone world public opinion"; furthermore, a protest demonstration would only let off "steam" without performing any constructive function. But a majority of the executive knew that the demonstration would go on regardless of their decision. They argued that if the "whipped up and tense" former Polish Jews were left on their own, the protest would surely be abusive and produce a public relations disaster. After two hours of occasionally acrimonious debate, the executive voted seven to three in favour of supporting the mass protest meeting. The only proviso was that support would be withdrawn if Caiserman could furnish "valid reasons to the contrary, in addition to those already given." All that remained was choose a date.[107]

Even this last stab at containing *amcha* passion was quickly thwarted. By mid-April the Workers' Conference, its ranks now including forty organizations, was understandably impatient to set a date. Relatives in Poland were under threat – daily telegrams and letters attested to the seriousness of the situation. These workers had no interest in waiting for Caiserman's approval for their actions. The Central Division executive had approved a protest – on with it! Their frustration and fear manifested itself as naked fury. Central Division secretary Mandell "escaped narrowly from being lynched ... when [he] ventured to point out the danger of mass protest and street parade." The *Zhurnal* abandoned the division and even Eisendrath was "puzzled by the whole situation." With the division leadership split, the Workers' Conference played its trump card and threatened not to participate in the elections (which had already been postponed to 3 May) unless a firm date was set for a public demonstration.

On 16 April Caiserman rejected any sort of public demonstration, even if Central Division did sponsor it. He instructed Mandell to select his delegates for a meeting with the Polish Consul and convince the Workers' Conference to change their plans. The workers were predictably unobliging and scheduled a mass parade. Through his friendship with the conference secretary, Mandell managed to convince the furious Polish Jews to move their demonstration indoors to Massey Hall rather than hold it in the streets. To gain time, he refused to pay the hall its deposit until the Division Executive could discuss the situation. This stalling tactic almost ended in violence. Many of the delegates brandished their fists and denounced Mandell as "a traitor and an anti-Semite." He grimly informed Caiserman: "If you read in the press that the executive secretary has been found dead, you will know that the Polish Jews in Toronto have shot him."[108]

With all the confusion, the conference agreed to delay its protest until after the Congress delegation had met with the Polish Consul General in Ottawa on April 23. The memorandum of protest was strongly worded and the Polish envoy appeared impressed with the delegation and promised to forward its message to Warsaw. In the light of this apparently successful *shtadlanut* exercise, the executive recommended that instead of a protest, the Workers' Conference hold a public meeting to raise money for relief purposes only. Acknowledging that the Polish political situation was cooling, the conference agreed. To consolidate its gains, the conference reorganized into the more permanent Federation of Polish Jews (Farband), and nominated candidates for the election of delegates to the Third Plenary. From Congress's point of view, *shtadlanut* had triumphed once again, but this time its larger victory was a hollow one. It had survived only because of the willingness of *amcha* to cooperate and consult with Congress. No one doubted that the conference could easily have organized a public protest independently of Congress.[109]

The upside to the whole affair was that it drew the Farband and Central Division together. Each needed the other. After the elections and a successful plenary, the backing of Polish Jewry in Toronto also gave the Central Division unprecedented financial security. The Farband's constituent organizations quickly ponied up almost $1,000 in cash for Central Division coffers. Given the strength of the Polish community in Toronto Jewry, it was clear that more money might be available. The suddenly flush Central Division no longer had to divert all its energy to fundraising. This new freedom allowed committees to do more efficient work in public relations, boycott work, and education.[110]

For the first time, the division was able to plan its November 1936 campaign well in advance. It hired a professional fundraiser and set a goal of $10,000 to cover office costs and its National Congress allocation. Congress scheduled a community meeting for 24 September at the Victory Theatre to kick off the campaign. Bennett was now chairman of the board (Roger was president). He left nothing to chance. The theatre was fully stocked with the paraphernalia of fundraising: adding machines, complimentary calendars, and promotional leaflets. Members of the Youth and Women's Committees served as money collectors. The program was well planned and fast-paced to build momentum. The campaign, which officially began on 2 November, was characterized by efficiency, professionalism, and, for the first time, an inflow of funds. The division sent out its workers, rather than Caiserman alone, to systematically canvass small Ontario communities. The Third Plenary attracted fewer delegates, but they were far more active and better informed, and were integrated into the division's work more effectively than ever before. Bennett, utterly devoted to the vision of Congress as the "Parliament of Canadian Jewry," "worked like a horse" during the campaign and insisted that anyone with a poor attendance record at meetings be counselled out of the organization. All hoped that Central Division was finally on its way to organizational self-sufficiency.[111]

The dismissal of executive secretary Mandell and his replacement by former *Jewish Standard* editor Oscar Cohen in early November 1936 also had far-reaching implications for Central Division's future. Unlike his predecessors, Cohen was non-Yiddish speaking and was unimpressed by Caiserman. Cohen's primary loyalty was to Central Division. He was determined to make what was formerly the weakest division into the most powerful one and he was in a good position to do so. The success of the campaign meant that Central Division had the economic resources to take up some long-awaited communal planning tasks on a full-time basis. An Economic Committee was struck to prepare a report on the problem of the Jewish unemployed, including the failure of Jewish employers to assist them in finding jobs. The Educational Committee was finally able to fund a province-wide conference on education. The executive even found money to investigate the vexing problem of restricted covenants, and hotel and resort discrimination.

Significantly, Central Division's re-invigorated spate of organizing and planning was carried on without consulting Caiserman. As the division grew more confident, his authority slipped. As noted, he never had been an effective administrator, and Montreal's state of perpetual financial disarray combined with the difficulties imposed by distance left him helpless in the face of Central Division's new activism. Nor did Bennett's ego make things any easier for Caiserman. The Toronto intellectual had decided that he was the man to lead his division out of the wilderness. His temper was legendary and he brooked no interference from Cohen, his own executive, or Caiserman.

To minimize executive interference, Bennett re-activated the Control Committee, renamed it the Inner Executive, and had it carry the burden of the executive's work. This had the advantage of ensuring greater policy continuity and speeding up decisions. On the other hand, it alienated many executive members, who suspected, not without reason, that they were becoming rubber stamps rather than decision makers. But Bennett controlled the Inner Executive, and Roger backed him because the system worked. Gathering the reins of power in his hands transformed Bennett from "*amcha*'s representative" to intellectual autocrat.[112]

Bennett proved more than willing to use his organizational leverage and stronger financial situation to increase divisional autonomy. The Third Plenary had passed resolutions that committed Central Division to cover 35 percent of head office expenses (budgeted at $12,000). This was 5 percent less than the previous rate, but when Caiserman claimed that Toronto had not lived up to its obligations, and still owed more than $2,300, he got nowhere with Roger. He was told to go back to his books and account for the funds spent by Montreal in its dual capacity as both National Congress headquarters and head office of the Eastern Division. Until he did so, it would be difficult, argued Roger, to justify $12,000 per annum in National expenses. He implicitly warned Caiserman against attempting to piggyback Eastern Division expenses onto Central's back by combining them with National expenses. The Toronto executive "would demand chapter and verse ... They would not pass ... irrespective of the Plenary Session in Montreal, a contribution towards National Expenses which, or the amount of which, cannot be conclusively established." After two drafts, Caiserman managed to compile sufficiently accurate expense accounting to convince the Toronto Executive to send more money to Montreal, but this episode sent a clear signal that power was shifting to Toronto.[113]

Events would keep Central Division from enjoying financial and organizational independence for very long. Like the rest of Congress, Central Division's rhetoric still exceeded its accomplishments. True, it had some important achievements to its credit. The formation of the Joint Public Relations Committee headed this list. It was born out of Eisendrath's anti-defamation work, Caiserman's insistence on a unified Canadian approach to anti-defamation work, and the negotiating skills of Roger and Catzman. In addition, Central Division had served as an important forum for communal cooperation between disparate economic and political groups. Nonetheless, by its own admission, Central Division had not fulfilled its mandate as the "Parliament of Toronto Jewry." The continued absence of organized Jewish labour from Congress mocked this claim and marked its most serious failure. Worst of all, Congress had failed to initiate systematic social planning, exerted no control over Jewish social welfare institutions, and had been unable to influence Jewish religious and educational activity. By 1936, as seen in chapter 3, the federation worked quickly to fill the vacuum.[114]

Perhaps it was too much to expect Central Division to have a track record of accomplishment after barely surviving its tumultuous first three years. Until January 1937 the financial situation of both Central Division and National Congress remained desperate. A good deal of this insolvency was due to the Depression. As noted, even the far better established Federation was in dire straits. In addition, both the federation and Congress had encountered stubborn resistance when they attempted to impose their visions of communal unity on fiercely independent *amcha* organizations. The federation had to take drastic action to seize control of the orphanage, and Central Division had tried, but failed, to take similar action in endeavouring to speak for the Polish *landsmanschaften*.[115]

Even if Central Division still lacked the communal clout it sought, its leaders could nevertheless boast of their independence from Caiserman and Congress headquarters in Montreal. By 1938 Montreal had been marginalized, and Toronto was financially autonomous and introducing innovative ideas. Central Division under Bennett was not democratic, but its governance was in far surer hands than Caiserman's. But what of relations between the Federation and Congress? Although the groups had overlapping aims, they had not yet come into conflict. Each claimed to speak to a different agenda. Congress hoped to be the communal political voice while the federation took care of communal services. Both organizations employed different building blocks to achieve communal solidarity. Congress courted support from *landsmanschaften*, synagogues, and unions, while the federation sought to control funding and rationalize policy making in communal social welfare institutions. Both aspired to leadership in social planning, but the federation had a huge head start because it had already professionalized most of the leading Jewish social service agencies. On the other hand, as European anti-Semitism loomed large, *amcha* suddenly took more notice of Congress, spurred by concerns about the fate of their families in Europe that gave them a new interest in unified political action.

Both Central Division and the federation struggled through similar problems of fundraising, organizational independence, and imposing a vision of communal unity. These issues would eventually draw the two organizations into fusion. The only question, and a bitterly contested one, was, whose terms would prevail?[116]

6

A Foundation of Unity: The Toronto Hebrew Free School and the Rise of the United Jewish Welfare Fund, 1933–39

By the end of 1936, it was clear that both the Central Division of the Canadian Jewish Congress and the Federation of Jewish Philanthropies would be unable to fully assert their organizational mandates. Congress had failed to build on the expectations associated with its re-emergence in 1933; the federation had indeed imposed professional standards on many social service agencies, but at the cost of alienating many volunteers. In addition, the federation's Uptown bias made it doubtful whether traditional *amcha* institutions would ever affiliate. Worst of all, the federation's consistent annual campaign shortfalls and, most crucially, its inability to demand audited budgets from constituent agencies, fatally limited its effectiveness.

No historian could have predicted that the movement toward Toronto's highly organized Jewish community of today would be catalyzed by a school-funding crisis. But the unique educational philosophy of the school in question attracted the young Uptown professionals and businessmen, whose education and values predisposed them to find solutions rooted in efficiency. The entire story, which took four years to fully unfold, began on 26 October 1933, when Rabbi Treiger, the newly hired principal of the Toronto Hebrew Free School, faced a sombre board of directors. He informed them that the teachers, who had not been paid for twenty-four weeks, were threatening to quit. The twenty-six-year-old school, colloquially known as the Brunswick Avenue Talmud Torah, was already in dire straits. The mortgage interest arrears on its impressive building on Brunswick Avenue just north of College Street were growing at a shocking rate. Even though the school's expenses had recently been reduced by

$2,500, it still carried an operating deficit of over $3,500 and had little prospect of attracting more money. The big donors had been bled dry. Half the students could not afford to pay tuition (a cost to the school of over $7,000), and the Ladies' Auxiliary was in a state of collapse. Closure of the widely respected communal institution seemed imminent.[1]

But instead, the school survived, prospered, and metamorphosed from a Sunday-through-Thursday after-school Hebrew program into what is now the Associated Hebrew Schools of Toronto, one of the largest Jewish day schools in the world. Its story epitomizes the difficulties faced by Toronto Jewish institutions during the 1930s and illustrates their resourceful responses.

The Talmud Torah's newly revealed financial turmoil sent shock waves through the community because of its unique nature. Its founder, Rabbi Jacob Gordon, had arrived in Toronto in 1905. Shortly thereafter he became rabbi of both the Goel Tzedec and McCaul Street synagogues. He was immediately accepted by the Lithuanian and Russian Jewish communities who formed the majority of Toronto Jewry before the First World War. Gordon was an unusual man – he was one of the few European rabbis from a top *yeshiva* (school of higher learning) to support Zionism. The Volozhin Yeshiva, which he had attended in its declining years, emphasized logical Talmudic scholarship – the trenchant analysis of Jewish legal texts. Significantly, it did not bar its students from discussing the latest discoveries in science and non-Jewish literature. Its students were given a breadth of vision that allowed them to mingle with religious and secular Jews alike. Many of its alumni became exemplars of this tradition and leaders of their generation – the most famous being Rabbi Kook, the chief rabbi of Palestine, who mixed more easily with Socialist Zionist kibbutz pioneers than with the ultra-Orthodox in Jerusalem.

Gordon fit the mould. Active in many communal areas, he made his most lasting contribution by founding the Toronto Hebrew Free School in 1909. The Free School was based on a then-novel concept unique to Volozhin: it was "ideology-free"; its mandate was to teach "ivrit b'ivrit," Hebrew language through immersion, and to instruct its students to be good Jews and good citizens. It made no pretense of ideological judgment but simply applied the latest teaching methods to a disciplined study of Judaism through its ancient and modern sources. The school went from kindergarten to Grade 8, and classes ran after public school hours and on Sundays. Depending on their age, students attended between eight and twelve hours per week.

This concept met with great success in Toronto. Many immigrants were anxious for their children to acculturate without assimilating, and the Free School seemed to offer the best of both worlds. The school developed rapidly, even though the difficulty of finding enough sufficiently trained teachers during the First World War initially inhibited its growth. Only educators who met its stringent criteria were hired, and the school usually had to rely on qualified immigrant teachers or find candidates in New York. Many teachers, and especially administrators, were men of copious secular and Judaic knowledge. The school was so adept at maintaining its mandate that Rabbi Barnett Brickner of Holy Blossom Synagogue was one of its greatest champions.

Brickner's approbation was so powerful that some students from Holy Blossom also attended the downtown Free School. By the 1920s, the student body was the most diverse in Toronto. The original building on Simcoe Street was too small and the community was rapidly moving west. Land was acquired on Brunswick Avenue, and planning began on an unprecedented scale. The new building was to be much more than a school; it was conceived as a Jewish Centre – a concept popularized by educational and ideological visionary Rabbi Mordechai Kaplan, later the founder of Reconstructionist Judaism. He envisioned a building where families could "play, pray, and learn together." Thus, fifteen classrooms were built for eight hundred students, complemented by a library, chapel, and auditorium/banquet hall seating twelve hundred. All this would be connected to the Young Men's Hebrew Athletic (YMHA) Centre, which housed a pool and a gymnasium. Fundraising for the new initiative proved challenging, however, and construction lasted over three years, with significant delays due to cash flow problems.

When the building finally opened in December 1925, it created quite a stir. Its evident extravagance led directly to the school's difficulties. Despite the Free School's amenities, many families still patronized cheaper (though less qualified) private tutors for their children's Jewish education. Nor did other schools conveniently disappear. Indeed, as Polish immigration increased, enrolment in the Eitz Chaim school (Orthodox), the Yiddishist Peretz School, and other secular

Yiddishist schools increased. However, the Free School had one key advantage: its parent body was overwhelmingly drawn from the wealthy Uptowners and upwardly mobile Downtowners attracted by its educational methods and excellent facilities. No other Toronto Jewish institution could boast such wide support. But enrolment never reached its target because of competition from other schools and the rise of congregational schools, as synagogues sprouted up along Spadina Avenue and as far west as the Junction Shul (Knesseth Israel) near Keele Street.

The onset of the Depression served a near mortal blow. In September 1929 the high school had to close, and adult classes were suspended. Only the classes from kindergarten through grade 6 were retained. By 1931 enrolment had fallen to five hundred from over eight hundred, and by October 1933, when the teachers gave their ultimatum, the financial situation was bleak. The board was eager to pay the teachers, but the massive decrease in tuition revenue made this impossible without declaring bankruptcy. Seeking a compromise, the board called a *Va'ad HaChinuch* (Education Committee) meeting for the next day. The *Va'ad* supervised school standards and curriculum, and dealt with other matters directly related to education. Although its decisions required board approval, in practice the board allowed the *Va'ad* to determine educational policy and rubber-stamped its decisions.[2]

The *Va'ad* told the teachers that they would be fired en masse and only those who agreed to reduced salaries would be rehired. The school would pay $5 per week toward each teacher's salary arrears. The teachers would have none of this, especially after the *Va'ad* cited "absolute necessity" to justify the continuation of Rabbi Treiger's $2,000 annual salary. The families of these dedicated teachers were hungry and the staff believed the school's survival was being based on their empty pocketbooks. They reacted with unexpected militancy and threatened mass resignation unless their salaries returned to their 1932 level. The *Va'ad*, recognizing that its teachers were uniquely qualified to deliver the school's pioneering curriculum, had to agree.[3]

The *Va'ad*'s retreat kept the increasingly sullen staff in the classrooms, but the school's perilous financial situation worsened. The operating deficit had increased steadily since the school had moved in late 1925. Despite cost cutting and a rise in tuition revenue, even in good times, there was never any hope of achieving a balanced budget, and certainly not an operating surplus. But the dilemma of maintaining a workable operating budget paled beside the difficulty of meeting the building's mortgage payments.[4]

From the outset, the mortgage had been a great drain on school finances. The decision to expand the function of the building beyond that of an educational facility and equip it as a Jewish Centre, with well-appointed athletic and social facilities brought financial and logistical headaches even before the mortgage difficulties began. The board had been compelled to secure a large bank loan to complete the building. Attempts to economize meant that contractors were forced to cut corners and incompletely fireproof the building, thereby causing a delay in obtaining the municipal building permit. When the building was completed, the school owed $15,000 and had to assume a huge ten-year mortgage of $78,000 at 6.5 percent interest. The lender, Canada Permanent Trust, allowed the payment of interest only (more than $5,000 per year) as long as the board agreed to discharge the principal in full when the term expired. Additional funds were secured by promissory notes underwritten by wealthy supporters. The total debt was over $100,000 and the carrying charges more than $7,000 a year. What was already a burdensome debt in the relatively prosperous years of the mid-1920s became a millstone when the Depression struck. The school was barely able to pay even the interest owed. By 1933 Canada Permanent Trust hinted at foreclosure.[5]

As long as the school continued to accumulate operating deficits, it could never pay off its capital debt burden. Like most Jewish institutions in similar straits, the school's annual campaigns focused on raising enough money to keep the school afloat, and little thought was given to systematically eliminating its rapidly accumulating capital debt. At this point, the Free School's story became unique. Its greatest resource was the diversity of its supporters. Its educational philosophy particularly attracted newly married and upwardly mobile young Jewish professionals, a demographic epitomized by Samuel Godfrey, a prosperous businessman on the board of directors. Alarmed at the spectre of foreclosure, he suggested that "the main problem in financing this institution was the large amount of interest paid yearly on the mortgages [and that] every effort should be made to pay off as much as possible on the mortgage [by the time] it expires in 1935." He had already run the school's annual campaign, and the board paid attention. Moses Gelber, who had just been re-elected president for the tenth consecutive year, directed the board to strike a sub-committee to look for subscribers to help to pay off the mortgage in three years. But this committee was doomed to failure by the economic climate of the Depression and the size of the mortgage. Nonetheless, Godfrey had pinpointed a key strategy for the school's eventual financial salvation.[6]

By August 1934 the teachers had been barely mollified by the payment of one week's back wages raised when the directors emptied their pockets at an emergency meeting. The school re-opened in September but it seemed only a matter of time until it would be forced to close. In October, Canada Permanent Trust demanded ten months' worth of outstanding mortgage interest, the operating deficit increased by another $3,000 despite a successful campaign and drastic cutbacks, and the school owed the teachers thirty weeks of back wages (totalling over $8,000). The directors dipped into their own pockets once again, but the teachers were understandably impatient and tired of their long-standing hand-to-mouth existence. On 8 March 1935, they delivered their final ultimatum: unless the board of directors guaranteed that half of their arrears would be paid out of the proceeds of the school's annual fundraising campaign, they would stop teaching on 15 March. The board responded by scheduling a massive special campaign for 5 May, but offered no guarantee to the teachers. The teachers kept their word. They walked out, and Rabbi Treiger was forced to close the school.[7]

On 20 March the board of directors held an emergency meeting. They realized that the school's only hope of survival lay in following Godfrey's suggestion and dealing with current and capital debts separately. A Building Committee was struck to take responsibility for all building expenses, while a newly created School Committee would raise the funds required for staff salaries. A Provisional Committee of Fifteen was appointed to work out the details of the two-committee plan, and an emergency appeal quickly secured enough to pay three weeks' wages to the teachers.[8]

The Provisional Committee soon decided that unless money was found to meet both the demands of the mortgagor (who had not been paid since 1 December 1933) and the teachers, there was no point in re-opening the school. It was senseless to pay the teachers three weeks' back wages and then hope for a miraculous infusion of campaign proceeds. And it was pointless to re-open the school until concrete solutions to its financial problems had been prepared. To otherwise might lead to another quick closing, which could completely destroy the school's reputation.[9]

Now out of options, the board began the fundraising campaign before its scheduled 5 May launch. At the urging of Joseph I. Oelbaum, a rising board member and businessman who had once served as executive director of the Federation of Jewish Philanthropies, the board hired Abraham Cohn, a professional campaign director from New York. Oelbaum insisted that Cohn's expertise would help the campaign overcome the "inactivity and disinterestedness of the leaders of the community and the public in general" to raise an unprecedentedly large amount of money and justify his salary of $1,500 plus $300 in expenses. Gelber was stunned by Cohn's fee, but Oelbaum and other members of the Provisional Committee allayed his concerns.[10]

Cohn proved the advocates of professional fundraising correct. He set up an efficient campaign machine, directed special attention to previously untapped friendly societies and *landsmanschaften*, and began the campaign in mid-April. Dashing from one speaking engagement to the next, and enthusiastically phoning prospective donors to cajole them into increasing their contribution, Cohn was a revelation of the power of professional fundraising. His dedication lifted the pall of despondency that surrounded the school. For the first time in more than a decade, a large segment of the community pitched in to ensure the school's immediate survival by raising over $18,000. True, the campaign goal had not been completely reached, but far more was donated than ever before, and in less than a month! Cohn's success guaranteed the continuity of professional fundraising in Toronto. Before he left, he reminded the Provisional Committee, composed mostly of young businessmen and professionals, that it was their duty to stay involved and organize a comprehensive plan to ensure the school's long-term survival.[11]

His advice was taken to heart both within and ultimately far beyond the Free School community. Teachers' salary arrears would be the first payment from anticipated campaign revenues, and the school would re-open as soon as possible. On 2 May a committee was empowered "to negotiate with the staff, pay back salaries, dismiss or hire with approval of Rabbi Treiger, and budget for the coming school year." The teachers were understandably nervous, and negotiations proved difficult. But within a week the staff accepted 25 percent of their arrears in cash and the balance in twelve equal instalments, and agreed to let a Board of Arbitrators decide other details. In return, the school rehired all the teachers and guaranteed their employment until October. The school re-opened on 20 May with less than half its pre-closure enrolment, but Treiger was confident that enrolment would return to normal by September.[12]

The fallout of the school's near collapse would decisively change the face of communal fundraising. The school's closure had galvanized the community precisely because other institutions affiliated with or administered by the federation were also on the brink of collapse. Uptowners, many of whom were involved with the school and with the federation, recognized that some type of financial rationalization on a communal basis was immediately required. Here was the chance to bring Toronto in line with other North American Jewish communities, and in the nick of time. Of course, the Downtown community was suspicious of joining a centralized fundraising, for fear of losing their independence. Downtown organizations rooted in traditional *tzedakah* practices preferred independent fundraising campaigns that allowed them to continue operating without any provision for paying off their capital burdens. But this was a dated and economically irresponsible view in the eyes of the federation and the Hebrew Free School Provisional Committee, both of whom shared a more scientific approach to fundraising and financial consolidation. Events would soon draw the two camps together.[13]

With the school re-opened, the School Committee was determined to profit from the lessons learned. It started planning future budgets and set up a Building Committee "to be fed regularly from the Campaign treasury" to make sure that the mortgage would be paid. Canada Permanent Trust, impressed by this approach, delayed foreclosure. The Building Committee then arranged that the YMHA, which already rented large parts of the Brunswick Street building for its own use, enter into a formal partnership with the school. A joint board was elected, and in May 1935 the building was renamed the Jewish Educational and Community Institute of Toronto (JECIT), thus fulfilling a 20-year-old dream of many "Jewish Centre" activists.[14]

Here was a model worth emulating. The financial innovations that would free the school, and ultimately Toronto Jewish institutions, from accumulated capital debts began in August 1935 when a group of young men, including Oelbaum, Godfrey, and Bernard Vise, took

Abraham Cohn's advice to heart. They recruited Charles Foster and Charlie Benjamin (both of whose fathers were active with the school) and drew up a financial plan that would enable the school to pay its capital liabilities and maintain its operating fund at the same time. On 12 September, at the first meeting of the Board of Directors in the 1935–36 academic year, Oelbaum described the plan:

> They [the group of young men] ... decided that they would suggest to the Board that the total liability which had been accumulated for a number of years must be set aside and the school should operate on its current income, without any interference of having to pay towards the old liabilities. They suggested that all the men who have guaranteed to the bank and to the mortgage should take it upon themselves to take care of the interest on the mortgage and the bank loans ... They also suggested that any surplus at the end of the year be handed over to this group to reduce the liability.[15]

Stunned, the board immediately interrogated the group. Vise, a chartered accountant, explained how the cumulative weight of the school's massive capital debts could eventually be eliminated. The board approved. Apt students of fundraiser Cohn, noting that big givers responded to peer pressure and social ambience, the young men determined to make fundraising a social experience. They quickly organized themselves into two groups. Group A took responsibility for paying off the capital debt, while Group B administered the school operating expenses. Group A held an auspicious opening meeting at David and Rose Dunkelman's magnificent estate, while the five founding members of Group B sent out letters to other young businessmen and professionals, inviting them to attend an organizing meeting at the Talmud Torah on 20 October. There, they distributed a number-crammed prospectus illustrating how, with diligence and economy, outstanding loans could be managed. Vise assured the gathering that the plan was simple to implement. In addition, he proposed enlarging Group B to include twenty-five members, and making an immediate start on planning a Spring Campaign while collecting outstanding subscriptions from the previous campaign. To attract communal interest, he proposed inviting Rabbi Mordechai Kaplan, the founder of Reconstructionist Judaism and a dynamic speaker and pioneer of the Jewish Centre concept in North America, to Toronto for a major address.[16]

The Group A and B financial system worked, although not quite as well as Vise had projected. Group A was able to pay over $3,000 of mortgage principal in the first year, while Group B made great strides toward paying off salary arrears, despite a rise in the overdraft. The 1936 Spring Campaign proved to be moderately successful, albeit significantly less so than Cohn's professionally run campaign.[17] The young professionals of Group B drew three vital conclusions from these results: operating costs could only be controlled through the use of proper accounting methods; a professional campaign manager was a good investment; and careful planning was essential to fundraising success in difficult economic conditions. While the school was still not out of its financial difficulties, the commitment to rational problem solving and professionalized fundraising boded well for the future.[18]

Meanwhile, other venerable Toronto institutions were facing a more dismal fate. Less than a mile away, Martin Cohn pondered the fact that the embattled executive of the FJP was experiencing problems similar to those of the Brunswick Avenue Talmud Torah but on a much larger scale. It was clear to him that the federation had lost its sway over its agencies because it had never been able to control their budgets. Furthermore, federation campaigns were insufficient to meet agency needs, not to mention satisfy the sudden demand for funds for educational and overseas relief funding. The federation had also failed to eliminate separate institutional fundraising campaigns and had not attracted new agencies.

At this point, most of the Downtown community's institutions still remained aloof from the federation. As separate institutional campaigns proliferated after 1935, the pressures on the community's largest donors increased – and so did their resentment. Cohn did not know what to do. He had tried everything and failed to attract new blood to the federation. But one day in 1936, as he contemplated the federation's surely approaching demise and the attendant loss of his job, he received a telegram from George Rabinoff. Rabinoff was the associate field director of the New York–based Council of Jewish Federations and Welfare Funds (COJFWF), an American agency founded in 1932 that served to integrate "the burgeoning number of funds that were multiplying because of the demands for overseas relief." He was a missionary for organized fundraising. Rabinoff was trying to organize a Community Chest for Montreal Jewry and told Cohn that he would be coming to Toronto as soon as he was finished. Cohn quickly telegraphed Rabinoff to put him off, but it was too late. Rabinoff was already en route. Cohn picked him up from Union Station and they went to the federation office to discuss the Toronto situation. This chance meeting irrevocably altered the course of Toronto Jewish institutional history.[19]

Rabinoff quickly convinced Cohn that Toronto needed a Welfare Fund. His rationale? A Welfare Fund allowed for non-local scientific fundraising, a key selling point, given the size of Toronto's Downtown community (well over 70 percent of the Jewish population). Given the European situation, demands for overseas relief would doubtless increase and a Welfare Fund model would allow for appropriate funds allocation. The Welfare Fund model would also provide for the maintenance of central financial control and scientific charity management over non-local agencies. This control was vital because separate campaigns were proliferating. Indeed, within minutes after Rabinoff had begun his presentation, Cohn realized that his visitor's ideas "were exactly what I needed." The two became friends and Rabinoff pressed his younger protégé to seek further professional training and apply it to organizing a Welfare Fund in Toronto. He introduced Cohn to Welfare Fund and Community Chest leaders in the United States. Cohn began an extensive correspondence and within a few months had built up a wealth of knowledge about community planning. Rabinoff arranged for Cohn to receive professional training and advice from the Detroit Jewish Federation, whose executive director, Kurt Kaiser, came to Toronto to assist Cohn in the fall of 1936. Cohn was soon thoroughly familiar with the techniques of Welfare Fund planning and became an advocate of systematizing Jewish community life. Now it was time to persuade the communal elite of Toronto to support the Welfare Fund idea.[20]

Cohn was following a path that elsewhere had extended well beyond the Jewish community. By the mid-nineteenth century efforts to coordinate charities were underway in Great Britain and the United States. In 1877 Buffalo, New York, had organized its charitable societies under one non-sectarian umbrella. This new group did not engage directly in fundraising but rather coordinated the work of affiliated agencies, thereby ensuring against agency overlap and helping direct clients to the proper social service after evaluating their needs. This central office eventually became the Buffalo Community Chest. Its methods spread rapidly through North America over the next three decades. Agencies appreciated keeping their financial independence while dealing with the appropriate clientele. By 1914 mass immigration and urbanization had raised new challenges, as agency caseloads soared and budgets became tightened. These challenges were met by the rapid rise of social work and sociology, which focused increased attention on the problems of urban living. Sociologists and social workers joined other reformers in insisting that community-wide fundraising was the only way to finance and eliminate overlap among social service agencies serving the poor. By the mid-1930s, the financial demands of the Depression on community institutions was accelerating the growth of Welfare Funds and Community Chests across North America. In fact, Rabinoff agreed to mentor Cohn because he believed that Toronto's lack of a Welfare Fund had left the Toronto Jewish community lagging behind its North American peers.[21]

Almost three decades behind, in fact. The first successful American attempt at community-wide fundraising had occurred in Cincinnati in 1908. There, Jewish social service agencies had convinced their Protestant and Catholic counterparts of the necessity of this approach. It was not surprising that Jewish agencies were the agents of change because communal fundraising was founded on traditional Jewish values. For centuries, organized Jewish communities had gone to great lengths to ensure that the poor among them would always be aided. Judaism looked upon giving as a form of social justice, and argued that the highest stage of *tzedakah* was helping the recipient attain self-reliance and financial independence through employment. This also became the ultimate goal of the social workers involved in charity in the late nineteenth and early twentieth centuries.[22]

The Cincinnati campaign was enormously successful and spawned similar Community Chests in other major cities, organizations that were inter-denominational, communally centralized, and which acted as fundraising agencies for social services. However, it was also clear to American pioneers of Jewish community fundraising that without communal planning and agency coordination to eliminate overlap and improve professional standards, the funds raised by the Community Chests would not be put to optimum use. Therefore, by the early 1920s, American social workers had convinced the businessmen who had initiated most Community Chests that "a federation of social welfare agencies of some kind was helpful to the community chest." This understanding led to the rise of the Protestant, Catholic, and Jewish federations, which combined federated fundraising and communal planning. They spread rapidly through North America between 1910 and 1940.[23]

In the United States, the movement toward federated fundraising often involved several religious groups uniting under one fundraising umbrella. Such ecumenism was impossible in a more sectarian country such as Canada, however. Toronto religious groups worked separately toward more intra-faith rationalized fundraising and communal planning. The Protestant community made repeated attempts between 1881 and 1912 to establish some form of central organization for the various charitable organizations. In 1913 Catholics established a charitable association that coordinated the work of several Catholic charitable and social welfare organizations but exercised no control over fundraising. However, Toronto's Jewish community lacked this unity. The formation of the Associated Hebrew Charities in 1912 had only "provided a central depot for the collection of information and the distribution of relief." It made no attempt to coordinate fundraising campaigns or set communal priorities.[24]

This tendency was mirrored in the non-Jewish community. The years between the end of the First World War and the Depression were filled with inter-organizational squabbles over the control of communal planning in Toronto. The non-sectarian Federation for Community Service (FCS) was founded in Toronto in 1919, but its first campaign raised only 38 percent of its $1.5 million objective. The FCS survived until 1943 but its impact remained limited. Toronto was just too divided by religious feuding. In 1927 the Catholics withdrew from the FCS over allegations that they had not contributed their share to the campaign. They formed the Federation of Catholic Charities, which proved to be very successful at both fundraising and social planning.[25]

The FCS did not invite Jewish agencies to affiliate, although the Federation of Jewish Philanthropies, founded in 1920, did establish working relationships with some FCS member agencies and embraced accepted social work techniques. Its development, as we have seen, was modelled on the Jewish Federation movement in the United States but, unlike the Protestant and Catholic federations and unlike Jewish federations in the United States at this time, the FJP never commanded the loyalty of the entire Jewish community. Thus, the years between 1927 and 1943 saw annual campaigns in Toronto run by the Protestant, Jewish, and Catholic federations. In the case of the Jewish community, as noted, many agencies also ran their own conflicting parallel campaigns.[26]

With parallel campaigns the order of the day, Cohn wondered how to gain support in Toronto for the idea of a Welfare Fund. He knew that the largest donors were indignant about the proliferation of appeals and he believed they would support a well-planned rationalization of fundraising. But how could he present this idea in a way that would entice the Jewish agencies to buy in? Not by reviving the federation. It was discredited and the Downtown community had never supported it. Cohn realized that only a completely new organization, a Welfare Fund such as Rabinoff had proposed, would be capable of drawing support from all major Jewish institutions.

He took his idea to Ben Sadowski. The son of eastern European immigrants, Sadowski had made a fortune in the automobile business and was now one of Holy Blossom's leading lights. He affected the lifestyle of an English gentleman and reminded Cohn of "some of the old German Jews – more sophisticated and more attuned to the *goyim* [Gentiles]." Sadowski, then in his mid-forties, was a University of Toronto graduate in Math and Physics who hated inefficiency and consequently had cut back on his charitable contributions to Jewish organizations. But his brother-in-law Bernard Vise had kept Sadowski abreast of developments in the Brunswick Avenue Talmud Torah and the Jewish community at large. When Cohn informed Sadowski that he needed his financial backing and personal help to make the proposed Welfare Fund a success, Sadowski agreed to become involved. He did not share Cohn's belief that Downtowner institutions were needed in the proposed Welfare Fund. But, tired of being hounded repeatedly for funds, and, most important, wishing to be perceived as a community leader, he agreed to help.[27]

After convincing Sadowski, Cohn approached Arthur Cohen, a prominent lawyer and also a member of Holy Blossom. Cohen had been active on the board of the FTP in its twilight years and believed in systematic fundraising. Cohen was perceived as a cynical and often aloof man, less than enamoured of Yiddish culture. He had been disappointed by the federation's failure to produce communal unity. He wanted ruthless institutional consolidation to eliminate overlapping services and supported Canadianizing immigrant-based institutions like the Folks Farein and *landsmanschaften*. Like Sadowski, Cohen regarded inefficiency as the supreme vice, and his federation experiences had convinced him that a centralized fundraising agency might be able to control communal planning successfully. In addition, he relished the company of others who shared his point of view and who were ready to use financial leverage to mould the community in a manner more compatible with their objectives.[28]

But the communal objectives and social aspirations of Sadowski and Cohen would certainly not attract Downtown support. The Uptowners still lacked the clout to impose their communal vision. Cohn realized that his proposal also needed someone who sympathized with the businesslike approach of Cohen and Sadowski but was in addition respected by the Downtowners and their institutions. Sam Godfrey was the perfect candidate. He was a Yiddish-speaking Orthodox Jew, but, as we have seen, he had used the most modern and administratively efficient business techniques to resolve the Brunswick Avenue Talmud Torah crisis. Although financially successful and religiously observant, he mixed easily with everyone. Cohn convinced Godfrey that his presence would ensure that the Talmud Torah and other Downtown institutions would share authority within the proposed fund. Godfrey, long an advocate of communal consolidation, agreed to help organize the Welfare Fund.[29]

The four men met in late 1936 and mapped out a plan to maximize institutional participation in the proposed fund. They then asked J.I. Oelbaum, a former federation executive director, to join them. Oelbaum's father, Moses, was a pillar of Toronto Orthodoxy, but like his friend Moses Gelber and like Godfrey, Moses Oelbaum was also a highly successful businessman. J.I. Oelbaum was not as observant as his father, but his background made him ideologically closer to Godfrey than to Sadowski or Cohen. While his tenure with the federation indicated his commitment to scientific administration, his desire to seek communal unity made him acceptable to the Holy Blossom group that dominated the federation board. All agreed to prioritize curtailing the multiplicity of campaigns, which had alienated the larger donors. Shades of difference persisted: Sadowski and Godfrey were especially interested in using the proposed fund to achieve greater communal unity, while Sadowski and Oelbaum were advocates of businesslike rationalization of spending.[30]

All five were in agreement that there was no hope of carrying on successfully under the federation masthead. But the Holy Blossomites and the traditionalists reached this conclusion for different reasons. As Cohn trenchantly observed: "Sadowski, Cohen, and I took for granted and tacitly agreed the strategy must be to ... appear to start afresh. Godfrey, typical of those close to the Orthodox community, took for granted that the Federation was outdated and had to be superseded." These seemingly small differences forced some delicate compromises. To avoid alienating the Holy Blossomites, it was announced that Cohn was "on loan" to the Welfare Fund from the FJP. Meanwhile, Downtown fears of being swallowed by the Uptown establishment were mollified by the creation of a completely new organization, which would allot equal representation to all constituent organizations.[31]

In early February 1937 the Committee of Five was ready to start organizing the United Jewish Welfare Fund of Toronto (UJWF). The first and most vital requirement was to have an accurate assessment of communal needs. The committee sent letters to the Toronto Hebrew Free School, the Canadian Jewish Congress, the Federation of Jewish Philanthropies (including its network of beneficiary agencies), Folks Farein, *geverkshaften*, the Jewish Immigrant Aid Society, the Joint Distribution Committee, *Mizrachi*, Mount Sinai Hospital, the Toronto Jewish Old Folks' Home, the People's Organization for Rehabilitation through Training (ORT), Toronto Hebrew Free Loan, Eitz Chaim Talmud Torah, and the United Palestine Appeal. These organizations represented virtually all of Toronto Jewry except for the Communists and the unions. Each organization was asked to send the committee audited financial statements for 1934 through 1936, as well as a list of subscribers and campaign workers. These documents would provide an accurate financial picture of the participating organizations, and the lists of workers and subscribers could then be consolidated into a master UJWF list.[32]

How could these five men expect to succeed where the FJP had failed? They had a simple answer: the paradigmatic Brunswick Talmud Torah experience and the continuing Depression. They gambled that access to an unprecedentedly large and deep-pocketed group of donors would convince all these agencies to file audited statements to guarantee their financial security. The stakes were high, but the group was resolute, recognizing that determination was the key to creating a systematic basis for the fundraising and allocation essential to the proposed UJWF's success.

Most invitations were accepted. Some agencies resented this intrusion into their books, but the Brunswick Talmud Torah's restructuring catalyzed the majority to commit to ensuring institutional survival in the Depression economy. What is more, it was impossible to deny the political and financial clout of the Committee of Five. Among themselves, they were connected to every major Jewish donor in Toronto.

The rest of the organizing work read like the script of a fundraising magazine. The Committee of Five canvassed the top one hundred donors and got them on side. Each constituent organization was informed that its workers would now canvass exclusively for the UJWF. Only after Cohn, Sadowski, Cohen, Godfrey, and Oelbaum were certain their proposal had the financial backing of the top community contributors did they present the plan for the fund to the organizations. By then, all the agencies had submitted the required lists and financial statements, and with the major donors onside, were at least willing to give the UJWF proposal a hearing.[33]

On 19 May 1937 the organizational representatives listened to Martin Cohn's presentation of the UJWF proposal. He was quick to allay concerns that the UJWF would impose its will on its constituents (this type of imposition had been partially responsible for the FJP's demise), pledging that "the Joint Campaign [would] not control the internal activities of the beneficiary organizations." In fact, during its first year, each organization could keep the proceeds of all bazaars, balls, and other small fundraising activities as long as these activities were disclosed to the UJWF in advance and the revenue received from them was recorded on its audited annual statements. Organizations would also be allowed to retain all annual membership dues of $5 or less. Each organization's initial annual allocation would be equivalent to the percentage its campaign target represented of the Welfare Fund's campaign target. To make calculations simpler, the fund omitted capital costs and dealt only with operating budgets. Cohn also explained that the leading donors had pledged to donate to the fund the total amount they had given to the various campaigns the year before. Most delegates responded enthusiastically; the others were at least willing to take the proposal to their boards.³⁴

Cohn also made it very clear that the UJWF prioritized rationalized fundraising as a means to scientific communal planning. He outlined what are now accepted as the standard reasons for supporting a centralized welfare fund:

> This project need not be considered only as a fundraising means of getting more money for each individual organization. A joint campaign is one of the most important ways of developing a better spirit of communal unity, and of planning in the best interests of the community as a whole. In entering into such a project, there must be a spirit of give and take among the organizations and a realization that they are joining not just in their own interest but in the interest of the community as a whole. It is the aim of each organization to serve the community as effectively as possible. The community can be served more effectively through joint and cooperative effort.³⁵

The organizations had two weeks to decide whether they wished to participate in the UJWF. The meeting concluded with the election of a "Committee of 21," which would serve as a Provisional Committee until a more formal organizational structure could be established.

Most of the organizations wasted little time debating the matter. Money was scarce and the fund's Committee of Five, unlike the federation, had consulted them before taking action. It had also made provision for continued consultation and had promised not to interfere in their internal affairs. It was too good a deal to refuse. Besides, the big donors were already in the UJWF's pocket, so to speak, and nothing would be forthcoming for organizations that refused affiliation. The Toronto Zionists were so delighted that they defied Archie Freiman's demand that the United Palestine Appeal never affiliate itself with another campaign and signed on to the Welfare Fund plan. On 16 June, when the top hundred donors met with organizational representatives to give final approval to the Welfare Fund proposal and to elect campaign leaders, only Mount Sinai Hospital, the Jewish Immigrant Aid Society, and Eitz Chaim Talmud Torah remained uncommitted. Eitz Chaim, bastion of immigrant Polish Orthodoxy, was soon persuaded by necessity to join the fund. Tellingly, its books were so muddled that it took over a year to meet the required standard. The Toronto JIAS was prevented from joining by Montreal headquarters, which feared any diminution of its power. Mount Sinai remained the sole agency that believed it did not need the Fund.[36]

On 16 June, Cohen, Godfrey, and Sadowski were chosen as joint chairmen of the first UJWF campaign. Other prominent men such as the Allen brothers, owners of many Toronto movie houses, Percy Hermant of Imperial Optical, David Dunkelman of Tip Top Tailors, and the two grand old men of Toronto Orthodoxy, Moses Gelber and Moses Oelbaum, were among those elected to serve as vice-chairmen. The campaign executive was composed of two representatives from each organization. Each was responsible for ensuring a quota of workers to assist in the campaign scheduled for 7 to 22 November, with an unprecedented goal of $170,000.[37]

The campaign organizers, leaving nothing to chance, hired Harold Altschul, a top-notch professional fundraiser, to run the campaign. He arrived in August to find work on the campaign organization well underway and quickly selected David Vise as campaign auditor. Vise methodically ensured the accuracy of each participating institution's audited statement so that budget allotments would accurately reflect need. Treasurers quickly learned that Vise expected facts, not estimates, and he wanted them yesterday. This often meant a dramatic tightening of accounting procedures, laying the groundwork for more efficient money management in future years. It also served as a reminder that all community needs would be seriously assessed. The simple act of organizational representatives meeting together under Welfare Fund auspices forced participants to confront both overlap in services and gaps in programming. It also helped these men and women to look beyond organizational parochialism. On this basis, the UJWF became the bedrock of community building from the moment of its inception.[38]

The campaign kickoff was a masterpiece of organization and deft public relations. With the top givers onside and the great majority of key communal institutions supporting the campaign, the public responded generously. Altschul built for the future by developing a large donor base supported by all classes of contributors. His public relations machine, based on well-trained, "homegrown" English and Yiddish speakers, was very successful in attracting smaller donors to the campaign – and every one of them was welcomed. Uptown and Downtown came together – everyone felt valued.

Altschul understood that the Welfare Fund's job went far beyond eliminating overlapping campaigns; he wished to make it the agent of community building. Its mission, he argued, was to train a new group of leaders in community planning and reduce the intra-ethnic and religious turf battles that plagued Toronto Jewry. Altschul knew that the Welfare Fund's success depended greatly on the efficacy of its canvassers, who, in contrast to previous campaigns, were formally trained in fundraising techniques to maximize potential contributions. Canvassing was distilled into a science, with best practices adapted from other successful North American Community Chest and Welfare Fund campaigns. There would be no telephone solicitation. Each canvasser was expected to make a personal call on each potential donor and, to induce maximum contributions, emphasize that "the Fund replaced 23 separate fundraising appeals and 23 knocks on the donor's door." The canvasser was also issued "assignment cards," which contained a donation history and the fraternal affiliations of all established subscribers. It was immediately clear to the canvasser whether a donor was contributing up to expectations and, if not, the donor was pressured to do so.[39]

Breakthrough techniques were introduced. Altschul's main target was the 2,500 prospects who had never contributed to any campaign. They were vitally important because they could widen the donor base and take pressure off the big givers. Canvassers for this group were given a special card. Altschul told them: "Most of [these 2,500 prospects] are able to give something ... Until now they have been a drain on the community and a source of fruitless expense in postage and literature." He calculated that "most of these prospects could give at least $10 per year." An extra $25,000 represented a significant amount in a city that "had the smallest number of contributors to Jewish social programs of any city of its size on the North American continent."[40]

This type of scientific campaigning created a great deal of paperwork. In addition to collecting funds, each canvasser had to fill in a special form if the prospect refused to donate or if there was reason to suspect that someone had not given enough. All reports were reviewed daily by campaign headquarters. Tedious it surely was, but the information produced a detailed community donor profile that would be vital for future campaigns. Canvassers were repeatedly told to emphasize that this was "a united campaign for a united community," that people who could afford a $10 cash donation could afford another $30 per annum on an instalment basis, and that all pledges of less than $5 must be paid in cash.[41]

Many volunteers found the work boring, but every contribution stimulated a feeling of accomplishment and solidarity. Canvassers socialized with each other at three "short and snappy" campaign report sessions combined with a much anticipated and nominally priced lunch at the spiffy King Edward Hotel.[42]

Canvassing of top givers was reserved for their peers, and wealthy canvassers had every reason to pull in all they could from those marked as likely big donors. Sadowski, Cohen, and Godfrey "got the hell out there and worked. If they were going to get stuck for money they wanted to make sure their associates got stuck for money." Playing on the desire of the wealthy to be seen as successful community leaders and stalwarts brought in record revenues. Leading donors competed with each other to donate, and persuaded others.[43]

On the eve of the campaign, despite careful preparations, a cautious Altschul warned his troops that "Welfare Funds are not always a howling success in their first years." Toronto's was. It exceeded its goal, enabling the fund to pay allocations in full, completely cover campaign costs, and set aside $5,500 as a surplus for 1938. This smashing success guaranteed the fund's continued existence, and more important, "it brushed away all continuing resentment and debate over the position of the Fund compared to that of the Federation." In May 1938, the UJWF applied to the Ontario government for a provincial charter. When the request was granted on 31 May, the fund formally replaced the federation as the key Jewish community agency responsible for communal fundraising and social planning. A watershed in communal organization had been reached.[44]

This success left other agencies eager to jump on the bandwagon. The 1938 campaign attracted some new agencies, among them the Jewish Community Centre Association (JCCA) and the Federation of Polish Jews, whose presence reflected unprecedented *amcha* support among the *landsmanschaften*. Fund leaders proved flexible recruiters: a number of schools not yet formally accepted into the fund received allocations because of their desperate situation. In turn, each recipient school promised to submit correctly audited statements the following year to qualify for admission. The 1938 campaign fell slightly short of its $170,000 goal, but the careful budgetary techniques, which included a 4 percent allowance for "shrinkage" (the difference between the pledge and the final donation), low administrative costs due to the large number of volunteer workers, and the 1937 surplus allowed the 1938 campaign to more than meet its goal.[45]

Success heightened expectations, and pressures on the UJWF increased. In 1937 and 1938, 4 percent of the campaign allocations had sufficed to cover overseas relief, but after Kristallnacht it became obvious that the fund would have to greatly increase its overseas relief allocations. Domestic needs were equally pressing. The assumption of the FJP debt and the huge allocations required to maintain the Family Welfare Bureau (FWB) were by this time straining the fund's capacity. In 1937, 74 percent of the funds raised had been spent within the community. Under the pressure of increased administrative and campaign costs, this proportion declined in 1938 to 65 percent.

It was clear that every effort had to be made to control these expenses, but how? Cohn and his UJWF publicity director, Florence Hutner, once again turned to Rabinoff for advice. He produced a Welfare Fund constitution that grouped the beneficiary agencies according to their common interests in order to keep the fund's administration from becoming overly complex as more organizations joined. The constitution divided the UJWF into four divisions. Division I included personal service and relief agencies, Division II was for Jewish educational agencies, Division III was the Central Division of Congress, and Division IV was for non-local agencies dealing with off-shore needs. This arrangement was formalized in late 1939 when a permanent Board of Directors was elected to replace the Provisional Committee, which had guided the fund through its first two years.[46]

The UJWF now wielded great power over its constituent agencies. Despite promises to the contrary, it was soon apparent that demands for financial order and accountability would by necessity lead to interference in agency internal affairs. By early 1939, the UJWF Budget Committee was complaining about agencies that deliberately incurred deficits and then passed their debt along to the fund. The committee recommended that the fund review its promise not to interfere in the internal affairs of the agencies where and when that policy might lead to "communal financial instability." A few agencies were unprepared for UJWF monitoring – monitoring that would tighten during the war years – but few member agencies and organizations challenged the fund's power. Most agencies were thrilled at their newfound financial security and embraced future planning with confidence. Others, most former FJP constituent agencies, had boards dominated by social workers committed to imposing professionalization and organizational accountability. They served as the UJWF's organizational cheerleaders.[47]

Predictably, only the Central Division of the Canadian Jewish Congress was perturbed by the success of the UJWF. The fund had appeared on the scene just as Central Division secured enough financial support to become independent of Montreal and was beginning to focus on raising its Toronto profile. But the Divisional Executive joined the UJWF because its exhausting battle for organizational survival and failed fundraising campaigns made the concept of an annual allocation irresistible. Significantly, the Divisional Executive believed that the UJWF would remain only a fundraising agency and that the field of community organization and planning would be left to them. By 1939 they learned the truth – but by then it was after the fact. Yet ironically, as we shall see, the fund would later shield Central Division from domination by a rejuvenated Montreal head office when Sam Bronfman became Congress president.

The Welfare Fund and Central Division make a study in contrasts. The division's workers were untrained volunteers recruited by the well-meaning Hannaniah Caiserman in an effort to forge communal unity. Until Oscar Cohen became its executive secretary in mid-1936, Central Division lacked capable professional direction. Caiserman's failure to present his "Congress plan" and delegate responsibility effectively left even dedicated supporters unsure of how to transform Caiserman's idealistic vision into organizational reality. The Welfare Fund, on the other hand, was the creation of professional community organizers whose businesslike methods lured donors with deep pockets. Using the progressivist belief in professionalism gleaned from their university training, UJWF leaders enlisted the support of businessmen who were committed to financial and bureaucratic efficiency and accountability and were determined to see these values reshape communal planning. With their overlapping agendas and different organizational styles, the Canadian Jewish Congress and the UJWF were destined for sparks. Their clash would last a decade.[48]

Given the fund's organizational advantages, Oscar Cohen undertook to ensure that Central Division did not become a mere administrative appendage of the UJWF. Cohen was determined to maintain Central Division as an independent centre of planning and research, especially on issues such as community relations, government affairs, anti-Semitism, and international concerns. This effort to remain independent became an ongoing struggle.[49]

In the years before the Second World War, Central Division became particularly restive in its efforts to steer a course between Montreal's orders and the embrace of the UJWF. The fund was not all-powerful, however. The United Palestine Appeal withdrew from the fund in 1939 when Freiman reasserted his insistence that Zionist campaigns had to proceed undiluted. It would take almost a decade for them to rejoin, but the other original agencies remained and new ones came on board. The birth of the UJWF had shown them that they shared many common goals. Working together at planning meetings and canvassing lunches helped bridge some of the Downtown-Uptown gap. This growing sense of accord came at an opportune time. But storm clouds were gathering over Europe even as Toronto's institutional unity finally emerged. The outbreak of war would propel the Canadian Jewish Congress forward as the voice of Canadian Jewry, undercut the already waning power of Downtown Jewry, and further strengthen the social service network that fell under the UJWF umbrella.[50]

Against this backdrop, Congress retained its pretensions to communal oversight. After January 1939 new president Samuel Bronfman spared neither energy nor expense to invigorate the creaking bureaucracy bound together tenuously by Caiserman's correspondence. From its revitalized Montreal headquarters, Congress would again seek to impose its hegemony over an often independent-minded Central Division, especially in the areas of immigrant absorption, lobbying for Jewish rights, and immigrant settlement. A clash was in the offing. An organizational turf war would shortly break out, not only between Uptown and Downtown but also between Toronto and Montreal. The prize to the winning organization? The right to impose its will and vision on Toronto Jewish community life. The following chapters narrate how this local war played out in the context of the Second World War, the revelations of the Holocaust, and the rebirth of the State of Israel.

7
Institutional and Communal Consolidation, 1938–43

Hannaniah Meir Caiserman may not have been a stellar administrator, but without his constant stream of entreaties, in both Yiddish and English, the Canadian Jewish Congress (CJC) would have collapsed again shortly after its rebirth in 1933. Indeed, if he had not kept the vision of the original Congress of 1920 alive, the organization would not even have been resuscitated. In response to his eloquently penned pleas, a trickle of funds continued to reach Congress's Montreal head office, but they were barely enough to sustain the organization, let alone pay Caiserman's salary. Fortunately his wife was a successful businesswoman, and he could spend his time fighting for the organization's existence. At the moment, Congress was on life support.

The weakness of the Congress headquarters made it easier for Toronto's Central Division to determine an independent course of action and increasingly assert its autonomy. And Caiserman, burdened by distance, a lack of administrative skill, and an empty chequebook, could only make occasional fruitless forays to Toronto or fulminate through correspondence. By 1938 a steady stream of money from the United Jewish Welfare Fund (UJWF) ensured Central Division's financial stability and augmented its autonomy. As the future of German and Polish Jewry darkened after 1936, Congress's ambition to be a national spokesagency was in jeopardy. Caiserman knew drastic action had to be taken to raise the organization's national profile quickly. He rose to the occasion, and recruited whiskey tycoon Samuel Bronfman to the Congress cause in late 1938. Bronfman's business acumen and funds would reinvigorate the Montreal head office and totally reverse the dynamic between head office and Central Division. A battle for organizational supremacy ensued that would last a decade and colour all national and regional Congress activities.

For many in Canada, the news of Bronfman's acceptance of the Congress presidency immediately made the Fourth Plenary worthy of particular attention. In ordinary times, the Fourth Plenary of the Canadian Jewish Congress in January 1939 would have been a gala event. Participants from Jewish communities coast to coast would have an opportunity to assemble, examine, discuss, and devise communal responses to the issues confronting Canadian and world Jewry. The networking would help establish and strengthen the personal and institutional ties on which Congress's existence depended.

But these were not ordinary times. The Plenary was overshadowed by a sense of foreboding as delegates exchanged reports of Kristallnacht and intensified Nazi anti-Jewish legislation, rampant anti-Semitism in Poland and Romania, and letters from anguished relatives begging their families to bring them to Canada. Few delegates yet knew of Canada's obstructionist performance at the Evian Conference and the Department of Immigration's refusal to admit qualified immigrants with substantial capital. Only top CJC officials realized that Mackenzie King's non-committal answers to the desperate requests of *shtadlanim* reflected Jewish political weakness. But even if Jewish concerns carried no weight in Ottawa, *amcha* still demanded that Congress take any action it could to save European Jewry. For many Canadian Jews "the oppressed had names and faces; each was a father or a sister, a cousin or a friend." Even if its efforts were rebuffed by Ottawa, Congress must do something. But what?[1]

The events of Kristallnacht had compelled Central Division to join a series of nation-wide public protests sponsored by Congress. In terms of publicity, the Toronto protest held in Maple Leaf Gardens on the afternoon of 20 November 1938 was highly successful. But when it came to the immigration of Jews, Prime Minister King remained unmoved even by a groundswell of English Canadian revulsion at the Nazis' actions. King's position, albeit morally unforgivable, could be rationalized in terms of Canadian political geography. The government reasoned that Canadians might be sympathetic to those being persecuted, but would reject any notion that they should be allowed, let alone encouraged, to enter Canada. Any political party that advocated Jewish immigration would be punished at the polls and no amount of Canadian Jewish lobbying would make it otherwise. "We would have needed zealots of stature," recalled Central Division Executive Secretary Oscar Cohen, "and even then, I doubt if we had the vigour or stature we needed to achieve success." The battle against immigration restrictions confirmed that techniques of mass protest were no more successful than the subtler approaches of the cap-in-hand *shtadlanim*. It became starkly evident to Congress and Canadian Jewry that they lacked political leverage.

But Canadian Jews could not acquiesce in political impotence. They had to do whatever was necessary to bring in their loved ones, and for many that meant doing whatever was necessary to obtain a permit. Their negative experiences with Canadian immigration authorities had made them desperate and wary. Immigration became a game of hardball between desperate families and the Immigration Department with the JIAS or steamship agents acting as middlemen. In early 1937 the society advised its member organizations: "Don't let anyone try and convince you that ... there are no immigration problems by reason of restricted immigration ... On the contrary, the less immigration permitted, the more complicated the problems that arise." Many discovered this first hand. Nathan Wilson, a prominent Toronto businessman and member of the JIAS board, for instance, sought to sponsor Polish relatives, a couple with three young children, in May 1937. He deposited $5,000 in their bank account (while the JIAS turned a blind eye) to provide the required assurance that they would not become "public charges." By July Wilson found that the government now regarded $5,000 as "insufficient" and that it would take "at least twice that to interest the department in the case and obtain a permit." The Department of Immigration also expressed concerns that if this family was admitted, they might in turn apply for their relatives. The family did not get a permit; they died in Treblinka. Similar stories abounded, and attentive observers drew conclusions. Even before Kristallnacht, observed JIAS executive director Solkin, the Canadian government was using every means at its disposal to block Jewish immigrants: "When the immigrant has parents, or other relatives, the case is refused outright, whether these parents are young or old, rich or poor." Thus united in despair, Canadian Jewry briefly closed ranks behind Congress, in the hope of somehow prying open Canada's bolted gates. But by late 1938, Congress was unsure how much longer it could keep *amcha* loyalty without winning any change in government immigration policy.[2]

Some had already given up on Congress. What use was it if it could not effectively lobby for increased immigration? And for that matter, what use was a Jewish Immigrant Aid Society that could not obtain immigration permits? By summer 1938 it was once again widely believed that Toronto steamship agents could more readily obtain permits than the JIAS. They certainly could not have done worse. In the two and a half years between January 1937 and the outbreak of war, with Frederick C. Blair in control of the Department of Immigration, the Toronto JIAS was only able to obtain thirty-two permits, allowing sixty-two immigrants to come to Toronto. This represented less than 5 percent of JIAS applicants.[3]

Of course, neither Congress nor the JIAS was to blame for this gloomy picture, but Jewish frustration was more easily turned against communal leadership than against government. If frustrated Canadian Jews withdrew their support, the financial reverberations could reach beyond Congress to the United Jewish Welfare Fund (UJWF) and its system of professionally administered communal fundraising. It was obvious to the leaders of Toronto Jewry that they needed to restore the authority of Congress, despite the inherent inter-organizational rivalry, to demonstrate that this "parliament of Canadian Jewry" could yet have impact.

No one realized this more than Caiserman, the indefatigable Congress executive secretary. He was still certain that a concerted and well-funded public relations effort backed by sympathetic non-Jewish organizations would increase European Jewish immigration. This effort, however, was an expensive proposition for the chronically debt-ridden Congress head office. Obviously a new source of funds would have to be found, and Caiserman accepted the unenviable task of persuading Bronfman to be that source. The wealthy and controversial whiskey entrepreneur and Liberal stalwart had scorned Congress when it was revived in 1933, and had shown little interest in the Downtown Jews of Montreal and Toronto, with their siren calls for action. He had refused to follow the lead of other members of the Canadian Jewish Committee who affiliated with Congress, choosing to devote his time and considerable funds to the Boy Scout movement, the Canadian Red Cross, and the Montreal Jewish General Hospital.[4]

The Caiserman-Bronfman meeting was not one of equals. Caiserman needed Bronfman and Bronfman knew it. But Caiserman led off with an attack, claiming that he held Bronfman "personally responsible for the fact that a group of the richest leaders in the community" did not contribute to Congress. Congress's failures were, in his view, Bronfman's failures. But Bronfman threw the blame back into Caiserman's court, claiming that certain Congress leaders had insulted him. He also averred that he was "seriously thinking of completely withdrawing all his support of Jewish causes and dedicating his philanthropy to such channels that [would] spare him a continuous crucifixion." Caiserman cannily sensed that Bronfman was not so much angry but demanding to be courted. He promised to obtain a letter of apology to salvage Bronfman's pride, and then invited the distiller to accept the presidency of Congress, left vacant by S.W. Jacobs's death in September 1938.[5]

Repairing Bronfman's wounded pride was a necessary prerequisite for ending his estrangement from Congress. But Bronfman, too, had an agenda. He also had been shaken by the events of Kristallnach and understood that Congress, despite its lack of prestige, remained the only national Jewish voice speaking out on the refugee issue. His money and an infusion of new leadership might give him and the organization a more powerful lease on life. And by helping the Jewish community in its hour of need he would also be doing himself little harm. Perhaps, just perhaps, if the Liberals were to recognize him as "King of the Jews," he would be rewarded with a senate seat and the social acceptance he had long craved.[6]

Bronfman demanded complete organizational control in return for his beneficence. He was already in charge of the Montreal Jewish General Hospital and would accept nothing less in return for opening his wallet to Congress. He wanted to reorganize the personnel and management system of head office completely and re-establish control over the divisions. He knew that Caiserman was a poor administrator and informed him that he would be replaced as executive secretary within a year. Caiserman predictably placed Congress above himself and wisely agreed. The whiskey magnate's business skills and financial clout offered the sole hope of reorganizing Congress into an effective lobby for Jewish refugee immigration and other issues of Jewish concern.[7]

As Congress president, Bronfman quickly put his stamp on the organization. He possessed excellent organizational skills, useful contacts, and a legendary ability to attract talented personnel. Whatever Canadian Jews thought of his business methods and his brushes with the law, he was generous with his money and connections. He believed the immigration campaign was winnable with sufficient funds, efficient organization, and careful publicity. Within a month of his formal election at the Fourth Plenary, Bronfman's presence was felt at Congress headquarters. The office was transformed from a sleepy little backwater staffed by the overworked Caiserman and a single secretary, into a modern suite of rooms with a tony address on rue Ste-Catherine, three secretaries, and an updated filing system. The aftershocks of Bronfman's assuming power were not long in reaching Toronto.

The vacuum produced by Caiserman's inefficiency and tendency to act as a mediator rather than a director had allowed the fiscally stronger Central Division to stake out an independent role. This suited Central Division president Bennett's plan to enhance the division's influence and prestige in Toronto. Until now, Congress's mere survival on a national level was an achievement that had been made possible by Central Division's monopoly status as the national voice of Canadian Jewry, however weak, and by the support of the Uptown Toronto elite. The successful establishment of the UJWF in 1937 assured the division of more funding. During 1938, the executive had expanded its role in Toronto Jewish communal planning: the Joint Public Relations Committee of Congress (JPRC) and B'nai Brith began its long uphill battle against anti-Semitism.

Bennett had also taken the first step toward Congress's long-stated goal of communal planning by striking a Youth Committee. Members of this committee, the majority of whom were between sixteen and thirty years old, felt alienated from communal life, and were frustrated by high unemployment and anti-Semitism in the workplace. Bennett worked with the Family Welfare Bureau to create vocational guidance programs and laid the groundwork for a systematic study of anti-Semitism in the workplace.[8]

The resurgent Central Division had also participated in the campaign to increase Jewish immigration to Canada. Before Bronfman became president, Caiserman had often looked to Toronto for assistance and consultation in his efforts to change immigration policy. Bennett, knowing the importance of immigration for *amcha*, led Congress into the immigration field both in their interests and in an effort to marginalize the JIAS.

Events conspired against any progress. Immediately after the *Anschluss* and Roosevelt's announcement of the Evian Conference, Toronto's *amcha* expected Bennett to endorse public meetings to lobby for Canadian attendance at Evian. None were sent. *Shtadlanut* reasserted itself. The Uptowners griped: couldn't *amcha* ever understand that influential insiders were working quietly behind the scenes to change immigration policy? Any heavy-handed public demonstrations would undermine their efforts. Bennett, a former *amcha* advocate, now demanded that Downtowners "take no action relative to the refugee question inasmuch as the Congress was making all necessary represenations."[9]

But in late March and early April 1938, when press reports hinted that Canada might not even attend the Evian Conference, impatient *amcha* tossed the principle of *shtadlanut* to the winds. By May the labour unions, long-time foes of Congress and its reliance on quiet diplomacy, had banded together to publicly protest immigration restrictions. In a new development, wealthy entrepreneurs and doctors formed two more independent anti-Fascist groups, which laid plans for protest demonstrations and delegations. Congress now recognized that conferences and quiet diplomacy would not be enough. Once again, it would have to do something to dispel an increasingly widespread belief that it consisted of little more than a group of talking heads lacking the will to act on behalf of Canadian Jewry.[10]

Revealingly, the Divisional Executive found itself in disagreement over a course of action. In a raucous meeting that extended over two days, accusations were hurled back and forth across the boardroom table. Bennett, sensing the *amcha* mood, blamed Eisendrath and Cohen for working behind his back to prevent public protest. He claimed that his attempts to initiate the more activist policy were being thwarted, and he offered his resignation. The executive refused to accept, but the obstinate Bennett refused to preside at subsequent executive meetings.[11]

Although Bennett's accusations were unfounded, they indicated his frustration at Congress's lack of political muscle. Most of the executive shared his frustration, but they faced a difficult dilemma. Despite the fact that continued adherence to *shtadlanut* made it difficult to maintain Congress's prestige, most of the executive still believed that subtle methods best served their interests. Thus, they had to risk further erosion of prestige and continue to "guard against any Jewish outburst ... that might rebound against the community at large." The executive promised a provincial conference on the refugee situation to appease *amcha*. Ads in the Yiddish press reminded readers that Congress was doing its utmost but that, "in view of the confidential matters involved, public statements might have unfortunate repercussions." To further assuage the anger of the *landsmanschaften* and disgruntled union members, the executive persuaded Sam Shapiro, whose *Zhurnal* often served as the *amcha* voice, to set aside his personal reservations and bring his editorial support to the concept of *shtadlanut*.[12] A fragile "coalition of silence" had survived until Kristallnacht. But, after November 1938, with the situation of Jews in Europe rapidly worsening and the *shtadlanim* having nothing to show for all their effort, dissent loomed afresh. Central Division leaders now looked to the newly elected Bronfman in the hope that a man of his financial stature and influence could win immigration concessions. They hoped to continue being consulted on national issues while retaining autonomy in local matters.[13]

Bronfman's presidency began favourably for Central Division's leaders. He focused immediately on the national issue of immigration, taking steps to establish Congress as an effective immigration lobbyist. The Central Division executive had already laid the groundwork for this even before Kristallnacht. In September 1938, Rabbi Eisendrath had complained "that no committee had been set up to deal with those few refugees who secure entry ... such refugees were being sent from agency to agency, with no body really equipped to give them assistance." His solution was the formation of a National Coordinating Committee sponsored by Congress, which would call a conference of "all groups interested" in the refugee situation.[14]

The suggestion was quickly implemented, and within two weeks, representatives of Congress, the UJWF, the JIAS, the Folks Farein, and the Family Welfare Bureau had convened under Congress auspices to deal with coordinating activities for refugees in need of assistance. In late November 1938, Egmont Frankel met with communal leaders active in the UJWF and the JIAS to plan a national refugee policy.[15]

In a letter to National JIAS president and CJC national executive member Benjamin Robinson, Frankel urged that a refugee committee be formed in Montreal as well. Robinson agreed: "We should endeavour to secure ... some individual who is not otherwise occupied in order to have someone who will devote his time exclusively to this situation." He wasted no time making the arrangements. In early December, Sydney Pierce was sent to Toronto by the national JIAS office to work out the mechanics of the proposed National Refugee Committee. Within two days he and his Toronto counterparts agreed to establish the Canadian Committee for Jewish Refugees (CCJR), which would deal with the refugee issue on a national basis.[16]

The committee decided to create a national secretariat, as well as divisional offices in Montreal, Toronto, and Winnipeg. Each division would be required to contribute a portion of the CCJR's initial budget and set up regional CCJR committees, each of which would determine what communal organizations would be represented. National policy would be determined by the Montreal-based national secretariat. The CCJR divisional representatives would meet at Congress's Fourth Plenary in January 1939 to begin the National CCJR formally. Thus, when Bronfman officially took office, the CCJR would be available to refugees who might reach Canada. All he would have to do was persuade government to open Canada's gates.[17]

After the Plenary, Bronfman renamed the CCJR the Canadian Jewish Committee for Refugees (CJCR) to reflect its dual mandate of caring for newly arrived Jewish refugees and lobbying for further immigration. By the end of March 1939, the CJCR executive had established a $50,000 line of credit to finance its work until a national fundraising campaign could be arranged. These funds were used to send Reverend Claris E. Silcox of the Canadian National Committee on Refugees (CNCR), a pro-refugee lobbying group, on a cross-Canada speaking tour designed to stir Canadian public opinion against immigration restrictions. This tour began a close cooperation between the CNCR and the CJCR. While encouraging links to non-Jewish organizations that promoted immigration, the CJCR secured Jewish inter-agency cooperation on refugee settlement. By mid-April 1939, the group had formed a sub-committee on refugee establishment that included all Jewish stakeholder agencies. In Toronto, that meant that the JIAS and six other organizations all worked together under the aegis of the CJCR. Systematization of communal services paralleled financial rationalization.[18]

Saul Hayes, a young Montreal lawyer who had begun his career in the firm of Montreal Jewish establishment lawyer Marcus Sperber, was hired as executive director of the CJCR. The self-assured Hayes moved confidently among non-Jews (something his detractors saw as a liability – one sniffed "he was more *goyish* than the *goyim*"), and soon proved a superb administrator and lobbyist. Most important, he knew how to work with the mercurial Bronfman. By the summer of 1939, in conjunction with the United Palestine Appeal (UPA) and the Joint Distribution Committee (JDC), the CJCR was already starting to plan a national campaign for $400,000.[19]

Congress was finally able to move, but time had run out for European Jewry. The outbreak of war cut off the anticipated flow of refugees, and the CJCR quickly shifted gears from coordinating pro-refugee lobbying to collecting funds for European relief. The UJWF had made great progress in coordinating communal fundraising in its first two years of existence, and its 1938 Campaign had raised over $150,000, of which $18,000 was sent overseas. But this change in direction challenged its control. Organizations that were part of the UJWF could take no financial contributions beyond annual membership dues, which were limited to $3.00 per person, a restriction that severely reduced the number of local overseas relief campaigns. The UJWF board that took office in January 1939 was eager to further centralize overseas relief fundraising. They focused on curbing appeals by itinerant representatives (known as *meshulochim* or "emissaries") of European Rabbinical schools (*yeshivot*), and tried yet again to convince the Zionists to merge their appeals with the UJWF annual campaign.[20]

In March 1939 the UJWF board eliminated fifteen *meshulochim* appeals by establishing a contingency fund to deal directly with their sponsors. But persuading the UPA to sign on proved more difficult. The 1938 UJWF and UPA campaigns had been combined, much to the satisfaction of Toronto Zionists (many of whom were among the leaders of the UJWF), and the UPA received a $12,000 allocation. However, this development angered ZOC president Archie Freiman, who passionately believed (as did the Zionists of Montreal) that Zionism could not be part of a "charity campaign." As he argued: "The great national implications of Zionism ... as an enterprise of national reconstruction is neither remedial in scope or palliative, but permanent in scope and objectives." Freiman thus concluded that a separate campaign was essential, "for only through a separate campaign can Zionism benefit from the moral assets attained from the teaching and spreading of Zionist philosophy." He also believed that separate campaigns would gather more funds for the UPA (in 1939 a separate UPA netted $35,000), and he convinced the 25th Zionist Convention to pass a resolution opposing joint campaigns. This decision was "not popular in Toronto," but it was obeyed for a decade.[21]

The resolution of the Zionist Convention led to two important developments, both with implications for communal fundraising in Toronto: the UPA withdrew from the 1939 UJWF campaign, and it broke off almost completed negotiations with the CJCR and the JDC which would have established the planned national CJCR campaign for $400,000. This setback made it imperative for the CJCR to establish control over all other campaigns, especially those gathering funds for European relief, and it therefore began de-emphasizing refugee settlement in favour of European relief. But this re-emphasis brought a head-on conflict with the UJWF campaign. The UJWF had originally supported the CJCR in the hope of rationalizing refugee settlement work in Toronto, but when it became apparent that most of the funds raised by the CJCR–JDC campaign would be sent overseas rather than to affiliated local agencies, the UJWF saw red. To complicate matters, the UJWF feared it could not restrain the *landsmanschaften* from launching independent overseas relief appeals. The nightmarish spectre of parallel CJCR-JDC, UPA, and *landsmanschaften* campaigns led UJWF leaders to fear its collapse into chaos.[22]

Fortunately this scenario didn't come to pass for two important reasons. The first was the fund's efficiency. Meeting its campaign goals assured its affiliate agencies of sufficient operating funds and thereby ensured the agencies' vested interest in keeping the fund strong and successful. The UJWF's first two years demonstrated that it was capable of raising large amounts and distributing them efficiently to organizations spanning the community's ideological and social spectra. Any agency that could properly maintained ledgers and commit not to engage in fundraising outside of membership drives was assured of an annual allocation that freed it from the expense and uncertainty of mounting individual campaigns.[23]

Second, and this proved the organizational trump card, the outbreak of the Second World War put the UJWF trend of centralizing and rationalizing communal work on a par with changes in Canadian society and the country's economy. Even if Canadian Jewry had failed to open Canada's gates, its concern for central organization was not to be denied. Indeed, the federal government insisted that it was the patriotic duty of ethnic groups to organize for war by creating national organizations to represent their political interests. For the first time, those wishing to impose communal rationalization were backed by legal fiat.[24]

On a national level, this role fell by default to the Canadian Jewish Congress – paradoxically, the war did more to impose unity than all of Caiserman's efforts. But not all Jews were yet willing to acknowledge Congress's primacy. This was particularly true in Toronto, where Congress again sought to bring the *landsmanschaften* and Jewish labour groups on side. Central Division executive deemed this allegiance a priority because the UJWF would not increase the divison's allocation without greater communal representation from *amcha* and Jewish labour.[25]

Central Division secured tenuous support from the *landsmanschaften* by giving them seats on its Council of Organizations and by including influential men like Shapiro on its executive. As noted, Congress already had a relationship (albeit sometimes rocky) with the Federation of Polish Jews (colloquially called the Farband) that helped bring the support of mutual benefit societies and the major *landsmanschaften*. Organized labour was far more reluctant to support Congress. Communist unionists were of course excluded from Congress, and other unions and democratic socialists supported their own organization, the Jewish Labour Committee (JLC). The Central Division executive saw the JLC as a competitor; two months before the war, Congress had recommended that the UJWF refuse the JLC membership because it "duplicated their own work." The fund obliged, reflecting its elitist bent, but organized labour continued to support the JLC. As long as it did, a key communal constituency remained alienated from Congress. (The JLC would survive independently and, as will be shown, provided important leadership in postwar human rights laws legislation in Ontario.)[26]

Once the war had begun, established priorities had to change. On 4 September Samuel Bronfman met with two representatives of Central Division to organize Congress's war agenda. The first obligation was enlistment. Congress's greatest concern now was that Jews would not enlist and would be branded "unpatriotic." Accordingly, it decided to begin a public relations campaign and open information and registration offices in Toronto, Montreal, and Winnipeg to encourage and facilitate enlistment. More staff and money would be needed, and new national and divisional budgets prepared. Volunteer work would be left in the hands of a newly created Women's Division.[27]

Canada entered the war on 10 September, and by the end of September Central Division was ready. It created four new committees: Military, Patriotic, Industry and Labour, and Liaison and Public Relations. These committees were shortly kept busy coordinating communal enlistment and assistance for Jewish soldiers. But in early September another agenda was afoot – dictated by *amcha*. Why the bureaucracy? shouted the *Zhurnal*. Why was Congress talking enlistment when Warsaw had fallen, Poland was partitioned, and families were trapped and unreachable? They demanded that the Farband coordinate a *landsmanschaften*-financed relief campaign for Polish Jewry. The Farband held off, "waiting to see what action Congress would take." Congress wasted little time. The divisional executive acknowledged that there was "great mass sentiment in favour of a large effort on behalf of European Jewry," but expressed the usual fears that there was "great danger of this sentiment expressing itself in an uncontrolled manner." This time, Central Division stepped forward to coordinate all European relief under the CJCR banner.[28]

The divisional executive's bold move infringed on the prerogatives of the UJWF, which was already irate at both Central Division and the CJCR for not appointing representatives to the fund and failing to schedule a meeting to coordinate activities. Significantly, the UJWF executive was less concerned about the possibility of a parallel campaign, because Central Division's budget was dependent on its UJWF allocation. Toronto's hard-won financial independence came at a high organizational price.

The UJWF was not shy about asserting its financial control. Even before the war, it had warned the CJCR that its proposed campaign would have to reduce its goal and be held under the auspices of the UJWF campaign. At an emergency board meeting on 8 September the UJWF outflanked the CJCR by officially adopting overseas relief as one of its 1940 campaign priorities. But the UJWF board wisely took no further action. It left the CJCR–JDC committee in place to administer whatever funds would be allocated for overseas relief. The mechanism was already in place; why create another? Further, many of the prospective donors to the CJCR–JDC campaign were not fund supporters. By cunningly pitching overseas relief to this group of donors, the UJWF obtained a risk-free opportunity to expand its donor base and widen its communal support. The divisional executive agreed to this plan.[29]

The CJCR received unexpected leverage in bringing the Farband and its affiliate organizations on side. The federal government assisted the acolytes of rationalization by controlling all offshore cash outflow. Government permits for overseas charitable fundraising were strictly limited so as to ensure that domestic fundraising for the war effort maintained priority. While a single Jewish overseas relief fundraising permit might be obtainable, multiple permits would be unlikely. Faced with that reality, the Farband's affiliate organizations abandoned all plans for a separate appeal and agreed in principle to cooperate in the CJCR–JDC campaign. The government's stance even compelled Jewish labour organizations to send out feelers about joining the UJWF campaign. Labour had organized a Peoples' Relief Project, which collected small sums from workers (the unions themselves continued to send funds to the JLC). Congress immediately offered these organizations representation on the Campaign Coordinating Committee and the Refugee Committee.[30]

Still, groups worked at cross-purposes. For several months there was no official word on how many overseas relief funding permits the government would grant. With no clear signal, the synagogues organized themselves into the Central Relief Committee, while the Mizrachi and other Zionist organizations continued plans for yet another independent Palestine campaign. But by early November 1939 it became clear that the UJWF and Congress had the inside track on obtaining permits for overseas campaigns. Congress mediation led to a meeting between the leaders of the People's and Central Relief committees in November. On 24 December came the breakthrough announcement that labour was on board and "the Congress Refugee Committee would symbolize the unity of all the organizations." Central Division could at last live up to its claim to be a communal spokesagency, at least in matters of refugee affairs and overseas relief.[31]

While Congress was busy extending its control of overseas campaigning, the UJWF opened its 1940 campaign. The demands of overseas relief pushed the campaign to an unprecedented $312,000, of which a stunning 25 percent was earmarked for offshore distribution, while agency allocations were frozen at 1939 levels. The UJWF board was confident of success. Their donor base was greatly augmented by new converts to centralized fundraising. The strengthening economy and the excitement of the war were a powerful inducement to maximize contributions.[32]

War excitement of the wrong kind was also in the air. The war also offered nativists an opportunity to raise accusations that Jews were staying at home as war profiteers while other Canadians marched off to fight. But Congress was ready with a two-pronged response. The

Military Committee boosted Jewish enlistment and publicized figures on Jews joining the armed forces. Congress's war efforts focused first on promoting Jewish enlistment, a challenging task. For some Jews, fighting Hitler was obvious after six years of Nazi persecution. Ben Dunkelman felt he "had a score to settle with Hitler," while Barney Danson recalled: "the evil of Nazism existed, and we had to be in it as Canadians and Jews." Morris, Solly, and Sidney Glass all were in uniform by 1942, leaving their widowed mother and two sisters at home to survive as best they could. Sidney recalled: "It was a hell of an adventure, and pretty scary too. But we never realized that until we actually went into Holland." But there were many who were personally or politically reluctant to risk their lives. Allan Grossman, a young insurance agent and Conservative party member, was quite content to join the reserves and was not overly upset when he was rejected for flat feet. David Lewis, secretary of the CCF, supported the party's pacifist line. Those who were Communists continued as party members despite the Molotov-Ribbentrop Pact and the partition of Poland between the Nazis and Soviets. Some Jews, remembering the German army as liberators in the First World War, still found it hard to change their views. Certainly Nazis were brutal to Jews, but the Wehrmacht was esteemed for its professionalism. In fact, this attitude was significant on both sides of the Atlantic.

The Military Committee was well aware that these intra-ethnic divisions had to be concealed because patriotism was the order of the day. The committee sent out weekly bulletins highlighting recruit numbers and stories of those who volunteered. Jewish recruitments were moderately successful: the percentage of Jewish soldiers roughly matched the percentage of Jews in the Canadian population. Consistent and often innovative effort was required. Comic books extolling "Johnny Canuck"–style stories of Jewish heroes such as pilot Sidney Shulemson were issued, recruitment posters were specially designed in Yiddish, and newly hired Jewish military chaplains drummed out patriotism. Newly ordained rabbi David Monson gave up his pulpit at Shaarei Shomayim Congregation to become a chaplain in 1940. He loved army life and often went up and down streets in Jewish neighbourhoods adjoining Spadina Avenue to persuade young men to enlist.

Jewish recruits received plenty of communal support. As they were sent off to basic training, Central Division continued to look after their needs. Servicemen's centres were established in Toronto and in the small Ontario towns that held army bases. Servicemen's clubs in smaller centres were non-denominational. They boasted a chapel/auditorium and meeting rooms where off-duty personnel could relax and fraternize. Central Division did such a fine job of supporting these centres that in 1942 it was placed in charge of provisioning servicemen's centres for an area that stretched from Port Credit in the west to Oshawa in the east – a vast undertaking, as the 142,000 servicemen visits between January and July 1944 indicate. With Congress's sponsorship and logo prominently displayed, this endeavour made for powerfully favourable publicity. The needs of Jewish servicemen were met by kosher meals at Passover, the hiring of three Jewish chaplains, and (outside of Toronto) the informal delivery of kosher food packages. Every Sunday Rabbi Slonim of the McCaul Street Synagogue would drive out to St Thomas, where there were over a hundred Jewish men at the British Commonwealth Air Training Station. After conducting services, he distributed the best of Spadina Avenue deli fare: "knishes filled with potato or kasha, almond rolls, and honey cake, pepper fish with plenty of sugar." Jewish servicemen stationed in Toronto had the additional benefit of free membership in the YMHA, with its gym and swimming pool.

All this of course came at a price. Central Division received $5,000 per year from 1943 onward to reimburse the "Y" for free military membership. Setting up and maintaining servicemen's centres cost $17,000 in the first six months of 1944, with additional costs for sending "Comfort Boxes" overseas to soldiers before the High Holy Days, and running recruitment drives. But this effort engendered much favourable publicity in the Canadian press, and the display of the Congress logo at servicemen's centres substantially increased Central Division's presence and prestige among Jews and non-Jews alike. It was not surprising that the UJWF became eager to assist the division, which, by 1944, had become the fund's leading beneficiary.[33]

Central Division's patriotic war work was expertly publicized. The Joint Public Relations Committee (JPRC) of Congress and B'nai Brith handled the public relations side of this challenge by making Jewish economic contributions known, scanning the press for articles unfavourable to Jews, and writing letters to the editor. Eisendrath, Roger, and other members of the JPRC went on speaking tours of small-town Ontario to dispel many anti-Jewish stereotypes.[34]

A particular canard that shadowed the Jewish community was the notion that "Jews formed the bulk of the Communist Party of Canada." This was not true, but the Jewish Communist presence in Toronto was undeniable. In the mid-1930s the Communists had made significant inroads into some unions and had made progress in municipal politics. Jewish Communist groups had applied for Congress membership in 1934, but were rejected because Congress leaders feared that their presence would undermine the organization's credibility. Until August 1939 Jewish Communists were virulently anti-Nazi. Although rejected by Congress, they secretly aided Central Division secretary Oscar Cohen by passing along to him Nazi propaganda material distributed in Canada, anti-Nazi pamphlets, and intelligence on anti-Jewish groups. But, on 23 August 1939 the Molotov-Ribbentrop Accord broke this link. Jewish Communists, already disliked by a segment of the community, were suddenly reviled and universally looked upon as traitors.[35]

So it came as no surprise that the potential negative public relations impact of Jewish Communist J.B. Salsberg's winning re-election as Ward 4 alderman in November 1939 Toronto municipal elections terrified the divisional executive. What message would be conveyed if he won in the heavily Jewish ward? The JPRC recommended a vigorous two-pronged anti-Communist campaign. The plan called first for an educational package, to include "an academic statement pointing out the attitude of the Congress to Communism," suitable for distribution in the Jewish and Canadian press. Second, it involved the unprecedented step of direct Central Division intervention among Jewish voters. Volunteers visited Jewish homes and businesses to persuade them to remove Communist campaign signs that might cast doubt on their patriotism. This "re-education" resulted in the removal of more than four hundred signs. The anti-Communist educational package was mailed to all Jewish voters in Wards 4 and 6. When Salsberg's support continued strong, Eisendrath made a radio appeal to Jewish voters. These tactics succeeded. Despite editorial support from the *Toronto Star*, Salsberg lost his seat.[36]

The high profile of Salsberg and other Jewish Communists made it all the more imperative that Jews be seen as doing their share for the war effort. In addition to encouraging Jewish military enlistment and announcing enlistment totals, the Military Committee issued press releases and invited reporters to meet Jewish enlistees. By 4 October, a month after the war had begun, 85 men had already enlisted. On 10 October Congress opened an enlistment office at 453 Spadina Avenue (near College). By 24 October, 180 more men had enlisted, most leaving jobs to do so. The committee also made sure that the enlistment program had a patriotic and non-sectarian air; the office was open to non-Jews. A great deal of time was spent planning Congress participation in multi-faith patriotic projects.[37]

This high-profile war work raised the Central Division's image among Jews and non-Jews. The federal government's recognition of the division as the coordinating agency of Jewish war work in Toronto brought practically all Jewish organizations under its umbrella. By early 1940 it had become a commanding force in organizing the communal war effort. Its major war project was to supply recreation and dormitory furniture for all bases and barracks in Military District #2, which included Toronto and surrounding areas. Central Division also assisted in fundraising for the Salvation Army, the YMCA, and the Canadian Legion, and, as noted, took care of Jewish soldiers' special needs.[38]

The UJWF executive watched Central Division's wartime ascendancy with mixed feelings. The division's efficiency was impressive, and the cooperation it attracted – or compelled – from other communal organizations indicated that a larger view of community was on the rise. But the UJWF had no intention of abdicating its social planning role. It insisted that Central Division take steps to ensure that its programs and responsibilities would not overlap or duplicate those of the UJWF or its affiliated organizations. There were areas of tension. The division had agreed to place the Refugee Campaign under the fund's umbrella, but it had not sought the fund's agreement before assuming responsibility for coordinating communal war work, much of which smacked of social service activity. In fact, the division executive continued to ignore repeated UJWF requests that it appoint members to the Welfare Fund executive and Budget Committee to ensure cooperation. The UJWF executive grew impatient, and in December 1939 insisted on a meeting to define mutual responsibilities and lay out a unified approach to communal problems.[39]

The meeting took place on 19 January 1940. Unexpectedly, cordiality proved the order of the day. The UJWF recognized that Central Division "represented the community in the sphere of public relations and constituted the democratic instrument of the community." The division in turn recognized that the fund "represented the community in the area of philanthropies." The top officers of both organizations acknowledged their shared interest in "stimulating and directing communal planning," agreeing upon their mutual interest in coordinating overseas relief and improving communal standards in Jewish education. Both would best be served by "close cooperation or a merger," and the best way to avoid misunderstandings would be to appoint representatives to each other's committees. Oscar Cohen directed each committee to ensure that it sent representatives to the parallel UJWF meetings. In turn, UJWF president Samuel Godfrey appointed representatives to the Public Relations Committee and the Refugee Committee. The considerable overlap in membership of the division and UJWF executives also helped smooth over the inter-organizational relationship and made it possible for both organizations to cooperate during the rest of the war and beyond.[40]

Although generally harmonious, this new relationship did not quite represent organizational equality. Congress had the broadest mandate of all UJWF-affiliated organizations, but it remained financially dependent on its annual allocation and Central Division programs had to receive advance approval from the fund. In practice, this was not problematic. But at times conflicts between Congress headquarters in Montreal and the Central Division, or between different factions on the Central Division executive, made it difficult for the UJWF and Central Division to see eye to eye. Overall, however, their cooperative relationship was never imperilled.

As the UJWF–Central Division relationship was being finalized in Toronto, Bronfman, as expected, accepted Caiserman's resignation as executive secretary of Congress and replaced him with the young lawyer Saul Hayes. Caiserman was put in charge of fundraising appeals among *landsmanschaften* and small communities. Hayes received the newly created title of national executive director of the Canadian Jewish Congress, where he would remain a leader for over three decades. He quickly centralized and consolidated Montreal's control over National Congress and took responsibility for policy development.[41]

The Central Division executive was uneasy with Hayes's increased authority. When the war began, the question of the division's autonomy had been raised, and Montreal had informed Central Division that "each Division would function autonomously, but with frequent consultation." The divisional executive had understood this as a definitive statement. It had become accustomed to independence of action during Caiserman's tenure, and was not eager to submit again to Montreal. Besides, by 1940 Toronto Jewry was more organizationally united than ever before. Wartime patriotism and the UJWF–centralized fundraising had somewhat repaired intra-ethnic and economic disaccord. In contrast, Montreal lacked a Welfare Fund, and the wealthier members of the community had seized control over Congress after Bronfman took over the presidency. Hayes spoke with Bronfman's authoritativeness and in a voice that rekindled the rivalry between Congress in Toronto and in Montreal. But if Bronfman's muscle made Montreal the dominant force in Congress affairs, Toronto's power could not be denied and would soon be used.[42]

Personal and organizational issues also explain why Central Division was intent on keeping organizational autonomy as it had existed under Caiserman. Cohen heartily disliked both Hayes's "non-Jewish" demeanour and his desire to centralize all policymaking in Montreal. He resented what he and many of his Toronto colleagues saw as the takeover of Congress by Hayes and Bronfman. No one questioned Hayes's ability or Bronfman's financial influence, but a strong head office meant less independence for Toronto. The UJWF also mistrusted any attempt to centralize power in Hayes's hands. When Hayes folded the CJCR into a newly created United Jewish Refugee and War Relief Agencies (UJRWRA) to coordinate war-related charity in line with federal government demands that ethnic groups consolidate their overseas relief efforts, the UJWF viewed this move as a looming threat to its hard-won control over Congress's overseas relief campaigning in Toronto and as an attack on its doctrine of rationalized communal fundraising.[43]

Fearing a Montreal takeover, the UJWF proved a vital ally in Central Division's effort to retain its autonomy. Its 1940 campaign had reached its goal, but the funds were inadequate to meet wartime demand. The UJWF now faced a very difficult situation. Its debt was still $10,000 (unchanged from 1939), the bank was again pressing for full payment of outstanding loans incurred by its organizational predecessor, and agency allocations had been frozen for two years to accommodate the demands of overseas relief. The UJWF needed to make internal changes that required the cooperation of all its affiliates. It thus was essential that Central Division, the only single organization to comprise an entire Welfare Fund division, remain loyal to the fund.[44]

Central Division president Archie Bennett found himself with divided loyalties. He had little love for the UJWF, understandably fearing that its control of the divisional purse would ultimately give it control over the division's policies. But, he was equally suspicious of Hayes's desire to expand head office's control and the potentially ensuing loss of local autonomy. Members of the divisional executive who also served on the UJWF executive were more sympathetic to the fund. When forced to choose between Congress's head office and the UJWF, they invariably chose the latter.

The UJRWRA therefore failed to gain the support of Central Division. The UJRWRA was incorporated under the *War Charities Act* to continue the CJCR mandate, but under far more stringent wartime fundraising and currency control regulations. As executive director, Hayes could issue licences permitting agencies affiliated with the UJRWRA to conduct fundraising campaigns for overseas relief and refugee settlement. UJWF officials were concerned that a separate, and therefore competing, UJRWRA campaign might be organized in Toronto, which could lead to the demise of the UJWF and a return to fundraising chaos. Central Division mistrusted the UJRWRA for different reasons. The divisional executive believed Hayes might use any funds raised in ways that were not in Central Division's best interests, if he even knew what those were – which many doubted. The UJWF was quick to show its sensitivity to Central Division's need to keep Hayes and the UJRWA at a distance, and when the UJRWRA was slow to reimburse Toronto for expenses incurred in refugee work, the UJWF quickly stepped in. It reimbursed the division for "extraordinary expenditures on behalf of refugees" and allotted $3,000 more to keep creditors at bay.[45]

The generosity of the UJWF bore fruit. The Central Division executive refused to ratify the UJRWRA's Articles of Incorporation until Hayes agreed not to launch a separate Toronto UJRWRA campaign. Instead, Hayes had to accept that the UJWF would incorporate refugee work into its allocation program. Between 1942 and 1945 UJRWRA allocations skyrocketed, running second only to those of the Jewish Family Welfare Bureau. The only inroad Hayes was able to make in Toronto was an affiliation of the United Jewish Relief Conference with the UJRWRA. Neither the fund nor Central Division minded this arrangement. Conference members were unionized workers whose financial contributions were negligible (less than 10 percent of the UJRWRA's Toronto allocation). The conference was also distrustful of Congress and in any case had never really supported the UJWF anyway. Both the division and the UJWF were delighted to cede this perceived nuisance to Hayes.[47]

The UJRWRA story typifies the overall relationship between the CJC head office and the UJWF until 1943. The head office of the JIAS soon found itself in a similar position. The Toronto JIAS office, strong under its founding executive secretary, Maurice Solkin, had stagnated after he assumed JIAS's national executive directorship in January 1937. When Manny Kraicer, a handpicked Solkin trainee, arrived in September 1939, the Toronto office was in serious financial and organization difficulty. The outbreak of war halted the flow of remittances and parcels that had supplied the bulk of JIAS's revenue. Kraicer requested financial aid from head office. Solkin refused. Echoing his mentor A.J. Paull, he claimed that Toronto had the potential to be self-supporting. In addition, he had not yet prepared a national JIAS budget; the Toronto JIAS would have to make do until the national office decided how to deal with them. Pressed for money, an enraged Toronto JIAS executive rebelled and applied for a substantial increase of its UJWF allocation in order to keep its office afloat. The fund agreed because the Toronto JIAS handled what few refugee and other immigration-related cases appeared in wartime Toronto – over the vociferous protests of both the JIAS National Office and Congress's Saul Hayes. UJWF support for the Toronto JIAS was granted over Solkin's protests that he had the right to control financial arrangements between head office and its local affiliate. His protests went unanswered. Hayes, still wanting to uproot the JIAS from its place in refugee work, exerted similar pressures for his own reasons. The fund's intervention in JIAS affairs seriously weakened the society's head office control over its Toronto office, and heralded a decentralization of the JIAS organization that was to continue for forty years.[47]

The UJWF's ability to assert its authority over fundraising and communal organization in Toronto underscored the weakness of national Jewish organizations in Canada at this time. Only four Jewish organizations in Canada even thought in national terms: B'nai Brith, the JIAS, the ZOC, and the CJC. Each organization's ability to assert itself nationally was hampered by circumstances: B'nai Brith's priorities were dictated by its American headquarters; the national JIAS office had already fumbled away control over its Toronto branch; the curb on Jewish immigration to Palestine hurt the ZOC, and, despite Bronfman's backing, the newly hired Hayes had just begun efforts to assert his control over Congress's scattered divisions. Under Caiserman, Congress had been little more than a paper affiliation of three very autonomous regions. Even under Hayes, national committees for Public Relations, War Efforts, Refugees, and the like were unable to impose national policies on the divisions. Daniel Elazar's observation that "the basic institutions of American Jewry are essentially local and at the most, are loosely confederated with each other on a countrywide basis for very limited purposes" also applies to Canadian Jewry until 1945.[48]

But the ability of the UJWF to plan and organize consistently successful fundraising campaign's trumped organizational weakness as an explanation for its primacy. The consequent predictability of allocations became the key to its retaining the loyalty of its affiliate agencies. To its credit, though, the UJWF refused to make the annual campaign its sole raison d'être. It used agency loyalty to encourage inter-agency cooperation in communal planning. Its professional workers consistently advocated for coordinated planning based on real needs, and the UJWF could never be faulted for favouritism. By 1941 it was such a dominant force that any history of communal organization in Toronto becomes of necessity a history of the UJWF. The fund's affiliated agencies did have their own interests to further, but their development cannot be understood without reference to that of the UJWF.[49]

The UJWF executive's ultimate goal was control over agency spending. The onset of war and the attendant tightening of fiscal controls expedited the process. Moves to curb spending had already begun in early 1939 when some agencies, finding their allocations inadequate, had requested supplemental funds. The executive's reply was blunt: "Requests for funds, either specifically or in principle, for items that could have been foreseen or are not on an emergency basis, cannot be considered." Furthermore, "supplemental funds would only be made available in unexpected circumstances beyond agencies' control and when needs cannot be met by budget readjustment." These responses sounded fine in principle, but what would happen if, as a result of being refused a supplementary allocation, an agency was forced into debt? Who would be responsible for paying off the indebtedness: the agency or the fund? Above all, did the fund, which was formed to rationalize fundraising and not to interfere in the internal affairs of its agencies, have the right to limit agency spending in the name of communal planning?[50]

The young professional leaders of the fund argued that such limits were necessary to avoid crippling communal fundraising. They had learned from the Brunswick Avenue Talmud Torah episode that capital debts had to be minimized or the pressure of accumulating debt and interest payments would reduce the allocations available for operating expenses to an impossibly low level. If the fund could not decide upon allocations, it would simply become a debt-paying operation and rational communal fundraising would be impossible. Therefore, even before the Second World War began, the UJWF executive changed its mandate to allow it to limit agency spending. As executive director Martin Cohn acknowledged in April 1939, "since this was a reversal of policies that had been originally suggested, it would require careful working out and a fairly lengthy educational process."[51]

The members of the UJWF executive assumed that simply presenting such "facts" would ensure instant acceptance of these onerous guidelines by the affiliated agencies. In late April 1939, they informed all local agencies, except Central Division, that their allocations would depend on their needs, as indicated by audited statements. They were free to use their allocation without the scrutiny of the UJWF, but the fund would not be responsible for any debts they incurred. If they needed a supplemental allocation, they would have to approach their division. If their request was granted, they had to use the funds according to the recommendation of the UJWF Budget Committee. The agencies were understandably furious at this alteration in the UJWF's purpose and the potential expansion of its power at their expense. But the outbreak of war and the subsequent government restrictions on charitable campaigns forestalled agency revolts.[52]

The fund retained its hegemony by ruthlessly disciplining agencies that attempted to defect. In January 1940, Mount Sinai Hospital threatened to resign, claiming "Fund interference in their internal management." The hospital's directors believed that as long as they submitted audited financial statements, they were entitled to receive their requested allocation without scrutiny. On 11 March the hospital formally objected to the UJWF's program of budget control but offered to send a delegation to negotiate its continued presence in the fund with the executive. The UJWF board understood that the hospital's go-it-alone attitude "seemed to centre around a limited number of individuals ... who did not consider themselves part of the general set up of communal affairs, but were ... interested in only the one agency." The UJWF had zero tolerance for narrow-minded organizational loyalists standing in the way of professional communal planning. There would be no return to the fundraising free-for-all of the past.[53]

The fund's response provided a cautionary tale to any affiliate agency that forgot its "communal place." The UJWF determined to educate the hospital board in the dangers of organizational parochialism. The "educational process" proved abrupt. After studying the hospital's audited statements, the UJWF lopped $2,000 off the hospital's requested 1941 allocation. The furious hospital executive demanded restoration of the full allocation as the price of continued affiliation. But Cohn observed that "the Welfare Fund could not put itself in the position of giving way under threat of an organization seceding" and refused to give in.[54] Facing an unyielding fund, the hospital's resistance collapsed immediately. Within a week, hospital executives acknowledged that "they had been perhaps somewhat lax in cooperating in the past, and that this situation would be corrected." After this no agency dared challenge the fund's policies.[55]

With complete control over fundraising now established, the UJWF shifted its emphasis to future planning. In 1941 it commissioned a series of studies by its own personnel working in cooperation with professionals from its affiliated agencies. For comparative purposes it also collected parallel American studies. These revealed that demand for care of the aged and the chronically ill would dramatically increase as the community both grew and aged. A new Jewish Old Folks' Home and a new Mount Sinai Hospital were needed. Other reports indicated that educational institutions were under strain and needed more funds for salaries and building expansion. Many agencies were still burdened with heavy capital debt loads that imperilled their efficiency and, in some cases, their existence, and these debts would have to be met before expansion could be considered. The pressures of wartime, with their unpredictable financial demands, increased social service agency caseloads, and restrictions on new building construction that aggravated already overcrowded conditions and increased the cost of living, made future planning all the more difficult. Paradoxically, these very pressures made planning the postwar world more essential than ever.[56]

In order to deal with both present needs and future plans, the UJWF modified its organization before the kick-off of the 1941 campaign. The composition of divisions I, III, and IV was left unchanged. Division II was now divided into Educational Institutions, which formed Division IIA, and Cultural and Recreational Agencies, forming Division IIB. Since all budgeting was done at the divisional level, this separation helped simplify educational budgeting, which was becoming increasingly complicated as school deficits mounted and enrolments increased. The formation of Division IIB reflected the absorption of the Jewish Centre for Educational and Cultural Activities (JCCA) by the Young Men's Hebrew Association (YMHA), a merger that helped reduce agency overlap and encouraged institutional rationalization. The JCCA was founded in the early 1920s by a group of merchants and young professionals to blend athletic activities with child and adult education classes. The YMHA traced its roots back to the same period, but emphasized athletics over cultural activities and was directed at the sixteen- to twenty-five-year-old group. The JCCA was reluctant to be merged into the YMHA, which it regarded as inferior. However, the UJWF used its power of the purse to impose the merger, which saved the fund thousands of dollars and allowed one strong, all-inclusive agency to flourish where two weak ones had stagnated.[57]

The same push for agency rationalization through merger produced the amalgamation of the Jewish Child Welfare Association (JCWA) and the Jewish Family Welfare Bureau (JFWB). Both these agencies had been associated with the Federation of Jewish Philanthropies, which had previously eliminated overlap by creating the JCWA in 1935 out of the Jewish Big Brothers, the Jewish Big Sisters, and the Jewish Children's Home. The JFWB was itself a consolidation of the Jewish Employment Service, Hebrew Maternity Aid Society, Joint Application Bureau, Mothers' and Babies' Rest Home, and the Toronto Hebrew Free Burial Society. During the Depression, the JFWB had been responsible for the administration of relief funds in the Jewish community. This role had produced more overlap because the JFWB increasingly dealt with entire families without consulting the JCWA as to the special needs of children. The FJP lacked the clout to impose a merger on the family welfare agencies; the UJWF had the clout and used it.[58]

The merger was not easy. Each agency had supporters who were also members of the UJWF executive. But, as always, the majority of the executive insisted on prioritizing communal needs over organizational parochialism. In May 1941, when the executive secretary of the JCWA took a one-year leave of absence, she was replaced by UJWF assistant executive director Florence Hutner, who supported the merger. In December 1941, the UJWF Executive sent a letter to the JCWA, which was having great difficulty finding foster homes because it paid below market price rates. It was intimated that an increased allocation would only be forthcoming if the agency agreed to a merger. Within two weeks both agencies agreed to initiate plans. On 24 March 1942, the agencies held a joint board meeting and agreed to fold into one agency, the Jewish Family and Child Services (JFCS), on 1 January 1943.[59]

Despite this admirable record of organizational and financial rationalization, emergency needs had led to a $12,000 deficit in 1939. In 1940 the fund's campaign goal was $312,000, but it collected only $256,000, leaving a deficit of well over $50,000. The deficits ran to over $30,000 in each of 1941 and 1942. In addition, the UJWF was still dealing with the FJP deficit that it had assumed at its inception. Immediate action was necessary.[60]

Wartime inflationary pressures had added fuel to an old fire. In December 1940 Division II representatives warned the UJWF of the schools' "pressing situation." Funds were needed immediately to satisfy teacher demands for cost-of-living increases. The executive was understanding; after all, education had fallen behind during the Depression when relief funding was prioritized. A large allocation to cover pay increases for teachers was quickly approved. But by March 1941 the Brunswick Avenue Talmud Torah, the largest of the schools, was once again seeking a supplementary allocation. Its old debt problem, the financial crisis that had catalyzed the UJWF's formation, had resurfaced. Once again the bank demanded an immediate payment against principal and the refinancing of the mortgage. Expeditious action was essential.[61]

The Talmud Torah's situation was not unique. A special executive meeting was informed that the combined debts of the Brunswick Avenue Talmud Torah, the FJP, the Eitz Chaim schools, the Workmen's Circle School, and the Mount Sinai Hospital totalled over $160,000, two-thirds of this in unpaid mortgages. Using the strategy that had saved the Talmud Torah writ large, the executive approved a Capital Debts Reduction Campaign to pay down half the accumulated debt over a three-year period. Any consequent savings in interest would also be applied to debt reduction. Fund subscribers would be allowed to designate any increase in their subscriptions to this plan. This special designation of funds marked a radical new stage in communal planning, and some dissenting voices on the fund executive wondered if the fund was not overstepping its power. But UJWF past president Ben Sadowski carried the day when he urged the fund "to bring order into communal financing" as part of "taking a wider view of the Welfare Fund responsibility for planning."[62]

Once again the UJWF's zeal for imposing order and planning for the future proved paramount. The Capital Debts Reduction Campaign was highly successful, and subscribers were so enthusiastic that by September 1941, when the UJWF campaign officially began, a number had earmarked donations for the Capital Debts Reduction Campaign. By early 1942 – within three years – contributions to this new scheme were sufficient to eliminate all of the accumulated debt and lift a great burden that had long troubled communal and institutional life.[63]

Thus, by late 1942 the fund had dealt with the burdens of the past through its Capital Debts Reduction Campaign, with present needs through its allocation system, and with future plans by functioning as a communal planning agency. In two and a half years, the UJWF had educated its agencies and the community at large to accept the merits of professional communal planning. Ideas that had been anathema to a significant portion of the community less than a decade earlier became accepted practice. This was a tremendous accomplishment, given the fractious state of Toronto Jewry before the Second World War. From the perspective of the historical development of communal fundraising in North America, however, Toronto still lagged far behind developments in other cities of similar size.[64]

Forces external to the Jewish community soon changed this. The Depression had triggered an unprecedented demand for social services and led to provincial intervention in municipal relief. The desperate rush to provide relief precluded rational social planning and angering the many Protestant, Catholic, and Jewish agencies that prided themselves on dispensing relief according to scientific principles. Now came a new push for coordinating social planning among Toronto social service agencies. This pressure bore fruit in 1937 with the formation of the Welfare Council of Toronto and District, which served as a communal planning agency. The Protestant, Catholic, and Jewish federations all supported the Welfare Council and elected members to its board. The Welfare Council, though divided along denominational lines, received its funding from the Protestant-backed Federation for Community Service (FCS), whose goal was non-denominational communal planning. Advocates of this type of planning hoped it would ultimately work for all social service agencies regardless of religious affiliation.[65]

The Second World War was the catalyst that consolidated communal fundraising. The federal government wanted to establish home-front organizations to coordinate the vast array of support services needed during wartime. The leaders of the Welfare Council, explained social worker Ben Lappin, "viewed this problem as a crisis ... The aim was to avoid at all costs duplication from organizations springing up overnight with assistance from Ottawa." The Welfare Council of Toronto quickly organized the Canadian Community Chest. This powerful, charity-funding lobby, consisting of the Red Cross, the Salvation Army, and social agencies across the country, demanded a moratorium on the creation of new social service agencies. The government agreed that only existing agencies would be authorized to meet wartime needs. This proved the major factor in bringing together the power of the UJWF and Congress's War Efforts Committee, resulting in the consolidation of Jewish communal unity.[66]

Even with the unifying pressure of war, it took three years to complete the rationalization of communal/social planning and fundraising under the direction of a Community Chest in Toronto. Businessmen on the Board of Trade pushed for a single city-wide campaign for a united Community Chest as early as 1940. This concept met resistance from social agency executives, who feared that their agencies might decline under Community Chest control. But pressures for consolidation were overwhelming. In June 1940 representatives of the Protestant, Catholic, and Jewish federations met at the Board of Trade to discuss the formation of a Community Chest, and each federation was mandated to sell the plan to its community. The Jewish response was typical of the others. Ironically yet predictably, the UJWF executive disliked the idea for the same reasons that its affiliates feared the fund: it would mean that Jewish social service agencies in Division 1 would leave the UJWF and receive funding from the Community Chest. The fund was concerned about its continued viability in the absence of these high-profile communal agencies. There were also concerns about whether a Protestant- and Catholic-dominated Community Chest could address the specific needs of Jewish agencies. Would the Community Chest provide adequate social planning and ensure the high social work standards at Jewish agencies? The UJWF executive was unprepared to deal with these questions and refused to discuss the plan between 1940 and 1942. Nonetheless, informal discussions about a multi-faith Community Chest continued among leading Protestant, Catholic, and Jewish businessmen.[67]

By 1943 it was clear that the lack of a Community Chest in Toronto was detrimental to the home front. Businessmen refused to donate to multiple campaigns and the government's desire to have free rein with its own patriotic fundraising forced other campaigns to compete with one another in the brief time period allocated for non-patriotic fundraising. The UJWF's deficit and needs increased, while Victory Bonds and other patriotic campaigns siphoned off funds. Wealthy business donors were increasingly beleaguered by appeals from all religious elements in the city. In response, businessmen of all faiths banded together under the auspices of the Board of Trade to lobby yet again for a Community Chest. This time, Protestants and Catholics quickly agreed to an experimental campaign, the United Welfare Fund (UWF), which set as its goal the combined total proceeds of all members' 1942 campaigns. Any extra funds raised would be disbursed according to the same ratio. There would be no scrutinizing of budgets or needs, and no need to submit audited statements. The FCS, the Federation of Catholic Charities, the Salvation Army, and other prominent organizations quickly agreed to participate.[68]

In early April 1943 the UJWF was asked to participate in the UWF. Now the fund executive had to confront the questions it had avoided for so long. At a special board meeting on 4 April, proponents of the UWF argued that a public relations disaster would result from a refusal to participate. Besides, if the campaign did not do well, it was only a one-year experiment without lasting impact on fund structure. Opponents of the idea countered that the establishment of a permanent Community Chest would play havoc with the fund's annual campaign. Government regulations that gave patriotic fundraising priority in fall campaigns would compel the UJWF to permanently move its annual campaign to the spring, thereby removing the traditional connection between community appeals and the autumn High Holy Day season. But in the end, the opportunity to participate in the UWF was too great to ignore, and the UJWF board approved participation by a vote of thirty to fifteen.[69]

The Community Chest campaign proved an unprecedented success, and it became an annual event. In 1944 it was aptly renamed the United Community Chest (UCC), following the model of more than five hundred similar North American organizations.[70]

Permanent UJWF participation raised a number of issues. The prime issue, as discussed, was the possible impact of the transfer of Division 1 social service agencies to the UCC in the event of a merger. Other questions also required answers. Would the non-sectarian UCC recognize the special needs of Jewish agencies? How could the UJWF coordinate proper social planning for the Jewish community if all the Jewish social service agencies were affiliated with the UCC and subject to its planning process? What of social service agencies, like the Jewish Old Folks' Home or Mount Sinai Hospital, which were planning or considering significant capital improvements? Would the UCC ensure that their needs would be met? The report commissioned to deal with such issues, like the social workers who wrote it, was concerned mostly with the UCC's plans for communal social planning. It argued (and the UJWF's history confirmed) that "a good fund must be more than a campaign and collection organization; it must be a planning tool in conjunction with fundraising activities." This meant that it was essential that the UCC develop a strong social services planning capacity and also that the UJWF receive enough representation to influence its planning. The report nevertheless advocated affiliation despite several unresolved issues. Its authors were convinced that, "with sound planning through a council of social work agencies," affiliation with the UCC would benefit the Jewish community.[71]

At the UJWF November 1943 board meeting, a succession of social workers affirmed their approval of the UCC and their eagerness to join. The board agreed to affiliation in principle. The UCC showed itself ready to meet the UJWF more than halfway on many issues of concern involving Jewish particularism. It allowed the UJWF to continue to be the sole canvassing organization for the Jewish community by inviting contributors to divide their contributions, at their option, between the UCC (33%) and the UJWF (66%). The Division I social service agencies that left the UJWF were still allowed to deal with UJWF on a "consultative basis." Agency capital costs were underwritten by the UCC, which soon became extremely adept both at fundraising and at social planning. The UJWF became even stronger and was able to give more attention to education and overseas relief just as communal emphasis on both peaked.[72]

The UJWF affiliation with the UCC marked yet another watershed in Jewish communal organization. Toronto Jewry had become important enough to have been invited to participate in the UCC because the Jewish community and its agencies were finally acknowledged as part of the larger civic society. By accepting the invitation, Toronto Jewry indicated that its interests were expanding beyond the parochialism of the pre-war years. A maturing community was beginning to look to Canadian norms. How to explain this vital shift? Certainly, the war played a catalytic role. But the lingering fractious intra-ethnic quarrels of Toronto Jewry and the sectarianism of Toronto and its deep cleavage between Orangemen and Catholics go far toward explaining why both the UJWF and community chest were established much later than Jewish federations and Community Chests in comparably sized American cities. In sum, the UJWF deserves credit for leading the integration of Toronto Jewry into a non-Jewish society. The fund would exploit its role to the full in the postwar world that could be anticipated after Allied victories at Stalingrad and El Alamein.

The consolidation of the UJWF's power over fundraising and future communal planning as well as professional standards, and its partnership with the Community Chest, underscored the triumph of the Uptowners' vision and imposition of will. It also indicated that the wealthiest of them were gaining acceptance into the wider Toronto community. Anti-Semitism and discrimination still existed in employment and housing, but wartime community-wide fundraising and the rationalization of social services greatly aided Uptowners' upward mobility. The coincident beginnings of a Jewish population shift to the suburbs verified the fund's vital role in future planning as it allocated money for educational expansion and planned communal eldercare and recreational needs.

At the same time, UJWF's success had not removed Congress from the picture. On the contrary. Backed by Bronfman's funds and Hayes's insistence on Congress's primacy as a communal organizer for Jewish recruitment, war relief, and refugee work, Congress swept the JIAS aside and received a huge UJWF allocation to fund its activities. As the postwar world came into focus, Congress envisioned continuing its primacy in local resettlement activity. This vision would lead to a head-on confrontation with the UJWF. The battle over social work professionalization was won, but the lay leaders of the Welfare Fund and of Congress were headed for a clash over the type of aid postwar immigrants would require, if and when Canada's gates finally opened.

8

"O Brave New World"?
The Imposition of Will, 1943–48

By the end of January 1943 a vital sea change had taken place in Allied war fortunes. The German surrender at Stalingrad coupled with Rommel's defeat at El Alamein made it clear that the pendulum was beginning to swing in the Allies' favour. Certainly, the postwar era was still far off, but by mid-1943 the organizational jockeying for peacetime hegemony was well underway. Winners and losers would not be sorted out until 1948, and their relative positions not confirmed until the 1950s.

This also held true in Toronto's Jewish and non-sectarian organizational politics. In the community at large, efforts to build a Community Chest supported by Catholics, Protestants, and Jews was well on the road to success by 1943. The fact that the Jewish community had been invited to participate, and the presence of Jewish leading lights on the Community Chest board portended the wider acceptance of Jews in the postwar world.

Similarly, the UJWF, Congress's Central Division, and the United Jewish Refugee and War Relief Agency (UJRWRA), the arm of Bronfman and Hayes in Toronto, all jealously guarded their respective organizational turf. Hayes and Bronfman expected that the UJRWRA would monopolize postwar immigration and refugee settlement, and hoped this monopoly would allow them to extend their sway over professional social work agencies such as the Jewish Family and Child Service. The UJRWRA might then be able to drive a Montreal-controlled wedge into the Welfare Fund's bailiwick. In addition, Hayes believed that ensuring the UJRWRA's monopoly of this field would pay postwar dividends in terms of Congress's visibility. Central Division bitterly opposed this incursion into its own autonomy and increased its visibility in combatting discrimination against Jews and other minorities. As we shall see, organized labour would also stake a postwar claim to hegemony in this area, with lasting impact. Central Division's foremost ally, the Welfare Fund, jealously guarded its monopoly over fundraising and its control over the rules for organizational allocations. The fund rightly regarded its methodology as trend-setting and was determined to ensure that, no matter how unpredictable postwar conditions would be, professionalism and communal future planning would carry the day.

Indeed, the fund's success in imposing its vision led one visionary to seek new worlds to conquer. UJWF executive director Martin Cohn resigned in early December 1943. His career epitomized social work's rise to pre-eminence in Toronto Jewish communal planning. Cohn's career began in 1927 as assistant executive director of the Jewish Boys' Club. At the time, he was one of the few employees of any FJP affiliate with social work training. As we have seen, during Cohn's tenure as executive director of the FJP, he worked with member agencies to develop professional standards for program delivery and staff development. He made progress despite the FJP's financial difficulties and the economic burdens imposed by the Depression. The establishment of the UJWF, with its fundraising clout and effective control, allowed Cohn to impose professional standards of social work methodology on the UJWF's ideologically diverse affiliate organizations. Cohn's crowning achievement was his role in the establishment of the United Community Chest (UCC) and the inclusion of the now professionally managed Jewish social service agencies under its umbrella. It was time to move on. Cohn left Toronto and became a fieldworker for the Chicago Jewish Federation. His timing proved exquisite.[1]

Cohn departed just as the Second World War was reshaping the practice of social work. Unprecedented wartime demand for trained social workers, little tainted by religious discrimination, offered Jewish social workers opportunities beyond their community. This made it difficult for the rapidly expanding Jewish social service agencies to find enough qualified personnel to serve their case loads. Overworked and underpaid staff was already straining to cope, and postwar planning pointed to further intensification of these trends.[2]

The UJWF and its affiliates worked to extend this insistence on professional qualifications beyond social workers. Two important organizational changes that began in this period proved key harbingers. In early 1944, the UJWF board of directors began meeting quarterly rather than monthly, leaving day-to-day policy oversight to the Executive Committee. This change had an immediate impact on the 1944 UJWF campaign. For the first time, daily campaign tasks were delegated to carefully trained volunteer workers drawn from UJWF affiliates, freeing up professional staff to deliver service.[3]

The UJWF executive thus signalled their ascendancy by prioritizing staff efficiency. The increased power of the executive derived from the rapidly changing nature of voluntary organizational operation. Although both UJWF executive and board members represented a cross-section of Toronto Jewry, those who were elected to the executive were generally higher on the economic ladder. They had more time to give, and in most cases, more money to donate. This further enhanced the Uptown bias of the executive. Professionals and independent businessmen predominated because they had the flexibility to attend hastily called meetings or spend time on the phone liaising with professional staff. In addition, because the executive met far more often than the board, the "knowledge gap" between the two groups quickly increased. Critics complained of UJWF's "lack of democracy," but it was simply the local manifestation of a North American trend.[4]

The quarterly UJWF Board meetings became more efficient, if lengthy affairs in which the board generally rubber-stamped the executive's agenda. In all but two cases between 1944 and 1949, the executive's agenda was accepted without amendment. Board meetings were four- or five-hour affairs and the executive's recommendations were discussed in great detail, but the board's activism extended no further.[5]

The decreased number of board meetings was not unique to Toronto; it reflected the growing complexity of North American Jewish communal life and the relatively small number of people who could afford to participate at the highest level. Most of the UJWF board members were fully occupied by their executive roles in UJWF's affiliates. With time at a premium, quarterly UJWF board meetings suited them just fine. Besides, a relatively small group formed Toronto's Jewish lay organizational elite, and the demands on their time grew rapidly.

Increased institutional complexity placed heavy burdens on all UJWF affiliates, adding to the responsibility and time demanded of board and executive members who served more than one communal organization. Thus the small group of elite communal leaders were often dashing between meetings. Sociologist Daniel Elazar offers an apt description:

> [T]o be a voluntary participant in the Jewish community one must be able to spend time – often a great deal of time – away from one's career or business ... Aside from successful businessmen and professionals and ... young lawyers ... the only people who can contribute the requisite time are academicians, and they are limited by their inability to spend the money required to maintain an active role. Thus of necessity wealth becomes an important factor in determining who the voluntary leadership will be.[6]

The few who had the time, interest, money, and ability divided their time between the organizations that interested them. Thus, the UJWF board was happy to delegate power to the executive and, increasingly, to the organization's professional leadership.[7]

The establishment of the United Community Chest compelled the UJWF to alter both the timing and methodology of its annual campaign. The UCC campaign took place in the fall when the UJWF's campaigns had previously taken place. The UJWF therefore organized a Spring Campaign, the first of which was scheduled to run from 19 to 31 March 1944, with a goal of almost $325,000.[8] The Campaign Committee sought volunteers from among the affiliate organizations and from the community at large. A Student Division was established to canvass the burgeoning Jewish university student population, while labour unions helped set up the Employees' Division. Clothing manufacturers on Spadina Avenue were divided into Men's and Women's Retail Divisions. This design proved a forerunner of later, far more targeted, UJWF fundraising campaigns, for which prospective donors would be canvassed by their peers. Similarly, the wealthy were canvassed separately in a Top Gifts category, which used peer pressure to maximize donations. These campaign tactics, a necessary response to the increased complexity of Toronto Jewish life, were based on extensive American Welfare Fund campaigning experience.[9]

The 1944 Spring Campaign is notable not only because of its new timing and methodology, but because it succeeded despite long odds. Jewish charitable appeals had always been timed to coincide with the High Holy Days, when synagogue attendance peaked and worshippers were inclined to donate. It was more difficult for the fund to campaign in late winter, when many wealthy donors were on vacation and poorer members of the community were putting away money for Passover, a very expensive holiday requiring special foods and preparation. In addition, despite a great deal of publicity, many donors still did not understand why major Jewish social service agencies were no longer part of the UJWF. A significant number of donors jumped to the conclusion that non-Jews had taken over Jewish agencies. Nonetheless, the well-briefed volunteer canvassers turned the tide. They proved adept at explaining the UCC/UJWF relationship and covering their pledge cards. The campaign exceeded its goal by more than $25,000.[10]

The campaign's success validated the fund's decision to rely on volunteer fundraisers. Granted, the campaign volunteers worked under professional guidance. Yet, scarcely a decade earlier, FJP professionals had closed the volunteer-run orphanage for failing to meet their standards. But North American Jewish Federation and Community Chest fundraising efforts in the 1930s demonstrated that properly trained volunteers were effective fundraisers. The successful canvasser did not need specialized knowledge. Peer pressure, a passion for the community, and a persuasive manner were more useful to a canvasser than knowledge of the psychology of donating. The UJWF soon learned that "no matter how much professional help is provided, only the voluntary leadership, the men who give the money, are able to influence others to give money."[11]

The campaign volunteers' ideological, religious, political and organizational diversity testified to the UJWF's organizational pre-eminence. In addition, the decision to prioritize overseas relief reflected communal concerns over the fate of European Jewry. Campaign volunteers mined a rich seam of communal support while applying the most current fundraising techniques. The numbers speak for themselves. The 1944 campaign received 7,656 pledges. Assuming that the average Jewish household contained 5.5 people, this would mean that over 42,000, or 78 percent, of Toronto's approximately 54,000 Jews were represented in the campaign.[12]

The highlighting of overseas relief was a sign of heightened communal anxieties. Although rumours of wartime atrocities against European Jews were widespread as early as 1942, it is doubtful that anyone, even among the leadership, could grasp the actual extent of these horrors. The Jewish public was desperate to help in any way possible. The UJWF executive shared these sentiments, and between 1944 and 1948 it consistently allocated all campaign surpluses to the UJRWRA–JDC, which already received the largest allocation of any UJWF affiliate. The prioritization of overseas relief came at the expense of Jewish educational institutions. In a rare indication of sensitivity to the *amcha* mood, the UJWF board vetoed the executive's January 1944 recommendation to allocate the campaign surplus domestically and redirected the entire $14,000 overseas.[13]

Jewish educators understood the need to prioritize overseas relief, but, the flat-lining of educational spending was a disappointment. Their patience was wearing thin. During the lean Depression years, the bulk of allocations had gone to the Jewish social service agencies of Division 1. The schools received allocations only for salary increases or essential repairs. Even though the schools enjoyed an unprecedented degree of financial security – their debts were being wiped out by the Capital Debts Reduction Campaign – they wanted to expand or build new facilities. But how to acquire the necessary funds?[14]

Separate fundraising campaigns were the obvious solution. The UJWF was no friend of such appeals. But the fund couldn't have it both ways. Thus, when the Borochov School asked for permission to conduct a special building fund campaign to finance a new building, the fund re-evaluated its stance. Impressed by the school's presentation, the fund executive authorized a sub-committee to consider the request. Its report cited the UJWF's overseas funding priorities as the central reason for recommending that schools be permitted to run pre-approved appeals for building projects. The executive agreed, noting that "if a demonstrated and proven need for a school building arises among the member agencies of the UJWF there should be no objection on the part of the UJWF to a campaign to fund such a building." As always, the executive demanded that no campaign conflict with the UJWF campaign and retained the right of final approval over all building details and the campaign goal.[15]

This logical and flexible response allowed many schools to mount campaigns. In recognition of this new trend, the UJWF established a

Permanent Committee on Capital Needs and Financing in November 1944. This committee presided over an impressive institutional renewal. Between 1943 and 1947 three schools raised funds for new facilities, while a $750,000 campaign for a combined YM & WHA/Canadian Jewish Legion/War Memorial Centre began, and the campaigns for the New Mount Sinai Hospital and a proposed Jewish Home for the Aged gained momentum. Of course, everyone was aware that communal pockets were only so deep. Special project fundraising, no matter how controlled, still competed not only with UJWF, UWF, and UPA campaigns within the Jewish community but also with the Victory Bond campaign of the federal government and the Community Chest campaign in the Toronto community at large.[16]

Wartime capital accumulation, economic prosperity, and institutional maturation were largely responsible for this surge of building plans. But fundraising and planning proved easier than construction. Wartime construction was stymied by quotas on construction materials, while skilled construction workers were diverted to essential war industries. Even with sufficient funds on hand, the UJWF and its affiliates were forced to defer all large capital building projects until after the war. In consequence, building campaigns made it clear that the funds collected must be earmarked for postwar use. Nonetheless, Toronto Jewry met or exceeded the quotas of every wartime UJWF, UPA, and UCC campaign, and still found the funds for special building campaigns. This success resulted both from the increased prosperity of Toronto Jewry and from the successful application of systematic fundraising methods.[17]

Prosperity also brought demographic change. In the late 1920s, wealthier Jews had begun moving north of Bloor Street into the St Clair and Bathurst area (often called Hillcrest) and into Forest Hill Village. The 1931 census had shown 1,293 Jews in Forest Hill, an almost tenfold increase over the previous decade. The completion of Holy Blossom's new building directly across Bathurst Street from the Village of Forest Hill in 1937 accelerated this trend. However, there was opposition to the Jewish movement northward. Forest Hill Village Council was uncomfortable with the increased Jewish presence, and it prevented the Brunswick Avenue Talmud Torah from using a storefront as its Eglinton Avenue branch. (The school moved further along Eglinton to a store outside the village boundaries.) Restrictive covenants also barred Jews from certain streets. Nevertheless, the Jewish population of the village increased to 6,073 by 1941 – a very noticeable 39.7 percent of its inhabitants. These wealthier Jews represented only 12 percent of the Toronto Jewish community, but they were the vanguard of the postwar suburban wave. In 1941 only 8 percent of Toronto Jews lived north of the Cedarvale Ravine; by 1951, over one-third of the city's Jews had settled there.[18]

Holy Blossom's move foreshadowed a northward institutional shift. Second-generation Jews whose immigrant parents had proudly affiliated with ethnic secular organizations switched their allegiance to religious-based institutions designed to meet the needs of the suburban family. This trend was epitomized throughout North America by the rise of the Conservative movement's "synagogue centre." Many second-generation Jews from traditional homes joined Holy Blossom or the suburban Conservative synagogues such as Beth Sholom on Eglinton Avenue, which were sprouting up in the 1940s and 1950s. Orthodoxy was not immune to suburbanization. The relatively few Orthodox congregations wanting a presence in suburbia also built comprehensive centres similar to those of the Conservative model. Shaarei Shomayim was a prime example. It began in the new Hillcrest area in the late 1930s, and soon began its building campaign. By 1942 it occupied a substantial property on St Clair Avenue.

Enrolment statistics at Toronto Hebrew Free School (THFS), formerly the Brunswick Avenue Talmud Torah, also reflected the northward flow of the Jewish population. In 1942 the greatest increases in enrolment occurred at the Free School branch in the Beth Yehuda Synagogue on Dovercourt Road (where enrolment tripled in a year) and the newly established Shaarei Shomayim branch on St Clair Avenue West (where enrolment merely doubled). When even these branches proved insufficient to handle the burgeoning Jewish population north of St Clair and west of Bathurst, a new branch was established in a storefront on Eglinton Avenue West in early 1943. These institutional demands kept the UJWF Committee on Capital Needs busy. Its successful coordination of myriad fundraising campaigns played a vital role in protecting the fund's hard-won hegemony over communal social planning and institutional rationalization.[19]

Judicious refusal of permission to campaign enhanced the committee's power. In early 1945 the Borochov School was not permitted a fundraising campaign for a new suburban branch. When the Borochov rebelliously built the branch, the UJWF refused to allocate funds for it. Protest was to no avail – the branch proved unsuccessful. The fund's strategy of strictly enforcing rational social planning remained intact into the postwar era. Indeed, the fund was always on the lookout for further rationalization. "There are some indications," noted the UJWF board of directors in March 1945, "that the community may be ready for the amalgamation of certain types of schools ... or at least the possibility of a more general coordination of Jewish education." In June 1945 the board further noted that there could be only one approach to fundraising: "The UJWF has a mandate for evaluating communal needs and meeting those needs." The formation of a centralized agency to oversee Toronto Jewish education was clearly on the horizon.[20]

War's end and continued suburbanization compelled the UJWF to zero in on communal planning to ensure growth without duplication of services. It was understandably concerned that fundraising chaos might follow the lifting of wartime controls on charitable fundraising. Hence its ceaseless effort to consolidate fundraising by minimizing separate campaigns even among member institutions and its continued insistence on proper accounting procedures from all its affiliates.[21]

But in the meantime, Jewish education continued to languish. Depression neglect, wartime constraints on finances and construction, and suburbanization left myriad schools demanding cash infusions. By the mid-1940s, the five major schools unaffiliated with synagogues all suffered from poor attendance, high staff turnover, and poor staff training. Although the fund's capital allocation program worked effectively to reduce the schools' mortgage debts, dealing with staffing issues proved more difficult. The lack of trained European teachers was especially troublesome. There were some local efforts to train Hebrew teachers under the auspices of Rabbi Abraham Price's Yeshivat Torat Chaim and the Eitz Chaim's Torat Emet Yeshiva School, but few of their graduates took positions in Toronto. Some prospective educators went to American yeshivot; most remained in the United States to teach. Thus the $12,000 per year that the UJWF allocated to teacher training produced few tangible results.

The end of the war allowed the fund to re-prioritize rationalizing Jewish education. Hiring an outside expert to examine the structure of Toronto Jewish education had been proposed in 1942, and by late 1946 further delay was untenable. Two new schools, the Jewish National Workers' School and the Morris Winchevsky School, joined the Fund. And there were fears that the growing congregational schools of Holy Blossom, Goel Tzedec, and Shaarei Shomayim would soon seek funding. The Associated Hebrew Schools (the new name of the Toronto Hebrew Free School and its associated branches in the city) began experimenting with a "day school" in 1944 at the senior kindergarten level. This concept involved students leaving the public school system and receiving both Jewish and general education in one school. The religious Zionist group Mizrachi funded this venture for the first two years. By 1946 this successful experiment extended to Grade 2, and Associated applied for an allocation. At the same time, Eitz Chaim Schools applied for a special allocation to pay the salary of a new principal. The UJWF executive was displeased and denied both requests. Its members decried the "parochialism" of Associated's day school, claiming it would prevent Jews from fully integrating into Canadian life, and noted that Eitz Chaim should have planned its budget more effectively. But the fund executive was galvanized into finally taking decisive action. Realizing that postwar prosperity presented a greater threat to its agenda than Depression and wartime austerity, the UJWF executive commissioned Uriah Englemann, a top-notch educational specialist, to investigate and report on the state of Jewish education in Toronto.[22]

To test willingness for educational reform, Division II hired Israel B. Rappaport, an expert on the communal organization of Jewish education. In December 1946 he presented a seminar on "Trends in Jewish Education" to principals and board members of Division II. Rappaport's seminar catalyzed opinion that communally coordinated educational planning under the UJWF banner was necessary and that the first step was to gather reliable information on the state of Jewish education in Toronto and the direction of its future growth. Englemann began his survey in fall 1946 and reported in early 1947. His report led to the formation of the Toronto Board of Jewish Education in 1949.[23]

The full revelation of the Holocaust brought renewed and unprecedented fundraising efforts for European relief. On 10 September 1945, Saul Hayes and Samuel Bronfman informed the UJWF executive that $1.5 million had to be raised immediately across Canada for European relief. Toronto's share came to $400,000. The UJWF executive was stunned. The fund had already increased its United Jewish Refugee and War Relief Agencies allocation by more than 30 percent to a record $175,000. Where would the extra $225,000 come from? The executive decided to approach the large donors of the community and canvass them so that the funds could be obtained immediately. Extraordinary times demanded extraordinary measures and in this case, the fund set aside its usual insistence on prior planning and budgeting in order to meet the demand. Faced with the horrific tales emerging from Europe, deep-pocketed philanthropists raised the funds in record time.

Postwar immigration posed a more formidable challenge. The fund had no control over the many organizations and different levels of government involved. While Joseph Kage, Harold Troper, and Irving Abella have explained the politics of postwar immigration, it is important to examine the effect of these new immigrants on Jewish organizations in Toronto. Dealing with immigrants provided a litmus test of communal professionalization and rationalization efforts.[24]

Since 1923, successive federal governments had worked overtly and covertly to minimize Jewish immigration. This action received approbation from some and a lack of attention from most, but it aroused great opposition among Canadian Jews anguishing over family separations amid growing European anti-Semitism. It had been an era of agonizing conversations about immigration, letters begging for entry that couldn't be answered in the positive, and relatives pleading with the JIAS, immigration lawyers, immigration consultants, and steamship agents for help that often did not materialize. Immigration restriction meant continued economic hardship for those trapped in Eastern Europe and worry for their extended families in Canada. By the late 1930s and during the Second World War, a denial of admission, written in the cold bureaucratic language of the federal bureaucracy, was a virtual death sentence.[25]

Revelations of the enormity of the Holocaust strengthened the resolve of Canadian Jews to bring as many survivors as possible to Canada. Many wished to sponsor the few family members that had somehow escaped. But the King government was adamant that, despite the tragedy of the Holocaust, "ultimate responsibility for these atrocities rested squarely on the Nazis" and therefore Canada had no obligation to offer Displaced Persons (DPS) a refuge. Preoccupied with demobilizing Canadian troops and maintaining economic stability, the goverment showed little interest in any refugee movement.[26] The Department of Immigration was in no hurry to send teams of inspectors to Europe to facilitate the processing of survivors. They claimed shipping was scarce, and, in the hope that the situation of Jewish refugees would sort itself out (and even disappear), did nothing.[27]

A shocking Gallup Poll revealed that well after the war, almost half of those polled did not want Jewish immigrants. Many even went out of their way to write anti-Semitic comments on the Gallup questionnaire. Yet, at the same time, as Walter Lacquer observed, the world was stunned by the revelations of Bergen-Belsen. The newsreels and stories in the press on the Holocaust were impossible to ignore. More important, by early 1946 it was clear that Jewish survivors could not conveniently repatriate themselves to homelands in which they were obviously not welcome. In mid-1946 the newly formed United Nations Relief and Rehabilitation Administration (UNRRA), of which Canada was a member, prioritized resettlement over repatriation. Pressure grew for Canada to open its gates. The JIAS inundated the Department of Immigration with streams of applications, while Hayes dashed from office to office in Ottawa vainly petitioning for some humanitarian discretion for survivors. Ultimately more significant pressure came from Department of External Affairs officials concerned that Canadian intransigence on admitting DPS was "giving Canada an international black eye."[28]

Finally, in early 1947 Cabinet agreed to a revision of Canadian immigration policy. King told a hushed House of Commons on 7 May 1947 – almost two years after V-E Day – that the long-term goals of Canadian immigration policy would shift from exclusion to selective admission. Family reunification was given the green light. An excited Hayes telegraphed the most relevant news to members of the CJC National Executive: "Admitted are: husband or wife; son, daughter, brother or sister together with their husbands or wives and unmarried children; father or mother; orphaned nephew or niece under 21." In addition, permission was given to admit a thousand Jewish orphans under the age of eighteen, provided that Congress would ensure that they would not become public charges and that their admission was acceptable to the provinces concerned. This was the government's sole open concession to Canadian Jewry – and it served only to replace the Vichy orphans who never made it.²⁹

From this point on, the CJC prioritized planning over lobbying. Hayes immediately planned two ambitious immigration projects to take advantage of the *Immigration Act*'s new provisions. The first, commonly called the "DP Project," aimed to quickly bring in as many survivors as possible to Canada." The second, the "Orphans' Project" was designed to ensure the speedy immigration of the thousand war orphans. Each project profoundly affected Toronto Jewish institutional life, and highlighted the organizational strengths and weaknesses of communal planning. Above all, these immigration projects would test the level of professionalism in the Jewish organizational bureaucracy.

At first blush, the Orphans' Project should have presented few difficulties. It originated in October 1942 when Hayes had successfully negotiated the admission of a thousand Jewish orphans from Vichy, France. Five hundred were to come immediately, with the balance to follow. Hayes had ruthlessly pushed aside the JIAS, which held prior responsibility for all immigration schemes, to ensure that Congress would both control and receive credit for the project.

The Toronto JIAS regarded this takeover as yet another in a series of humiliations at the hands of Hayes. As earlier mentioned, when he became executive director of the United Jewish Relief Agencies (UJRA) immediately after its formation in 1939, Hayes had established refugee committees in Montreal, Winnipeg, and Toronto. The Toronto JIAS protested this incursion into its domain, but JIAS national president Benjamin Robinson overruled their objections, likely persuaded by Bronfman and Hayes, his fellow CJC executive members, that in these desperate times organizational unity was essential.

But the Toronto JIAS begged to differ. Local president Ben Forer complained bitterly to his national counterpart that the UJWF's Sam Zacks had told a public meeting that "the JIAS now occupies the place of a Ladies' Auxiliary meeting immigrants upon their arrival and also takes care of passport applications for people." Forer charged that Robinson and Solkin had stood by while the Toronto JIAS lost credibility. Solkin's *volte face* in his new role was especially painful since he had been behind efforts to earn the Toronto JIAS credibility in the mid-1930s. Hyman Latch, Forer's successor as Toronto JIAS president, continued sniping at Robinson and Solkin for allowing Hayes's UJRA to run roughshod over the prerogatives of the JIAS. They accused Hayes, with justification, of undermining the Toronto JIAS's authority and lowering its funding allocations from the UJWF.[30]

Hayes had adeptly used political pressure to stonewall the JIAS. In early 1941, just as UJWF allocations were being determined, UJWF executive director Martin Cohn expressed his belief that "the JIAS was doing the work well, and why bother with the Refugee Committee in the amount being given?" Hayes, anxious to ensure that the UJRA's large allocation remained untouched, wrote a confidential letter to former UJRA committee chairman Sam Zacks, who was slated to become UJWF president in April 1942. Hayes's letter indirectly criticized Cohn by noting: "I have nothing personal against Martin ... but I always felt that he was quietly sniping at *your* Refugee Committee in Toronto." Hayes was also capable of head-on assault. He openly dissuaded leaders of other Jewish organizations from pleading immigration cases in Ottawa without his prior approval. Backed by Bronfman's money and prestige, Hayes criticized all who ignored this protocol. JIAS national presidents and executive director had continued to defer to Hayes, fearful of the dressing down they received whenever they crossed him.[31]

By November 1942, when the Allied invasion of North Africa had derailed the Vichy Orphans' Project, Hayes established the UJRA's hegemony over immigration. But, much to his chagrin, Toronto's UJRA committee was moribund. Without immigration and refugees, there was no point in calling meetings. Its chairman Samuel Kronick acted as a one-man office, and the local JIAS secretary took charge of financial matters.[32] Though Hayes disapproved, this expedient relationship worked well. Between April and October 1944, sixty-nine refugee families arrived from Lisbon. Central Division retained tight control of the paperwork, but still needed JIAS's organization when it came to local settlement. The 174 individuals arriving from Lisbon were quickly and efficiently settled, an impressive feat given the scarcity of housing in Toronto.[33]

This small influx of refugees proved the worth of communal settlement resources. Volunteers supplied interim housing while Congress sourced rental accommodation. By early January 1945, fifty-two refugee families had been placed in furnished apartments through the generosity of the Women's War Efforts Committee of Hadassah, Congress, and the Council of Jewish Women (COJW). In 80 percent of the families at least one member was employed full time; these families did not need further rental assistance. The Lisbon refugee families were also offered employment counselling and medical and dental care. Refugee children quickly enrolled in public schools and the Brunswick Avenue Talmud Torah, and attended summer camps courtesy of Congress. All the major Jewish organizations of Toronto, including the *landsmanschaften*, pitched in to help the Lisbon refugees.[34]

The Lisbon group represented a new type of migrant who had been traumatized by what they had seen and experienced. "Many of these people," noted the "UJRA–JIAS Report on the Lisbon Refugees," "are agitated and nervous due to years of wandering and suffering." The community handled the Lisbon refugees well from an organizational point of view. Thirty agencies, both Jewish and mainstream, were mobilized to coordinate their settlement. The "Report on the Lisbon Refugees" explained the success in the self-congratulatory and paternalistic detail that characterized the social work of the period:

> We are regarded by them [the refugees] as their parent organization; they consult with us on all manner of problems. Jobs have to be found, old ones changed to new ones, new flats have to be obtained, children and adults fall ill, need surgical services. Nursery schools have to be found for children of working mothers, refugees plan to go in business and consult us for advice, emergencies of all kinds occur, disputes occur with employers, verification of wages when financial assistance is sought, follow-up investigation of homes, help with Free Loans, clothing and furniture ... They receive from us professional case work services to meet their individual needs and requirements and make their adjustments to Canadian life with the minimum amount of tension and conflict.

This statement masked a grim reality, however: this tiny refugee influx had stretched communal resources to the limit. What would happen if and when immigration rules allowed Jews to enter in greater numbers? Success wasn't cheap either – the Lisbon refugees program cost the UJRA Central Division almost $24,000. Not that anyone complained. The refugee settlement bolstered communal pride and provided a solitary happy note among the grim tidbits of news that escaped wartime Europe. What was money if not a tool to aid rescue? Toronto Jews who gave generously to a wide variety of charitable causes were called upon to give more each year, and per capita generosity became a hallmark of Toronto Jewry.[35]

The Lisbon refugee influx also tested the newly formed Jewish Family and Child Services (JFCS) formed on 1 January 1944, through the merger of the Jewish Family Welfare Bureau and the Jewish Children's Bureau. From the outset, these agencies exemplified adherence to professional social work principles and a willingness to apply these principles to communal planning. The JFCS consistently worked to broaden its mandate. After a 1944 survey of community social service indicated many students in Jewish schools could benefit from social work intervention, the agency moved quickly. UJWF affiliate schools began the 1944–45 school year with social workers paying regularly scheduled visits. This successful program allowed earlier intervention with problem children, expanded the JFCS client base to non-Jewish nursery schools, and provided increased revenue, since many of these educational services were fee-based. Once again the UJWF divisional system had proved its value by providing a framework for members of organizations to meet, exchange ideas, cooperate, and learn how to work together to optimize resources.[36]

However, a shortage of social workers soon threatened these ambitious plans. In June 1944 it was reported that with present staffing it was evident that the agency "could not undertake additional responsibility." The immediate creation of two and a half more staff positions was recommended. By December, the JFCS had a caseload of 382; two-thirds were family cases, and the other third dealt with children. This caseload increased by 118 in November alone. It was impossible to increase staff because social work graduates were in demand and salaries were rising continually to cover wartime inflation. In January 1945 the board agreed to hire one and a half more workers, less than than recommended. This began a five-year period in which the JFCS was understaffed and its social workers overloaded. Its board had little time for proactive policy making as it struggled to retain staff, pay them competitive wages, and maintain morale. Future planning indicated no relief was in sight. The "Report on the Extension of Case Work" noted that the Jewish elderly were underserviced, and more workers would have to be assigned to both eldercare and future planning. This need led directly to planning the Baycrest Hospital and Home for the Aged.[37]

Thus, the JFCS was seriously overextended just as it confronted the pressure of postwar Jewish immigration. It had managed the relatively small number of Lisbon refugees, but could it cope with the flood of Holocaust survivors requiring heavy social work intervention? Not likely. On 10 January 1946, well before large-scale postwar Jewish immigration began, JFCS executive secretary Dora Wilensky painted a bleak picture:

> In the Family Service Department there are at present 5 and one-half workers, in May 1945 there were seven. The part-time worker has been ... unable to give part time. The five students [from the University of Toronto School for Social Work] require half of Miss Greene's time for 6 months of the year. In the Child Placement Department, we have one half-time worker less than in May of last year. The total shortage of professional staff at this point is three workers ... Efforts at recruiting staff have not met with success.[38]

These conditions eroded staff morale. The JFCS staff association told the board that chronic overwork accounted for the increased number of sick days. The association demanded longer vacations (one month instead of three weeks) and complained that staff shortages had forced employees to work overtime and accept more responsibility than many of them could handle. The sympathetic board increased vacation times but, despite raising salary levels, could not find more trained social workers.[39]

It is crucial to note that money was not the issue. The Community Chest of Toronto funded the JFCS, and the UJWF made up any fiscal shortfalls due to additional wartime expenses. The ongoing problem was a lack of trained social workers. Many skilled personnel were at war, others were in "essential industries," and there simply weren't enough graduates of social work schools to go around. The JFCS could not provide the required level of professional service. As early as May 1945, Wilensky noted that "we need a worker for Refugees." When a worker was finally hired, she was only "partially trained." Soon, even partial training would be a luxury.[40]

War's end brought no respite. Inflation drove salaries upward and the demand for social workers spiked. The few newly minted graduates who could be found to replace departing staff lowered the level of experience at the agency. By 1947 the JFCS was less ready than ever to deal with the psychological issues of refugee immigrants.[41]

Naturally, these staffing deficiencies could not keep Canadian Jewry from seeking increased immigration, and the UJRA was also wrestling with these problems. In February 1946, Hayes began to pick up signals from Ottawa that a change in immigration policy was forthcoming. He instructed the Toronto UJRA to reactivate the organizational framework that had facilitated the integration of the Lisbon refugees, and asked the JFCS to report on "what steps should be taken with regard to the future provision of casework services."[42]

Wilensky was blunt. She replied that the JFCS lacked the staff to carry out such an investigation. She lamented that in any case "it would be almost impossible to ... implement the conclusions of such a study." But the UJRA was insistent. Hayes had received assurances that the government would finally relent and renew the permission for the thousand war orphans to enter Canada to replace those prevented from immigrating by the Nazis' seizure of Vichy in November 1942. The UJRA had to guarantee that these children would be placed according to acceptable social work standards. The JFCS was the key player and its board was worried. Knowing how inadequate their staffing was, they agreed to study whether the JFCS could fulfill its mandate, but added the warning that only "a cursory study would be undertaken involving minimum of staff time ... it being clearly understood that a comprehensive survey cannot be undertaken at this time."[43]

The unionization of JFCS employees in May 1947 drove costs even higher and cut the amount of permitted overtime work. Already overburdened staff members were compelled to handle more cases in less time. Yet the JFCS further expanded the range of its operations. In early 1947 it set up the Jewish Vocational Service (JVS) to find work for unemployed Jews and others. It also continued to spearhead the investigation of Jewish eldercare in Toronto and convened a committee to begin discussions on future planning for the aged. Thus, the JFCS was still woefully overextended when the admission of the war orphans was authorized on 29 April 1947. As anticipated, the UJRA accepted responsibility both for financing the project and for ensuring that foster home placement was in accord with "the accepted standards of social work" required by each province.

This issue would lead to considerable conflict between the JFCS and potential foster parents. Three days after the Order-in-Council approving the Orphans' Project, the government amended the *Immigration Act* to allow first-degree relatives to immigrate. After over two decades, the possibility of family reunification became a reality. Ironically, this change would impact negatively on the Orphans' Project because families that might have welcomed orphans understandably preferred to open their homes to family members.⁴⁴

How would an understaffed and underfunded JFCS cope with these new pressures? Could it expand its reach while retaining its commitment to professional standards? For that matter, could Toronto Jewry, extended to the maximum by the arrival of a few Lisbon refugee families, handle the larger influx on its way?

It seemed that there was in fact little cause for worry. Few children had survived the Holocaust, and many of them were bound for Palestine. The sketchy information available from the CJC's European contacts suggested that it would be unlikely that more than three hundred orphans would be available. That would mean a hundred each for Toronto, Montreal, and Winnipeg. It was agreed that the first group of orphans would go to Winnipeg and the second group to Toronto. The JFCS took a sanguine approach. It should be relatively simple to accommodate this number – smaller than the number of Lisbon refugees. Besides, the Lisbon refugees had been settled successfully under wartime conditions. And these were children – survivors of the Holocaust – surely placement would not be an issue.⁴⁵

The JFCS staff put the planning for the children on hold. Wilensky didn't even send the outline of the Orphan's Project to the JFCS executive until late June. They proved equally unconcerned, endorsing her decision and moving the annual meeting to the fall. After all, it had been a challenging year and everyone needed a rest. With European refugee movments in constant flux because of erratic ship schedules and screening procedures, the orphans' arrival time was unpredictable and likely months away. And, with offers of private foster homes pouring in, the JFCS executive could be excused for being a bit smug about its ability to handle the orphans. After all, it was August – high season for summer vacation – and a good time to take a well-deserved break. All seemed ready.⁴⁶

It did not take long to disturb the summer's relaxed attitude. Just after Labour Day 1947, reality checked in with a vengeance. On 9 September, CJC central executive secretary Solomon Grand was glancing over his weekly memo from Hayes in Montreal when he noticed an apparent typographical error. It was a reminder that the first contingent of orphans would arrive in Winnipeg around the middle of September and the Toronto contingent would arrive around 7 October. Grand immediately called Wilensky to confirm the error. Wilensky recognized it, but reminded him that shipping schedules were subject to change and warned that if this indeed turned out to be the orphans' arrival date, the JFCS wouldn't be ready. She recalled that they had agreed to allow "time to prepare for a Reception Centre, etc. at least until the third transport."[47]

When a worried Grand in turn called Hayes, he heard an earful. Not that it helped – the orphans were coming and Toronto wasn't ready. Furious, Hayes rerouted the second contingent to Winnipeg to maximize Toronto's preparation time. However, that only delayed the inevitable. When the JFCS board convened on 18 September, it was already racing against time. The board members listened attentively as Wilensky told them the Toronto JFCS was "to take the responsibility for the reception, placement, care and planning for these children and youth now coming to Toronto and to Ontario." The CJC would reimburse all costs, "including those for additional staff and supervision." Wilensky recommended the immediate establishment of a reception centre staffed with a social worker, cook, and maintenance person. The children would remain there while prospective foster homes were screened in accordance with accepted social work practices.[48]

At this point the immensity of the Orphans' Project dawned on the board. Members grilled Wilensky about the age and characteristics of the orphans, noting that they actually knew nothing about the groups coming to them. They were met with silence. Even the professionals did not know who or what to expect – and this at the very moment the first orphans were disembarking! Undeterred, and stirred by the opportunity to finally do something for these precious child survivors of the Holocaust, the board quickly agreed to establish a Committee on European Youth. It was made up of representatives from various community organizations including the JIAS, JVS, UJRA, women's service organizations, trade unions, and religious groups. Wilensky jotted down the committee's mandate: find and equip a reception home;

publicize the need for foster homes and other living arrangements; plan the agency's program for this group; recommend the required budget and staff; and act as a case committee.[49]

The "one-stop" mandate of the Committee on Youth marked a key departure in refugee settlement. The government's insistence on settlement in accordance with accepted social work practices led to a confrontation between the JFCS and UJRA that would have far reaching consequences. The committee put the JFCS in the driver's seat for the Toronto end of the Orphans' Project. The agency used "accepted social work practices" as its excuse for a confrontation with Hayes, the CJC head office, and their Toronto representatives. Simply put, the JFCS intended to ally with the UJWF to wrest control over refugee settlement in Toronto away from the Montreal-based Congress.[50]

The battle between the Toronto-based and Montreal-based agencies had deeper roots in social work and immigrant settlement methodology than geography. By the end of the war, Hayes had made the UJRA pre-eminent in immigration by usurping the role of the JIAS. He confirmed the CJC's primacy by travelling across Canada to negotiate the orphans' admission with provincial authorities. The UJRA believed that all immigrants required only minimal intervention. Many older Toronto community leaders likewise assumed that most immigrants needed little more than a welcome and a brief orientation to Toronto. There was no reason for reinventing the wheel of immigration settlement for immigrants who arrived via the Tailors', Domestics', or Furriers' projects, for example. They were already assured of work and would only need housing. Sponsored immigrants would initially live with their sponsoring relatives and would not encumber scarce communal settlement resources. The "catch all" approach assumed that only a few immigrants in dire straits would require referrals to the social services offered by the JFCS.[51]

This approach of the "old guards" was hotly disputed by younger community leaders, who comprised the Committee on European Youth, and who strongly supported the rigorous application of professional standards in all realms of communal life. The JFCS was a model agency in this regard. It valued and rewarded professionalism, and often undertook self-surveys and shared the costs of continuing education to ensure that its social workers met the most current professional standards. The Committee on European Youth viewed the UJRA's approach as the well-meaning but misguided thinking of untrained volunteers. All immigrants were not created equal and many required professional social agency care. As Ben Lappin, a social worker who took part in the Orphans' Project and later analysed it, explained: "It was one thing ... to settle a man on a farm where he could continue the work he had done in Europe; it was another matter entirely to take a child who had been orphaned in Europe and to bring him to a strange family environment in Canada to start life anew. Both the Canadian home and the European child would face certain problems ... that would require the help of a trained professional case worker."[52]

In sum, it was Montreal's organizational clout that brought the orphans to Canada, but Toronto's organizations that determined how they would be settled. The Committee on European Youth used the "accepted social work standards" mandate to take control of the settlement and supervision of the orphans arriving in Toronto. This determination proved fortunate, as these orphans were different from other immigrants and were now guaranteed professional casework assistance. As in the case of Jewish Children's Home struggle almost a decade earlier, the view of the young professionals prevailed.

Nonetheless, the triumph of the professional social workers was not unimpeded and was frustrated by factors beyond their control. The Committee on European Youth held its first meeting on 8 October. Its roster was a veritable "who's who" of key lay and professional leaders in CJC Central Division, the UJWF, and the JFCS. Hayes, in attendance, stressed the importance of the JFCS's responsibility for "the technical and social service work of the Youth movement." He insisted that the UJRA would remain responsible for "broad policy and financing." Therefore, although the Committee on European Youth was technically only a sub-committee formed by the JFCS board, it would have hands-on responsibility for the project.[53]

Hayes also stressed the importance of speedily organizing the orphans' reception. He had decided to send a few orphans from the first group to Toronto, although most had been diverted. The ship carrying the first eighteen orphans destined for Toronto would arrive around 23 October. At least one Toronto representative should be dockside to meet them. Hayes predicted that these would be the first of about three hundred orphans who would be settled in Toronto. The energetic young Toronto leadership frantically prepared for the orphans' arrival. They organized furnishings for the reception centre, advertised for new staff, and convinced the Toronto Board of Education to provide special English and Civics classes for the orphans. However, the search for a home that could be converted into a Reception Centre was still unsuccessful because of a serious housing shortage. The JFCS decided to retrofit a building previously used to store used clothing for shipment to camps for displaced persons. To lower medical costs, Hayes recommended that JFCS encourage doctors and dentists to donate their services.[54]

The committee assumed that orphan placement would be the simplest part of the puzzle. After all, these were the first group of Holocaust survivors to reach Toronto, and many came from the same towns as Downtowners. Surely, with the horrors of the Holocaust now known, every Jewish house would be ready to accept an orphan. Not so. Toronto Jewry did not yet appreciate the scope of the Holocaust and naïvely believed that most of these orphans were babies and toddlers. In fact, more than half of them were seventeen years old, and a third were fifteen and sixteen. Not one child was under five. But when the newly graduated social workers tried to explain this to prospective foster parents among the communal elite, they received an interesting reception:

> They interpreted the act of giving shelter to an immigrant youth as an extension of their communal activities. To the agency worker ... they were a client. But the elite group balked at the client role in no uncertain terms. One worker recalled: ... the reception ... would often be cordial; the worker would be ushered into the living room where there were cocktails and chit-chat ... The moment the conversation turned on the war orphan residing in the home, another cocktail was offered and the subject changed ... Community leaders ... tended to regard many of the workers as youngsters hardly older than the war orphans.

When community members realized how old the orphans actually were, many offers of homes were withdrawn. Some felt incapable of handling teenaged survivors. And it was not easy; many of these children were distrustful and fearful. It was understandably hard for a boy who had been a partisan leader at fourteen to suddenly be asked to act "like a normal teenager," go to school every day, and obey his foster parents. It is not surprising that almost 10 percent of the orphans needed more than one foster home. As stories of these "difficult children" circulated, the supply of free foster homes dried up, threatening the project's success. The normally unflappable Hayes exploded. "A scare must be thrown into the Jewish community at once," he furiously wrote. "The whole of the Canadian Jewish community must be apprised ... that if homes are not offered ... we must go back to Europe to cancel many of our plans and go back to Ottawa and confess our inability to absorb ... even several hundred war orphans." This threat inaugurated a year-long series of campaigns asking people to "open their hearts and homes" and "rescue the children from *shmad* [forced conversion], shame, and shambles." Even these deliberately crass appeals to communal guilt proved unsuccessful. Eventually, paid homes were found to accommodate most orphans, though the original foster parents often tried to remain in touch.[55]

The initial inability to predict the number of orphans available for immigration had exacerbated the home-finding issue. Conditions in Europe were chaotic, and since the orphans' visas had no time limit, they had a lower priority than other immigrants and were often able to board ships only at the last minute. This issue dogged the entire Orphans' Project and played havoc with the professionals' carefully laid plans. Time and again, improvisation would trump organization. This uncertainty extended even to knowing how many orphans would actually settle in Toronto. The hunt for foster homes for 150 orphans began in late August of 1947. By early October, Hayes told Toronto to expect about 300; in the end, 418 settled. The lack of foster homes produced overcrowding in the reception centre, which, as early as December 1947, was reported to be facing "a considerable crisis." It was already filled to capacity with twenty-nine orphans and seventy-three more were expected to arrive in less than a month. The committee was warned that this problem might well continue for some time after that. It did: until the end of the project in early 1949. The increasingly strident and urgent appeals for foster homes mirrored the the dwindling number of "free" homes ready to take in teenagers.[56]

Housing remained a divisive issue. A furious debate developed over "paid" versus "free" foster homes. This debate was not new. It had been part of the discussion behind the takeover of the Jewish Children's Home. Paid foster care was a growing trend in North America. It was cheaper than running orphanages – a fact that Welfare Funds and

Community Chests appreciated. Childcare professionals preferred to screen and pay foster parents rather than accept volunteers, who often resisted scrutiny as an imposition on their voluntary generosity. Since the closure of the Jewish Children's Home, the JFCS had far more children in paid homes than in unpaid ones.[57]

But communal feeling mitigated against paid care in the Orphans' Project. The orphans were the children who had survived Hitler, the "remnant that had returned, the stick saved from the fire." They were the living link between the slaughtered millions in the "old homeland" and North Americn Jews. There was a strong sense that everything should and must be done for these "orphans of the storm." Therefore the Jewish community was generous with financial support – but not with their homes – and many offered to volunteer. The orphans at the Reception Centres became "stars," their presence eagerly sought out by girls checking out the new boys in town. "Many an evening," wrote an observer, "girls would predominate in the visiting parties, bent on lounging and flirting with the older members of the European youth group" and Toronto Jews seeking news from long-lost relatives.[58]

All this was flattering, but professionals, concerned with the project's mandate, fussed that "instead of being a place for reception, the [reception] centre began to take on the character of a neighbourhood settlement serving the immediate area rather than the war orphans." The carefully articulated divide between the orphans and their supervising professionals on one side and the Jewish community on the other collapsed. This process was expedited by the numerous high-profile community members who had immediately stepped forward to offer "free homes" to the young immigrants. Wealthy professionals often spontaneously appeared at the reception centre and zoomed off on shopping sprees with happy orphans in tow. The delighted teens descended on local stores, and quickly spent their benefactors' money to acquire the coveted "American look." Their sartorial splendour was immediately displayed to admiring crowds at the centre, which of course both charmed the opposite sex and elicited the jealousy of their peers. Social workers expressing concern were perceived as interlopers, keeping the children from people who cared for them, controlling access and offering dire prognostications on the deleterious effect of all this communal attention.

Such outpourings of open-hearted generosity and spontaneity met a wall of rejection from the social workers. Nothing, declared the professionals, must interfere with the carefully staged adjustment of these youths. They had to relearn the routine of civilized society. For children like ten-year-old Celena, who grew up "with the screams of people being taken away ... a sound I thought I would never get out of my head," coming to Canada meant huge adjustments. They had survived by their wits and by breaking rules. Now society demanded they follow rules and procedures in a foreign language and try to make up the lost years while becoming accustomed to a new culture. Social workers insisted on controlling access to the children, mapping out their lives, and searching out proper homes for them – all under their mission of handling the orphans "in accordance with accepted social work practices."

The Toronto Jewish community, and some of the orphans, responded by "uniting in their distrust of social workers." Most of this reaction was misguided. The Toronto Reception Centre files indicate confusion caused by orphans who were already placed in foster homes trying to stay for a few nights with their friends awaiting placement. Certainly orphans and visitors who suddenly "discovered" they were relatives only aroused suspicion on all sides. Sometimes orphans did meet relatives, who then concealed this fact so that they would not be financially liable. Most important, however, it was essential that the centre be run smoothly and permanent foster homes be found quickly so as to allow sufficient space for the next group of orphans – whose time of arrival could not be predicted. But quickly found homes were not necessarily good homes. The Committee on European Youth rejected "free" homes because some people were "offering a home out of a sense of duty only," with no idea what was involved in meeting the orphans' needs. Better to pay for homes with experience than accept free accommodations from people with good will but little experience. Even with the most careful screening, approximately one-fifth of the children had to be removed from their first home placement because of incompatibility.[59]

This situation brought the clash between lay and professional value systems into the open. As Fraidie Martz wrote:

> The result [of these antagonisms] was an irreconcilable conflict between the volunteers who were in every way indispensable to

the Project and the professional agencies, especially in ... Toronto ... Emotional appeals called upon people of good will to act like family. When they came forward, however, they were treated impersonally as "clients," and brusquely screened and evaluated by newly trained "professional social workers"—the graduates of a young, still-to-be-tested profession. Instead of being recognized for their altruism, even men and women who were acknowledged pillars of society were told they must be examined for the suitability of their homes or the wholesomeness of their marital and family life.[60]

Social workers could not hermetically seal off the orphans. Indeed, as Lappin observed, "the formalized relationships between the agencies and the general public ... simply gave way." Communal misunderstandings on all sides were responsible for a constant shortage of both "free" and "paid" homes. The shortage persisted despite frequent, and increasingly desperate, appeals for housing which drew on images of the Holocaust and played on the traditional Jewish value of protecting widows and orphans. Almost twice as many orphans stayed at the reception centre than it was designed to accommodate and for far longer than anticipated. This overcrowding exacerbated tensions and diminished the orphans' sense of self-worth. Many felt that no family wanted them. Pressure increased as the staff noted the longer children remained in the centre, the more difficult it became to place them successfully.[61]

Many placements proved challenging. Nathan came to live with a family that had a nine-year-old son and had lost a son that would have been Nathan's age. Things began well but then went downhill. The family perceived Nathan as "aloof ... and played the role of boarder rather than the child in the house." After some time "the S's decided he was not what they wanted and asked that Nathan be replaced. He was distressed and embittered to learn of their desire to have him leave and found it difficult to contemplate another experience in a family home".

This story had a happy ending – another family took Nathan and nurtured him so that he was able to catch up on his education and find employment. Moniek Lewkowitz, on the other hand, was one of the many who had a positive experience: "Congress really looked after us – they did the utmost for us ... it was a tremendous feeling to be given clothes and be put in a house."

The Orphans' Project successfully placed most of its children and they begin to reassemble their shattered lives. But it was a near thing. To the dismay of social planners, planning could not cover all contingencies. The vagaries of refugee movement, immigration screening, and trans-Atlantic transportation were beyond the project's control. However, Toronto's lack of preparedness on the ground was all too obvious. The leading professionals had miscalculated everything, from the arrival date and number of the first contingent, and had failed to educate the community on the demography of the new arrivals.

The political fallout of this need to improvise proved far reaching. According to one review, the Orphans' Project suffered "from chronic problems of understaffing, staff turnover, and union trouble" and was ill-equipped to meet the orphans' basic needs. In August 1948, at the height of the Orphans' Project, its six caseworkers saw 229 of the 250 youth then in Toronto. Secretaries were busy typing lengthy semi-annual reports on each youth and keeping up with a heavy flow of correspondence generated by proper adherence to social work procedures. Bookkeepers were issuing six hundred cheques per month for the Orphans' Project, and balancing its three separate bank accounts. When the related activities of the JFCS's other fourteen caseworkers is taken into account, it is obvious that the Orphans' Project was drowning the agency in a sea of paper.[62]

Overburdened bureaucracy was exacerbated by communal lack of understanding of the orphans' experience. Frank Bialystok reveals that Canadian Jewish leaders, like those in other countries, "could not comprehend the scope of the event [the Holocaust] or its catastrophic effects" even after reports from 1942 onward. Neither would the Jewish public listen to the survivors' stories. No one wanted to listen to them. "There was a war here too," they were told. The *Canadian Jewish Chronicle*, voice of Uptown Jewry, did not publish a single account of survivors' experience in 1948, even though twelve thousand survivors had arrived. Rabbi David Monson recalled running from store to store in the Kensington Market asking for contributions to help purchase homes for the orphans. He found few takers. Many simply responded: "Since when do teenagers need so much help?" Some European Youth Committee members themselves questioned why so much time was being spent on European youth "while Canadian youth do not receive this casework service." Some members went so far as to ask why it was taking so long for these young people to settle down and become independent. One even inquired, "Are we not pampering and overprotecting them?" Communal inability to comprehend the magnitude of the Holocaust's impact on the individual was reflected in caseworkers' repeated reminders to the committee (who should have known better!) of these children's uniquely tragic history and the provincial government's insistence that the project be administered under professional guidelines consistent with the *Ontario Child Protection Act*.[63]

Surprisingly the Orphans' Project seemed efficient compared with the administration of both the Tailors' and Furriers' Projects, and the influx of refugees immigrants. The Tailors' Project grew out of a government-approved program to bring European DPs to Canada to fill jobs in Canadian industries with a demonstrated shortage of labour. Under the joint direction of the Jewish Labour Committee (JLC), an umbrella organization representing many unions with significant Jewish membership, and the overwhelmingly Jewish owners and employees of clothing factories in Toronto and Montreal, an application was made to bring "skilled workers" needed by their industry. Their efforts were rewarded with the passage of PC #2180 in October 1947, authorizing the admission of 2,136 tailors, 500 furriers, and their families.[64]

Hayes kept in touch with the industrial lobbying effort from a distance. He was all too aware that until now Jewish labour in Canada had kept Congress at arm's length despite frequent efforts to remedy the situation. In the past, the heavily Jewish needle and fur trades unions preferred to deal with the JLC on issues of communal Jewish interest. In Toronto, organized labour's absence from the Congress table was keenly felt, as Jewish unions were important in communal life. After the war the JLC played a key role in convincing the previously anti-immigrant Canadian Labour Congress that immigration would increase employment opportunities for Canadian workers. The JLC worked with factory owners to lobby Ottawa to approve a labour scheme. But it was politically essential that Congress remain in the background so that Ottawa could be convinced that industries needed workers – not that Congress wanted Jews.[65]

The postwar Canadian Jewish community demanded increased Jewish immigration. The existence of government-approved bulk-labour schemes in other sectors fuelled the desire of the fur and clothing industries to appeal for similar schemes. Both industries contained significant numbers of Jewish bosses and workers. In late February 1947 Samuel Posluns, owner of Superior Cloak, convened a committee of Toronto manufacturers to help prepare the brief. Hayes got wind of the plan, most likely because similar efforts were taking place among the Montreal clothing manufacturers and workers. He covertly offered access to Congress's research department and its experience in dealing with the Department of Immigration. Hayes reminded Posluns that the scheme would only win government approval if it appeared that the trades and unions had approached Ottawa independently; that this was a legitimate labour scheme and not a backdoor to Jewish immigration. Everything depended on Congress's maintaining a low-profile relationship with the clothing industry representatives.[66]

On 14 March the newly formed Needle Trades Immigration Committee, composed of both management and labour representatives, met in the office of CJC Central Division executive secretary Solomon Grand. He showed them a draft of a proposed brief that had been prepared at Hayes's request by CJC chief statistician and research director, Louis Rosenberg. The brief documented meticulously the importance of the needle trades to the Canadian economy. The statistics showed that the skilled craftsmen then employed in clothing factories were aging, and that there were insufficient Canadian workers available to replace them, even though training could be obtained upon discharge from the Canadian Armed Forces. The needle trades representatives quickly decided to use Congress's text as the basis for their brief, and obtained additional documentation from Tip Top Tailors and the National Association of Women's Wear. In the meantime, they requested entry permits for at least fifteen hundred tailors.

Beneath the statistics and documentation, though, the whole project was a scam. Industry did not really need labour. The workers and owners of the Jewish-dominated industry saw the proposed labour scheme as a way to bring Jews from Europe. Needle Trades Immigration Committee representatives pressured less eager firms to accept a specified number of workers they did not need; the desire to bring Jews to Canada trumped business sense. By 17 March the Toronto Cloak Manufacturers and the International Ladies Garment Workers' Union had found employers for up to two hundred workers "who would add a measure of relief to our industry." By month's end, Max Enkin, owner of Cook Clothing and president of the National Council of Clothing Manufacturers, reported that the brief had been endorsed by the influential Retail Men's Wear Association of Canada.[67]

The briefs were sent to Ottawa in late April and a meeting with the ministers of Immigration and of Labour arranged for 2 May. The ministers were clearly interested in the scheme, which now called for the admission of 2,000 tailors for the men's wear industry and 500 for women's wear. The representatives of these industries warned that without imported labour, factories could close and Canadian jobs might be lost. For once, government moved quickly. On 21 May, the ministers called the clothing industry representatives to finalize transportation and work arrangements. The lobbying effort succeeded despite C.D. Howe's discomfort with the project. Howe unilaterally reduced the number of Jews among the immigrant tailors to no more than 50 percent of the total and demanded that most approved Jewish tailors be single or at most married with no more than one child. This was not easy. Everywhere the selection team went, they were met by desperate crowds. "Everyone was a tailor," recalled selection team member Max Enkin. The pressure on the team was enormous, as Bernard Shane of the JLC wrote: "They [the refugees] looked upon us as saviours in whose power it was to liberate them and give them a new lease on life." In theory, the applicants had to pass a job test demonstrating proficiency on the sewing machine or with hand sewing. But there were exceptions. A selector recognized the name of one of the men. He asked the man: "Was your father Jacob Y. of Lodz?" "Yes," came the reply. "Prove to me that you are telling the truth," insisted the selector. He was given a detailed description of the house and family business. "I played with your father and went to school with him!" exclaimed the selector. "What happened to him?" "Chelmno," came the brief answer. The selector overlooked the "job test" and pronounced the man "an excellent tailor." Years later the selector recalled: "What else could I do? His father was my best friend before we emigrated to Canada." By October 1947 over two thousand DP tailors (and over a thousand of their dependants) had been selected and awaited passage.[68]

The speed of the scheme's approval proved a mixed blessing. The numbers permitted represented a clear breakthrough, but the tailors would begin arriving just as the straitened Toronto Jewish communal organizations were trying to service the Orphans' Project. Immigration, including family reunification, was slowly opening up as well. From late 1947 on, Jewish immigration to Canada surged – of the twelve thousand Jews who arrived between 1947 and the end of 1949, over half came to Toronto.[69]

Once again, communal foresight lacked clarity. Neither Congress nor the agencies associated with the Tailors' Project had expected this major influx to cause problems. The logistics of the two immigration projects seemed very different. The orphans would require supervision and services in accordance with proper childcare laws and social work standards. The tailors were adults, going to assured positions in an industry for which they had (or were supposed to have) prior experience. It seemed straightforward enough: welcome the tailors, take them to their places of work, give them a brief introduction to Canadian life, and let them carry on from there.[70]

This assumption was once again based on a tragic misunderstanding of the unprecedented nature of the survivors' experience. The established community, many with their immigrant experience still fresh, would not – could not – understand how the Holocaust had created a completely different type of immigrant: the survivor. Survivors had lost not only their homes and all or most of their immediate and extended families, but also every personal possession. Then, they had had to languish in refugee camps like prisoners while the world moved on and forgot them. But when they tried to communicate their experiences, no one listened. Even worse, they were labelled *greener* ("greenhorns") and joked about. One recalled: "What was the use of even trying to talk to the *gayle* ("the ones who made it") about what happened? They looked cross-eyed at you." Perhaps "didn't look" would have been a more correct view. Except for a ten-part series in the *Canadian Jewish Chronicle* by Bernard Shane that recounted his experiences as a member of the selection team, neither the English nor the Yiddish press would risk discussing the Holocaust. The yawning void between the two communities lasted for two decades.[71]

In this light, the communal agencies' focus on transportation and housing arrangements rather than social and psychological services sent a negative message to the survivors. Indeed, barriers between the survivors and the host community were first raised on planning boards and around committee room tables. But, given the community's lack of comprehension and empathy, nothing was done about more sensitive needs. On the other hand, arranging transportation was a complex issue that demanded considerable bureaucracy. Transportation from Europe to Canada was provided free by the International Refugee Organization (IRO). Travel costs from dockside to Montreal, Toronto, or Winnipeg were covered by the Canadian Overseas Garment Commission (COGC), the corporate body formed to handle the Tailors' Project. The tailors would reimburse the COGC through payroll deductions of not more than 10 percent of their salary per pay period. Reimbursement seemed certain since all the tailors had contracts to stay in their new jobs for at least ten months before being legally permitted to turn to the open labour market. The COGC was also responsible for arranging small cash loans that would enable the immigrants to purchase household goods and place the first month's rent on an apartment. The COGC was given charge of payroll deduction schemes to facilitate repayment of these charges.[72]

The JIAS assumed responsibility for reception and temporary housing, a task that would prove daunting given the housing situation in Toronto, particularly lower- and lower-middle class housing. In 1941 only 41 percent of Toronto homes were occupied by their owners; the balance were rented. More than one Torontonian in five shared residences with another family. The housing situation worsened during 1944–45 as workers streamed into the city to find employment in war industries, as well as after the war, when returning servicemen married and started families. "The whole project," wrote Hayes on 30 October, "depends on the ability of the selected to find accommodation in Canada. If there are insuperable difficulties and insoluble problems it is obvious that Mr. McNamara [the Deputy Secretary of Labour] would want to terminate the project."[73]

The lay leadership of the community begged anyone who would listen to donate space for immigrants. But it was an uphill struggle from the start. Placing the JIAS in charge of coordinating accommodation was organizationally disastrous. Hayes's insistence on the UJRA's pre-eminence throughout the war had displaced the Toronto JIAS from its traditional place in immigrant work. Now a weakened Toronto JIAS was suddenly responsible for housing in the midst of an unprecedented housing shortage. To make matters even worse, in February 1947 Toronto JIAS executive secretary Manny Kraicer left to become a front-line European refugee camp worker. A replacement for the five-year veteran administrator was not found until September. There would be four more administrators in the next two years. This left the already weak Toronto JIAS office burdened with an inexperienced administrator just as the office came under unprecedented pressure.[74]

The demography of the Tailors' Project exacerbated the difficulties of the JIAS. When C.D. Howe imposed a Jewish quota of 50 percent for the tailors (later raised to 60 percent), Max Enkin did "an end round past him." In defiance of Howe's verbal orders, Enkin and the COGS commission selected Jews who had large families and among non-Jews made sure to select as many as possible who were single or married without dependants. Ironically the housing shortage made the families the hardest to accommodate. By mid-November Hayes complained to the JIAS that the Toronto office had located only 10 out of 71 interviewed homes that "might be persuaded to take in a child." A further 38 would only take a single man. There were still 99 more homes to check on the JIAS master list. Hayes over-optimistically noted that they would "be utilized for family units with children" even though their owners hadn't yet been consulted![75]

The scramble to find homes had begun in earnest. The first group of tailors was due in less than two months, and eight hundred more would arrive by year-end. Where could they be housed? Some space was being used or reserved by those who had applied for close relatives to immigrate. The orphans occupied another hundred homes. Housing was in short supply both in the larger community as well as within Jewish neighbourhoods. In January 1948 over 4,000 Toronto families lived in overcrowded conditions and even the municipal government was unable to locate more vacant rental space. Even rabbinic appeals at Rosh Hashanah 1948 services failed to find room for the newcomers.[76]

The accommodation crisis forced the three main Jewish sponsoring organizations in the Tailors' Project to reassess their roles. By the beginning of December it was clear that the JIAS would not be able to find enough homes for families with children. On 14 January, 1948, Grand ousted the JIAS and informed Hayes that other arrangements for accommodation would have to be made. Hayes gave Grand permission to "assume responsibility for the initial expenses in connection with the placement of the tailors." The CJC was even authorized to pay for room deposits, cooking utensils, and emergency medical expenses. For its part, the COGC also would have to move beyond merely providing work placements. Tailors would require start-up loans. But what kind or how much? The COGC wasted valuable time dithering over such administrative trivia. It spent weeks deciding what types of cash advances would be counted as advances against salaries and which, such as transportation costs, would be charged as loans and deducted from pay.[77]

Time ran out. Organizational turf wars suddenly became academic. On 15 and 16 January, 1948, 391 tailors and close to 350 of their dependants landed in Halifax. The immigrants were not informed or didn't care whether they were destined for Toronto or Montreal. And, in a huge foul-up, Jewish officials in Toronto were not informed of their landing and had no idea they were en route to Toronto. Most of the tailors got off at Montreal because rumour held that job prospects were superior to those in Toronto. On the weekend of 17–18 January, 266 tailors and their dependants disembarked at Union Station. No one was there to meet them. "Their arrival," noted a fact-finding report, "created the first of a long series of crises which bedevilled the program [Tailors' Project] for the rest of the year." Word of the unexpected arrival quickly reached the CJC and created panic. A vast fleet of cabs was immediately hired to haul luggage, and volunteers' cars conveyed the new arrivals to the Labour Lyceum, a building owned and used as a meeting place by a number of non-Communist unions. Exhausted and disoriented, with their children running underfoot, the tailors were given their work assignments. Housing was not ready. Many single men and women and couples were given accommodations, but families with children were taken to the Folks Farein and to the Community House. Sheets were quickly hung from the ceiling to separate families, bunk beds were gathered, suppers were purchased at nearby Spadina Avenue restaurants, and, amid great confusion, the families settled in for their first night in Canada.[78]

This was quite a feat of improvisation, and the JIAS Toronto president boasted that they had "accommodated each and every one in the two groups that reached Toronto." His braggadocio ignored the reality that handling immigrants was a far cry from settling them. Only one of the 110 available rooms was suitable for families. The Beth Yehuda Synagogue was pressed into service: it could hold up to 75 people and was suitable for families with children. Enkin took issue.

After a visit he complained, "the Beth Yehuda synagogue is not fit for human habitation." Hayes, for his part, viewed the Toronto confusion as yet another example of the JIAS's inability to deliver. The fact that 250 immigrants in whom Congress had invested so much time, money, and effort, had arrived to such confusion became a public relations fiasco of the first order – so much so that Hayes avoided mentioning it directly in his daily briefing to senior Congress leaders. He knew the project would be jeopardized if the federal Department of Labour discovered the situation. This sloppy beginning, however, catalyzed organizational preparedness and streamlined chains of command. Both Congress and the JIAS realized that they would have to press ahead with even greater determination and speed to organize future tailor arrivals in Toronto.[79]

Organizational retribution came quickly after this debacle. On 19 January Hayes met with Solkin and minced no words. Displeased with what he regarded as JIAS's failure to live up to its housing commitment, he determined to ensure that the events of that January weekend not be repeated. He demanded that the JIAS honour its commitments by renting rooming houses or hotel rooms. If the JIAS wouldn't do it, he told Solkin, Congress would. For that matter, he added, the JIAS needed to supply linen and cooking utensils for the families in the Folks Farein or in the large number of rooms without cooking facilities, if only to give the immigrants a sense that their situation was not permanent. When Solkin turned to the 1944 CJC–JIAS agreement on immigration to argue that emergency aid did not fall into the JIAS's jurisdiction, Hayes exploded. "If Congress takes over JIAS' role the tailors certainly won't complain." He then announced that he was personally taking charge of search for suitable housing. Solkin, livid, was left to vent his spleen on the hapless Toronto JIAS office.[80]

Hayes's intervention brought results. On Thursday, 22 January, the COGC opened a Toronto office under the management of Tom Aplin. Here was further evidence of poor planning: the office was to have been up and running well in advance of the tailor immigration. As Grand, of CJC Central Division, observed to Hayes, "both times – tailors and children – the project started much ahead of schedule and we didn't have time to plan properly."[81]

Hayes's hand was now clearly visible in the administration of the COGC office. Central Division paid for a full-time office assistant, and the Canadian Polish Congress provided a half-time secretary to deal with the non-Jewish tailors. The garment industry was eager to divest itself of administrative responsibility. Its members made it clear that they assumed no responsibilities beyond placing the workers and ensuring that transportation costs were reimbursed through payroll deductions: if Congress wanted more, Congress could pay for it. Hayes opened the coffers.[82]

Congress's poor planning and desperate improvisation was unfortunately typical of Canadian Jewish communal organizations' response to immigration projects or postwar immigration. The government's success at keeping Jews out of Canada had left Jewish immigration reception systems rusty and displaced from their former importance. Canadian Jewry lacked an efficient response mechanism when the influx was renewed. In addition, as Franklin Bialystok has observed, the needs of Holocaust survivors were not yet understood, and, as we have seen in regard to the Orphans' Project, the assumption that they had the same needs as pre-war immigrants caused serious misunderstandings and untold grievances.[83]

Now that Canada's gates had opened a crack, each organization wanted to do its all to validate its claim to leadership. The squabbles and turf wars between Congress, the JIAS, and the COGC must be understood as a result of the tremendous pressure each organization was under to settle Holocaust survivors successfully. And memories of past failures loomed large. Hayes saw Congress as the coordinating agency of Canadian Jewry and was determined to ensure that it assume the lion's share of responsibility and credit for being the *éminence grise* behind the tailors' movement. Solkin, angry at Hayes's usurpation of the JIAS's pre-eminence in immigration matters, demanded more than the understaffed and poorly directed Toronto JIAS office could deliver. The COGC, for its part, felt that its contribution was being overlooked. It believed that its members had done more than their share by initiating the Tailors' Project and giving employment to workers above and beyond the industry's real needs, all as a cover for immigration. This task had been complicated by the 50 percent non-Jewish quota, but the garment industry went along – knowing full well that many of the non-Jews they selected were unsuitable for the industry – because every non-Jewish tailor accepted meant another Jewish family given a new life in Canada.

By February 1948 Hayes's vision seemed about to prevail. The JIAS had been shunted aside, and the COGS office had become a Congress subsidiary. But the UJWF's executive director, Florence Hutner, believed that Congress's primacy interfered with the UJWF's control over professionalized program delivery – the fund's raison d'être. The bitter battle between these organizations prevented cooperation in both the Tailors' and Orphans' projects. Each organization attributed the continual crisis atmosphere to the others' failure to deal with the situation properly. But given the pressures of the moment, there was no time for a full airing of grievances. Confrontation was postponed and inter-organizational tensions persisted and proliferated. Hayes and Hutner, both organizational rationalizers from the same generation, battled over whose vision would define "the search for order." Hayes emphasized the broad picture. When he heard that the UJWF had approved the creation of the Jewish Vocational Service (JVS) to specialize in finding jobs for new immigrants, he scoffed: "This is the wrong way to do things. I want to strengthen existing agencies ... This is the thin edge of the wedge where agencies take on staff at our expense. They respond to conditions rather than solve problems." But the UJWF disagreed, deeming the vocational service crucial to professionalized job placement in Toronto.[84]

The JVS office provided centralized monitoring of the Tailors' Project worker placement, a role that it fulfilled smoothly, although some problems arose as the industry shed workers in late 1948 during the slow post-holiday season. The agency dealt with unemployed tailors and the 10 percent of the tailors who were unsuited for the Canadian industry. It showed great flexibility, placing some clients in valet services or small neighbourhood stores, while relocating others to Hamilton garment factories. Nonetheless, it became difficult for the JVS to place the majority of the tailors referred by the COGC. Some had never been tailors and didn't want to be. The European selection process had focused on family numbers rather than skill, and many non-tailors were selected simply to fill quotas. Even some experienced tailors found the Canadian garment industry too different from what they had known in Europe. A backlog of supposed tailors seeking jobs had built up even as other tailors arrived.[85]

Throughout 1948 about 150 tailors a month arrived in Toronto. Slowly, very slowly, the housing crisis for non-family accommodation eased and the administrative snags were smoothed out. A protocol for newly arrived tailors was developed. Congress money allowed the JIAS to provide rental deposits on flats for single and married tailors. JIAS representatives met the new arrivals at Union Station and took them to the Labour Lyceum, where the COGC assigned jobs and provided a $25 advance against future wages. Each tailor signed an undertaking to accept the arranged accommodation and to allow the COGC to deduct a portion of his or her wages to repay transportation costs. Each was then outfitted with clothing from the clothing depot, where the Council of Jewish Women sorted donated clothing by size. Donated furniture was also distributed to rental flats. Tailors were eligible for a loan of up to $250 as a deposit on up to $800 worth of new furniture and appliances, but they themselves were responsible for handling all credit purchases with merchants. The loans could be repaid as slowly or as quickly as the borrower wanted.[86]

These arrangements also applied to families with children, although accommodating them remained a challenge. Until 1949, rents remained exorbitant. But these immigrants had survived far worse; many simply refused occupancy until Congress agreed to pay the difference between the rent asked and the amount the immigrants believed affordable. In February 1948 a detailed survey of the Jewish community by the Council of Jewish Women (COJW) concluded: "Permanent housing accommodation can be provided only by the rental or purchase of large homes suitable for multiple occupancy." In late July, after lengthy negotiations, the JIAS obtained an $11,500 UJWF grant. The funds were used to purchase a house at 147 Beverley Street, which was renovated and furnished to accommodate four to five families and the JIAS Toronto office.[87]

The flood of tailor immigrants soon made even this expensive renovation inadequate, and Congress responded by getting into the housing business. The Congress Holding Corporation was constituted in October 1948 and by the end of that year it had purchased fourteen homes and rented two others at a cost of almost $150,000, exclusive of the cost of renovations (which averaged over $500 per unit). These houses could accommodate seventy-five couples and their children, almost three hundred individuals in all. Volunteers from the COJW and B'nai Brith provided on-site English classes and social activities to ease immigrant acculturation.[88]

This inter-organizational process for immigrant absorption was not exempt from the now familiar petty squabbles. What was worse, even when the system ran smoothly, it was evident that immigrant arrival exceeded communal absorptive capacity. The fourteen Congress homes were soon full, and although some singles and families found accommodation in private homes, many remained in temporary quarters for months. Some ended up in makeshift accommodations in Jewish communal buildings where there were no cooking facilities and little privacy was possible.[89]

In retrospect, most young immigrant families coped remarkably well, sensing that their housing problems, while difficult, were temporary. And a crowded auditorium on Davenport Road offered more hope than a wooden barracks at a Displaced Persons Camp. Both were infinitely preferable to ghetto conditions. And the immigrants were innovators. They learned to cope with Toronto conditions and how to use – even manipulate – the Jewish organizational structure very quickly. They dealt with the lack of kitchen facilities at the Folks Farein by strolling en masse to various restaurants that lined Spadina Avenue a block away, ordering meals, and telling the owners, "Congress will pay." Congress did: the bill totalled over $1,000. Some immigrants approached both the CJC and the Toronto Hebrew Free Loan to borrow money, after discovering that poor record keeping and collection methods made the loans almost impossible to recover.[90]

This did not mean that all immigrants took advantage of the situation. Far from it. Such irregularities simply reflected the fact that the Tailors' Project was a course in improvisation from the start. In early January, Grand bluntly told Hayes, "I don't know what we are responsible for," and confessed to CJC central president, Ben Sadowski, "We are disorganized." After the January crisis, agencies still continued to react to events rather than plan. Even major expenditures became ad hoc. When the UJWF asked Grand about controlling expenditures, he could only reply, "I'm not sure yet ... the financial and loans provisions have plenty of loopholes." The agencies expected the tailors would repay the cash advances for rent, furnishings, and transportation through payroll deduction. However, Hayes prophetically observed in early February 1948: "All this adds up to is that we will be advancing a great deal of money and we will not know until a period of ten months how much of it we will be getting back."[91]

Hayes' suspicions were well founded. The COGS payroll deduction scheme remained a bone of contention from the beginning. Like the whole Tailors' Project, it was a study in knee-jerk responses to crisis rather than the result of any ordered planning. Originally the deductions had been intended to cover the cost of transportation from the point of disembarkation to the tailor's destination. But Hayes was determined to keep a ceiling on costs and insisted that payroll deductions should be used to repay all funds loaned by Congress without interest until the full account was settled.[92]

Repayment looked reasonable on the drawing board but became a public relations disaster in practice. The plan raised community ire at "overly demanding" immigrants who felt that the loans had been misrepresented as gifts by some overzealous or overly well-intentioned volunteers. One angry COGC worker wrote to Grand "about the g.[od] d.[amned] tailor who complained about an $11.00 deduction on a 2 week paycheck of $110," while an equally angry tailor complained that he would not allow his wages to be deducted to repay for furniture he had taken with him (against the rules) from one of the Congress's houses because he had been told, "all of this is a gift." Besides, he complained, "I did not choose the furniture. It was given to me." In Montreal, tailors went so far as to elect a delegation that successfully met with Hayes and other top Congress officials and obtained a radical revision in the payment schedule. Henceforth, loan repayment would only commence at the end of the first year of Canadian residence and repayment of the total would be left to the discretion and goodwill of the borrower. This arrangement became policy in Montreal.[93]

But Toronto rejected the resolution. The COGC office had been careful to ensure that the payroll deductions were fine-tuned to what it judged to be each individual's payment ability. By the end of October 1948, over $10,000 had been repaid, which included both transportation costs and money loaned. "It is felt," argued the Committee on Financial Assistance, "that chaos would be created among the immigrants if these deductions were discontinued because we would be faced with the problem of requests for reimbursements from immigrants who have had the deductions made."[94]

Were the tailors treated unfairly? An exhaustive outside report commissioned by Hayes to analyse the response of communal organizations to mass immigration noted that the payroll repayment scheme was inequitable because it subjected the tailors and furriers to provisions not imposed on others. A needy immigrant sponsored by relatives under the Close Relatives Scheme was eligible for "free loans" not subject to repayment, while a tailor or furrier could only qualify for loans requiring repayment. It was rumoured that some tailors and furriers received "free loans" by phoning Toronto Hebrew Free Loan and pretending they were sponsored immigrants in need. The chronically overworked staff could not keep accurate records and errors were frequent. While some immigrants obtained free loans, others had to move to cheaper and more crowded quarters because their salaries were reduced by payroll deductions. The Toronto and Montreal Yiddish press criticized the payroll deduction scheme as simply grabbling for money from immigrants before they had a chance to put down roots.[95]

This critique missed the mark in one important respect. As the COGC staff gained experience, they modified the original sliding scale of deductions, and Aplin was always ready to lower deductions when asked. Some poorly paid tailors were repaying as little as $1.00 per week. On the other hand, the report was right in criticizing the intrinsic unfairness of the various types of loans. Of course, in the Tailors' Project, the Jewish community had assumed travel and housing costs not covered for other immigrants, and a justifiable case could be made that the tailors should repay them. But the inconsistency of allowing some immigrants forgivable loans and denying them to others caused friction and cheating. By 1950 the COGS had abandoned its concern for "the bottom line" in favour of Montreal's example.[96]

The Furriers' Project, modelled on the Tailors' Project, was the second Jewish labour scheme inaugurated in 1947. The fur industry, heavily represented by Jews, approached the Canadian government to import workers. Using briefs supplied by Congress, the fur industry claimed that domestic craftsmen who had pioneered the industry were dying out and that new blood was needed. Once again, the JLC assisted, this time through a formal agreement with the CJC that assigned the JLC the role of supervising furrier repayment schemes. In May 1948 the government authorized the admission of five hundred furriers and sent a two-man selection team representing the Canadian Fur Association to Europe. They met scenes of desperation similar to those encountered by the Tailors' Project selection committee. Once again, the Department of Immigration imposed a 50 percent Jewish quota, which was later raised to 60 percent when it became apparent that there weren't enough non-Jewish applicants.

Again, the non-Jewish quota could not be filled sufficiently and so, in order to maximize the number of Jews selected, the industry agreed to train the unskilled non-Jews it selected. The selection teams worked quickly and the government expedited matters so that the furriers would arrive in time for the busy holiday season from September to November. By the end of August the final preparations for the sailing of five hundred "furriers" and their three hundred dependants were well underway.[97]

Lessons recently learned in the Tailors' Project were applied to the scheme. Each furrier and his family were assigned a number on a master list. In addition, Max Federman of Toronto's International Ladies Garment Workers' Union was a member of the selection team. He told each selectee where he would be going even before he left Europe. This information was communicated immediately to Toronto, along with the list number and name of each furrier and the number of their dependants. Avoiding the confusion that attended the first tailors' arrivals, the Toronto JIAS and Congress knew exactly who was coming and where they would be working.[98]

To ensure inter-agency and inter-ethnic cooperation in the Furriers' Project, newly appointed CJC central executive secretary, Ben Lappin, invited representatives of the JIAS and the JVS, along with important members of the Croatian, Lithuanian, Polish, and Hungarian communities who were prepared to assist the non-Jewish furriers. Enkin, Aplin, and Federman shared their selection experiences.[99]

Lappin, a trained social worker, emphasized the importance of delineating the function of each agency before the furriers' arrival. As the UJWF looked on benevolently from a distance, the agencies involved constituted themselves as a "Steering Committee" to coordinate the Furriers' Project. Immediately after the meeting, the committee sent a lengthy letter, written in question and answer fashion, to outline clearly the responsibility of each agency. The Canadian Fur Commission (CFC) would establish an office to handle payroll deductions just as the COGC had done for the Tailors' Project. The JIAS and Congress would assume the roles they played in the Tailors' Project, while non-Jewish furriers would be directed to agencies organized by their own ethnic communities.[100]

The higher level of planning that characterized the Furriers' Project was evident particularly in the role assigned to the fledgling JVS. The CFC found only fifty-nine qualified non-Jewish tailors, but the project could only go forward if the non-Jewish quota was filled or the Jewish quota would be proportionately reduced. As a compromise, the fur selection team was allowed to fill the non-Jewish quota by choosing 141 unskilled non-Jews to be apprentices for the industry. The industry insisted that these be single females. In the interim, the JVS was told in advance which furriers would have to be trained for other service in accordance with National Selective Service criteria. On 5 October 1948, Deputy Minister of Labour McNamara agreed to allow all these women to "pass through the ranks" and leave the project if they were found unfit by the industry and could be properly outplaced by JVS.[101]

Lappin, the methodical social worker, was determined to avoid the last-minute débacle that had confronted the first group of tailors to arrive in Toronto. When he was informed that the first group of 141 furriers and 160 dependants had left Genoa on 16 September 1948, he called together his steering committee to ensure that all would proceed smoothly. It would have to, since a second group would follow a week later. In September alone, 221 furriers and their dependants were en route to Canada. The committee arranged a temporary staging area for new arrivals to give them two or three days of orientation before they were dispatched to new jobs and housing.[102]

Although the Furriers' Project ran more smoothly than the Tailors' Project, it too had its share of problems. The first glitch was caused by an organizational lapse. The fur industry had not opened the promised office to coordinate placement and payroll deductions. Placement was left to the union, and payroll deductions were haphazard at best.[103] Problems also arose because of the seasonal nature of the fur industry. Between May and October furriers worked frantically to prepare coats, stoles, and caps for the winter clothing and Christmas seasons. For the balance of the year, there was little for them to do. In economic downturns, such as the one that occurred in late 1948, even less work was available. Thus by late September only 70 of 120 furriers in the first group to reach Toronto were still working in the industry. Only 14 had legally switched to other industries through the JVS. The other 36 were suitable workers, but there was no work for them. The fur industry worried about a government crackdown.[104]

The problems that arose with the Furriers' Project reflected all that was wrong with the way Canadian bulk labour schemes had been applied to Jews. In the Domestics, Lumber Workers, and Nurses schemes, the government sought to import qualified personnel to fill waiting jobs. Even experience and ability to do the job did not qualify Jews for these schemes, as government and industry worked to bar Jews from selection to these programs. This discriminatory attitude was what created the need for the Tailors' and Furriers' projects. But when the Jewish community launched these plans, the Department of Immigration retained its emphasis on ethnic origin over skill and imposed ethnic quotas.[105] These had their most severe impact on the furriers' movement. With characteristic rigidity and anti-Semitism, the Departments of Labour and Immigration refused to drop the quotas even when the International Refugee Organization certified that there were no qualified non-Jewish furriers available. The furrier selection team thus found itself in the economically untenable position of selecting unskilled non-Jewish workers. It was the only way to bring Jewish refugees to Canada who could not qualify under the Close Relatives Scheme. If furriers' dependants were included, the entire project had the potential to bring in up to eight hundred Jews to Canada.[106]

This analysis goes a long way toward explaining Federman's refusal to place unskilled workers in Toronto fur shops. The fur industry was a closed shop and Federman its undisputed ruler. He held court daily at union headquarters on Cecil Street and lunched at United Bakers Dairy restaurant, where he met with those seeking jobs and other favours. He strongly objected to the quota forcing him to place people who were not only unskilled, but who "might even have engaged in anti-Jewish activities." Max won. None of the unskilled non-Jews ended up in the Toronto fur trade.

The flood of postwar immigrants changed the face of the Jewish community, which grew by almost 10 percent between 1946 and 1950. Immigrants arriving in Toronto swamped the Congress and JIAS offices. Caiserman, visiting from Montreal, reported that "the entire office was overwhelmingly busy with the housing and the aid of the orphans and DPs who arrived daily." Stairways were clogged and some employees worked in the halls. Every Congress employee became a *de facto* full-time immigrant worker. Caiserman couldn't even get any secretarial assistance for the first three weeks of his five-week stay in Toronto. At one point, Grand was without a secretary when she was transferred to full-time work at the COGC. He reported that in her absence: "I have had to take on her entire case-load [of the Central Division Refugee Committee]. This means that I am spending about half of my day collecting money for transportation, writing letters to the IRO and JDC offices, and worrying with lost relatives about applications. The load seems to be increasing, and it is really knocking hell out of my personal operations here."[107]

But the fundamental issue, which remained unaddressed for over a decade, was the deep divide between the survivors and the Toronto community. Survivors who tried to tell their stories to their families were told, "There was rationing here too." After hearing comments like this, survivors confined their commiserations to their own peer group. Why talk to people who could have no understanding of what they had experienced? Incomprehension was found at all levels of the community. Ben Lappin, thoroughly involved in the Orphans' Project and a trained social worker, remarked: "We couldn't believe it happened and they [the survivors] disbelieved it happened." Was it any wonder that by 1954 survivors had withdrawn from the community and formed their own social groups?

Unremitting pressure affected the well-meaning but overburdened staff of the receiving agencies and generated high turnover and low morale. A number of full-time employees performed three or four extra duties simultaneously, and even this proved insufficient. Immigrant needs swamped the division and overshadowed all other matters. Congress headquarters at 150 Beverley Street became a beehive of activity, with newcomers everywhere, pleading their cases to anyone available. As one eyewitness recalled: "The immigrants milling around the Congress offices gave it the appearance of a chaotic depot." The state of confusion made routine office work all but impossible.[114] Thus, the Refugee Committee's caseload on farmers languished, while the Societies and Youth divisions fell dormant. All employees were reassigned to work full time on the Tailors' and Furriers' projects. By November all non-refugee work at Central Division had ground to a standstill.[108]

Hayes looked on in anger from Montreal. Congress's carefully nurtured stature as a national spokesagency was undermined by Central Division's paralysis. As far as he and his board were concerned, Congress existed to rationalize Jewish life – not to allow its Toronto headquarters to resemble a marketplace. Toronto was out of control –

anathema to the patrician Hayes, who lashed out: "We cannot have responsibility without some control."[109] He seethed over spending huge sums while ceding effective control over immigration projects to UJWF-sponsored social service agencies. More fuel was added to the fire when many sponsors of relatives under the Close Relatives Scheme refused to live up to their commitments.[110]

When Lappin reported these latest developments, Hayes vowed drastic action. He resuscitated the UJRA as the coordinating body of all refugee and immigrant work, and vowed to restore its primacy even if the process involved a head-on clash with the UJWF and its affiliates.[111]

Hayes saw Lappin's July 1947 appointment as Central Region executive secretary as an opportunity to fulfill this agenda. He summoned Lappin to Montreal for three days of consultation and reminded him that since Congress was funding all the major immigrant movements it had to regain overall control. Lappin was already on side, but his social work training predisposed him to professional efficiency and weeding out duplication of services.[112]

On his return to Toronto, Lappin attempted to impose order on the local scene. He fought against the developing shift from "catch all" to "specialized" immigrant absorption tasking by agencies. At a joint meeting of the Central Division and UJWF executives in August, Lappin proposed that the UJRA assume responsibility for working with those arriving under the Close Relatives Scheme. He also suggested that the UJRA provide social services for the Orphans', Tailors', and Furriers' projects.[113] The fund was sceptical, arguing that each immigrant group's needs could be met by existing agencies. Rather than accept coordination, they pressed for more money to hire staff for JFCS to further extend its counselling services.[114] The fund also wanted more money to purchase housing for immigrants. Hayes saw red. Decentralized spending would only strengthen local agencies at Congress's expense.[115]

Lappin was ordered to proceed with Hayes's agenda. To gain the professionals' support for a more centrally coordinated operation, he called a meeting of all agency executives on 27 August. They listened intently as Central Division president, Sadowski, informed them that "in addition to the needs presented by the Close Relatives Scheme, a set-up was required by which immigrants ... could be referred out of a central office to the agency equipped to give the specific service the immigrant needs." This agency, in effect a resuscitated UJRA, would also be a central filing agency for reports and would coordinate the provision of social services to the refugees who had arrived under the Close Relatives Scheme

When the committee members agreed, Sadowski moved on to the CJC's proposed second, and more controversial, role for the restructured UJRA. He proposed that the UJRA assume responsibility for the overall coordination of the Orphans', Tailors', and Furriers' projects. This was delicate ground. After a lengthy discussion, Sadowski's motion was endorsed, with the proviso that Congress would supply a director versed in administration and social work, and that the JFCS, the agency that would be most affected by the proposal, give its consent.[116]

There is no mention in the records as to whether JFCS was indeed consulted. It is possible that the JFCS board simply did not complain. Perhaps it was glad to give up part of its responsibilities. It had already been forced to cut back some key programs because of the Orphans' caseload after the Community Chest refused to increase its allocation. In addition, three key board members of the revitalized UJRA also sat on the JFCS board to ensure that its interests would not be overlooked.

Thus, in early October the president and executive director of the JFCS gathered, along with leaders of all the other major communal organizations, for the first meeting of the reconstituted UJRA. Fifty-one percent of its members were from Congress and the remainder represented the organizational gamut from JIAS to the Peretz School. After more than three hours of frank discussion, the meeting unanimously approved the new UJRA's structure and mandate.[117]

The UJRA now assumed complete control over Jewish immigration to Ontario, including coordinating policy and services among the various agencies that dealt with immigrants. The hope was that this control would avoid duplication and that a system of monitored referrals would guarantee that "agency shopping" would stop and immigrants would be directed to the agency or agencies that best met their needs. An experienced social worker and administrator agreed to head the UJRA. Five committees (Housing, Budget, Financial Assistance, Health-Welfare, and Public Relations) were established. To ensure that there was no gap in services as the new order was put in place, Congress would temporarily maintain the existing committee structure for the

Orphans', Tailors', and Furriers' projects.[121] At last, Hayes and Congress were firmly in the driver's seat.

This coup marked the apparent triumph of what Lappin called the "direct service" approach. It assumed that if agencies did their part, most immigrants would be settled quickly and easily, while only a few would need special help. It also assumed that supervised lay volunteers could handle most immigration issues, and that professionals would be required only in a few problematic cases. While these assumptions certainly underscored communal ignorance of the survivors' serious needs, its main thrust complemented Hayes's long-standing ambition for the primacy of Congress in immigration policy making and implementation.

Hayes's championing of the abilities of the UJRA's lay workers might at first seem puzzling. He had consistently attempted to bring young professionals and professional methods to both the CJC and the UJRA. Why revert now to lay-led committees? The answer is simple. His belief in professionalization was inextricably linked to his desire to impose Congress's leadership on every aspect of Canadian Jewish life. Thus, he rode roughshod over the JIAS's attempt to protect its long-established role in immigration. This goal also explains his desire to ensure that Congress received sole credit for every favourable development in Canadian Jewish immigration and the pervasive efforts to diminish the JDC's vital role. The renaissance of the UJRA, a Congress agency, was designed above all to impose Congress's will indelibly on refugee work in Toronto.[118]

Hayes's overzealous desire for Congress domination blinded him to the fact that the single UJRA worker in Toronto was impossibly overworked in her efforts to service the Orphans', Tailors', and Furriers' projects simultaneously. All Hayes had accomplished by redesigning the UJRA was to "creat[e] a committee whenever a problem reared its head." The renewed organization had the nominal responsibility of coordination but no staff to carry out that responsibility. What worked on paper didn't work in practice; there was a vacuum at the top. Hayes's appetite for authority was trite in the face of the ongoing needs of the new arrivals, which should have driven agency priorities.

The UJRA's sudden resurrection begs a number of questions. Why was the UJWF apparently asleep at the switch during most of this process? Why did the UJWF not intervene? Tougher still, how to explain why UJWF executive director Hutner remained a silent spectator at the meetings that led up to the reorganization? Why did influential UJWF laypeople vote for the revival of the UJRA? Why do the executive and board minutes of the UJWF for this period contain no reference to the UJRA and its new role?

Here again, the answer is disarmingly simple: the power of the purse. As we have seen, the UJWF imposed its will on most of its affiliate organizations by taking control of all other appeals for funds. These were allocated to member agencies only if funds were spent in a professionally responsible manner. By 1948 the UJWF had been in complete control of communal fundraising for a decade and enjoyed unchallenged primacy. Even Central Division was dependent on UJWF funding. And its allocation was huge – $380,000 in 1948, the largest allocation for any Canadian agency. With money tight, and Hayes apparently ready to foot the bill on terms that accorded with UJWF's vision, there was no reason to deny his request. There is no evidence that any fund executive or board member realized Hayes's real motives.[119]

By now Hayes's objective was almost accomplished. All the UJWF had to do was submit a budget, like any other fund agency, and the entire deal would be approved. Then came a shockingly unexpected turn of affairs. Neither Lappin nor Hayes could submit a proposed budget for the reconfigured UJRA because the "old" UJRA's bookkeeping system had completely broken down. Perhaps the old secretary knew where most of the records were, but she had been seconded to the COGC office the previous year. A succession of bookkeepers had quit. No figures were available; nor would they be until March 1949. By then it would be too late – and the irony was rich. The organization busily trumpeting its intent to rationalize immigration work had not kept its own books in order. Lappin desperately searched for a remedy, but other forces were already in play that would keep him from fulfilling Hayes's mandate.[120]

By now it was apparent to everyone in the know that, despite all pretensions to the contrary, Toronto refugee reception had been seriously mishandled. A Self-Study Committee was struck under the direction of long-time lay leader Gurston Allen. In early November Allen told Lappin that while the JFCS had done a good job with European youth, it had spent sums "out of proportion to ... expenditures in relation to other DP groups." This was certainly true. The orphans required individual casework attention in accordance with the CJC's guarantee of professionalism to the Ontario government. But, like all supporters of "direct service," Allen found it hard to justify these "extra" expenses and recommended against similar expenditures on the Tailors', Furriers', and Close Relatives schemes. The Self-Study Committee also recommended that Central Division determine an allocation for the new UJRA only after National Congress programs for immigrants had been evaluated by an authoritative outside group.[121]

This recommendation echoed Hayes's expressed desire for an outside assessment of the new UJRA proposal. Lappin too endorsed the idea, for two reasons. First, it would put the imprimatur of outside authority on the new UJRA structure. Second, and more significantly, he expected that the report would endorse and thus reinforce Congress's role as the prime organizing force in refugee settlement in the Toronto Jewish community. Lappin and Hayes envisioned a resurgent Congress controlling Canadian national and communal Jewish life through a pyramid-like structure. At its apex the National Executive would preside over the regional divisions. Central Division would organize the Jewish communal agenda in Toronto and the rest of Ontario. The UJWF would simply be responsible for rationalized fundraising. All that was seemingly required was the imprimatur of a respected outside agency. Lappin naively believed that the UJWF's primacy was tenuous, and spilled considerable ink warning Hayes about carefully selecting who would evaluate Congress's immigrant programs: "Certain care must be taken that Congress is understood by the expert. Otherwise, the same old 'piffle paffle' about national restrictions on local economy [autonomy?] may emerge in this study." This warning proved prophetic.[122]

Hayes shared Lappin's unease. "In principle," he suggested, "I am for it and will contact New York early in the week for suggestions." But he then cautioned: "The difficulty is finding an objective person. An USNA [United Service for New Americans] or Council of Welfare Funds professional is almost sure to bring in a report on American methods and the advisability of maintaining social welfare standards through social welfare techniques." Herein lay Hayes's dilemma. His willingness to seek outside advice collided with his organizational loyalty. He knew full well that the "direct service" model was no longer in keeping with professional social work standards, but it was the only model that would afford Congress organizational control over immigration, which was his priority. He may also have taken to heart Lappin's caveat about American experts. They tended to value local communal structures over national bodies because the latter did not function effectively on the communal level in the United States. If imposed on Canada, this perception would also work against Congress's vision. The other key question, of course, although neither Lappin nor Hayes dared mention it, was how the UJWF would respond if the report were favourable to Congress.[123]

The die was cast; Hayes travelled to New York in December 1949 to ask the Council of Jewish Federations and Welfare Funds to undertake the study. It agreed and selected Mary Palevsky, deputy executive director of the USNA, to research and write it. Palevsky was an experienced social worker who had worked for the UNRRA in China before returning to New York and the executive suite. She received research assistance and complete cooperation from Hayes and all of the Jewish social service agencies. In mid-October 1949 she submitted her report.[124]

Palevsky gave an often-scathing review of the way in which Congress and other Jewish social service agencies had directed immigrant absorption in 1947 and 1948. As Hayes had prophesied, Palevsky took it as axiomatic that the "social agency" model was *de rigueur*, and repeatedly noted Congress's failure to provide trained staff to serve immigrants. The basic thrust of her argument was predictable given her predisposition, but her excellent research allowed her to cite examples that drove her point home forcefully and effectively. She rated the level of service the Orphans' Project had received as "adequate," noting: "Housing on the physical side is fair, family care ranges from poor to very good, medical and dental care are excellent. Recreational facilities ... are growing better. Educational services ... are good ... Financial assistance ... is well planned." She added that counselling, the heart of the project, was good, but that employment placement was difficult because of the special problems of the young people and the level of placement skill required. The work of the fledgling JVS was inadequate, and the economic downturn at the end of 1948 had only exacerbated an already difficult situation.

Predictably, Palevsky had few kind words for the "direct service" model of the Tailors', Furriers', and Close Relatives schemes. She noted that the community had put forth a great effort, but that its preoccupation "with the affairs of the orphans" had not allowed it to plan the Tailors' Project adequately. The COGC, on the other hand, was praised for its efforts. The JFCS's failure to deal effectively with the tailors was explained by its lack of staff and the failure to allocate funds to hire extra staff. Similarly, the JIAS, "lacking qualified staff," had proven unable to provide social services. The report correctly noted that "the problem of temporary shelter was never solved" and blamed this failing on a lack of organization.

The worst example of poor organization, Palevsky observed, was loans to immigrants. She decisively documented the "double-dipping" and "agency shopping" that went on, and the lack of properly applied criteria, which she attributed to the absence of pre-planning and the insufficient numbers of trained staff. Here was the core theme of the entire report: well-meaning but unqualified staff worked hard but failed to serve the new immigrants' needs properly; the lack of trained social workers made program delivery impossible. But, even if there had been enough social workers, she argued, they were so hated by all concerned. By implication, the report made clear that Congress, as the lead agency, had failed the new arrivals.

Palevsky saved her worst excoriation for the Close Relatives Scheme. She noted that many people, anxious to bring in European relatives, had lied on their Affidavits of Support to the immigration authorities. This forced many Close Relatives Scheme arrivals to turn to social agencies for loans and job placement. The report exhaustively documented how the JIAS, the Toronto Hebrew Free Loan, and Congress had duplicated each other's efforts. It cited examples of immigrants who hopped from agency to agency, getting loans at each. Poor record keeping meant that most of these loans were "thinly disguised relief grants."

Palevsky also condemned the lack of social facilities for immigrants, who were mostly left "to gather on Sundays in rather forlorn little groups on Spadina Street [sic]." Although the English and Citizenship classes were usually scheduled at a time when working men could attend, the lack of nursery facilities and afternoon classes made it impossible for women with children to learn English even though they wanted to. The report also predictably complained that these immigrants received a level of counselling insufficient to their needs.

Palevsky agreed with Hayes on one key issue: that by autumn of 1948 the entire immigrant absorption system had ground to a standstill. But she did not endorse the proposed UJRA solution. "The need for coordination of services under UJRA has not materialized. The Executive Secretary's [Mrs Hallowitz] relationship to other workers on the refugee program has never been defined ... By the time problems are sifted through the cumbersome committee machinery the opportunity for effective action has passed." To rub salt in the wound, she noted that the JIAS in Montreal had done a better job than the Toronto UJRA for half the cost.

Palevsky recommended that the UJRA be dissolved and that its functions be divided among other agencies. Its refugee caseload should be transferred to JFCS because "it is the only agency whose staff has the experience and knowledge to do the job." The report envisioned an augmented JFCS staff organized into a special immigration unit to serve all immigrants until they attained citizenship. Loans to immigrants would only be granted after JFCS approval. Palevsky believed that JFCS would now be able to serve other immigrants because the bulk of the Orphans' Project work was complete. However, the Toronto JIAS, unlike its Montreal counterpart, was not to provide social services. The report proposed that it be restricted to the fields of "technical migration and naturalization work."

Palevsky did not mince words in her judgment: "The Jewish community of Toronto was not equipped to cope successfully with the multitudinous and complex problems imposed suddenly upon it by the arrival of several thousand immigrants. In general, the services for all immigrants *outside of the orphan youth*, are below minimum adequate standards, and the administration of these services under the existing structure is cumbersome, inefficient, and wasteful."

Hayes, the consummate community professional, knew when he had lost. To cut his losses, he took care to minimize the distribution of the report, and it became a dead letter within months. Central Division leadership reluctantly followed Hayes's lead, ceding control and supervision over immigrant affairs to local agencies. They were already under pressure from some of their number who also sat on the UJWF Executive and correctly saw the Palevsky Report as a vindication of UJWF primacy. Edward Gelber, to cite just one example, told Hayes that the Palevsky Report was: "fairly well dated as far as Toronto is concerned. The only point of real interest to me is her recommendation that Congress get out of the social welfare business."[125]

Hayes left the field to the victorious UJWF, and began setting up a thorough damage control protocol for the 1950 Plenary. Only the positive contributions of Congress to the refugee effort were mentioned, and failures studiously avoided. The Palevsky Report provided the final stamp of approval to the UJWF model of communal planning based on the highest level of trained personnel and the "social agency" system – which applied across the board to all the fund's affiliated agencies. For example, as previously noted, before the Palevsky Report was released, the UJWF had followed this mandate by commissioning the Englemann Report on Jewish Education, and in late December 1948 American Jewish education expert Uriah Englemann had visited Toronto to present it. It called for the creation of a Board of Jewish Education (BJE) to coordinate the various schools in the city and establish standards for salary and curriculum. The BJE became a reality in 1949.[126]

The affirmation of UJWF methodological supremacy brought the attainment of its long sought goal of rational communal planning. The UJWF Future Planning Committee carefully mapped out the medical, educational, and social needs of the burgeoning postwar community. Planning for a new Mount Sinai Hospital was already well underway under the leadership of former UJWF president Ben Sadowski. An expert from the Council of Jewish Federations and Welfare Funds was soon hired to write a report that would lead to the transformation of the Jewish Old Folks' Home into Baycrest Hospital, which later expanded to become the Baycrest Centre for Geriatric Care. The UJWF also initiated discussions on improving recreational facilities, which led to the building of the Bloor Street YMHA in the mid-1950s. This institutional growth was undertaken against a backdrop of the gradual abandonment of the area of second settlement for the more northern suburbs of Forest Hill, Cedarvale, and North York. Communal agencies organized to meet this rapidly changing Jewish population base under UJWF control of communal financing and planning were finally solidified between 1945 and 1948.[127]

The last element of communal fundraising to fall under control of the UJWF was the United Palestine Appeal (UPA). The Fund's efforts to rationalize campaign allocations led to discussions with the Zionist

Organization of Canada (ZOC) about merging their campaigns. The ZOC had cooperated in the first two UJWF campaigns of 1937 and 1938. But fiery ZOC president Archie Freiman's insistence on holding a separate Zionist campaign for ideological reasons had terminated the relationship. Freiman argued that the ZOC was a well-established national organization that had raised funds across Canada since 1920 and was financially independent of any local fundraising organizations. Its member groups, such as Hadassah, Habonim, and Mizrachi, were also well established and backed by loyal financial supporters. Their appeal proved extremely successful in Toronto. The 1941, 1942, and 1943 United Palestine Appeals collected more than $160,000, while those of 1944 and 1945 collected over $277,000.[128]

This stream of funds made it easy for the ZOC to ignore UJWF attempts to control and rationalize local fundraising. Even though there was overlap between the ZOC board and that of the UJWF, local Zionists affiliated with the UJWF lacked the clout to persuade National ZOC to override Freiman's order. The ZOC and the UJWF continued their competing campaigns. This was the Fund's one significant failure, and it rankled.[129]

But corrective forces were in the making. The postwar Jewish world refocused on Palestine. *Amcha* – the average Jews – cared little about the organizational turf wars engrossing Congress, the JIAS, and the federation. Their attention was riveted on the revelations of the scope and horror of the Holocaust and the dramatic events taking place in Palestine. The tragedy of the Holocaust and the battle over the British mandate for Palestine dominated the overseas Jewish agenda. Canadian Zionist ranks swelled as *amcha* increasingly aligned themselves with Zionist organizations of various political and religious leanings. Donations rose apace. The UPA campaigns of 1946 and 1947 raised a total of more than $422,000. In fact, the Toronto UPA almost tripled its yearly revenue between 1941 and 1946. The Zionist cause, always strong in Canada, had caught fire.[130]

Freiman's sudden death in 1944 was a great blow to the ZOC, which he had dominated since 1919. But it also removed his fierce opposition to an alliance between the UPA and the UJWF. His death left a power vacuum: from Freiman's death until 1946, the ZOC was run by a presidium of Michael Garber, Sam Schwisberg, and Sam Zacks.[131]

In 1946, Zacks was elected president. He had already served as president of the UJWF and was a strong proponent of its vision. One of his

ZOC vice-presidents was Edward Gelber, also heavily involved with the UJWF and a supporter of its aims. It did not take long for this new leadership to reverse Freiman's policies. In late 1946 the UJWF and the ZOC began negotiating the creation of a joint campaign, but agreed harmoniously in early January 1947 to break off negotiations. It appears from the minutes of the UJWF board that there was still resistance from some Montreal-based Freiman loyalists on the ZOC executive, even though the Toronto Zionist Council (TZC), the umbrella organization of Toronto Zionist groups, was ready to proceed.[132]

Whatever disagreement existed between Montreal and Toronto Zionists became unseemly as pro-Zionist fervour pulled in more and more supporters. "No Jew who thought of himself or herself as a part of the Jewish people could remain unmoved," observed historian David Bercuson. "Palestine became the focus for the hope of redemption from the horror and shame of the Holocaust." Given this atmosphere, Zacks was able to convince the ZOC that Canadian Jewish unity and the cause of a national state in Palestine required its affiliation with the UJWF.[133]

It is also possible that Zacks, noting how much local Jewish interest was centred on the refugee problem, saw a chance to stimulate fundraising by emphasizing the shared responsibility for refugee settlement in both Palestine and Toronto. The slogan of the 1948 campaign "Do – or they die," coined by Zionist leader Bernard Laxer, certainly suggests this linkage. And passion for Zionism had never been greater. The Herzl Zion Club, a general Zionist group, reported that "hundreds of new members had joined." The constant media coverage of events in Palestine kept attention focused on the Middle East. Passionate Toronto Jews packed an auditorium to volunteer for service in Palestine, and surreptitiously raised more than $100,000 to finance the arming of the future Israeli Army. The pull was irresistible. By late November, on the eve of the United Nations partition vote, the Toronto Zionists were formally permitted to negotiate with the UJWF.[134]

The partition vote of 29 November 1947 provided the final impetus toward a joint UPA–UJWF campaign. To this point the Toronto UPA campaign had already raised more than $200,000. In the wake of the partition vote campaign leaders were sure they could do better. The UJWF knew that it would need unprecedented revenue to handle refugee settlement. In order to allocate funds properly, it also needed to know how much money Central Division would require. In early

January 1948 Hayes informed the UJWF that Central Division would require 26 percent of the CJC national budget. This gave the UJWF Budget Committee the key numbers they needed to complete their planning for the UJWF campaign itself. Both the UJWF and Toronto Zionists now knew where they stood and by late January 1948 executives of both organizations, ready to go all-out in fundraising but not wanting to trip over one another's campaigns, agreed in principle to a campaign merger. All that remained was an agreement on the allocation that each organization would receive.[135]

On 23 January 1948, the UJWF proposed a joint campaign goal of $1.84 million, to be divided equally. Seventy-five percent of the funds received above the goal would be allocated to the UPA. The goal was ambitious but not unreachable. The $920,000 goal of the UJWF was a large jump over its $774,000 goal of the previous year. However, it was anticipated that the improving economy and the visibility of the refugee crisis at home and abroad would be sure to stimulate donations. But was it reasonable for the UPA to expect to raise a similar $920,000, a four-fold increase over the previous year? It seemed so. After all, just months before Golda Meir had managed to raise over a million dollars in one evening in New York.[136]

On 1 February the TZC accepted the UJWF proposal. Eight TZC board members and seven top officers of the UJWF met to finalize the agreement. The Zionist representatives quickly agreed that, following the American United Jewish Appeal (UJA) model, refugee settlement would be the first priority of the campaign. However, the TZC delegates believed that it was unfair for them to have to wait until $920,000 was raised for UJWF purposes before getting any money for the UPA. The UJWF Budget Committee promptly accepted a compromise, agreeing that the first $430,000 would go to local needs (JIAS, CJC Central, campaign costs, and refugee settlement), and the next $835,000 would be divided equally between the UPA and the UJWF. After this point, with $1.26 million raised, 75 percent of the next $170,000 would go to the UPA. Anything above $1.43 million to a total of $1.76 million would go entirely to the UPA. This historic agreement went into effect on 3 February. It recognized that the appeal of Zionism gave it a chance to earn more than the UJWF if the campaign goal was even 75 percent subscribed, while guaranteeing the immediate needs of local agencies and refugee settlement.[137]

The resulting UJA campaign was an unprecedented success. It began in March, and by June over $1.46 million had been raised. The full campaign goal was reached by September. In fact, the Canadian UPA campaign of 1948, bolstered by overflowing passion for a new Jewish state, almost tripled that of 1947. In November 1948, it was suggested to the UJWF Board that it admit the Canadian Palestine Appeal (which ran the UPA) to membership and thus make the UJA a permanent arrangement. But the board feared this move might be premature, and recommended "the continuance of this ad hoc arrangement." Despite this caution, the Canadian Palestine Appeal was admitted in 1949 and the UJA became a permanent part of the Toronto fundraising landscape.[138]

It had taken eleven years for the UJWF to fulfill its founding mandate and assert the primacy of its vision over Toronto Jewish communal life. The UJA campaign, the Palevsky Report, and the agreement to begin the Board of Jewish Education stamped the fund's imprimatur of control, rationalization, and professionalization on communal institutions, planning, and fundraising. This vision had been challenged by many, including the CJC, and its growing acceptance had caused considerable resentment on the part of a significant minority. At times, this minority had been vociferous, at times powerful. But UJWF had held its course, and its single-mindedness, which at times bordered on arrogance, never abated. In the end, the fund's staunch defence of its modernized vision and growing control of the communal purse strings defeated even its most stalwart opponents. Even Saul Hayes, and by extension Sam Bronfman, had to acknowledge the fund's power.

The ascendance and dominance of the UJWF entrenched the role of the "educated professional volunteer" who had to be trained to perform optimally. While some deprecated this trend as a move away from *tzedakah* and traditional Jewish voluntarism, it is clear that the increasingly specialized social and community services required by the postwar community demanded this type of volunteer. In addition, growing numbers of highly educated people who wished to volunteer their services could be used to best advantage when carefully matched with an appropriate designated volunteer position. Each volunteer would feel more fulfilled, stimulated, and challenged, and would perform better under professional guidance. This was the crux of the entire "social agency" model that the UJWF advocated and successfully imposed.

The UJWF's ultimate control over communal planning was directly related to the successful and orderly relocation of key institutions into the suburbs during the 1950s and '60s and to the rationalized coordination of major institutional building campaigns with the annual UJA campaign. The ability to raise funds for the expansion of the Baycrest Centre for Geriatric Care, Mount Sinai Hospital, the Bloor and Northern YMHAS, and the building campaigns of many day schools while continuing to meet annual UJA goals, could only have been accomplished by the professional methods pioneered by the UJWF. These methods became the basis for the now-vaunted institutional completeness of Toronto's Jewish community and the high quality and institutional diversity of its Jewish life – the cornerstones of community. Though not yet in place in 1933, they stood strong and steady by 1948, the year of the end of the beginning.

CONCLUSION

Entering the Mainstream

In 1955 Torontonians chose Nathan Phillips as their mayor. Phillips was the first non-Orangeman to assume the office. Revealingly, the campaign of his opponent Leslie Saunders had floundered over a letter extolling the importance of the Battle of the Boyne written on municipal stationery. Phillips was hailed as "the mayor of all the people" – a title that acknowledged the changing face of Toronto. The defeated Saunders became Grandmaster of the Orange Lodge just as its membership and political clout began its precipitous decline over the next two decades. Phillips's victory was a political and social watershed in Toronto history.[1]

Few living in 1945 would have predicted mayoral victory of Phillips, a Jew. But the factors that made it possible had deeper roots. Most important among them was increased inclusion of Jews and other minorities in roles of political responsibility. This development was spearheaded by the same group that founded the UJWF and catalyzed Jewish involvement in the Community Chest. The long and indirect route toward political inclusion began in 1943 when some Ontarians began to wonder why racism was tolerated at home while Canadian soldiers were dying as they battled Nazism and Fascism abroad. One observer recalled that "Jews [and other minorities] were barred, both formally and informally, from renting or buying houses in certain parts of Toronto and Ontario, that very few Jews were employed in banks or insurance (except as salesmen)... Jewish high school teachers were as rare as hen's teeth ... Discrimination was the norm." Blacks were shunted to jobs as hotel and railroad porters, while Asians languished in the restaurant and laundry businesses. For Jews, current times were scarcely better than their situation in the 1930s, the only "improvement" being that Nazi propaganda had been stifled by wartime legislation.[2]

The winds of change that began to blow in 1943 only had an effect because the minority Drew government depended on the votes of some MPPs who sought to diminish discrimination. These were led by MPPs John J. Glass (Liberal), a pioneer in this legislative area, and two Labour Progressive Party MPPs, Joseph B. Salsberg and Alistair Macleod, who spearheaded the passage of the *Racial Discrimination Act* in March 1944. The Act's reach was more symbolic than real – in keeping with the sentiments of Drew and most of his ministers – it only banned egregious displays of words, signs, or symbols indicating racial discrimination. But it proved powerless against restrictive covenants and resorts, restaurants, and golf clubs that sported "restricted clientele" signs, stationery, or advertisements. These remained popular into the 1950s. Discrimination just became more covert, and minorities were expected to "know their place" or face the embarrassing consequences. Pierre Berton's surveys in *Maclean's* and Gallup polls at the time also revealed support for discrimination at resorts and hostility towards Jewish immigration.[3]

The sponsors of the *Racial Discrimination Act* were fully aware of its limitations but they believed that the educational value of the Act trumped its legal efficacy. This judgment reflected careful alignment with the long-standing approach to race relations of the Joint Public Relations Committee (JPRC). In addition, the overwhelmingly Jewish source of funding for community relations campaigns was kept under wraps for fear of Jews being accused of self-interest. Nonetheless, it is clear, as Carmela Patrias and Ruth Frager have shown, that Ontario Jews were "the most influential and effective campaigners against discrimination." Long-standing Jewish communal organizations provided the wherewithal to engage these issues. We have seen how the JPRC, formed between the Canadian Jewish Congress and the B'nai Brith, from the outset employed the latest educational techniques to convince employers to hire more Jews and other minorities and battle discrimination at all levels. The JPRC's lay leadership, constituting a who's-who of Uptown Jews, turned their attention to gaining the passage of fair employment practices legislation.[4]

From 1947 on, the JPRC carefully formed alliances with sympathetic groups inside and outside the Jewish community. The Jewish Labour

Committee (JLC) proved a key partner. Established in 1926, the JLC opened a Canadian office around 1937, and was backed by Jewish socialists and unions, and closely affiliated with the CCF. During the war it emphasized rescue operations. Its Spadina Avenue factory constituents supported it financially, both at the union and individual levels, and this support allowed it to remain independent of both Congress and the Welfare Fund. But, as we have seen, in Toronto economic lines did not always coalesce into political barriers. Even when economic and political lines clashed, as they did during strikes, the fault lines were far less deep than in American communities. Certainly, unionized workers supported left-wing parties and distrusted their bosses. But these same bosses made common cause with the unions in both the Furriers' and Tailors' Schemes. But as war and its attendant labour shortages increased prosperity, and postwar brought the Rand Formula and the recognition of union bargaining rights, the economic gap between workers and bosses temporarily receded. The JLC's postwar repudiation of Communism made cooperation with Congress more politically acceptable. However, these reasons alone do not account for the JLC's suddenly higher profile. It was the desire to increase Jewish immigration, that ever-continuing thread of communal unity, which proved the key factor in the JLC's arrival as a mainstream Jewish organization.[5]

The close cooperation between factory owners and unionized labour in the Furriers' and Tailors' projects served to knit the two sides together organizationally and personally. The structure of the immigration schemes placed the onus on industry to substantiate a need for workers. Thus, as we have seen, Saul Hayes funded and provided research to manufacturers to demonstrate their need for workers; the manufacturers in turn partnered with the unions to select workers in refugee camps, arrange for their transport and provide subsequent job placement. The unions were left in charge of much of the bureaucracy of the immigration schemes. Indeed, JLC Toronto representative Bernard Shane played a crucial role in administering the Tailors' Project, attracting and commanding considerable respect from Congress and UJWF leaders. On 14 January 1948, as planning for immigration movements shifted into high gear, the JLC and Congress officially entered into an agreement to cooperate on immigration and community education matters. The JLC had responded to the community education challenge by hiring Kalman Kaplansky, a veteran American union organizer familiar with various American approaches to racism, as executive director in 1946. Kaplansky's experience and ability to adapt American research to Canadian conditions eventually proved decisive in the battle to pass the *Fair Employment Practices Act* (FEPA) and design effective public education campaigns to increase tolerance.[6]

Many of the JPRC's leading lights, on the other hand, were veterans of the communal politics that led to the formation of the Welfare Fund. Abraham Feinberg, the charismatic rabbi of Holy Blossom, chaired the committee. He was a well-known radio host and brilliantly passionate orator whose sense of social justice would transform his synagogue. Feinberg, a civil rights crusader and peace activist – dubbed the "Red Rabbi" when he later became famous for his role in the March on Washington and for meeting Ho Chi Minh – took up the battle for the FEPA with tremendous vigour. The rabbi was assisted by Professor Joseph Finkelman, the first Jewish member of the University of Toronto Law School, who had been involved with the JPRC for over a decade. He was joined by his colleague Bora Laskin, the 1934 gold medalist, who went on to Harvard Law School and returned home in 1937 only to find that no significant firm employed Jews. Laskin was given a university lectureship only after the department chair assured the president that although "Laskin is a Jew...he will not disgrace the university." Laskin lived up to this promise, eventually becoming Chief Justice of Canada. This experience explains Laskin's commitment to the JPRC's agenda. These men were ably assisted by Joseph I. Oelbaum, who had moved beyond his role at the Brunswick Avenue Talmud Torah to the UJWF presidency and the vice-presidency of Central Division. When Feinberg completed his term as chair, he was replaced by lawyer Fred Catzman. Catzman, the silver medalist of the class of 1929, had shared Laskin's job hunting experiences. Unlike his classmate, gold medalist and celebrated legal eagle John J. Robinette, Catzman was forced to work solo for most of his career. He also had a long history of communal involvement that began with Central Division in 1933.[7]

Thus, many of the same men who had imposed a measure of order on their community had now moved to the next level of political challenge. They sought a wider role in society for themselves, their community, and other minorities hobbled by racism and discrimination. As we have seen, this group had many characteristics in common.

They had received most or all of their education in Canada and came from homes that supported a hyphenated Canadian-Jewish identity. They shared a passionate belief in the power of education and a dedication to rational problem solving. And this was by no means just a "boys' club"; key women such as Florence Hutner and Dr Wilensky, as well as the veritable army of mostly female social workers who had professionalized almost every Jewish organization, attested to the vital role women played in communal rationalization. This group were fervent Canadian patriots, who believed that loyalty entitled them to be listened to when they spoke to government – politely of course – about vital communal issues. They were rudely disappointed with the government's deafness to all appeals to allow Jews to escape the Holocaust.

But in the area of race relations, Uptowners' reach did not exceed their grasp. This segment of the Jewish community played an essential part in the ultimately successful battle against racial and religious discrimination in Ontario. The JLC's role proved equally decisive. Congress and the JLC built a broad consensus of organizations, including the YMCA, the Canadian Labour Congress, and the Canadian Civil Liberties Association, to support their goals and to raise public and political awareness of the need for a *Fair Employment Practices Act*. The fact that "Hitler gave racism a bad name," along with the historic passage of the United Nations Charter of Human Rights, provided added impetus. By 1949 the movement was gaining traction as the vanguard of thousands of immigrants came to Toronto. Both the *Star* and the *Telegram* contributed their editorial voices, arguing not only that tolerance was a postwar virtue but that immigrants could hasten postwar prosperity. Organized labour spread the news to its members. As these educational and networking efforts began to bear fruit, the JPRC and JLC, now openly funded by Congress, selected a large delegation from over twenty organizations to meet with Ontario's newly elected premier, Leslie Frost, in early 1950. They asked for the elimination of racial covenants, the introduction of a FEPA, and an end to all informal discrimination that kept minorities from certain amusement parks, ice arenas, resorts, and clubs. They were heard. Within six months, future restricted covenants were banned, despite the vociferous complaints of Frost's supporter *Globe and Mail* publisher George McCullagh. Encouraged, the JPRC-led coalition continued its campaign in January 1951 by bringing in Republican Senator Wayne Morse of

Oregon, one of the few states that had enacted an act regulating fair employment practices. Morse, a liberal Republican, gave a talk at the formerly all-establishment Empire Club – whose president Sydney Hermant of Imperial Optical had been one of the Welfare Fund's earliest supporters – and spoke on CBC Radio about equity in employment. By chance, Premier Frost heard the five-minute speech and was impressed that a Republican could support such laws and that they worked. At a confidential meeting with a JPRC delegation, he promised to enact such legislation. Frost kept his word; Ontario enacted the FEPA in 1951.[8]

Just before this, in November 1950, the Supreme Court found a racial covenant *ultra vires* in *Noble and Wolf* v. *Alley*. Though the decision was based on a narrow reading of the covenant's language and nothing was said of the dangers that racism posed on the public policy level, the JPRC hailed it as a victory. Its effusive comment that the case was "further evidence that there is no place in Canada for racial and religious intolerance" was validated in retrospect. No other racial restricted-covenant cases have been reported. With the dam of resistance broken, reform in Ontario streamed forth. After the enactment of the FEPA, Frost approached Jacob Finkleman to draft further reforms in labour relations – reforms that became the *Labour Relations Act* (1954), which removed the last vestiges of workplace discrimination. Further legislation banned discrimination at skating rinks, taverns, music halls, and other public places. Therefore, less than a decade after Gallup polls had indicated widespread aversion to Jewish immigration and considerable anti-Semitism, roadblocks to the progress of Jews and other minorities were disappearing. Thus, Phillips's victory was simply the most public manifestation of this new trend, which Phillip Givens's 1963 election as mayor further underscored. Some barriers remained, especially on Bay Street, but the main work was done.[9]

As we have seen, many of the leaders of this battle against discrimination began their careers in the UJWF. It is thus appropriate to ask, who among the host of leaders encountered in this study were the most effective in bringing a new vision to Toronto Jewry? Certainly men and women like Florence Hutner, Professor Finkleman, Samuel Zacks, Ben Sadowski, who leveraged their UJWF participation into positions of influence beyond the Jewish community, merit consideration. But they stood, as most would readily have admitted, on the shoulders of one man who paved the way: Martin Cohn. It was Cohn who coaxed the Federation of Jewish Philanthropies through the Depression by never abandoning his vision, well honed in the School of Social Work, of professionalized service delivery funded by rational and professional fundraising. Even more impressive was Cohn's willingness to learn new behaviours in mid-career. He constantly kept up with the latest developments in welfare funds and community chests and went to seek advice when it was needed. He was a man who knew when he was in over his head, and when there was nothing more to accomplish. He presided over the UJWF's takeover of his own organization, fully realizing that the obsolescence of his job meant the salvation of a vision he wished to preserve and impose. Indeed, he saw this takeover as an opportunity to keep leading and learning, and headed off to Chicago, where his successes paralleled those in Toronto.

Immigration and Zionism were the two key issues uniting Toronto Jewry. Uptowners and Downtowners may have disagreed about politics, but the "little blue box" of the Jewish National Fund adorned practically every Jewish home. A wide array of Zionist organizations gave opportunities for adherents from all religious streams, and practically all ideologies save the Communists, to follow and debate developments in Palestine. Reform Judaism was uncomfortable with Zionism, but this discomfort never became a major issue at Holy Blossom. Rabbi Eisendrath may have insulted some congregants with his eloquent pre-war anti-Zionist sermons and sharp editorials in the *Canadian Jewish Review*. Indeed, some, like the Dunkelmans of Tip Top Tailors, were so offended to hear, "Zionists are like our oppressors [who wish] to incarcerate us once more," that they switched allegiance to Goel Tzedec. But Holy Blossom valued its tradition of a "free pulpit," and the majority of its congregants remained Zionist supporters. Eisendrath's ideas began to shift after he visited Germany in 1933, but even before then his sentiments were out of synch with Reform Judaism, which was reinventing itself in order to attract the children of the immigrant boom. Abba Hillel Silver, famous Reform rabbi and Zionist leader extraordinaire, was born in Lithuania and grew up on the Lower East Side; other Reform rabbis of similar background graduated during this time from Hebrew Union College. It is thus not surprising that when Rabbi Eisendrath left Holy Blossom in 1943, his successor, Rabbi Feinberg, did not share his views. And well that he did not. In the postwar years Zionism ran at floodtide in Toronto. The drama (often shown on newsreels) of immigrant ships filled to the brim with the shattered survivors of the Holocaust struggling to break the British blockade catalyzed generous Toronto Jewry to attain new heights of charitable commitment.

Significantly, Zionism – along with immigration – also became one of the proxies in the battle over control between Toronto and Montreal that characterized the period of this study. As mentioned, there was considerable overlap between the Welfare Fund and the Zionist Organization of Canada (zoc) leadership. Archie Freiman's insistence on "stand-alone" zoc campaigns halted a nascent attempt to merge the two campaigns in 1939. But his passing, and Torontonian Sam Zack's increasingly influential role in national Zionist affairs, gave the nod to Toronto's vision of a united zoc-Welfare Fund campaign. This union became a reality in late 1948 and subsequent results validated Zack's vision, experience, and loyalty to both organizations. It was also an affirmation of the vital and consistent importance of Zionism in Canadian Jewish life, one of the primary contrasts between Canadian and American Jewish experiences. The unification of the UPA and the federation marked yet another repudiation of Montreal's and Congress's claim to continued postwar primacy in Canadian Jewish life.

Indeed, as illustrated throughout these chapters, the battle of Toronto's Jewish organizations such as the JIAS and Congress to secure independence from their Montreal headquarters formed a vital underlying theme in organizational behaviour until 1948. While the Toronto JIAS remained under Montreal's control, much to the chagrin and embarrassment of its officers, Central Division followed a very different path. As we have seen, under H.M. Caiserman's weak leadership, the Canadian Jewish Congress lurched from crisis to crisis. Organizational independence therefore fell by default into the hands of the Central Division executive. Given their talents and predilections, it is not surprising that by 1939 Central Division had come into its own and was flexing its organizational muscle. Samuel Bronfman's sudden foray into organized Canadian Jewish life, highlighted by his accession to the Congress presidency in 1939 and coupled with his appointment of Saul Hayes, was justifiably perceived by Central Division loyalists as a shot across their organizational bow.

As we have seen, Hayes first sought to impose Montreal's authority in immigration and refugee affairs, but found himself stymied partly by the rise of the Welfare Fund and mainly by wartime fundraising restrictions. He chafed at the bit, glowering from afar as the Welfare Fund imposed fiscal responsibility and professionalism on its constituents, waiting eagerly to impose his centralizing authority when peace arrived. When it finally did after six gruelling years of war, the tide seemed poised to flow in Montreal's direction. Hayes fully expected the Orphans' Project to be completed on Montreal's terms. As noted, the Canadian government's key requirement was that the orphans be placed in accordance with accepted child welfare procedures. Knowing that Quebec law placed responsibility for child welfare in the hands of the churches, Hayes must have viewed this requirement as a slam dunk: with Jews as Quebec's "third solitude," Congress would control the entire placement procedure and receive all the credit for saving a key remnant of European Jewry.

The Welfare Fund had other plans. In stark contrast to Quebec, Ontario law mandated that child welfare standards be enforced by professionally trained social workers at both provincial and municipal levels. In response to this, as we have seen, one of the fund's greatest impositions of will was exerted in relation to the development of professionalized Jewish social welfare delivery services. The Jewish Family and Child Service was created at the Fund's behest to do just this, and it was backed by significant allocations. Given these conditions, Hayes's plans never had a chance. His worst case scenario quickly developed: when the orphans were placed after considerable communal struggles, the lion's share of the credit fell to the JFCS and the Welfare Fund. Montreal was stuck with the transportation costs and had to be content with the knowledge that Hayes had at least forced the government to make good on its 1942 pledge of admitting a thousand Vichy orphans.

The rise of the JLC to prominence in Ontario, and its partnership with the JPRC, marked another stinging defeat for Hayes's Montreal-centred vision. Once again, the differences between the Ontario and Quebec varieties of anti-Semitism proved so substantial as to nullify what little expertise Hayes possessed in this area. In addition, the signing of the JDC-CJC memo of cooperation was an acknowledgement that Congress's long-stated vision of itself of "the Parliament of Canadian

Jewry" never extended to Jewish unionized labour. Henceforth the battle against discrimination became provincially based, demarcating further autonomy for Central Division at Montreal's expense. The success of the approach led by the JPRC/JLC between 1948 and 1955 in the *Fair Employment Practices Act* battle continued to underscore Toronto's advantage. The pre-eminence of the Welfare Fund and Central Division was further confirmed when the organizations merged in January 1976 to form the Toronto Jewish Congress.

These developments resulted from the Welfare Fund's successes in rationalizing fundraising campaigns and imposing professionalization on Jewish social service organizations. The fund could now control future planning and their programs by the power both of the purse and of like-minded professionalism. Montreal could not match this record. Indeed, Toronto Uptowners went even further. Economic success and improved social mobility allowed many of them to assume positions of importance in the United Community Chest, where they mingled with some of Toronto's elite and applied the communal organization strategies they had honed in a wider population. Montreal had no Community Chest during this time. Most of Montreal Jewry, trapped between Quebec's "two solitudes" could not enjoy this type of leverage. The most successful of Montreal Jews made no impact on francophone Quebeckers.

The rise of Toronto's Jewish community at the expense of Montreal's epitomized the rivalry between the two cities. Postwar Toronto was a boom town with relentless suburban growth driven by immigration. It was the premier destination of postwar immigrants, while Montreal languished. Toronto industries burgeoned and head offices began to move from Montreal to Toronto in the 1950s and '60s. In the meantime, Montreal stagnated economically. Montreal Jewish cultural life remained richer than Toronto's until the "Montreal Exodus" that followed the election of the Parti Québécois in 1979, but the irrevocable tilt toward Toronto was heralded by the events of 1948.

Given the significant differences between Toronto and Montreal, it would be logical to compare Toronto Jewish organizational behaviour between 1933 and 1948 with that of other North American federations and welfare funds. Most of these American organizations were founded by and led by descendants of Jews who emigrated from Bavaria, Western Prussia, Posen, and Alsace (often misleadingly lumped together with other Jews from Hungary and Austrian Poland as "German Jews"). Many of these were successful businessmen and were affiliated with Reform Temples. But by 1931, the number of Reform Jews was evenly divided between those of German and Russian/Polish parentage. Many of their children, and the children of the Russian immigration of 1881–1914, headed to university. Thus, the 1930s saw the rise of a large number of educated young Jewish men and women, many of whom could not find employment outside the Jewish community during the Depression. A significant number of these entered the New Deal at various levels, and many others were hired as professional workers by the growing number of American Jewish federations and welfare funds. These were the pioneers of what would become a huge "Jewish bureaucracy." The demands of the Depression decimated charitable giving and spurred the founding of more federations and welfare funds: their number increased by almost 50 percent between 1931 and 1936. Even these proved insufficient to meet communal needs: by 1935 almost half of the federations were forced to ask Community Chests or United Ways for allocations. In addition, the care of many Jewish families was outsourced to the federal relief agencies that sprang up in the wake of the New Deal.[10]

Many observers, noted economist I.L. Rubinow and federation expert Maurice Karpf among them, feared that the "future of Jewish agencies would depend entirely on the federal and state governments." They also believed that even if Community Chest leaders were not anti-Semitic, they were unfamiliar with the special needs of Jewish agencies. Thus allocations would likely be insufficient. Of most concern to contemporary observers, there was also a fervent belief that Diaspora Jews should take care of their own. "American Jews," observes Hasia Diner, "believed passionately in the separation of church and state. They feared the political and cultural costs associated with a new paradigm in which sectarian agencies would come to the government for money."[11]

Of course, there was no New Deal north of the border. While Roosevelt opened the vaults of the Treasury, Canadian politicians proved downright stingy. The "Bennett buggies" moniker targeted the misplaced frugality of the prime minister, one of Canada's richest men. Besides, there was no Community Chest in Toronto until 1943 and, when it arrived, once again in contrast to the American experience, many Welfare Fund leaders were involved in or consulted about its creation. This overlap goes far toward explaining the Community Chest's responsiveness to the needs of its Toronto Jewish constituent organizations. But even before the Community Chest existed, the fund's predecessor organization, the Federation of Jewish Philanthropies (FJP), was very careful about allowing clients to opt out of municipal relief services completely. As we have seen, the FJP only turned to governmental authority if it suited their agenda. The desire to transfer orphans to foster homes, which were both cheaper and more in keeping with the social work principles of the day, and the FJP's acquiescence in Jews receiving municipal relief on condition that the community provided kosher meet and received reimbursed for it by the city, are but two examples. It is notable that even when the FJP was on the verge of financial collapse, its leadership held to this course of maximizing communal control – once again in sharp contrast to the American experience. In the end, this consistent pursuit of communal order utterly denied the CJC's attempts to exert control over communal politics and gave the fund its pre-eminence.

Close scrutiny of Toronto Jewish communal organizational behaviour therefore casts grave doubt on scholarly assumptions about the similarity of communal organization in Canada and the United States. Other scholarly assertions about Canadian Jewish polity also do not square with the experience examined in this study. For example, the assumption of some Canadian Jewish researchers that leaders progress from the local to the divisional to the national level is not borne out by the facts. The great majority of the communal leaders wore many organizational hats simultaneously. This multi-tasking can be explained by the small size of the leadership pool in Toronto, a situation that persisted well into the 1960s. This alone makes comparisons between the American and Canadian experiences problematic.

The fact that Jewish Toronto's leaders were typically united by age, a primarily Canadian educational experience – which often included university – and a desire to identify both as Jews and Canadians flies in the face of those who speak about Holy Blossom and its "German-English" leadership clashing with the "Polish immigrants" over their vision of community. The simple fact is that there never were enough German Jews in Toronto to make their presence felt. Holy Blossom's very gradual evolution from Orthodoxy to Reform testifies to this.

What is more, the leaders of the FJP, the UJWF and its constituent organizations were unconcerned with the battle between Reform and Orthodox Judaism. Rabbis Sachs and Eisendrath may have disagreed about Judaism, but both supported the FJP and the Welfare Fund. Besides, by the 1930s the economic and social status of Goel Tzedec and Holy Blossom was roughly equivalent – choosing between them was largely a matter of religious preference and family custom. There was also significant movement both ways, often because of marriage. Community leaders who went to different synagogues on Saturday shared the same federation boardroom table on Sunday mornings and many a weekday evening.

In the final analysis, this interrelationship proved decisive. The entire process of creating a welfare fund, and listening to requests for allocations from both local and non-local institutions created a broad sense of Jewish community among its participants. At one time or another between 1933 and 1948, every Jewish ideology was represented around the boardroom tables of the FLP or the UJWF. The Communists came and went, and unionized labour eventually arrived to stay – thus rectifying the fund's greatest failure – and the fund facilitated their inter-organizational dialogue. The fund's long-standing insistence on proper accounting compelled representatives of different ideologies to justify their organization's contributions and rationale for existence to sceptical ears. Organizational participants had to look beyond their noses at a time of rampant parochialism. This requirement produced a breadth of vision that eventually transcended much factionalism and helped unify the community. In short, the UJWF represented the triumph of methodology over ideology.

Did ordinary people – *amcha* – notice all this in their daily lives? Did all these boardroom discussions have any impact on the street? At first glance, it is tempting to answer "no" and "none." Few among the Spadina throngs or those buying freshly slaughtered chickens in the Kensington Market cared much about the organizational machinations of 1933–48 beyond the snippets carried by the *Zhurnal*. *Amcha* were primarily concerned with the daily grind of life, often made worse by the Depression, and the ensuing war-time economic constraints, and coloured by continuous concern over European relatives who had suddenly stopped writing. The *landsmanschaften* remained busy and their memberships steady, unions generally increased their economic and social importance, and religious life continued to offer relevance to its adherents, although rabbis moaned about the decrease in religious observance with astounding regularity. In sum, for *amcha* – many of the goings-on of the Welfare Fund, Congress, and the JIAS had little relevance.

But by 1948 *amcha* could not ignore the change mediated by the Uptowners' imposition of will. At work many garment and fur workers' unions asked their members to participate in FJP fundraising campaigns as contributors or canvassers. Many *amcha* had relatives who had arrived through an immigration scheme, and had first-hand knowledge of some of the complex cooperation that brought them to Canada. Every Jewish school received funding from the federation and advertised it. If *amcha* used the pool or gym at the Brunswick YMHA, signs reminded them that these facilities benefitted from federation funding. There was no way of avoiding the annual federation campaign: *amcha* could perhaps ignore the knock on the door without difficulty, but then they would be canvassed by mail. The more religiously minded could not escape – the rabbis of the larger congregations were not shy about sermonizing on the importance of communal *tzedakah*. Most important was the obvious part the UJWF had played in immigration. By 1948 it was impossible for *amcha* to ignore the role of Uptown organizations or their reach.

But all this paled beside the overwhelming presence of the federation in Toronto communal fundraising after Israel's birth on 14 May 1948. Canadian Jews had always embraced Zionism, but the dramatic struggle for statehood and survival played out in the final years of the British mandate in Palestine stirred Canadian Zionist involvement to fever pitch. Zionist organizational membership swelled and donations reached record amounts. And now, with an alliance between the Toronto Zionists and the UJWF, and with unionized labour firmly in the communal fold, more and more *amcha* would be canvassed by their own peers in the annual fund campaign. After 1948 the annual campaign truly embraced the whole Toronto Jewish community. Certainly, the average *amcha* had a far more inclusive vision of community in 1948 than in 1933.

This was a great achievement, but was it worth the price? As Hasia Diner has rightly observed, albeit about the American situation: "In their attempts to manage the organizational chaos, the federations compromised the essential democracy of American Jewish life. They centralized authority in the hands of professional staff and big donors, depriving Jews of control over community funds." Her analysis has weight in Toronto. Certainly the imposition of organizational will caused great pain to some – as the volunteer mothers of the Jewish Childrens' Home could attest – and was enacted with considerable arrogance and condescension. Intra-ethnic quarrels did not end immediately, although the consensus on communal needs and future planning built around the UJWF committee tables did trickle down by the 1950s. But as leaders like Martin Cohn recognized at the time – not only in the 20/20 roseate glow of hindsight – the alternative was worse. Given the reality that the Jewish community requires significant institutional completeness, how else could a small ethnic community maintain the comparatively vast and expensive network of services they needed to retain their identity? What would have happened if Brunswick Talmud Torah and a host of other institutions had defaulted on their mortgages and ceased to exist? Imposition of will proved the price of ethnic survival. The fact that the architects of survival crafted a system that allowed for mass participation speaks volumes about their sense of community. On that glorious day of 14 May 1948 when Israel declared its independence, the Toronto Jewish community boasted unprecedented unity and financial security. The major paradigms of leadership set out between 1933 and 1948 would last for another three decades. The foundations of community were secure enough to withstand a suburban march from Richmond Street to Richmond Hill with stops in between. The pain of those swept aside may not justify the means, but the final results and their achievement against long odds attest to the necessity of their imposition of will.

Glossary of Individuals

A.B. Bennett	VP CJC Central, 1934–36 Executive member throughout period Queen's University graduate
Alexander Brown	Executive Secretary CJC Central, 1934–36 University of Toronto graduate
Dr Abraham Brodey	President, Toronto JIAS, 1925–40 University of Toronto Medical School graduate
Samuel Bronfman	President of the CJC, 1939
Hannaniah Meir Caiserman	General Secretary of the CJC, 1933–48
Fred Catzman	Lay leader of CJC Central in 1930s Osgoode Law School graduate
Oscar Cohen	Publisher of *Jewish Standard* Secretary of Central Division 1938–41, 1946
Martin Cohn	Headed Federation of Jewish Philanthropies, 1928–43 University of Toronto graduate
Maurice Eisendrath	Rabbi of Holy Blossom Temple, 1929–1943

Abraham Feinberg	Rabbi of Holy Blossom Temple, 1943–1961
Egmont Frankel	President CJC Central 1934–36
Archie Freiman	President of ZOC, 1922–44 Ottawa businessman
Jacob Gordon	Founder of Toronto Hebrew Free School
Saul Hayes	Headed the UJRA 1938–48 Executive Director of CJC 1942–78 McGill Law School Graduate
Florence Hutner	Headed the Federation of Jewish Philanthropies 1944–72 University of Toronto graduate
Samuel W. Jacobs	MP Cartier, 1917–38 President CJC, 1934–38 McGill Law School graduate
Sam Kronick	Chair of the Toronto UJRA 1938–50s
Ben Lappin	Executive Secretary Central CJC Central 1941–55 University of Toronto graduate
Joseph I. Oelbaum	Key figure at Toronto Hebrew Free School and one of the founders of UJWF University of Toronto graduate
A.J. Paull	National Executive Director, JIAS, 1927–37
Benjamin Robinson	President of the JIAS, 1929–40 Harvard BA, McGill Law graduate
Otto B. Roger	Leadership roles in CJC Central in mid-1930s English Shell Oil Executive

Samuel Sachs	Rabbi of Goel Tzedec Congregation, 1927–46
Ben Sadowski	Leading Toronto businessman President of the UJWF and later Mt Sinai Hospital
Shmuel Myer Shapiro	Publisher of the *Yiddisher Zhurnal* On Executive of the JIAS in 1920s and Central Division in 1930s and 1940s
Maurice A. Solkin	National Executive Director of the JIAS, 1938–40
Dr Dora Wilensky	Took over Jewish Children's Home Head of Jewish Family and Child Service Wife of J.B. Salsberg University of Toronto graduate
Samuel Zacks	A founder of UJWF President of the ZOC, 1943–49 Queen's University BA (1924) Harvard MA (1926)

Notes

ABBREVIATIONS USED IN THE NOTES

AA	Associated Hebrew School Archives, Toronto
ADL	Anti-Defamation League
BBM	Bnai Brith Minutes, Public Archives of Canada
BOC	Board of Control, Central Division
CJC	Canadian Jewish Congress
CJCA	Canadian Jewish Congress Archives, Montreal
CJCA-IOI	Inter Office Information, weekly news sent Out by Saul Hayes in CJC headquarters to the Central and Western Divisions of Congress, Montreal
CJCP	Canadian Jewish Congress Papers, Montreal
CJCR	Canadian Council for Jewish Refugees
CNCR	Canadian National Committee on Refugees
COJW	Council of Jewish Women
CTA	City of Toronto Archives, Toronto
ECC	Eastern Canadian Conference, Bnai Brith of Canada
FPR	Federation of Jewish Philanthropies Reports 1934, Ontario Jewish Archives, Toronto

IOI	Inter Office Information Bulletin, Montreal
JECIT	Jewish Educational and Community Institute of Toronto
JFCS	Jewish Family and Child Services
JIAS (M)	Jewish Immigrant Aid Society of Montreal Papers (held in CJCA)
JIAS (T)	Jewish Immigrant Aid Society of Toronto, OJA
JPRC	Joint Public Relations Committee of Canadian Jewish Congress and B'nai Brith
JWB	Jewish Welfare Bureau
LAC	Library and Archives Canada, Ottawa
MBD	Minutes of the Board of Directors
MBE	Minutes of the Board and Executive
OJA	Ontario Jewish Archives, Toronto
THFS	Toronto Hebrew Free School—predecessor of Associated Hebrew Schools of Toronto
PAO	Public Archives of Ontario, Toronto
UJWF	United Jewish Welfare Fund
UJRA	United Jewish Relief Agencies
UPA	United Palestine Appeal, predecessor of United Israel Appeal
UTA	University of Toronto Archives, Toronto
YMHA	Young Men's Hebrew Association
ZOC	Zionist Organization of Canada
ZOCFR	Records and Minutes of the ZOC, Ottawa

INTRODUCTION

1 This is a Glass family story that my mother-in-law, Elaine (Glass) Geller, recounted to me many times. She was a participant at the picnic.

CHAPTER ONE

1 See Creighton, *Empire of the St. Lawrence*, which stresses the centrality of the St Lawrence in Canadian history, and Craig, *Upper Canada*, 1–3 for a fine discussion on how geography made this land so impenetrable. On early Jewish settlement in Canada see Godfrey and Godfrey, *Search Out the Land*, and Gerald Tulchinsky, *Taking Root*.
2 Godfrey and Godfrey, *Search Out the Land*, ch. 12; Tulchinsky, *Taking Root*, 12–13.
3 For a good overview see Careless, *The Union of the Canadas*. The quotation in the text is from 144.
4 Armstrong, "Metropolitanism and Toronto"; Careless, *Union of the Canadas*, ch. 8; "Toronto: A Place of Meeting" at http://ve.torontopubliclibrary.ca/TPM/sec2.html (15 July 2005).
5 Rosenberg, *Canada's Jews*, 10; Speisman, *Jews of Toronto*, 11–15; Tulchinsky, *Taking Root*, 71–2; Godfrey and Godfrey, *Burn this Gossip*, 1–21, 39–42, 136–8.
6 Speisman, *Jews of Toronto*, 16–17; Tulchinsky, *Taking Root*, 72–3.
7 Speisman, *Jews of Toronto*, 13, 21–3.
8 Ibid., 22–4.
9 Ibid., 31–4.
10 Godfrey and Godfrey, *Search Out the Land*, 200–4, 214.
11 Speisman, *Jews of Toronto*, 57. There is a growing literature on the importance of these organizations in North America and Europe. For some excellent examples see Cordery, *British Friendly Societies*; Schmidt, *Fraternal Organizations*; Beito, *From Mutual Aid to the Welfare State*.
12 For a good overview of medieval Jewish *tzedakah* in action see Katz, *Tradition and Crisis*, 79–212; also Splane, *Social Welfare in Ontario*, 16, 18, where Splane quotes the *Globe* of February 27, 1874; for a similar view to Splane see Fraser, *The Evolution of the British Welfare State*, 124.
13 Speisman, *Jews of Toronto*, 56–7.
14 Ibid., 62–3; Ben Lappin, "Toronto's Tombstones: An Old Cemetery reveals interesting history," *Shem Tov* 20:1 (March 2004): 1,12 (translation of original article in Yiddish by N. Shemen, *Jewish Standard*, 1 October 1959); "Lewis Samuel" in *Dictionary of Canadian Biography On-Line* http://www.biographi.ca/EN/ShowBio.asp?BioId=39942&query=.
15 Speisman, *Jews of Toronto*, 62–4, 118–19; Lappin, "Toronto Tombstones," 1.
16 Fraser, *Evolution of the British Welfare State*, 108, 125–31; Beito, *From Mutual Aid to the Welfare State*, 7, 10.

17 Ibid., 7, 15.
18 Ibid., 18–19; Fraser, *Evolution of the British Welfare State*, 110–12; Splane, *Social Welfare in Ontario*, 103–5, 165–8, 242–5.
19 Fraser, *Evolution of the British Welfare State*, 126; Beito, *From Mutual Aid to the Welfare State*, 18.
20 Speisman, *Toronto Jews*, 71, 76.
21 Ibid., 120–5.
22 Ibid., 149; Deuteronomy 15:8.
23 Speisman, *Jews of Toronto*, 123.
24 Ibid., 106–7; on the whole issue of doctors and friendly societies see Beito, *From Mutual Aid to the Welfare State*, ch. 6; for a personal memoir on the difficulties of this job in Toronto see Willinsky, *A Doctor's Memoirs*, 47–9; LAC. Louis Rosenberg Papers, MG 30 C119, Volume 26, File 19, "Jewish Mutual Benefit and Friendly Societies in Toronto," 22, Tables 22a and 22b; Tulchinsky, *Branching Out*, 21.
25 Frager, *Sweatshop Strife*, 80–1, 29 16, 124, 62–3, 70–2.
26 Nathanson, "Jewish Peddlers"; Wyman, *A Forest of Trees*, 2, 44–5; for a large number of anecdotes that bear this out see Abella, Goodman and Sharp, *Growing Up Jewish*, and Oliver, *Unlikely Tory*, 11.
27 Speisman, *Jews of Toronto*, 82–4, 145–9; no author, "The Rise of the Jewish Community," 62.
28 Nathanson, "Jewish Peddlers," 34–5; Speisman, *Jews of Toronto*, 45, 97.
29 Ibid., 43, 64, 168–9.
30 Ibid., 171–8.
31 Fraser, *Evolution of the British Welfare State*, 170–1; Lurie, *Heritage Affirmed*, 30–4; Jewish Social Service Association, *Fifty Years of Social Service*, 11–16.
32 Speisman, *Jews of Toronto*, 156–9.
33 Ibid., 92, 159.
34 Jewish Social Service Association, *Fifty Years*, 19–26; Howe, *World of Our Fathers*, 31; Lurie, *Heritage Affirmed*, 90–3.
35 Ibid., 45–58.
36 Ibid., 41–2; 419 fn 10.
37 Speisman, *Jews of Toronto*, 150–3.
38 Ibid., 145, 149–50.
39 Ibid., 260–1, 43.
40 Ibid., 261–2. Allen would remain a powerful community leader for the next three decades both in the new federation and later in the Canadian Jewish Congress.

41 Ibid., 261–3.
42 Ibid., 263–6.
43 Ibid., 265–8.
44 The calculation is based on Rosenberg, "Mutual Benefit Societies," Table 6; Speisman, *Jews of Toronto*, 90; on Jewish student groups at the University of Toronto see Speisman, *Jews of Toronto*, 183.
45 Tulchinsky, *Taking Root*, 265–7.
46 Ibid., 268–71.
47 Ibid., 269.
48 Ibid., 274–5; Tulchinsky, *Branching Out*, 33.

CHAPTER TWO

1 For a more complete discussion see Speisman, *Jews of Toronto*, 324–8.
2 All immigration was sponsored. The JIAS files in Toronto are packed with remittance forms noting that Jews sent copious amount of money to their European relatives. A fuller account of the activities of the JIAS will be found in chapter 4.
3 *Yiddisher Zhurnal*, 1 February 1933; Figler and Rome, *Caiserman: A Biography*, 115–17.
4 CJCA, 1933 Year Box, Caiserman, "The History of the Canadian Jewish Congress," 1.
5 Ibid., 1–2.
6 *Canadian Jewish Chronicle*, 5 May 1933, 1.
7 On the league see Levitt and Shaffir, *Riot at Christie Pits*, 113–19 and Speisman, *Jews of Toronto*, 331, 335.
8 CJCA, 1933 Year Box. Graner to Caiserman, 17 May 1933, contains a reference to this earlier letter.
9 Ibid.; Freiman was elected to the post of honorary vice-president but he refused the position and his name was not listed on the Congress letterhead; CJCP, Minutes of the Dominion Executive, 12 November 1933; CJCA, 1934 Year Box, Frankel to Caiserman, 5 and 10 March 1934; CJCA, 1933 Year Box, Caiserman to Kramer, 29 May 1933.
10 Ibid.
11 Speisman, *Jews of Toronto*, 240–1; Levendel, *Canadian Jewish Press*, 32–4; Kayfetz, "Only Yesterday," 3–4.
12 Interview with Brown; interview with Rome.
13 Interview with Brown.

14 On Eisendrath, see Speisman, *Jews of Toronto*, 219, 242; Kayfetz, "Development of the Toronto Jewish Community," 6–7, and Eisendrath, *Can Faith Survive?* 35–6.
15 Though Eisendrath was out of the country by this point, he must have written to his officers, allowing them to go to the conference. There is good evidence that Frankel did nothing for Congress without Eisendrath's explicit approval. For example CJCA, 1934 Year Box, Frankel to Caiserman, 21 March 1934.
16 Tulchinsky, *Branching Out*, 87–106; Frager, *Sweatshop Strife*, 180–2, 225–8; OJA, Goldstick Papers, File 2, "Platform and Resolutions adopted by the Preliminary Conference on June 10 and June 11, 1933, for creating a permanent all-Canadian Jewish Organization." Eisendrath's opinions on Zionism were well known, see Speisman. *Jews of Toronto*, 242.
17 OJA, Goldstick Papers, File 2, "Platform and Resolutions," 1933; CJCP, 1934 Year Box, Minutes of the Dominion Executive, 12 November 1933, 3.
18 Ibid.
19 OJA, Goldstick Papers, File 2, "Platform and Resolutions"
20 Ibid.
21 Delisle, *Traitor and Jew*, ch. 7; the quotation is from 126; for a slightly different view see Anctil, "The Interwar Period"; on the entire issue of restrictive covenants see Walker, *"Race," Rights and Law*, ch. 4; Dunkelman, *Dual Allegiance*, 11–12; Shaffir and Weinfeld, *Christie Pits*, especially ch. 1. Quotation is from introduction (by Fulford), ix-x; Speisman, *Jews of Toronto*, 331–5; Lita-Rose Betcherman, *Swastika and Maple Leaf*, 45–61; Interview with Wise.
22 OJA, Morris Goldstick Papers, Box 2, "Platform and Resolutions" 5.
23 Ibid. The community did not want a messy repeat of the Kehilla Inquiry of 1926. In this case, a dispute over kosher meat supervision ended up in the hands of Gentile judges, much to the embarrassment of the community. On this, see Speisman, *Jews of Toronto*, 283–92.
24 CJCA, 1933 Year Box, Caiserman to Bennett, 22 June 1933.
25 Figler and Rome, *Caiserman*, 120; Irving Abella, *Coat of Many Colours*, 190–1.
26 Ibid., Caiserman to Bennett, 22 June 1933.
27 Interview with Cohen.
28 Ibid., Caiserman to Eisendrath, 4 September 1933.
29 Ibid., Altschul to Rev. D. Kirshenbaum, 13 September 1933.
30 Ibid., Goldstick to Caiserman, 14 September 1933.
31 Ibid., Catzman to Caiserman, 14 October 1933.

32 Speisman, *Jews of Toronto*, 331; interview with Catzman.
33 CJCA, 1933 Year Box, Caiserman to Catzman, 11 September 1933; ibid., Catzman to Caiserman, 14 September 1933; ibid., Minutes of the Dominion Executive, 12 November 1933, 3. The Western Division had first hinted at a delay in early September. OJA, Morris Goldstick Papers, file 2, Caiserman to Catzman, 11 September 1933; ibid., CJCA, 1933 Year Box, Caiserman to Catzman, 11 October 1933; ibid., Catzman to Caiserman, 20 October 1933; as early as 11 October 1933, Catzman noted: "Owing to the holiday season, it has been impossible to hold a meeting in the past couple of weeks." CJCA, 1933 Year Box, Catzman to Caiserman, 11 October 1933.
34 OJA, Morris Goldstick Papers, File 2, Caiserman to Goldstick, 11 September 1933; CJCA, 1933 Year Box, Caiserman to Catzman, 27 September 1933.
35 Ibid., Catzman to Caiserman, 1 October 1933; ibid., Catzman to Caiserman, 11 and 20 October 1933.
36 Ibid., Catzman to Caiserman, 7 November 1933; ibid., Minutes of the Dominion Executive, 12 November 1933, 3–5; ibid., Catzman to Caiserman, 14 November 1933.
37 Ibid., Catzman to Caiserman, 23 November 1933; ibid., Caiserman to Bennett, 24 November 1933; ibid., Caiserman to Catzman, 26 November 1933.
38 Ibid., Catzman to Caiserman, 7 November 1933; ibid. Minutes of the Delegates' Meeting, 28 November 1933.
39 "The Anti-Nazi Boycott of 1933," www.ajhs.org/publications/chapters/chaptercfm?documentid=230l; Frager. *Sweatshop Strife*, 36–7.
40 For an example of this kind of thinking, see "Congress Preliminaries Take Place," *Canadian Jewish Chronicle*, 16 June 1933, 4.
41 CJCA, 1933 Year Box, Minutes of the Toronto Division Executive, 6 December 1933.
42 Ibid., Goldstick to Belkin, 10 December 1933; ibid., Belkin to Goldstick, 7 December 1933.
43 Ibid., Bennett to Caiserman, 19 December 1933; ibid., A. White and Chaikes to Caiserman, 30 December 1933.
44 Ibid., undated, Caiserman to Chaikes, but based on internal evidence, written between 31 December 1933 and 3 January 1934.
45 In all the files, there is no reference to the postponement of the elections. However, a perusal of the minutes and correspondence of early January reveals that the elections were postponed without Caiserman's input. He did not know of the decision until after it had been made. CJCA, 1934 Year Box, Caiserman to Chaikes (Yiddish), 3 January 1934, my translation.

46 Ibid., Goldstick to Caiserman, 17 January 1934; ibid., Minutes of the Toronto Executive, 14 January 1934; for proof that Caiserman knew nothing of Goldstick's plans, see Belkin to Goldstick, 8 January 1934 and Caiserman to Freiman, 8 January 1934.
47 Ibid., Goldstick to Caiserman, 17 January 1934; Goldstick to Belkin, 16, 17, 19 January 1934.
48 *Canadian Jewish Chronicle*, 2 February 1934, 4–5.
49 Ibid.
50 Ibid.
51 Ibid.
52 Other observers agreed with this critique, labelling Eisendrath and his group "Bourbons," *Canadian Jewish Chronicle*, 9 February 1934, 2.
53 *Jewish Standard*, 2 February 1934; *Yiddisher Zhurnal*, 30, 31 January 1934. This attitude continued until June 1935.
54 CJCA, 1934 Year Box, Caiserman to Eisendrath, 13 February 1934.
55 Ibid.

CHAPTER THREE

1 Speisman, *Jews of Toronto*, 265. This is part of a fuller account on 260–5.
2 Schottland, "National Conference of Jewish Social Welfare Agencies": 134–45, 141.
3 OJA, Federation Office files, FPR, 9.
4 Ibid., 5.
5 Ibid., 65 provides the basis for the data used in this calculation.
6 Ibid., 64, Table C.
7 Ibid., Table C.
8 Ibid., Table C for the source of figures used in these calculations.
9 OJA, FPR, 60–2.
10 UTA, McGregor, "The Department of Social Science, 1919–40," 9–32, especially 10–11; on the development of social work in the United States, see Lubove, *Professional Altruist*.
11 Latimer, "An Analysis of the Social Action Behaviour of the Canadian Association of Social Workers," 56, citing "National Council of Women," *Social Welfare* 4 (1 January 1922), 71.
12 McGregor, "Department of Social Science," 20; on Rabbi Brickner, see Speisman, *Jews of Toronto*, 232, 241–2.
13 FPR, "Family Welfare Bureau Report," OJA, 24; Ben Lappin has argued that social workers advocated this change because it allowed the City of Toronto to take care of clients in need of financial assistance, thus leaving "the case-

workers to deal with the clients that were deemed to need treatment." This had the key outcome of maintaining the image of the caseworkers as professionals who counselled clients and remained distinct from welfare functionaries. Social workers could therefore remain "disinterested enablers" who helped their clients solve problems. Bernard Lappin, "Social Work Activism," 5–6. For a discussion of general trends in social work in Toronto during the 1920s, see Lappin, "Community Organization Work," 240–3.

14 Ibid., 224–37; on the question of relief and social services in Canada just before the Depression, see Strong, *Public Welfare Administration in Canada*.
15 OJA, FPR, 31–2.
16 For Cohn's thoughts on this matter, see OJA, FPR, 32–3.
17 Ibid., 7; FPR, "Family Welfare Bureau Report," 11–12; on the Folks Farein, see Speisman, *Jews of Toronto*, 153, 162.
18 OJA, FPR, "Family Welfare Bureau Report," 43–5.
19 All statistics are from the various appendices to the FPR, bound at the back of the report.
20 Ibid.
21 Ibid., "Family Welfare Bureau Report," 22.
22 PAO, RG, 18 E5, Campbell, Report on Direct Relief in the Province of Ontario (28 July 1932), 3–9.
23 CTA, RG 273. City of Toronto, Civic Unemployment Relief Committee, Report (May 1931), 42–3, 45; CTA, SC 35A, Box 3, Minutes of the House of Industry, 28 April 1932, 1–2, and 21 June 1932, 3.
24 CTA, RG 273. Civic Unemployment Committee. Report, 33 and Appendix IV, which recommended a $13,000 appropriation for this purpose.
25 It is important to resist the theoretical Progressive assumption that this consolidation was carried out in a completely logical manner. Lappin, "Community Organizational Work," 270–1, notes that when the Department of Public Works took over relief, fifteen trained social workers were fired and replaced by ill-trained investigators. Ironically, the investigators had more clout than their professional predecessors. Nonetheless, Lappin notes (287) that the overall trend was toward consolidation and rationalization of social service. This same conclusion was reached independently by a contemporary civil servant. See PAO, MG 19, Box 12, Administration File, Rupert, "Financing Public Welfare"; OJA, FPR, "Family Welfare Bureau Report," 23.
26 Speisman, *Jews of Toronto*, 306.
27 Ibid., 149–50. As proof of eastern European weakness, see Spiesman, "The Jews of Toronto," 5, 2 (PhD diss., Toronto, 1975), 577.

28 OJA, FPR, "Child Care Activities," 8; Jolliffe, *History of the Children's Aid Society of Toronto*, 52.
29 OJA, FPR, "Child Care Activities," 1–5; for a good example of the trend to "outplacement" see Lipman, "Change from Institutionalization to Foster Home Care in the Infants' Home."
30 Ibid., 8–9.
31 On the CJC campaign, see chapter 2; OJA, FPR, "Federation Office," 3 gives the figures on the amount collected in their campaign.
32 Ibid., Minutes of the Personnel Committee, 21 May 1934, 1.
33 Ibid., 3.
34 OJA, FPR, "Dora Wilensky's Report on the FWB," 44; ibid., "Family Welfare Bureau Report," 1–2.
35 Ibid., "Jewish Children's Bureau Report," 9.
36 Ibid., Minutes of the Personnel Committee, 22 November 1934, 2.
37 Interview with (Hutner) Rosichan.
38 OJA, Minutes of the Personnel Committee, 22 November 1934, 1; anonymous interview
39 OJA, FPR, "Personnel Committee Report," 22; ibid., "Child Care Activities," 8; Cohn and Wallace, *Problems of Administration in Social Work*, 35.
40 Ibid., "Jewish Children's Bureau Report," 16, 20; ibid., "Federation Office," 65; the turnover is interpolated for the annual reports of the Provincial Department of Public Welfare, *Third Annual Report of the Minister of Public Welfare for the Year Ending 30 September 1933*, 107–13 and idem. *Fourth Annual Report of the Minister of Public Welfare for the Year Ending 30 September 1934*, 100–5 for cost comparisons and other useful statistics.
41 OJA, FPR, "Federation Office," Appendix; Speisman, *Jews of Toronto*, 336.
42 Ontario, *Report of the Minister for Public Welfare for 1936–1937*, 100; *Report of the Minister for Public Welfare for 1937–1938*, 75; Speisman, *Jews of Toronto*, 336; PAO, MG 19, Box 12. "Order-in-Council File" indicates that on 15 October 1934 the Provincial Department of Public Welfare assumed full control of all relief distributed to the Toronto Department of Public Welfare. On the problems of convincing Jews to accept relief see Speisman, *Jews of Toronto*, 341, note 14.
43 OJA, FPR, Minutes of the Personnel Committee, 4 June 1935; Cohn drew his ideas from Louise C. Odenkrantz, *The Social Worker*, which he signed out of the University of Toronto Library between 29 May and 18 December 1934 (the card was still in the book!). This coincides with the time during which most of the Personnel Committee's work was carried out. It should be noted that this book bore the imprimatur of the American Association of Social Workers.

44 On this issue see chapters 4 and 5 of Lipinsky, "Progressive Wedge."
45 OJA, FPR, Minutes of the Personnel Committee, 18 July 1934, 2; ibid., "Federation Office," 65 is the source for the extrapolation of these figures; there is evidence to support each of these hypotheses. On the Depression see Gathercole, "City of Toronto in Depression," 40; on Poland see Sachar, *The Course of Modern Jewish History*, 359–60; on Germany see Lipinsky, "Progressive Wedge," chapter 1; OJA, FPR, Minutes of the Personnel Committee, 18 July 1934, 2.
46 Speisman, *Jews of Toronto*, 337. The full story of the United Jewish Welfare Fund and the Toronto Hebrew Free School (Brunswick Avenue Talmud Torah) is discussed in chapter 6; for parallel developments in the United States see Lurie, "Developments in Jewish Community Organization," 34–41.
47 Speisman, *Jews of Toronto*, 340.

CHAPTER FOUR

1 Belkin, *Narrow Gates*, chapters 9–12 for a full account of the role of the JIAS in bringing Russian and Romanian Jews to Canada. There is a literature on this topic. See Troper, "Jews and Canadian Immigration Policy," 52–6, and Tulchinsky, *Branching Out*, 40–5.
2 For this attitude, see Abella and Troper, *None is Too Many*, 10; on the Orders-in-Council, see Belkin, *Narrow Gates*, 10, 124–5, 128, 130, 148, 150, 152, 153–5, 169, 170.
3 Troper, "New Horizons in a New Land," 12.
4 Belkin, *Narrow Gates*, 142; JIAS (T), "Report for September 1925," 1.
5 Ibid.; Belkin, *Narrow Gates*, 146–8; on Jacobs's importance during this period see Figler, *Jacobs*, 161–3. Note that the Montreal Yiddish paper urged a protest vote against the incumbent Jacobs over the Liberal failure to admit more Jews and the resultant large number of votes won by Jacobs's Jewish Conservative opponent. King's government was in a precarious position in 1925 and 1926. It had failed to win a majority in the election of 29 October 1925, and clung to power in Parliament from January until it fell on 28 June 1926. This is why Jacobs had so much leverage at this time and why he pressed his advantage. On 28 June the Conservatives formed a government under Arthur Meighen. After Meighen's government fell on 1 July, another general election took place on 14 September 1926. On this issue, see Neatby, *William Lyon Mackenzie King: 1924–1932*, 74–157; calculation based on the table of immigration statistics in Belkin, *Narrow Gates*, 160, 211.

6 JIAS(T), "Report for 1925," 1–2; Belkin, *Narrow Gates*, 148–52 on quota negotiations; comment about Jacobs's office is on 152, on Jacobs's career during this period see Figler, *Jacobs*, 162–5.
7 JIAS(T), Minutes of the Special Executive Meeting of the Jewish Immigrant Aid Society of Ontario, 7 June 1926; for Stewart's biography, see his biography at the Parliamentary website: http://www.parl.gc.ca/information/about/people/key/bio.asp?lang=Eng&query=2630&s=M&Source=hochist; on Jacobs's methodology, see Paris, *Jews*, 76–8, and for some of his clever speeches see Figler, *Jacobs*, especially 127–32.
8 On *landsmanschaften* and their role in immigration in Toronto, see Speisman, *Jews of Toronto*, 111; Ruth Frager, *Sweatshop Strife*, 15–16; Tulchinsky, *Branching Out*, 19–21; on *landsmanschaften* in general, see Howe, *World of Our Fathers*, 183–90.
9 Tulchinsky, *Branching Out*, 37; Troper, "Jews and Immigration Policy," 153; Belkin, *Narrow Gates*, 127, 148.
10 On Singer's role at Mount Sinai in this period see Barsky, *Mount Sinai*, 29–30; Speisman, *Jews of Toronto*, ch. 17, especially 290–1 and relevant footnotes; Haltrecht's guilt was a matter of common knowledge. Belkin hints at it in his book by leaving Haltrecht out completely, whereas Tulchinsky alludes to it obliquely in *Branching Out*, 41. In a confidential interview I was told that since Singer was never formally charged he was never named, but the JIAS feared that opening criminal proceedings against him would only confirm everyone's suspicions; on the permits left over, see Troper, "Jews and Immigration Policy," 54.
11 JIAS(T), Minutes of 7 June 1926 Special Meeting; on the Kehilla Inquiry, see Speisman, *Jews of Toronto*, ch. 17, especially 290–1 and relevant footnotes; on PC #534 and its effects, see Belkin, *Narrow Gates*, 148–50; Tulchinsky, *Branching Out*, 54–5; Troper, "Jews and Immigration Policy," 55.
12 Barsky, *Mount Sinai*, 36–7; confidential interview, 23 May 1983; Stephen Speisman, conversation, 5 August 2002.
13 Even Belkin commented: "[PC #534] placed the Department in an even more dominant position. We had a foreboding that it was to be used for granting only special quotas." Belkin, *Narrow Gates*, 148; JIAS(T), "Report for 1936."
14 *Der Kanader Adler*, 12 December 1926, 5 January 1927, cited in Tulchinsky, *Branching Out*, 41; Belkin, *Narrow Gates*, 151–2; I do not mean to minimize the importance of the department's argument that Jews were not agriculturists and hence didn't fit immigration policy. I emphasize the reasons why even concessions became less and less available to the JIAS and other agents trying to obtain permits.

15 Lipinsky, "The Apprenticeship of an Executive Director," 72; Caiserman, "Names in Jewish Immigration History," *Canadian Jewish Chronicle*, 3 September 1948, 5.
16 JIAS(T), Minutes of 21 September, 22 November, and 7 December 1927; there is some evidence that the Toronto JIAS was offered a chance to formally affiliate with the FTP on 9 November 1927, but that the board chose to postpone the decision for six months and nothing further happened. This would have been symptomatic of the strange interrelationship between the two agencies that shared space in Scheuer House on Beverley Street from 1920 to 1935.
17 JIAS(T), Paull to H. Narrol, 31 March 1930; Belkin, *Narrow Gates*, Appendix 1; JIAS(T), File 10A, Extract of the Minutes of the Fourteenth Annual Meeting of the Jewish Immigrant Aid Society of Canada, 13 May 1934; Colonel G.R. Geary, Conservative MP for Toronto South from 1925 to 1935 is a good example of those who engaged in the permit business around election time. He was a former mayor of Toronto and the epitome of a WASP establishment figure. *Canadian Parliamentary Guide 1926* (Ottawa: Mortimer, 1926), 157, and *Canadian Parliamentary Guide 1935* (Ottawa: Labour Exchange, 1935), 171, provide a brief biographical overview.
18 Confidential interview; Brodey did little; in 1928, 386 permits were issued to Jews, of which Montreal received 125 and Toronto only sixteen. MP Geary obtained nine and Hocken, another MP, obtained two. Agents got the others. None went to the JIAS. Brodey's attitude is substantiated by JIAS(M), File 4082, Brodey to Narrol, 21 March 1930.
19 Ibid., Narrol to Paull, 21 February 1930; JIAS(T) "Report for 1936"; Belkin, *Narrow Gates*, 169; JIAS(M), File 4082, Paull to Brodey, 29 August 1930; ibid., Narrol to Paull, 2 September 1931; confidential interview; ibid., Robinson to Brodey, 21 January 1933. For Brodey's opinion of his Sunday morning activities, ibid., Brodey to Paull, 3 March 1933.
20 Ibid., Robinson to Brodey, 21 January 1933.
21 Ibid., Brodey to Robinson, 21 February 1933; ibid., Brodey to Paull, 29 August 1934; ibid., Brodey to Robinson, 6 October 1934; ibid., Robinson to Brodey, 15 October 1934; ibid., Paull to Berk, 4, 23 October 1934.
22 Ibid., Brodey to Robinson, 3 March 1933, 4 November 1934.
23 For Brodey's opinion of Paull ibid.; for Robinson's opinion of Paull, ibid., Robinson to Brodey, 21 January 1933; Abella and Troper, *None*, 14; JIAS(M), File 4082, Brodey to Robinson, 3 March 1933, 4 November 1934.
24 Confidential interview.
25 Ibid., Brodey to Robinson, 3 March 1933; JIAS(T), File 10A, Brodey to Robinson, 4 November 1934.

26 JIAS(M), File 4082, Brodey to Paull, 28 April 1933; ibid., Brodey to Paull, 23 November 1933; ibid., Brodey to Paull, 7 June 1933; ibid., Paull to Brodey, 13 June 1933; ibid., Paull to Shapiro, 8 June 1933.
27 Ibid., Berk to Paull, 15 February 1934; ibid., Paull to Brodey, 27 March 1934; ibid., Brodey to Paull, 29 March 1934; on these developments in a broader context see Abella and Troper, *None*, 6; confidential interview; also see JIAS(T) File 10A, Brodey to Robinson, 3 March 1933, in which Brodey boasts: "We have never competed with the steamship agents, except where the public needed protection and proper guidance in the intricacies of their problems." Lest he be misunderstood, Brodey prefaced these remarks by stating, "I wish to explain to you now our slower and safer progress."
28 Canada, Report of the Department of Immigration and Colonization 1934, Tables 6, 14, 37; JIAS(T), File 10A, Minutes of the Fourteenth Annual Meeting of the Jewish Immigrant Aid Society of Canada, 13 May 1934.
29 Ibid.; JIAS(M), File 4082, Robinson to Brodey, 11 June 1934.
30 Ibid., Brodey to Robinson, 18 June 1934; ibid., Narrol to Robinson, 22 June 1934. Robinson continued to exert pressure steadily; ibid., Paull to Brodey, 29 June 1934, and 16 August 1934; ibid., Brodey to Paull, 17 August 1934; ibid., Paull to Brodey, 21 August 1934.
31 Ibid., Brodey to Paull, 29 August 1934; ibid., Brodey to Robinson, 6 October 1934; ibid., Robinson to Brodey, 15 October 1934; ibid., Paull to Berk, 23 September, 4 October 1934.
32 Ibid., Robinson to Brodey, 4 November 1934.
33 Ibid., Brodey to Robinson, 14 November 1934; ibid., Paull to Brodey, 14 November 1934.
34 Ibid., Paull to Berk, 3 December 1934.
35 Ibid., Berk to Paull, 15 February 1934; ibid., Paull to Brodey, 27 March 1934; ibid., Brodey to Paull, 29 March 1934; Neatby, *The Prism of Unity* , 278; Abella and Troper, *None*, 14.
36 JIAS(T), Minutes, 6 March 1935; JIAS(M) File 4082, Paull to Brodey, 8 March 1935, ibid., Paull to Dominion Bank, 12 March 1935.
37 Dominion Bank to Paull, 13 March 1935; ibid., Paull to Dominion Bank, 15 March 1935; JIAS(T), Minutes, 17 March 1935; JIAS(M), File 4082, Brodey to Paull, 17 March 1935.
38 Ibid.
39 Ibid., Robinson to Brodey, 19 March 1935; ibid., "Our Mutual Responsibilities," 19(?) March 1935.
40 Ibid., Paull to Dominion Bank, 19 March 1935; ibid., Brodey to Paull

(telegram), 23 March 1935; ibid., Dominion Bank to Paull, 29 March 1935; JIAS(T), Minutes, 17 March 1935.

41 Ben Kayfetz, telephone interview, 31 December 1984; JIAS(M), File 4082, Brodey to Paull, 17 March 1935; ibid., Solkin to Paull, 4 April 1935; ibid., S. Kaplan to Paull, 11 April 1935; Cohen, *Canadian Jewry*, 115; Speisman, *Jews of Toronto*, 153.

42 JIAS(M), File 4082. Paull to Brodey (telegram), 26 March 1935; ibid., Solkin to Brodey, 7 April 1935; ibid., Paull to Solkin, 3, 4 April 1935; ibid., Paull to Kaplan (memo), 10 April 1935.

43 Ibid., Paull to Brodey, 13 April 1935; ibid., Kaplan to Paull, 11 April 1935; ibid., Kaplan to Paull (telegram), 10 April 1935.

44 Ibid., Kaplan to Paull, 14 April 1935.

45 Ibid.

46 Ibid., Paull to Frost, 17 April 1935, Paull to Jolliffe, 17 April 1935.

47 Ibid., A.L. Jolliffe to Paull, 25 April 1935; ibid., Frost to Paull, 26 April 1935; ibid., Paull to Solkin, 2 May 1935.

48 Ibid., Paull to Berk, 4 October 1934; informal talk with Mr Albert Wise (no relation to the agent), 6 January 1985; JIAS(T) Minutes, 2 May 1935.

49 Ibid.; JIAS(M), File 4082, Solkin to Paull, 3 May 1935; ibid., Solkin to Wise, 3 May 1935.

50 Ibid., Paull to Solkin, 4(?) May 1935; ibid., Paull to Brodey, 8 May 1935; JIAS(T), "Solkin Report," 30 April 1935, 1935 Minutes File; the Toronto JIAS tried to obtain a contribution whenever they obtained a permit. On some rare occasions, permits were given away for free. Tobie Taback, interview, 18 March 1983. Also see JIAS(M), File 4082, Paull to Brodey, 28 April 1935.

51 JIAS(T), Solkin to Paull, 13 May 1935; ibid., "1935 Report" claims that over this period 78 of 162 appeals were successful (48%). See Abella and Troper, *None*, 17; JIAS(T), "Reports 1935–1939," 12; JIAS(M), File 4082, Paull to Solkin, 16 December 1935.

52 JIAS(T), File 190. In the period April 1935 to August 1939, there were 1,615 applications for relatives, but the Toronto JIAS forwarded only 162 of them. Certainly judicious weeding was done, but this practice could also explain why so many Torontonians preferred steamship agents.

53 JIAS(M), File 4082, Solkin to Paull, 4 June 1935; ibid., "Reports 1935–37"; Solkin was allowed to charge less than Montreal for remittances in order to undercut the steamship agents. See JIAS(T), Minutes, 18 June 1935.

54 Solkin to Paull, JIAS(M), File 4082, 8 September 1935; ibid., Paull to Solkin, 26 August 1935; Paull was very diligent and quick to spot the slightest lag

in business which might weaken the Toronto office. Ibid., Paull to Solkin, 26 June 1935; Solkin to Paull, 8 July 1935. Brodey now respected Paull and Solkin both personally and professionally. Ibid., Brodey to Paull, 8 July 1935.
55 Ibid., "Toronto Expenses April to August 1935," no date, but probably around October 1935; ibid., Paull to Solkin, 5 September 1935; ibid., Solkin to Paull, 12 September 1935.
56 Ibid., Paull to Solkin, 15 September 1935; ibid., Paull to Brodey, 25 September 1935; ibid., Solkin to Paull, 15 October 1935, Brodey to Paull, 16 October 1935.
57 Ibid., Paull to Robinson, 17 October 1935; ibid., Paull to Brodey, 21 October 1935; ibid., Solkin to S. Kaplan, 27 October 1935; ibid., Solkin to Paull, 19 December 1935; ibid., Brodey to Robinson, 12 December 1935.
58 Ibid., Paull to Solkin, 27 December 1935; Abella and Troper, *None*, 14; JIAS(M), File 4082, Brodey to Paull, 13 January 1936; ibid., Paull to Solkin, 12 December 1936.
59 There appears to have been only one formal board meeting during this whole year. JIAS(T), Minutes, 11 June 1936; JIAS(M), File 4082, Solkin to Paull, 6 January 1936 ; Solkin to Paull, 28 April 1936.
60 Ibid., Paull to Solkin, 6 January 1936; ibid., Solkin to Paull, 25 April 1936.
61 All figures compiled from JIAS Toronto monthly reports sent by Solkin.
62 Canada, Department of Immigration and Colonization for the Year Ended March 31, 1936, Report, Table 38; Canada, Department of Immigration and Colonization for the Year Ended March 31, 1938, Report, Table 32.
63 JIAS(M), File 4082, Solkin to Paull, 8 January 1936; ibid. Paull to Solkin, 12 January 1936; ibid., Solkin to Paull, 9 December 1936; ibid., Paull to Solkin, 11 December 1936.
64 Ibid., Paull to Solkin, 11 December 1936; Immigration Branch, "Report for 1937," Table 5; "Report for 1938," Table 5; JIAS(M), File 4082, Solkin to Paull, 24 March 1937.
65 Ibid., "Cost of Operating the Toronto Branch of JIAS, April 1935 to December 1936," enclosed in Paull to Solkin, 30 December 1936; JIAS(T), "1936 Report"; JIAS(M), File 4082, Solkin to Paull, 16 December 1935.
66 Ibid., Solkin to Paull, 24 March 1937; JIAS(T), "1937 Report" indicates that in this year the U.S. consulate was visited ninety times, and that sixty-five of these visits were to obtain U.S. visas. On Ben Forer, see Cohen, *Canadian Jewry*, 289.
67 JIAS(M), File 4082, Paull to Solkin, 11 February 1937.
68 Confidential interview; JIAS(M), File 4082, Solkin to Robinson, 29 April 1937; ibid., Robinson to Brodey, 10 February 1937; JIAS(T), "1925 Report."

69 JIAS(M), File 4082, Brodey to Robinson, 22 February 1937; ibid., Solkin to Paull (telegram), 26 February, 7 March 1937; JIAS(T), Minutes, 28 February, 7 March. On the entire Solkin-Paull relationship, see Lipinsky, "The Apprenticeship of an Executive Director."
70 JIAS(M), File 4082, Paull to Solkin, 1 July 1937; ibid., Solkin to Paull, 2 July 1937.
71 Ibid., Paull to Solkin, 25 October 1937.
72 Ibid., Brodey to Robinson, 23 October 1937.
73 Ibid., Robinson to Brodey, 30 October 1937; ibid., Paull to Solkin, 12 November 1937; ibid., Robinson to Brodey, 11 November 1937; ibid., Solkin to Robinson, 15 November 1937.

CHAPTER FIVE

1 See chapter 1; CJCA, Caiserman to Catzman, 8 March 1934.
2 Ibid. Caiserman to Catzman, 26 December 1933.
3 Ibid. Catzman to Caiserman, 3 January 1934; ibid., Caiserman to Catzman, 8 January 1934.
4 Ibid. Caiserman to Catzman, 9 January 1934.
5 Cohen, *Not Free to Desist*, 158–66.
6 For a good account of the history of the order, see Moore, *Challenge*, Grusd, *B'nai Brith*, and Schick (ed.), *B'nai Brith in Eastern Canada*.
7 Moore, *Challenge*, 118–19; Grusd, *B'nai Brith*, 151; LAC BBM, 6 May 1934, 6--7). The suggestion that the ADL operated in Canada in the 1920s is not tenable, as it is not supported by the documentation of B'nai Brith itself. See Scheinberg, "From Self-Help to National Advocacy: The Emergence of Community Activism," 57. The methodology of the article is suggestive, but the historical precision is marred by a failure to have consulted the primary sources or key secondary accounts of B'nai Brith's history.
8 BBM, 5 November 1933, 19–21; Grusd, *B'nai Brith*, 151.
9 As early as November 1933, the ECC noted that "Congress was to meet in Toronto in January 1934 and that delegates from all over Canada were invited. As B'nai Brith was not representative of every class of Jewry it could not speak on behalf of the Jewish people. But the Canadian Jewish Congress, being composed of all classes might very well do so, and it would be wise to determine whether B'nai Brith should affiliate itself with such an organization." This motion was referred to the executive for further study. BBM, 5 November 1933, 2010; Grusd, *B'nai Brith*, 189–93; it should be noted that financial and organizational difficulties engendered by the

Depression seriously undermined the order in the United States, and probably made its leaders even more unwilling to share their powers with rival organizations.

10 Moore, *Challenge*, 116; Grusd, *B'nai Brith*, 190–2.
11 Moore, *Challenge*, 116–19; Cohen, *Not Free to Desist*, 162–3, 219–21; Lazin, "The Non-Centralized Model" offers an interesting argument that will be explored.
12 Grusd, *B'nai Brith*, 192.
13 Moore, *Challenge*, 118–19; Cohen, *Not Free to Desist*, 161; Grusd, *B'nai Brith*, 193–200; Catzman, interview, 24 October 1984.
14 Grusd, *B'nai Brith*, 207, hints at this; Lazin, "Non-Centralized Model," 309.
15 CJCA, Catzman to Caiserman, 16 January 1934; ibid., Caiserman memo, n.d.
16 BBM, 6 May 1934, 2017; ibid, 6–7, 18; the B'nai Brith would later claim that Congress had formally agreed to this arrangement. This was understandable in view of Rabbi Eisendrath's speech, but it is not known if the rabbi spoke for himself or in his official capacity as chairman of the Central Division's Public Relations Committee; CJCA, Goldfield to Jacobs, 16 August 1935.
17 CJCA, Caiserman to O. Cohen, 13 April 1934; O. Cohen to Lipinsky, 13 October 1983 (author's possession).
18 CJCA, Caiserman to O. Cohen, 6 April 1934
19 CJCA. For hints of this, see Eisendrath to Caiserman, 8, 13 February 1934; for an example of newspaper attacks demanding action from the CJC, see *Canadian Jewish Chronicle* (Montreal), 9 February 1934, "The Congress Stumbles," 2.
20 O. Cohen to Lipinsky, 13 October 1983; CJCA, Caiserman to O. Cohen, 5 April 1934.
21 CJCA, Eisendrath to Caiserman, 20 February 1934; ibid., Eisendrath to Caiserman, 6 March 1934; ibid., Minutes of the Central Division Executive Committee, 8 March 1934; Frankel's father had been president of Holy Blossom in 1916, according to Speisman, *Jews of Toronto*, 262; *Canadian Jewish News* (Toronto), "Lecture Honours Christian Businessman," 1 December 1984, 21.
22 Catzman interview; a great deal more about many of these people can be found in chapter 2.
23 CJCA, Minutes of the Central Division executive, 26 April 1934; ibid., Caiserman to Frankel, 5 March 1934; on the compromise at the Second Plenary, see chapter 2.
24 CJCA, Frankel to Caiserman, 13 March 1934.
25 On Canadian Jewry and Zionism among first-generation Jews, see Speisman, *Jews of Toronto*, 200–1; Feingold, *Zion in America* (New York: Hippocrene, 1974), 279–84.

26 The hagiographic but important Bernard Figler, *Lillian and Archie Freiman*, and Tulchinsky, *Branching Out*, ch. 6, especially 168–71; CJCA, Caiserman to Brown, 4 April 1934; Brown interview. His pay was soon increased to $20 per week, and the division began to pay his secretary thereafter. See CJCA, Minutes of the Central Division Executive Committee, 10 May 1934.
27 This conclusion is based on an examination of all available correspondence between Caiserman and Brown, Eisendrath, Frankel, and Roger between April 1934 and November 1936. Some specific instances will be cited later in this chapter.
28 Catzman, interview.
29 CJCA, Minutes of the Central Division Finance Committee, 10 April 1934; ibid., Caiserman to Brown, 12 April 1934; ibid., Brown to Caiserman, 16 April 1934; ibid., Caiserman to Brown, 19 April 1934; ibid., Minutes of the Central Division Executive Committee, 28 May, 6 June 1934.
30 CJCA, Caiserman to Eisendrath, 11 February 1934; ibid., Caiserman to Eisendrath, 20 February 1934; ibid., Eisendrath to Caiserman, 8 April 1934; ibid, Eisendrath to Caiserman, 17 April 1934; ibid., Eisendrath to A. Lipson, 27 May 1934; ibid., "Report of the Committee on Public Relations," 3 June 1934.
31 Graeme Decarie, "Review of *None is Too Many*," in *Labour/Le Travail* 15 (spring 1985): 201–2; Betcherman, *Swastika*, 45–54; Speisman, *Jews of Toronto*, 318–20; CJCA, Eisendrath to C.C. Goldring, 31 May 1935; ibid., Minutes of the Central Division Executive Committee, 27 September 1935; ibid., Brown to Caiserman, 18 September 1934; CJCA, "Arbitration Court," (Vertical Reference File). The arbitration court was set up in early 1934. There had been earlier attempts to set up this court, and Congress's version of it did not begin to function efficiently until 1936. It handled quite a few cases between individuals and institutions that would certainly have been as embarrassing to the community as the celebrated Kehilla Inquiry of 1926. Speisman, *Jews of Toronto*, 288–99; on the much earlier origins of Jewish courts see Katz, *Tradition and Crisis*, 95–9; and for another attempt to transfer this concept to North America, see Goren, *The Kehillah Experiment*, especially 77–9; Eisendrath to Editor of *Mail and Empire*, 25 April 1935.
32 Cohen, *Not Free to Desist*, 204; Feingold, *Zion in America*, 140–1; Betcherman, *Swastika*, 40; *Jewish Standard* (Toronto), June 1936, 12.
33 For a finely nuanced interpretation of the milieu of Toronto Jews in this era, combining oral and documentary history with sociological analysis, see Levitt and Shaffir, *Christie Pits*, especially 1–50,; this quotation from Ben Kayfetz is on 34. A number of biographical sketches indicate the constant

state of "street fighting" and tension felt by the children of immigrants in this era. For some evocative examples, see Sharp, Abella, and Goodman (eds.), *Growing Up Jewish*, particularly 91–9, 119–25.

34 Levitt and Shaffir, *Christie Pits*, 13; for a larger perspective, see Speisman, "Anti-Semitism in Ontario," especially 120–7.

35 There is very little Canadian literature on this issue. Some sociologists suggest that this era saw the "beginnings of advocacy" but adduce little historical support for their position. As suggested here, the confluence of many trends laid the groundwork for ADL-style advocacy. On this, see Scheinberg, "Self-Help to Advocacy," 52–65; a very sparse account that (understandably, given the focus of the text) fails to validate whether its hypothesis is relevant to this period is presented in Elazar, Waller, and Glicksman, "The Toronto Jewish Community Through Four Generations," 158–61; the American literature on the attempts of the Uptowners to acculturate the Downtowners is truly voluminous, and a full description is beyond this narrative. For an outstanding overview of the key issues, see Howe, *World of Our Fathers*, especially 127–9, 229–35, and Feingold, *Zion in America*, ch. 10 for a brilliant synthesis of many approaches to "Americanization" later echoed in Canada; *Jewish Times* (Toronto), 28 March 1911, 1, quoted in Speisman, *Jews in Toronto*, 123.

36 The number of Jewish university students began to increase sharply in the 1920s. Jews were especially noticeable in medicine and law. In 1930 Jews made up almost 5 percent of all Canadian university students at a time when they made up 1.5 percent of the general population. Rosenberg, *Canada's Jews*, Table 175, Table 3; for the attitude of the ADL to mass demonstrations see Cohen, *Not Free to Desist*, 213–15, in which the ADL was also concerned with the labelling of Jews as Communists by Coughlin and his cohorts; on the stereotyping of Ontario Jews as Communists, see Speisman, "Anti-Semitism in Ontario," 123–4.

37 There is very little information on the Henry government. See http://www.kids.premier.gov.on.ca/english/history/henry.htm; on the Singer exposé of the insurance companies, see Speisman, *Jews of Toronto*, 332, who claims the legislature took action against the insurance companies but supplies no supporting evidence; Levitt and Shaffir, *Christie Pits*, 35, merely notes that Singer raised the issue in "early 1932" without any further documentation; Tulchinsky, *Branching Out*, 183, sees this as an example of a strengthened Jewish response to anti-Semitism; on Argue Martin's bill see Tulchinsky, *Branching Out*, 9–10, the quotation from the *Star* is on 10; Sohn, "Human Rights Laws in Ontario," 104, emphasizes Singer's effort and men-

tions the failure of the Martin Bill. No source provides any documentary evidence.

38 Betcherman, *Swastika*, 31–2; Esther Einbinder, "An Exploratory Study of Attitudes Toward Jews in Toronto," 20–3; despite all this, Singer still thought legislation was possible – at the very least, it was the only possible methodology. CJCA, Singer to Caiserman. 6 May 1934.

39 CJCA, Caiserman to Frankel, 22 May 1934; ibid., Minutes of the Central Division Executive Committee, 10 May 1934; it should be noted that Brown knew nothing of Caiserman's impending visit before he actually arrived. Brown to Caiserman, 30 May 1934,

40 Ibid., Minutes of the Dominion Executive, 3 June 1934.

41 There are many important parallels to the American situation here that are beyond the scope of this book. For an excellent introduction see Hawkins, "Hitler's Bitterest Foe."

42 CJCA, Minutes of the Actions Committee, 10 April 1934; for American parallels, see Cohen, *Not Free to Desist*, 160–6; Brown was put in charge of the boycott correspondence and, overburdened by other duties and poorly informed by Caiserman, had a hard time of it.

43 CJCA, Minutes of the Actions Committee, 3 May 1934; ibid., Caiserman to Brown, 10 May 1934; ibid., Brown form letter to all firms, 22 May 1934; ibid., Olivier Ltd. to Brown, 23 May 1934; ibid., Brown to Olivier Ltd., 25 May 1934; ibid., Olivier Ltd. to Congress Central Division, 26 May 1934; ibid., S.D. Cohen to Brown, 20 June 1934; ibid., Brill Neckwear to Glass, 26 June 1934; on Mrs Schwartz see chapter 1; CJCA, Minutes of the Actions Committee, 3 May, 20 June 1934.

44 On the boycott in general see Tulchinsky, *Branching Out*, 180–1, which argues that it did achieve some limited success, although he doesn't distinguish between the roles played by the Montreal and Toronto Actions Committees.

45 Ibid., Minutes of the Actions Committee, 26 June 1934; ibid., Minutes of the Central Division Executive Committee, 6 June 1934, at which Caiserman was present.

46 Ibid.,

47 Ibid., Caiserman to Kaufman, 14 June 1934; Brown, interview.

48 Speisman, *Jews of Toronto*, 335; Since the CJC grew out of organizations such as the League for the Defence of Jewish Rights and the Canadian Jewish Committees, many of the participants assumed that Congress's primary role would be that of anti-defamation. But, for Caiserman, these goals were secondary to the idea of Congress serving as the "Parliament of Canadian

Jewry," as the instrument of unity for its people; Speisman, *Jews of Toronto*, ch. 17; Cohen, *Not Free to Desist*, 160; Speisman, *Jews of Toronto*, 299; CJCA, Minutes of the Central Division Executive Committee, 27 October 1934; ibid., Roger to Caiserman, 11 October 1934.

49 Ibid. Freiman had to constantly intervene to keep Toronto's Zionists loyal to his cause, since many of them were also Central Division members. Freiman would not countenance the "admixture of local and Zionist campaigns." See Figler, *Lillian and Archie Freiman*, 248, 276–7; CJCA, Roger to Caiserman, 11 October 1934; ibid., Minutes of the Central Division Executive Committee, 27 September 1934; ibid., Brown to Caiserman, 18(?) October 1934.

50 Ibid.
51 Ibid.
52 Ibid.
53 Ibid., Caiserman to Roger, 16 October 1934; ibid., Caiserman to Roger, 24 October 1934.
54 Ibid., Caiserman to Bennett, 2 November 1934; ibid., Caiserman to Shapiro, 2 November 1934; ibid., Minutes of the Congress Delegates, 21 October 1934.
55 Confidential interview; O. Cohen, interview.
56 CJCA, Minutes of the Central Division Executive Committee, 8 November 1934.
57 CJCA, Brown to Caiserman, 22 February 1935; ibid., Brown to Caiserman, 21 February 1935; Speisman, *Jews of Toronto*, 336–7; CJCA, Minutes of the Central Division Executive Committee, 2 February 1935. Caiserman attended this meeting and left for Montreal that night.
58 CJCA, "Caiserman Report," 15 February 1935. The weakness of the FJP allowed this campaign to take place. With the rise of the UJWA, a separate campaign would have been impossible without prior permission.
59 Ibid., Frankel to Caiserman, 22 February 1935; ibid., Caiserman to Frankel, 28 February 1935; ibid., Frankel to Caiserman, 5 March 1935; ibid., Frankel to Brown, 5 March 1935; ibid., Brown to Caiserman, 10 March 1935; ibid., Frankel to Brown, 11 March 1935; ibid., Caiserman to Eisendrath, 28 February 1935.
60 Ibid., Minutes of the Central Division Executive Committee, 14 March 1935.
61 Ibid., Minutes of the Planning Committee, 18 March 1935.
62 Ibid., Minutes of the Central Division Executive Committee, 14 March 1935; ibid., Minutes of the Planning Committee, 15 March 1935; Eisendrath went so far as to demand that the Planning Committee be "ruthless" in its

quest for control of the division. Ibid., Caiserman to Brown, 5 November 1935.
63 Ibid., Minutes of the Elections Committee, 1 March 1935, in which another reason for the apparent lack of democracy is given: "Despite the fact that the best method [of elections] would be by popular vote, there is nevertheless the fear that the majority of people will not come out to vote ... therefore the proper means of elections under the prevailing conditions shall be representation of organizations." Obviously, communal apathy was a serious issue.
64 CJCA, Caiserman to Brown, 5 November 1935.
65 Ibid., Minutes of the Central Division Executive Committee, 2 April 1935.
66 Ibid., Minutes of the Central Division Executive Committee, 9 April 1935.
67 Ibid., Minutes of the Actions Committee, 21 August 1935.
68 Ibid., Minutes of the Anti-Nazi Consumer League, 2 October, 12, 21 November 1935; for a very general assessment of the effectiveness of the overall CJC campaign, see Tulchinsky, *Branching Out*, 140–1.
69 CJCA, Eisendrath to Caiserman, 21 March 1935; confidential interview.
70 Ibid., Report of the Public Relations Committee, 9 June 1935; ibid., Eisendrath to Caiserman, 15 September 1934; ibid., Caiserman to Eisendrath, 15 October 1934; ibid., Caiserman to Eisendrath, 17 October 1934; ibid., Eisendrath to Caiserman, 1 November 1934.
71 BBM, 28 April 1935; Cohen, *Not Free to Desist*, 184–7; Sachar, *Course of Modern Jewish History*, 358–61; CJCA, Minutes of the Committee Appointed to Draft a Protest, 5 August 1935; ibid., Brown to Caiserman, 2 August 1935; Bennett heard out the delegation and promised to investigate the situation. The committee probably expected no better, but it was essential that the *shtadlanim* make an appearance to ensure that *amcha* did not resort to less politically acceptable modes of dissent.
72 CJCA, Minutes of the Committee Appointed to Draft a Protest, 5 August 1935; ibid., Caiserman to Goldfield, 20 August 1935; ibid., Goldfield to Jacobs, 16 August 1935; ibid., Brown to Caiserman, 9 August 1935; ibid., Caiserman to Brown, 27 August 1935; ibid., Brown to Caiserman, 29 August 1935; ibid., Minutes of the Actions Committee, 24 August 1935; ibid., M. Goldstick and M. Kramer to Caiserman, 14 August 1935.
73 Ibid., Caiserman to Catzman, 22 August 1935; ibid., Caiserman to Catzman, 1 October 1935; ibid., "Action Taken by Conference of Canadian Lodges," 10 November 1935; ibid., Roger to Caiserman, 12 November 1935; BBM, 10 November 1935. Abella, *Coat of Many Colours*, 203–4, observes accurately that B'nai Brith leaders "realized that the unity of Canadian Jewry was far

more important than the autonomy of their organization," although he fails to note that the impetus came from Toronto in 1935 rather than from Samuel Bronfman in Montreal in 1938.
74 CJCA, Roger to Gordon, 14 January 1936; ibid., Roger to Caiserman, 17 June 1935; ibid., Roger to Caiserman, 23 September 1936.
75 BBM, 5 May 1933, 6 May 1934, 11 November 1934, 28 April 1935, 3 May 1936, 25 April 1937, 21 November 1937; CJCA, "Conditions of Agreement Regarding the Conduct of Anti-Defamation Work in Canada Between the Canadian Jewish Congress and the Eastern Canadian Council of B'nai Brith," 20 February 1938; O. Cohen interview.
76 There is a wide literature on anti-Semitism in Quebec during this period. See Delisle, *Traitor and the Jew;* Anctil, "Interlude of Hostility"; Betcherman, *Swastika and Maple Leaf,* 32–44, 85–98; Rome, *Clouds in the Thirties,* 6 vols.; Tulchinsky, *Branching Out,* 176, 190; Abella, *Coat of Many Colours,* 179–86; Paris, *Jews,* 49–54.
77 Cohen interview; CJCA, Brown to Caiserman, 2 August 1935, and Caiserman to Brown, 27 September 1935, hint at this situation. Oscar Cohen discussed it post-facto from his perspective of almost forty years in ADL work during our interview and suggested that the ADL was aware of its failure to bring unity to the American scene and sought to learn from its errors.
78 CJCA, Caiserman to Brown, 27 August 1935; ibid., Minutes of the Central Division Executive Committee, 29 July 1935.
79 On the Workman's Circle, see Speisman, *Jews of Toronto,* 316–18; for the American Jewish Committee's approach to this issue see Cohen, *Not Free to Desist,* 166–73; for the role the Arbeiter Ring played in labour politics in Toronto, see Frager, *Sweatshop Strife,* ch. 2, especially 53–4, and 57–9.
80 CJCA, Caiserman to Brown, 27 August 1935; on press opinion, see CJCA, "Report of the Public Relations Committee," 21 October 1935; for a similar analysis of communal unity see Speisman, *Jews of Toronto,* 339–40; CJCA, Roger to Caiserman, 21 November 1935.
81 Ibid., Roger to Caiserman, 25 August 1935; ibid., Roger to Caiserman, 4 September 1935; ibid., Caiserman to Roger, 27 August 1935; ibid., Conference of Delegates, 8 August 1935.
82 Ibid., Langsner to Mandell, 7 August 1936; ibid., Eisendrath to Caiserman, 31 October 1935; Caiserman and Eisendrath devoted a great deal of time and energy to the boycott issue. For further information on Eisendrath's efforts, see CJCA, Eisendrath to Caiserman, 9 September 1935,; ibid., Caiserman to Eisendrath, 11 September 1935; ibid., Eisendrath to Caiserman, 9 October 1935; ibid., Caiserman to Eisendrath, 15 October 1935.

83 Guttman, "Nazi Olympics," 31–2, 50.
84 Ibid.
85 Hart-Davis, *Hitler's Games*, 107–11.
86 Kidd, "The Popular Front and the 1936 Olympics," 13–16. The "turn" in Comintern policy was very significant in terms of allowing Communists to ally themselves with the Socialists in the boycott struggle. The fact that they still failed attests to the power of sport and to the unwillingness of the world to anger Hitler. Appeasement was part of sports policy at this time.
87 Guttman, "Nazi Olympics," 35–40.
88 Ibid., 40; Kidd, "Canadian Opposition to the 1936 Olympics," 22–4.
89 Ibid., 29–31, 33; the YMHA was actually pushed into this embarrassing situation by the promoter of the boxing event. He somehow managed to suppress a circular from the COA that announced that a percentage of ticket revenue from all member organizations was required if athletic events were held before the Canadian team left for Berlin. The YMHA executive discovered the truth when it was too late to call off the event. Cohn called this "a piece of inexcusable blundering on the part of the "Y" Board." CJCA, "Olympic Boycott," M. Cohn to H. Golden, 19 June 1936. It is interesting to note that even Edmund Scheuer, the grand old man of Toronto Judaism, signed the protest letter. He was very acculturated and moved in the high levels of Toronto society, yet this issue resonated for him. Even the very discreet and socially accepted Sigmund Samuel enjoyed going to his home in London where, he commented, "we enjoyed freedom from the religious prejudice we often encountered in Canada." Samuel, *In Return*, 106.
90 Luftspring, *Call Me Sammy*, ch. 5, 9.
91 Ibid., 62, 84–5; Luftspring gave a similar answer in an interview with Bruce Kidd in 1977. Kidd, "Canadian Opposition to 1936 Olympics," 35, note 45. It is clear that Luftspring here is confusing what his family wanted with the political objectives of the Canadian Jewish Congress.
92 Luftspring, *Sammy*, 86–8; Kidd, "Canadian Opposition to 1936 Olympics," 36. Luftspring's memoirs reflect his uncertainty. He was only twenty, had devoted the last few years of his life to fighting, and had to make difficult decisions quickly. He wasn't sure if the games organizers "had enough bread to get me over there and get me back." Then, he wrote, "[I] ran into Harry Sniderman on the street one day ... Harry would arrange my financing from the Jewish community." According to Luftspring, Sniderman, a well-known athlete, appointed himself as Luftspring and Yack's mentor and then took him to a meeting of the Central Division executive. As Luftspring told it, Roger praised them for their stand, "the kind of stand that would have the

support of Congress. Within minutes, we had a pledge from the meeting for the money we needed." Sniderman then arranged a Stag at the YMHA in order to "allow the bookmakers to sweeten the cake" even further. This raised another $1,000.
93 Luftspring, *Sammy*, 83.
94 CJCA, "Olympic Boycott." There are other facts as well. Luftspring was suspended from boxing between December 1935 and April 1936 for assisting a gambling operation. He desperately needed money and was thinking of turning professional. After his reinstatement, he was still angry at the way he had been treated, and was upset even further when he was made to pay his own way to the Canadian Championships in Edmonton. He placed second and on 30 May he was offered a chance to join the Olympic team. He "had a tremendous desire to go and thought about it for days." But Luftspring was torn between the desire to participate, family concerns about his safety, and his considerable Jewish pride. Luftspring, *Sammy*, 87–95.
95 Kidd, "Canadian Opposition to 1936 Olympics," 36–40.
96 CJCA, Roger to Caiserman, 10, 23 September 1935.
97 Ibid., Caiserman to Roger, 30 September 1935; ibid., Caiserman to Roger, 25 October 1935; ibid., Caiserman to Roger, 1 October 1935; ibid., Caiserman to Brown, 22 October 1935.
98 Ibid., "Statement Made by Mr. A. Brown," 23 October 1935, confidential interview; Caiserman to Brown, 29 February 1935; ibid., Minutes of the Central Division Executive Committee, 7 November 1935.
99 Ibid., "Statement Made by Mr. A. Brown," confidential interview; Caiserman to Brown, 20 February 1935. A number of confidential interviews reveal that Brown's critique was well aimed and not well received. His anger at the situation was still palpable when I interviewed him almost fifty years later. One can well imagine what drove him to write this letter. This career change eventually proved to be beneficial. Brown became a key teacher at the Brunswick Avenue Talmud Torah and went on to a very distinguished career as a Jewish educator in Toronto who became a consultant to the Board of Jewish Education before his retirement.
100 CJCA, Minutes of the Central Division Executive Committee, 7 November 1935. Goldstick was later persuaded to withdraw his resignation but was defeated and left Congress after the 1936 elections.
101 CJCA, Roger to Caiserman, 29 October 1935; ibid., Caiserman to Roger, 5 November 1935; ibid., Roger to Caiserman, 2 December 1935; ibid., Jacobs to Roger, 12 December 1935. The financial plight of all these institutions

will be the subject of chapter 6. Ibid., "Report of the Central Division," 23 February 1936.
102 Ibid., Report of the Central Division, 25 February 1936.
103 Sachar, *Modern Jewish History*, 360; CJCA, Mandell to Caiserman, 25 March 1936. On the role of socialism and unions in caring about Jewish world affairs, see Frager, *Sweatshop Strife*, 57, who calls anti-Semitism in Europe "a cause that united different classes."
104 CJCA, Caiserman to Mandell, 26 March 1936; Caiserman planned to follow the same procedure as a combined delegation from the American Jewish Congress, B'nai Brith, and the American Jewish Committee had used at the Polish embassy in Washington, DC, in early February; CJCA, Mandell to Caiserman, 31 March 1936; Cohen, *Not Free to Desist*, 158, 179; CJCA, Minutes of the Central Division Executive Committee, 1 April 1936.
105 Ibid., Minutes of the Central Division Executive Committee, 1 April 1936; ibid., Mandell to Caiserman, 2 April 1936.
106 Ibid., Caiserman to Mandell, 18 April 1936; ibid., Mandell to Caiserman, 17 April 1936.
107 Ibid., Eisendrath to Caiserman, 20 April 1936.
108 Ibid., Minutes of the Central Division Inner Executive Committee, 28 April 1936. Ibid., Mandell to Caiserman, 20 April 1936.
109 On the elections, see CJCA, Minutes of the Central Division Executive Committee, 10 February, 5, 11, 17, 22 March, 12 May 1936; Minutes of the Elections Committee, 1, 9 March 1936; and "Rules Governing the Election of Delegates to the Third Plenary"; on coal dealers and the boycott, see CJCA, Glass to Frank, 18 August 1936; ibid., Frank to Mandell, 20 August 1936; ibid., Mandell to Frank, 28 August 1936; ibid., Frank to Glass, 20 August 1936; Report of the Actions Committee, 15 November 1936; on Divisional finances, see CJCA, Minutes of the Ontario Delegates, 16 June 1936; Report of the Central Division to the Third Plenary, 15 November 1936.
110 Ibid., Minutes of the Central Division Executive Committee, 19 August, 24 September, 18 October, 2 November, 9 December 1936; ibid., Campaign Committee, 10 November 1936; ibid., Roger to Caiserman, 12 November 1936.
111 Cohen interview, 17 May 1983; Cohen to Author, 13 October 1983; CJCA, Roger to Caiserman, 12 November 1936; ibid., Caiserman to Roger, 13 November 1936.
112 Inner Executive meetings became far more frequent after the results of the Third Plenary elections had placed Bennett as Chairman of the Board. CJCA, Minutes of the Central Division Executive Committee, 1937–39, Cohen interview.

113 CJCA, Caiserman to Roger, 9 December 1936; ibid., Roger to Caiserman, 11 December 1936; ibid., Caiserman to Roger, 17 December 1936. This was the version that was sent; its original draft of 15 December reveals that Caiserman was a careless accountant who failed to pro-rate the salaries of those workers who did "national" work and Eastern Division work.
114 CJCA, Report of the Central Division, 15 November 1936, 6, in which the Kehilla Committee reported that "this Committee has accomplished nothing."
115 The orphanage matter is fully discussed in chapter 3; Speisman, *Jews of Toronto*, 340, makes some reference to this in passing but in a slightly different context.
116 A basic account of this matter, which will be discussed in detail in chapter 6, is found in Speisman, *Jews of Toronto*, 337–8.

CHAPTER SIX

1 AA, MBD, 26 October 1933.
2 Ibid., MBE, 24 August, 27 September 1933.
3 After his contract was renewed in 1934, Treiger agreed to accept a pro-rated salary like the rest of the teaching staff, to assuage any bad feelings.
4 On Gordon's background and relationship to the school see Speisman, *Jews of Toronto*, 166, 171–3, 310–12,; Shapiro, *Toronto Jewish Community*, 89–90; Caplan *"No Precious Stones,"* 150–3; AA, MBE, 3 October 1933; ibid., MBD, 20 March 1935.
5 Speisman, *Jews of Toronto*, 310–12; Speisman, "The Jews of Toronto: A History to 1937," vol. 2 ch. 19, fn 28, 558–9; AA, "Group B and the Jewish Center of Educational and Communal Activities: An Outline of a Plan Approved by the Board of Directors of the Toronto Hebrew Free School to Place the School on a Sound Financial Basis for Future Operations," 22 October 1935, Schedule 1.
6 AA, MBD, 9 May 1934.
7 Ibid., 5 July, 15 August, 1934; ibid., MBD, 17 October 1934; ibid., "Audited Statement for the Year Ending 30 June 1934."
8 Ibid., 20 March 1935.
9 Ibid., Minutes of the Provisional Committee, 24 March 1935.
10 Ibid., 24, 28, 30 March, 4 April 1935; S.A. Kurtz, interview, 12 August 1985.
11 Kurtz, interview; AA, MBD, 28 April 1935.
12 Ibid., Minutes of the Provisional Committee, 30 March 1935.
13 Ibid., Minutes of the Board of Directors, Committee of 15, and the Cam-

paign Committee, 2 May 1935; ibid., Report of the Campaign Committee, 2 May 1935; ibid., Report of the Committee of 9, 15 May 1935; ibid., MBD, 27 June 1935.
14 Ibid., Minutes of the Building Committee, 19, 23 May 1935; ibid., Minutes of the Annual Meeting of the Toronto Hebrew Free School, 18 June 1935; Speisman, *Jews of Toronto*, 171–3, 182–4, 310–14.
15 AA, MBD, 12 September 1935; in social work terms, the success of these young men at convincing their older and better-established peers to support their ideas can be traced to the fact that these young men were recognized as leaders and thus their proffered advice was legitimate. See M.G. Ross, with B.W. Lappin, *Community Organization*, 123.
16 AA, MBD, 12 September 1935.
17 AA, MBD, 16 October 1935; ibid. "JECIT Report"; ibid., Minutes of Group B Meeting, 22 October 1935.
18 Ibid., "JECIT Report." Vise had hoped to decrease the loan principal by about $5,000. All statistics are from the annual audits for 1934–36 in the Associated Archives. I am indebted to Mr Samuel Kurtz for his aid in analysing and interpreting them.
19 A complete examination of the federation may be found in chapter 3; M. Cohn interview.
20 Ibid., Karpf, *Jewish Community Organization*, 115.
22 Ibid., 95–8; Katz, *Tradition and Crisis*, ch. 10; for a fine summary of how this relates to North America, see Harry L. Lurie, *A Heritage Affirmed*, 15–19, and Goldin, *Why They Give* for a very general overview.
23 Lappin, "Community Organization Work," 99.
24 Ibid., chs. 5, 6; ibid., 218–19; Lappin, 249, 256–65.
25 Ibid., ch. 6
26 Ibid., 264; the social work theory behind these organizations is mapped out in Ross, *Community Organization*, ch. 2 and in Lappin, *Community Workers and the Social Work Tradition*, especially III.
27 Cohn interview.
28 Ibid.
29 Ibid.; Kurtz interview.
30 M. Cohn's comments on my draft of chapter 3.
31 Ibid.
32 AA, M. Cohn to Kurtz, 5 February 1937; ibid., Minutes of the May 19 Meeting.
33 M. Cohn's comments on my draft of chapter 3: AA, M. Cohn to Gelber, 7 May 1937.

34 Ibid., Minutes of the May 19 Meeting.
35 Ibid.
36 Ibid., Godfrey and M. Cohn to Kert, 21 May 1937; ibid., Provisional UJWF Executive to Gelber, 17 June 1937; confidential interview provided this information about Eitz Chaim. The Freimans were furious at the Toronto Zionists, led by Henry Rosenberg, who was an important figure in the CJC, UJWF, and Brunswick Avenue Talmud Torah. See Figler, *Freiman*, 145, 249–50.
37 AA, "List of those elected on 16 June 1937"; ibid., Altschul to Gelber, 18 August 1937.
38 Ibid.; M. Cohn, interview. For a sophisticated analysis of the science of fundraising see Seeley et al., *Community Chest*, ch. 10. On the basis of these criteria, the UJWF campaign was certainly "cutting edge" in terms of practice.
39 "$170,000 Campaign of the United Jewish Welfare Fund of Toronto," October 1937, pamphlet, CJCA.
40 Ibid.
41 Ibid.
42 Ibid.
43 Cohn interview.
44 CJCA, Altschul, "Facts About the UJWF of Toronto"; ibid., "UJWF Folder," vertical reference file; PAO, RG19, Box 96, File "Sadowski, Cohen, Godfrey, and Rosenberg to the Provincial Secretary, "Provincial Secretary's Dept., 1937–45," 3 May 1938; M. Cohn's comments on my draft of chapter 3.
45 OJA, Minutes of the UJWF Board of Directors, 10 March 1939, CJCA "UJWF Folder," vertical reference file.
46 Ibid.; (Hutner) Rosichan, interview; CJCA, "UJWF Statement of Assets and Liabilities," 31 December 1938.
47 OJA, Minutes of the UJWF Board of Directors Minute Book, "Report to the Board of Directors on Financial Policy for 1939," 24 March 1939.
48 CJCA, "What is the Canadian Jewish Congress?" November 1936, pamphlet.
49 Cohen interview.
50 On Freiman's decision, see Figler, *Freiman*, 276–7; M. Cohn, interview; (Hutner) Rosichan, interview.

CHAPTER SEVEN

1 Abella and Troper, *None*, 23.
2 Cohen interview. This is shown by Abella and Troper, *None*, and also argued effectively by Draper, "Fragmented Loyalties"; JIAS(T) File 441, Advertise-

ment for Council of Organizations, February 1937; ibid., File 343 Solkin-Taback, 18 March 1938; on the $10,000 requirement being generalized see File 198, Solkin to Frank, 21 February 1938; ibid., File 339, Solkin to Taback 13 October 1938.
3 JIAS(T), "Reports and Statistics 1933–1939." I have used these as the basis for my calculations.
4 Marrus, *Mr. Sam*, 260–4, describes Caiserman as the catalyst in getting Bronfman involved in the Refugee Committee of the Congress, while Labour Zionist leader Moshe Dickstein ensured that he would actually become president. Newman, *Bronfman Dynasty*, 60–2; PAC, MG 27 III C3, S.W. Jacobs Papers, 2695, 2767.
5 CJCP, Caiserman to Eisendrath, 20 October 1938.
6 Newman, *Bronfman Dynasty*, 61; O. Cohen to author, 13 October 1983.
7 M. Cohn interview; Kayfetz interview, 30 May 1986.
8 CJCP, Minutes of the Central Division Executive Committee, 6 January 1938; ibid., Minutes of the Central Division Joint Public Relations Committee, 29 August, 30 October, 1938; the UJWF believed that the JPRC's work was so important that they allotted it $12,500 for 1938 in contrast to the $6,000 allocation for Central Division. CJCA, 30 October 1938.
9 Ibid., Minutes of the Central Division Executive Committee, 31 March, 5 May 1938.
10 Ibid.
11 Ibid., 5, 9 May 1938.
12 Ibid.
13 Kayfetz interview.
14 CJCA, Minutes of the Central Division Executive Committee, 11 September 1938,.
15 Ibid. Central Division thus scored a key organizational coup by filling the vacuum left in the Toronto JIAS office after Solkin's departure in November 1937. The Toronto JIAS would remain weak until August 1939, when Manny Kraicer took the reins. Other agencies had their own priorities and did not challenge Central Division.
16 Ibid., Frankel to Robinson, 28 November 1938; ibid., Minutes of the Montreal Refugee Committee, 11 December 1938; ibid., Minutes of the Eastern and Central Regions, 13 December 1938, Congress Central File, Box 10, file 54.
17 Ibid.
18 Ibid., Minutes of the CJCR Central Division, 1 May 1939; Abella and Troper, *None*, 57–8; on the role of Silcox and the CNCR in general, see

Davies and Nefsky, *How Silent Were the Churches?* ch. 3; Nefsky, "The Shadow of Evil."

19 LAC, MG 27 III C3 S.W. Jacobs Papers, vol. 9, 3333; Cohen interview; Abella and Troper, *None*, 57; CJCA, Minutes of the CJCR Actions Committee, 25 June 1939.

20 Ibid., Minutes of the CJCR Central Division Executive, 13 September 1939; CJCA, UJWF Reference File, "UJWF Annual Report for 1938," 10; JIAS(M) file 4082, Solkin to A. Brodey, 23 July 1938; OJA, UJWF Minutes, 17 March 1938.

21 CJCA, UJWF Reference File "After Two Years: Achievements of the UJWF of Toronto," 3; this allocation represented the average of the amounts raised by the Toronto UPA in its 1935–37 campaigns; LAC, MG 28 V81 Zionist Organization of Canada Papers vol. 8 "ZOC Financial Report, 1 January 1935 to 31 December"; Figler, *Freiman*, 276–7, 278, 282, 232; Hadassah, the women's Zionist group, was also "unalterably opposed" to combined campaigns. Ibid, 145. Their fear may well have been based on the U.S. experience, which featured constant arguments among the JDC, the UPA, and Community Chests over fund allocation. On this issue, see Karp, *To Give Life*, 71, 78; Shapiro, *From Philanthropy to Activism*, 31–3; and OJA, UJWF Minutes, 2, 24 March, 10 April, 5 May 1939.

22 CJCA UJRA Files, Box 11, File 59 Minutes of a National CJCR Actions Committee, 25 June 1939; OJA, UJWF Minutes, 30 August 1939.

23 Ibid., UJWF Minutes, "Minutes of a Joint Meeting of the Executive and Budget Committee," 30; ibid., August 1938 and 9 June 1939.

24 CJCA, Minutes of the Central Division Executive Committee, "Conference of Organizations Round Table Report on Labour Organizations," April 1939; on the Canadian government's efforts to control ethnic information and win the loyalty of ethnic groups, see Kirkconnell, *Canadians All*, Young, "Making the Truth Graphic," and "Chauvinism and Canadianism: Canadian Ethnic Groups and the Failure of Wartime Information"; Kordan and Luciuk, "A Prescription for Nationbuilding: Ukrainian Canadians and the Canadian State, 1939–45"; N.F. Dreisziger, "The Rise of a Bureaucracy for Multiculturalism."

25 Ibid.

26 On the Jewish Labour Committee, see Wyman, *The Abandonment of the Jews*, 68; OJA, Minutes of the Central Division Executive Committee, 23 July 1939.

27 Ibid., 7 September 1939.

28 Ibid., 20 September 1939; ibid., Minutes of the Inner Executive Committee, 20 September 1939.

29 Ibid., UJWF Minutes, 5, 28 May, 30 August, 8 September 1939.

30 CJCA, Minutes of the Central Division Executive Committee, 3 October 1939; Abella and Troper, *None*, 68; another example of the centralizing effect of the war was the Polish remittance business. This was an important source of Toronto JIAS revenue. But the war had completely disrupted communications with Poland, and the JIAS was forced to abandon its remittance service and its tracing service for relatives. The only organization with enough clout to approach the government and obtain the necessary permit for foreign remittances was the UJWF, and smaller organizations were forced to turn to it. This, and the subsequent closure of all mail service to Poland, shut down remittance business for the war's duration.
31 CJCA, Minutes of the Central Division Executive Committee, 24 December 1939; ibid., Minutes of the Conference of Organizations, 4 October 1939. This conference was attended by 172 representatives of 109 organizations. OJA, Minutes of the UJWF, 22 September 1939.
32 Ibid., 18, 22 September 1939.
33 CJCA, "JPRC Central File for 1940"; on the formation of this committee see CJCA, Minutes of the Central Division Executive, 26 September 1939; Much of this material is taken from the excellent summary of Congress's war efforts in Tulchinsky, *Canada's Jews*, ch. 11; CJCA, Minutes of the War Efforts Committee, 13 September 1944 for the expenses of the Servicemen's Centres; the War Efforts Committee also looked after War Guests – the euphemism for British evacuees in Canada. Central Division took care of about fifteen families at considerable expense – over $7,000 per year. CJCA, Minutes of the War Guest Executive Committee, 23 August 1940.
34 Ibid., Minutes of the Central Division Executive, 12 October 1939.
35 On this topic, see Avakumovic, *The Communist Party in Canada* and Kirkconnell, *Canada, Europe, and Hitler*; Cohen interview.
36 OJA, Minutes of the Central Division Inner Executive Committee, 22, 29 December 1939; for an excellent analysis of the Salsberg campaign, see Manley, "Audacity, audacity, still more audacity: Tim Buck, the Party, and the People, 1932–1939."
37 OJA, Minutes of the Military Committee, 26 October 1939.
38 Ibid., Minutes of the National Emergency Committee, 11 February 1940; ibid., 19 April 1940; ibid., Minutes of the Central Division Inner Executive Committee, 27 February, 16 April 1940; ibid., Minutes of the Women's Committee, 19 February 1941; ibid., Minutes of the Central Division Executive Committee, 1 May 1941; ibid., Minutes of the War Efforts Committee, 6 May 1941.
39 See chapter 6 for a detailed analysis of the FJP and the birth of the UJWF.

CJCA, Minutes of the Central Division Executive Committee, 23 November 1939; OJA, Minutes of the Executive of the UJWF, 26 May, 22 September 1939.

40 Ibid., "Meeting re: Congress-Welfare Fund Relationship," 19 January 1940; CJCA, Minutes of the UJWF Executive, 23 January 1940.
41 Ibid., UJRA, File 83A, "Report on People's Committee on War Sufferers – Winnipeg," 6 April 1942.
42 A classic comparison is D.C. Masters, "Toronto vs. Montreal"; Montreal remained the pre-eminent Jewish community in Canada until the late 1970s. Tulchinsky, *Branching Out*, 338.
43 Hayes was remarkably qualified for his job and performed it brilliantly. However, his competence was considered a threat to Toronto's authority, and this is the point of view argued here. Cohen interview; Marrus, *Mr. Sam*, 282–3; OJA, Minutes of the UJWF Executive, 27 December 1939; CJCA, Minutes of the National Emergency Board (Central Division), 4 October 1939.
44 OJA, Minutes of the UJWF Executive, 22 January, 13 May 1940.
45 CJCA, UJRA File 100C, "President's Report," January 1941; ibid., File 158, Hayes to A. Bronfman, 22 August 1941; ibid., "Report of the CJC Central Refugee Committee," 16 January 1941; OJA Minutes of the UJWF Executive, 27 December 1939, 13 February 1941.
46 Ibid., unnumbered file folder, no date, "UJWF Budgets"; ibid., Minutes of the Central Division Executive Committee, 21 August, 5 November 1942, 20 January 1943.
47 JIAS(T), File 666; OJA, Minutes of the UJWF Executive, 26 November 1941.
48 Elazar, *Community and Polity*, 132; for a critique of Elazar, see Lazin, "The Non-Centralized Model."
49 OJA, Minutes of the UJWF Executive, 26 December 1941.
50 Ibid., "Report to the Board on Financial Policy for 1939," 24 March 1939.
51 In fact the Report to the Board cited above argued that the UJWF's purpose was "planning for communal financial stability as a foundation for the provision of more adequate communal activities"; OJA, Minutes of the UJWF Executive, 28 April 1939.
52 Ibid., Minutes of the UJWF Executive, 8 and 18 September 1939.
53 Ibid., 10 January, 29 March, 13 September 1940. Barsky, *Mount Sinai*, is mute on this issue, probably because the board minutes for this period have been lost.
54 The concept of educating agencies to perceive each other's needs was drawn from social work theory of the time. On this idea, see Lappin, "Stages in the Development of Community Organization," 350–1, which hints at this. Lap-

pin was hired in 1947 to work at Congress by Saul Hayes as part of this drive to professionalize the operation. Marrus, *Mr. Sam*, 295.
55 OJA, Minutes of the UJWF Executive. 11 and 18 March 1940.
56 Ibid., "Report to the Executive Committee re: Care of the Aged," 6 June 1941; ibid., Minutes of the UJWF Executive, 6 June 1941.
57 On the JCCA, see Speisman, *Jews of Toronto*, 338; on the YMHA, see JCCA, 313; OJA, Minutes of the UJWF Executive, July 1940. The allocations saved totalled over $6,000.
58 Ibid., "Federation Personnel Report," 7, had recommended as far back as in June 1934!; Speisman, *Jews of Toronto*, 336.
59 OJA, Minutes of the UJWF Executive, 2 May, 17 December 1941; ibid., 14, 23 January 1942; ibid., 8 February, 12 March, 6 April 1942; Speisman, *Jews of Toronto*, 336.
60 OJA, undated file folder "UJWF Budgets."
61 Ibid., Minutes of the UJWF Executive, 17 December 1940, 14 March 1941; see chapter 6 for the details of the financial plight of the Toronto Hebrew Free School.
62 OJA, Minutes of the UJWF Executive, 21 April, 2, 21 May 1941; ibid., "Proposal re: Debt Reduction Allocation in the Campaign," 8 September 1941, included in "Report of the Budget Committee to the UJWF Board," 9 September 1941. For more on Sadowski, see chapter 6 and Marrus, *Mount Sinai*, 49–50.
63 OJA, Minutes of the UJWF Executive. 14 January 1942.
64 Elazar, *Community and Polity*, 181–94.
65 Ross, *Community Organization*, 264, and chapter 3
66 Ross, *Community Organization*, 289–91.
67 Lappin, "Joint Fundraising in Toronto," 30; Ross, *Community Organization*, 293–4; OJA, Minutes of the UJWF Executive, 7 June 1940; similar trends can be discerned in the United States, where cooperation between Jews and other ethnic groups (especially elites) had begun after the First World War. See Seeley et al., *Community Chest*, 157–9; LaMonte, *Politics and Welfare in Birmingham*, especially 21, 46, 57, 58, 59. Note the observation that in Birmingham the impetus for creating a Community Chest came from the social workers, 96.
68 Ross, *Community Organization*, 300–1; OJA, Minutes of the UJWF Executive, 4 April 1943.
69 Ibid.
70 Lappin, "Joint Fundraising," 35–9; OJA, "Memo to Community Chest," 22 November 1943.
71 Ibid.; Lappin, "Joint Fundraising," 39–40; there is an entire literature on the

rise of Community Chests in North America. Among the most relevant studies are Seeley et al,. *Community Chest* and the extensive bibliography appended. An interesting subsequent study is Tittle, *Rebuilding Cleveland*. Both these accounts briefly mention that Jewish Welfare Funds joined larger Community Chests. It does not raise issues of how this merger affected giving, or the reasons behind these decisions, or how accommodating the communal chests were to ethnic welfare funds. This issue is addressed to some extent in Ostrower, *Why the Wealthy Give*, especially ch. 2. Her evidence suggests that elite Jewish donors advanced through stages of fundraising, with communal fundraising viewed as a higher sphere than Jewish fundraising. Many donors rose through the ranks of Jewish Federations to become important players in Community Chests. This is very suggestive material, and will be touched on the Conclusion.

72 Lappin, "Joint Fundraising," 35–9.

CHAPTER EIGHT

1 Cohn interview.
2 (Hutner) Rosichan interview.
3 OJA, Minutes of the UJWF Executive, "Report on the 1944 Campaign to 21 April."
4 Ibid. Minutes of the UJWF Executive, 1944–48.
5 See chapter 7 for information on the role of peer pressure in fundraising.
6 Elazar, *Community and Polity*, 266; S. Kronick interview. Mrs Kronick recalled that her husband, Sam, "was out all day on business and all nights of the week except on Friday and Saturday with community meetings." This engagement parallels the American examples cited in Seeley et al., *Community Chest*.
7 (Hutner) Rosichan interview; Elazar, *Community and Polity*, 267.
8 OJA, Minutes of the UJWF Executive, "Meeting of the Board of Governors and the Service Council," 25 January 1944.
9 Ibid.; Seeley et al., *Community Chest*, ch. 4.
10 OJA, Minutes of the UJWF Executive, "Report on the 1944 Campaign to 21 April."
11 Elazar, *Community and Polity*, 272–5, 277.
12 OJA, Minutes of the UJWF Executive, "Report of the Executive Committee to the Board of Directors," 24 April 1944; this population estimate is based on Louis Rosenberg, "Distribution of Toronto Jewish Population," 5 and LAC, Louis Rosenberg Papers, MG 30 C119 v26 File 119, "Jewish Mutual Benefit

Friendly Societies in Toronto," 27, which estimated at 56,500 the 1946 Jewish population of Toronto.
13 CJCA, UJWF File "Statement of Income of the UJWF for 1941 to 1945"; Laqueur, *The Terrible Secret*, 204, argues that by late 1942 everyone knew that extermination was taking place "though the news about the murder of many millions of Jews was not accepted for a long time and even when it had been accepted, the full implications were not understood." Certainly Saul Hayes was convinced of this by September 1942. He wrote that "Hitler intends eventually to make Europe *Judenrein*," and enclosed numerous documents that bolstered his argument. CJCA, CJC Central File Box 23, file 198B, Hayes to Zacks, 3 September 1942; on this issue in Canada, see Tulchinsky, *Branching Out*, 205–6, and for a very complete account, see Bialystok, *Delayed Impact*, 22–6, which agrees that "those who wanted to know knew by December 1942."
14 OJA, UJWF File "Report of the Budget and Executive Committee for 1944 Needs" 15 January 1944.
15 Ibid., Minutes of the UJWF Executive, 25 January 1944.
16 Kurtz, interview; AA, MBE, 11 May 1943, 10 January 1944, 2 January 1946, all of which refer to "the impossibility of obtaining teachers qualified for our curriculum"; the desire to erect some sort of community centre can be traced to the rise of this idea in North American Jewish community-planning circles. It came to the fore in the influential "JWB Report," which envisioned these centres, first promoted by Rabbi Mordechai Kaplan, as playing a key role in the postwar Jewish community. See Janowski, *The JWB Survey*, 6–8; on the growth of Mount Sinai Hospital in this period, see Barsky, *Mount Sinai*, 60–6.
17 OJA, Minutes of the UJWF Executive, "Report of the Board of Directors," 11 January 1944 and "Report on Borochov School Capital Campaign," 24 April 1944.
18 Rosenberg, "Distribution of Toronto Jews," Tables 8 and 12; Tulchinsky, *Branching Out*, Table 2; Seeley et al., *Crestwood Heights*, 41, claims there were no residential covenants, but anecdotal evidence suggests otherwise. Jews who did settle in Forest Hill generally settled in the "Upper Village" and were banned from the "Lower," which was south of the Village centre and far more prestigious; on the entire "Eglinton Branch Affair," see AA, MBD, 29 August 1943; 20, 27 February; 5, 12, 19 March 1944; and especially 9 May 1944, which noted "perhaps it might be better to erect a building in a *nonrestricted area*" [my emphasis]; the best source on the suburbanization of Orthodox Jews in Toronto (with some information on Shaarei Shomayim

in this period) is Diamond, *And I Will Dwell in Their Midst*, 46–47, which does not mention the "Forest Hill/Eglinton" phase of Associated's growth; on the entire subject of racial covenants, see Walker, *"Race," Rights and the Law in the Supreme Court of Canada*, ch. 4 and Walker, "The 'Jewish Phase' in the Movement for Racial Equality in Canada."

19 AA, MBD, 28 November 1942; on Eglinton Avenue, ibid., 14, 29 July, 25 August, 10 November 1942. On the latter date it was noted that there were four classrooms in the Eglinton building and that it would open for registration on 29 February 1944; OJA, Minutes of the UJWF Executive, 29 November 1944. It is only fair to note that eventually Reeve Gardiner (who later became famous as Metro Chairman) persuaded the village council to allow THFS to rent the Forest Hill Public School from 4:30 to 7:30 p.m. on Mondays through Thursdays for $30 per week for all students attending THFS, even if they lived "beyond the Village boundaries." Ibid., 26 June 1945; there is also a significant literature on the relocation of North American Jews to the suburbs and the parallel rise of large Conservative and Reform congregations. Among the most suggestive studies are Sklare, *Conservative Judaism*; Gans, "The Origins of a Jewish Community in the Suburbs"; and Seeley, *Crestwood Heights*; Tulchinsky, *Branching Out*, 276–9.

20 OJA, Minutes of the UJWF Executive, "Report on Borochov School Capital Campaign," 24 April 1944; ibid., Minutes of the UJWF Executive, 21 March, 20 June 1945.

21 Ibid., "1945 Budget Report"; ibid., 29 November 1945, at which the "Day School" request was made; and the meeting of 7 March 1946 at which the school formally withdrew its request; Rosenberg, "Toronto Jewish Community," Table 13.

22 OJA, Minutes of the UJWF Executive, 4 November 1946, 28 January 1947.

23 Ibid.; Raben, "History of the Board of Jewish Education of Toronto, 1949–1975," ch. 1.

24 Joseph Kage, *With Faith and Thanksgiving*, 113–31; Abella and Troper, *None*, 238–79; Lappin, *The Redeemed Children*; Martz, *Open Your Hearts*; additional information is found in Bialystok, *Delayed Impact*, ch. 2; Troper, "Canada and the Survivors of the Holocaust."

25 Hawkins, *Canada and Immigration*, 2nd ed., 33; some examples of these recollections are Tulchinsky, *Taking Root*, 1; Martz *Open Your Hearts*, 12; for a brief and revealing example (one of thousands), see Paris, *Jews*, 86–8.

26 For a useful discussion, see Belkin, *Narrow Gates*, 150–4, 169–71; and for a glimpse of the political background see Kage, *Faith and Thanksgiving*, 79–81.

27 Abella and Troper, *None*, 211–13.

28 Ibid., 190–5, 196–7; Hayes, 101 (Inter Office Information Bulletin) #64, 8 January 1947; Laqueur, *Terrible Secret*, 1–2, 204; Abella and Troper, *None*, 195–6, 204–6; on the Kielce pogrom and its effects, see Gilbert, *Atlas of the Holocaust*, Map 314, on 241, which also notes that over a thousand Jews were murdered in Poland in the two years following liberation; there is further information in Bialystok, *Delayed Impact*, 38, 50; Abella and Troper, *None*, 236; on postwar pressure from the Jewish community in general, see Abella and Troper, *None*, 207–13; Bialystok, *Delayed Impact*, 43–8; Troper, "DP Crisis," 269–74; Kage, *Faith and Thanksgiving*, ch. 8; Hawkins, *Immigration*, 91.
29 Ibid., 91–3; Hayes, 101 #144A, 7 May 1947. These were to replace the Vichy orphans who never came. On the children, see Abella and Troper, *None*, ch. 4, especially 112–18; Martz, *Open Your Hearts*, 32–3, Bialystok, *Delayed Impact*, 48–50; and Kage, *Faith and Thanksgiving*, 124–6.
30 On the JIAS–UJRA relationship, see Abella and Troper, *None*, 114.
31 JIAS(T), no file number, Forer to Robinson, 14 November 1941; CJCA, CJC Central File #75, Hayes to Zacks, 1 February 1941.
32 Abella and Troper, *None*, 168–9.
33 JIAS(T), "Report of the UJRA–JIAS Committee on the Lisbon Refugees," 3 January 1945, 1.
34 Ibid.
35 Ibid., 3.
36 OJA, UJWF File, Minutes of the First Meeting of the Committee on the Extension of Case Work, 7 June, and subsequent meetings on 21, 30 June 1942; eventually an agreement on allowing social workers to be guidance counsellors was reached, but the distrust of the teachers and their refusal to take part in orientation and training kept the plan from getting underway. Nonetheless, it was a harbinger of things to come: the JFCS later provided these services to the Jewish Day Schools under the Board of Jewish Education. Ibid., "Report of Subcommittee on Plans for Co-operation between Jewish Schools and the JFCS," 4 October 1944, and the follow-up in Minutes of a Meeting between Educationalists [sic] and Social Case Workers, 5 October 1944.
37 OJA, Minutes of the JFCS Board, 10 January 1946.
38 Ibid.
39 Ibid.
40 Ibid., "A Report on the Current Staff Situation," no date, but was attached to JFCS Board Minutes of 10 January 1946; ibid., Minutes of the JFCS Board, 29 January, 7[?] February 1946.
41 Ibid., 29 August 1946.

42 Ibid., 7[?] February 1946.
43 Ibid., 7[?] February 1946.
44 Ibid.
45 Abella and Troper, *None*, 222; OJA, Minutes of the JFCS Board, 29 January, 28 February, 5 March, 29 May, 28 June 1947.
46 Abella and Troper, *None*, 241, 270–2; Lappin, *Redeemed Children*, 24–28, 161–3; Martz, *Open Your Hearts*, 50–1.
47 OJA, Minutes of the JFCS Board, 22 May 1947; ibid., Grand to Hayes, 9 September 1947, Congress Central file #10; Lappin, *Redeemed Children*, gives the date of this meeting. Nothing of this meeting is mentioned at the 11 June board meeting minutes, or even at the Executive Committee minutes of its meeting of 8 July, the last before September. On 24 July, Hayes noted: "There is no likelihood that the full number [of permits] will be granted." IOI #196, 27 July 1947; Martz, *Open Your Hearts*, 17, gives the date of their arrival as 15 September. This is incorrect. Lappin notes that the ship left on 13 September, and no ship could cross the Atlantic in two days. Lappin, *Redeemed Children*, 13.
48 Ibid. Grand was reading IOI #226, 8 September 1947, Item 1; OJA, Minutes of a Meeting of the JFCS Board, 22 May 1947; Abella and Troper, *None*, 272–3; OJA, Minutes of the JFCS Board, 18 September 1947.
49 Ibid., Minutes of the JFCS Board, 18 September 1947.
50 Ibid. It is notable that the CJC Central Region executive approved the JFCS's decision to set up the Committee on European Youth, since the JFCS had acknowledged Congress's control of policy making and it would therefore be a waste of effort to form a separate committee under the aegis of Congress and thus duplicate services. This decision was reached only after a lengthy and passionate debate and a vote that defeated a motion to set up a separate committee. OJA, Minutes of the Central Region Executive Committee, 19 September 1947.
51 Lappin, *Redeemed Children*, 32–3.
52 Ibid. 33, where Lappin contends that this rift developed after the establishment of the JFCS Committee on European Youth. This thesis argues that the differences in philosophy of service were latent and that the creation of the committee mirrored the existence of these points of view and brought the clash into the open.
53 OJA, Minutes of the First Meeting of the Committee for European Youth, 8 October 1947.
54 Ibid.

55 Lappin, *Redeemed Children*, 37, 53, 75; Martz, *Open Your Hearts*, 70, and 73, where Martz has mistranslated *shmad* and has misdated Hayes letter by a year.
56 OJA, Minutes of the First Meeting of the Committee for European Youth, 8 October 1947; ibid., Minutes of the Central Region Executive Committee, 22 December 1947; Lappin, *Redeemed Children*, 68.
57 On this debate, see Lappin, *Redeemed Children*, 53–4, 65, 73–5, and Martz, *Open Your Hearts*, 53–4.
58 These two Biblical expressions, from Isaiah 7:3 and Zechariah 3:2 respectively, convey the idea of the miraculous redemption of the Jewish people in the face of all odds; on the nature of these children and their interaction with foster parents and social workers, see Lappin, *Redeemed Children*, 72–85, and Martz, *Open Your Hearts*, ch. 7.
59 Martz, *Open Your Hearts*, 50–3.
60 Ibid., 51.
61 Lappin, *Redeemed Children*, 72–85.
62 OJA, Minutes of the Case Committee on European Youth, 4 November 1948; ibid., "Memo on the Time Spent by Case Workers on European Youth in August 1948"; ibid., Palevsky, "Survey of Immigrant Work of the CJC," 25; on this report and its subsequent history, see Bialystok, *Delayed Impact*, 61–7.
63 OJA, Minutes of the Case Committee on European Youth, 4 November 1948.
64 This study focuses on the role Toronto institutions played in these immigration projects. For fuller information on the projects themselves, see Abella and Troper, *None*, 256–70, Bialystok, *Delayed Impact*, 48–56, and Troper, "DP Crisis."
65 OJA, Minutes of the Central Division Labour Committee, 1934–35. This committee became defunct because unionists ignored Congress; LAC MG 30 C119, Louis Rosenberg Papers vol. 20 file 18; see also Rosenberg, *Canada's Jews*, Table 116, Bialystok, *Delayed Impact*, 51, 55–6.
66 It is impossible to judge the truth of the "shortage of skilled tailors" claim empirically. Rosenberg had raised this point in his 1935 study "Toronto Jews in Industry," but judging from the text of this monograph, he may have been attempting to convince the Department of Immigration to allow for the admission of more "skilled workers." Troper argues that the industry knowingly misled the government and certainly there was plenty of incentive to do so. See Troper, "DP Crisis," 282, Abella and Troper, *None*, 256–61; CJCA, File 300T, Posluns to Hayes, 14 February 1947; ibid., Minutes of Needle Trades Immigration Committee, 14 March 1947; ibid., L. Rosenberg to Hayes, 7 March 1947.
67 Ibid., Draft of Brief Requesting Inclusion of Needle Trades Workers Among

Immigrants to be Admitted to Canada. This draft was completed on 7 March and the final draft on 18 March. It was sent to Ottawa in advance of the meeting between the needle trades representatives and the Departments of Immigration and Labour. LAC, RG 27 Vol. 278 File 1-26-5. Department of Labour Papers, Hereford to McNamara. 10 May 1947.

68 CJCA, File 300T 1947, "Petition of Toronto Cloak Manufacturers and the ILGWU," 19 March 1947; Charles Lloyd to M. Enkin, 21 April 1947, W. McCaig to M. Enkin. 28 March 1947, M. Enkin to S. Hayes, 29 March 1947. My own father's story attests to this. He was seventeen when his hometown of Pabianice (a suburb of Lodz) was overrun by the Wehrmacht in 1939. He wanted to be a textile engineer, but he had no formal training in the garment industry. Max Federman had known my grandfather, and when he met my father at the DP camp he recognized the name Lipinski and asked him, "Are you Jacob Lipinski's son from Pabianice?" When he received an affirmative reply, and after further questioning established that my father was telling the truth, he added my father's name to the Canadian garment list, without even giving him the test for proficiency in the needle trade.

69 Ibid., J.J. Spector to Hayes, 23 May 1947; CJCA, 101 #147A, 7 May 1947; the Cabinet delayed approval because C.D. Howe got involved in the whole affair. For an account of this and further delays and complications, see Abella and Troper, *None*, 262–8; Enkin interview.

70 Abella and Troper, *None*, 246–7; "Palevsky Report," 17.

71 Bialystok, *Delayed Impact*, 50–67.

72 "Palevsky Report," 12; JIAS (T), Minutes of the Toronto JIAS Executive, 30 November 1947. This method of repayment was mandated by the government in all bulk immigration schemes of industry workers. See LAC MG26 J4, William Lyon Mackenzie King Papers, vol. 241, 2 June 1947; Cabinet Documents, Cabinet Document #469, C.D. Howe to Cabinet.

73 Ibid.; Wade, "Wartime Housing Limited, 1941–47," 41–59, 42–3; CJCA, 101 #248, 17 October 1947.

74 JIAS(T) Minutes of the Toronto JIAS Executive, 22 February, 8 June, 30 October 1947.

75 Enkin interview; CJCA, 101 #269, 17 November 1947.

76 Ibid., 101 #280, 2 December 1947; OJA, Rabbis to Community, 24 September 1947; Martz, *Open Your Hearts*, 69–75, emphasizes the use of guilt in this campaign.

77 CJCA, 101 #316, 25 January 1948.

78 The number cited is taken from the JIAS Board minutes of 22 January,

which noted "266 tailors and dependants arrived," which implies that the 266 is an inclusive number. Minutes of the Toronto JIAS Board of Directors, 22 January 1948. This number is supported by the "Palevsky Report," 26, which notes "over 200 people." Where they all came from is not such a mystery. It is clear that two transports carrying tailors left Germany in December 1947. Hayes was told they would arrive "between 10 and 20 January" carrying 342 tailors, or 522 adults in total and 125 children (IOI #298 of 29 December 1947). But on 14 January, now equipped with passenger lists, Hayes noted that the two boats contained a total of 391 tailors and 726 people. The *General Sturgis* docked on 14 January. It also contained 69 orphans (1 bound for Toronto). It was followed by the *General Heizlemann*, which contained tailors only (IOI #309 of 14 January 1947). What is mysterious is how they came to Toronto unannounced and unexpected. There is a lacuna in all the documentation. Nothing more was heard from Hayes until after the weekend incident. None of the correspondence files of the JIAS and Congress contain any clear discussion of what happened during the weekend. Neither does the Jewish or non-Jewish press. But there are clues to what happened scattered through the correspondence. See, for example JIAS(T), File 2774, especially M.I. Simpson to Solkin, 23 January 1947.

79 Ibid.
80 CJCA, File 300T, Minutes of a Meeting on Thursday 22 January 1948 at the Office of the Canadian Jewish Congress; JIAS(T), File 2774, Solkin to M. Latch, 27 January 1948.
81 CJCA, File 300T Hayes to Grand, 22 January 1948; ibid., File 36D, Grand to Hayes, 4 March 1948.
82 Ibid., File 300T Hayes to Grand, 22 January 1948.
83 OJA, CJC Central Correspondence, microfilm #7, Clothing Campaign File, yields a figure of 5,000 based on newspaper clippings (paper title missing) from December 1948; Bialystok, *Delayed Impact*, ch. 2.
84 On this idea, see Wiebe, *The Search for Order*; OJA, Tailors' Immigration File, Hayes to Grand, 26 February 1948.
85 Ibid., "Form Letter on Placement"; Lappin to Rubin, 20 September 1948. On the methods used and the issue of oversupply, see Abella and Troper, *None*, 258, 261, 265.
86 CJCA, File 300T, Hayes to Grand, 22 January 1948; OJA, CJC Central Correspondence 1947–49, microfilm #9, file "Tailors" Grand to Stack, 5 May 1948; ibid., Minutes of a Meeting of the Canadian Overseas Garment Commis-

sion, 15 May 1948; CJCA, File 300T, A.C. Cowan to COJW and CJC, n.d. [February 1948?]; JIAS(T), File 3148, L. Herman to Mr. Duck, 29 July 1948.

87 The JIAS even tried to obtain an army barracks used by the Department of Public Welfare, but without success. CJCA, File 300T, Grand to Hayes, 22 January 1948, A.C. Cowan to COJW and CJC; on the JIAS purchases of 145 and 147 Beverley Street, see JIAS(T), Minutes of the Toronto JIAS Executive Committee, 22 January, 29 February, 28 March, 11, 22 April, 9 May, 27 July, and 21 November 1948; ibid., File 3210/1, "Report from the Housing Committee," 2 November 1948; ibid., File 3148, L. Herman to Mr. Duck, 29 July 1948.

88 Ibid., "Report of the Housing Committee of the UJRA," 15 February 1949; ibid., UJRA Housing Committee to Taback, 24 December 1948, file 3210/2; ibid., "Report on Service to New Canadians," n.d., file 3210/3; OJA, Minutes of an Emergency CJC Central Region Budget Committee Meeting, 20 October 1948.

89 Ibid., Grand to COJW, 28 April 1948; ibid., "Canadian Fur Commission Report: 22 September to 31 October 1948."

90 Ibid., "Palevsky Report," 26–7; JIAS(T), File 576/1, Minutes of the Financial Assistance Committee, 16 December 1948.

91 CJCA, File 300T, Grand to Hayes, 14 January 1948; OJA, CJC Central Correspondence, 1947–49, microfilm #9; CJCA, File 300T, Grand to Sadowski, 20 January 1948, Hayes to Grand, 16 February 1948; on payroll deduction, see CJCA, File 300T, Hayes to Grand, 16, 26 February 1948.

92 Ibid.

93 OJA, CJC Central Correspondence File, 1947–49, microfilm #9 Bertha G. to Grand, 18 May 1948; CJCA, File 300T, Representatives of Delegates of Garment Workers, 1 September 1948; OJA, Central Correspondence File, 1947–49, microfilm #8, S. Levine to S. Hayes, 16 September 1948; Lappin to Dr. Hallowitz, 19 September 1948.

94 JIAS(T), File 576/1, Minutes of the Sub-Committee on Financial Assistance, 1 November 1948.

95 OJA, "Palevsky Report," 30.

96 For some examples of Aplin's methodology, see JIAS(T), File 576/1, Minutes of the Sub-Committee on Financial Assistance, 1 November, 29 December 1948. At the latter meeting, interviewers for loans were empowered to give those in the Close Relatives Scheme "an outright grant or a loan, at their discretion, depending on the circumstances of the immigrant." It was also noted that some tailors were only being deducted $1.00/week if their circumstances warranted it; the number of Jews is from JIAS(T), File 576/1,

"Partial Report of Debits and Repayments Concerning Immigrant Tailors in Toronto to November 30, 1948"; OJA, September 1948, CJC Central Correspondence File, 1947–49, microfilm #7, Furriers File, "Report of Daniel Drutz"; the estimate of $180,000 is based on the fact that the houses cost $150,000 just to purchase and that at least another $11,000 was spent on furniture and repairs. OJA, DP Housing Policies File, Lappin to E. Gelber, 19 November 1948, adds that $12,000 was spent on the tailors and over $7,000 on the furriers through 31 October; "Palevsky Report," 8, made this recommendation and it was accepted at the CJC 1950 Plenary.

97 Abella and Troper, *None*, 268–70; CJCA, 101 #478, 10 September 1948; OJA, CJC Central Correspondence, 1947–49, microfilm #7, Furriers file, Lappin to Carbell and Rubin, 20 August 1948. Bialystok, *Delayed Impact*, 51, lumps the Tailors' and Fur Workers' schemes together and focuses more on the former.
98 OJA, CJC Central Correspondence, 1947–49, microfilm #7, Furriers file, Lappin to Carbell and Rubin, 20 August 1948.
99 Ibid.; OJA, CJC Central Correspondence, 1947–49, microfilm #7, Furriers file, Minutes of a Fur Project Planning Meeting, 18 September 1948.
100 Ibid.; Lappin to Kerbel, 7 September 1948; ibid., Lappin to Rubin, 20 September 1948.
101 Ibid.; CJCA, 101 #478, 10 September 1948; CJCA, Minutes of the Executive Committee of the UJWF and CJC, 17 August 1948; CJCA, CJC Central File, 36A, 101 #489, 10 October 1948.
102 101 #477, 17 September 1948; 101 #480, 22 September 1948; 101 #489, 10 October 1948.
103 OJA, "Palevsky Report," 27; 101 #514, 20 November 1948; OJA, Furriers File, D. Drutz to H. Diamond, 29 December 1948.
104 Ibid., "Report on Furriers to 30 September 1948."
105 Abella and Troper, *None*, 247–71.
106 See Troper, "Jews and Immigration Policy," 44–58, especially 55.
107 CJCA, Central File 36D, Caiserman to Hayes, 9 November 1948; ibid., File 300T, Grand to Hayes, 9 March 1948.
108 OJA, "Palevsky Report," 31–2; Lappin, *Redeemed Children*, 33.
109 CJCA, Central File 36D, Caiserman to Hayes, 9 November 1948.
110 Ibid., File 300T, Hayes to Grand, 15 January 1948.
111 OJA, "Palevsky Report," 33.
112 CJCA, CJC Central File 36D, "Summary of Conversations in Meetings with Mr. Ben Lappin on July 12th, 13th, and 14th, 1948"; ibid., Lappin to Hayes,

5 August 1948; ibid., Minutes of a Meeting between the Executive Committees of Congress and the UJWF, 17 August 1948.
113 Ibid., Minutes of a Meeting of All Agencies, 27 August 1948.
114 Ibid.
115 OJA, Minutes of the JFCS Executive, 8 October 1948; these key board members were Sadowski, Gelber, and Kronick. Sadowski was president of CJC Central and a former UJWF president, who would soon go on to direct the building of Mount Sinai Hospital on University Avenue; Arthur Gelber was named UJRA chairman on 3 October 1948 and elected to the JFCS board the same year; Sam Kronick was "Mr UJRA" to many people, especially Jewish farmers in Ontario; CJCA, CJC Central File 36D, Minutes of the UJR Committee, 3 October 1948; for evidence of Lappin as the originator of the UJRA restructuring, ibid., Lappin to Hayes, 20 August 1948; "Memorandum on the Re-Establishment of the UJR Committee," n.d.; and Lappin to Mrs. Hallowitz, 12 October 1948, (five separate memos delineating in detail the workings of each of the proposed UJRA committees); OJA, Central Division Correspondence, 1947–49, microfilm #7, Hallowitz File, Lappin to Mrs. Hallowitz, 22 November 1948.
116 Ibid., Minutes of the UJR Committee, 3 October 1948.
117 On Hayes's professionalization of the UJRA and Congress, see Marrus, *Mr. Sam*, 207–8; it is interesting to note that Hayes's communal interests before joining the UJRA paralleled those he later opposed at the Toronto JFCS: ibid., 278; for evidence of Hayes's consistent insistence on CJC's primacy, see Abella and Troper, *None*, 113–16, and Bialystok, *Delayed Impact*, 55–6.
118 On the issue of lack of staff at the UJRA, see OJA, "Palevsky Report," 33–5; on UJRA representation on the European Youth Committee, see OJA, Minutes of the Committee on European Youth, 17 October 1947, which indicate that CJC Central Division executive secretary Grand attended the meeting; and on the essentiality of proper casework procedures, see Lappin, *Redeemed Children*, 13, who quotes PC #1647 in its entirety, #5 and #7 are especially relevant.
119 See chapter 6 for a discussion of the methodology; OJA, "Report of Budget and Executive Committees for the Combined Campaigns of the UJWF and UPA," 3 March 1948, 2.
120 Ibid., "Palevsky Report," 33.
121 CJCA, File 36D, Lappin to Hayes, 19 November 1948; the Self-Study Committee could not decide which model was best and made no recommendation. See OJA, Minutes of the Self-Study Committee, 5 December 1948.
122 Ibid.; for the social work theory behind this, see Lurie, *Heritage Affirmed*,

220–31 and Lurie, "Character of Relationships of Jewish Agencies with Public or Non-Sectarian Agencies in the Field of Public Welfare."
123 OJA, File 300T, Hayes to Lappin, 26 November 1948.
124 Ibid., for the fact that Hayes was travelling to New York; Introductory letter from E.L. Lurie to the Survey Committee, OJA, "Palevsky Report," 13 October 1949.
125 Ibid., 61–4.
126 Raben, "Board of Jewish Education," chs. 3, 4; Raben, "Bringing Order to Chaos"; OJA, Minutes of the UJWF Executive, 9 January 1948; ibid., Minutes of the Scholarship and Sponsorship Committee of the Coordinating Committee on European Youth, 25 January 1948.
127 OJA, Minutes of the UJWF Executive, 9 January, 22 December 1948; on the plans for expanding Mount Sinai Hospital, see Barsky, *Mount Sinai*, 61–8.
128 LAC MG 28 V81, Zionist Organization of Canada Papers, vol. 8, "Zionist Organization of Canada Financial Report 1943–45," (hereafter cited as ZOCFR and year).
129 On the original inclusion of the ZOC, see chapter 5. Note that Freiman applied this principle to all fundraising. The ZOC Toronto campaign collected $386,000 between 1941 and 1943, and over $560,000 in 1944 through 1946. These were princely sums that the UJWF might well have appreciated. ZOCFR 1941, 1943, 1946, 1947.
130 Ibid., ZOCFR 1946–47; background to the Zionist boom of 1945–48 is in Tulchinsky, *Branching Out*, ch. 9, Troper, "Crisis of Displaced Persons," 284–5, Bialystok, *Delayed Impact*, 40–1, and Abella, *Coat of Many Colours*, 227–30.
131 For a tribute, see *Canadian Zionist*, 25 June 1944, 5; ZOCFR 1946–47.
132 OJA, Minutes of the UJWF Executive, 28 January 1947.
133 Figler, *Freiman*, 145, 278, 276–8, 283; Bercuson, *Secret Army*, 71.
134 PAC MG 30 C177 V5, Samuel J. Zacks Papers, Minutes of the National Council of the Central Division, 5 February 1948; ibid. Robert H. Soren File, Soren to Zacks et al., 25 March 1946; Bercuson, *Secret Army*, 62–3; David Dunkelman, *Dual Allegiance*, chs. 16, 17.
135 ZOCFR 1947, LAC; OJA, Correspondence of the CJC Central Division, 1947–49, microfilm #8, Hayes to Hutner, 23 January 1948.
136 Ibid., Collins and Lapierre, *O Jerusalem!*, 168–71.
137 OJA, Minutes of the UJWF Executive, 28 January 1948; LAC MG30 C144, Samuel J. Zacks Papers, vol. 3, Gelber Brothers Correspondence File, Minutes of Meeting of Representatives of Toronto Zionist Council and the United Jewish Welfare Fund, 1 February 1948.
138 Ibid., 9 June, 22 November 1948; LAC, ZOCFR, 1949.

CONCLUSION

1 Phillips, *Mayor of All the People*, 1967. 130; certainly it is true, as Leslie Saunders asserted, that one of the factors in Phillips's victory was that the mayoralty race was three-sided and that he and Arthur Brown "split the Christian and Gentile vote," allowing Phillips to win. This analysis ignores the fact that both the *Star* and the *Telegram* backed Phillips's candidacy – which would have never happened a decade before. Saunders, *An Orangeman in Public Life*, 128.
2 Kayfetz, "On Community Relations in Ontario," 59.
3 Walker, "Race," 185.
4 Patrias and Frager, "Minorities and Human Rights," 17.
5 On the JLC see Patrias and Frager, "Minorities and Human Rights," 26–8 and Lambertson, "Jewish Labour Committee," 331–2.
6 Patrias and Frager, "Minorities and Human Rights," 16–17.
7 Walker, "Race", 185 for Laskin; on Feinberg see Feinberg, *Storm the Gates of Jericho*, 1964.
8 Kayfetz, "Community Relations," 58–61.
9 Ibid., 64–5; Walker, "Race," 231.
10 Diner, *The Jews of the United States*, 81, 233–4.
11 Ibid., 234.

Bibliography

PRIMARY SOURCES

Archival

I LIBRARY AND ARCHIVES CANADA, OTTAWA
B'nai Brith of Canada Papers
Canadian National Committee on Refugees Files
Department of Labour Papers, 1946–48
Immigration Branch Records and Reports, 1933–45
Samuel W. Jacobs Papers
Jewish Labour Committee Papers
William Lyon Mackenzie King Papers
A.M. Klein Papers
Louis Rosenberg Papers
Samuel Jacob Zacks Papers
Zionist Organization of Canada Papers

II ARCHIVES OF ONTARIO, TORONTO
Holy Blossom Synagogue Papers and Records
Ontario. Report of the Committee on Direct Relief. Wallace C. Campbell, Chairman. 28 July 1932
Ontario. Department of Public Welfare Records. Files on "Relief" and "Orphanages," 1930–37; Annual Reports, 1930–39
Ontario. Ministry of Public Welfare. *Annual Reports*, 1933–37

III CITY OF TORONTO ARCHIVES, TORONTO
Civic Unemployment Relief Committee, Minutes and Reports, 1933–37
House of Industry, Minutes, 1933–37

IV ONTARIO JEWISH ARCHIVES, TORONTO
Canadian Jewish Congress Central Region Correspondence, 1933–48
Canadian Jewish Congress Central Region, Clippings File, 1933–39
Federation of Jewish Philanthropies Records, 1925–37
Morris Goldstick Papers
United Jewish Welfare Fund Records, 1937–48

V CANADIAN JEWISH CONGRESS ARCHIVES, MONTREAL
Canadian Jewish Congress Papers, 1933–48
Jewish Immigrant Aid Society of Canada, Correspondence Files

VI ASSOCIATED HEBREW SCHOOL ARCHIVES, TORONTO
Board of Directors Minutes, 1933–48
Vaad Hahinuch (Board of Education) Minutes, 1933–48

VII JEWISH IMMIGRANT AID SOCIETY, TORONTO
Board Minutes, 1923–48
Case Files #1-4500 (1933–48)
Correspondence 1925–48
Reports 1933–48

VIII UNIVERSITY OF TORONTO ARCHIVES
School of Social Work, Administrative Files, 1920–25

Personal Interviews

Dr John Atkins, 12 April 1983
Dr Alexander Brown, Toronto, 27 August 1983
Fred Catzman, Toronto, 23 March 1982, 24 and 27 November 1984
Martin A. Cohn, Toronto, 8 April 1985
Max Enkin, Toronto, 27 May 1985
Ben Kayfetz, Toronto, 31 December 1984, 30 May, 13 June 1986
Samuel A. Kurtz, Toronto, 8 June, 12 August 1985
Oscar Cohen, New York, 31 May, 1 June 1983
Joe Kronick, Toronto, 5 March 1985
Mrs S. Kronick, Toronto, 17 October 1983, 13 April 1985
David Rome, Montreal, 24 July 1983
Florence (Hutner) Rosichan, Toronto, 14 January 1985
Montague Raisman. 11 July 1982

Rabbi Reuben Slonim, Toronto, 14 and 23 July 1982
Stephen Speisman, Toronto, 3 August 2002
Tobie Taback, Toronto, 18 March 1983
Albert Wise, Toronto, 6 January 1985

SECONDARY SOURCES

Abella, Irving. *A Coat of Many Colours: Two Centuries of Jewish Life in Canada*. Toronto: Lester & Orpen Dennys, 1990.
– and Harold Troper. *None is Too Many*. Toronto: Lester & Orpen Dennys, 1982.
Armstrong, Frederick H. "Metropolitanism and Toronto Re-examined, 1825–50." *Canadian Historical Association Review* (1966), 29–40.
Anctil, Pierre. "Interlude of Hostility: Judeo-Christian Relations in Quebec in the Interwar Period, 1919–39." In *Anti-Semitism in Canada: History And Interpretation*, edited by Alan Davies. Waterloo: Wilfrid Laurier University Press 1992, 135–66.
Avakumovic, Ivan. *The Communist Party in Canada*. Toronto: McClelland & Stewart, 1985.
Barsky, Lesley Marrus. *From Generation to Generation: A History of Toronto's Mount Sinai Hospital*. Toronto: McClelland & Stewart, 1998.
Beito, David T. *From Mutual Aid to the Welfare State: Fraternal Societies and Social Services, 1890–1967*. Chapel Hill: University of North Carolina Press, 2000.
Bercuson, David. *The Secret Army*. Toronto: Lester & Orpen, 1983.
Betcherman, Lita-Rose. *The Swastika and the Maple Leaf*. Toronto: Fitzhenry & Whiteside, 1976.
Bialystok, Franklin. *Delayed Impact: The Holocaust and the Canadian Jewish Community*. Montreal and Kingston: McGill-Queens's University Press, 2000.
Breton, Raymond. *The Governance of Ethnic Communities: Political Structure and Processes in Canada*. New York: Greenwood, 1991.
– *Ethnic Identity and Equality: Varieties of Experience in a Canadian City*. Toronto: University of Toronto Press, 1990.
– "Institutional Completeness of Ethnic Communities and the Personal Relations of Immigrants." *American Journal of Sociology* 70:2 (1964): 193–205.
Caplan, Kimmy. "There is no interest in precious stones in a vegetable market: The Life and Sermons of Rabbi Jacob Gordon of Toronto." *Canadian Jewish Studies/Études Juives Canadiennes* 13–14 (2005/6). 149–67.

Careless, J.M.S. *The Union of the Canadas.* Toronto: McClelland & Stewart, 1977.

Cohen, Naomi W. *Not Free to Desist: A History of the American Jewish Committee, 1905–1966.* Philadephia: Jewish Publication Society, 1972.

Cohen, Zvi. *Canadian Jewry.* Toronto: Canadian Jewish Historical Society, 1926.

Cohn, Martin and Elizabeth Wallace. *Some Problems of Administration in Social Work.* Toronto: University of Toronto Press, 1944.

Collins, Larry and Dominique Lapierre. *O Jerusalem!* New York: Pocket Books, 1973.

Cordery, Simon. *British Friendly Societies: 1750–1914.* London: Palgrave Macmillan, 2003.

Craig, Gerald M. *Upper Canada: The Formative Years, 1784–1841.* Toronto: McClelland & Stewart, 1977.

Creighton, Donald G. *Empire of the St. Lawrence: A Study in Commerce and Politics.* Toronto: University of Toronto Press, 2002.

Davis, Alan F. and Marilyn E. Nefsky. *How Silent Were the Churches? Canadian Protestantism and the Jewish Plight during the Nazi Era.* Waterloo: Wilfrid Laurier University Press, 1998.

Decarie, Graeme. "Review of *None Is Too Many*," *Labour/Le Travail* 15 (spring 1985), 201–2.

Delisle, Esther. *The Traitor and the Jew.* Translated by Madeleine Hébert. Montreal and Toronto: Robert Davies, 1993.

Diamond, Etan. *And I Will Dwell in Their Midst: Orthodox Jews in Suburbia.* Chapel Hill and London: University of North Carolina Press, 2000.

Diner, Hasia. *The Jews of the United States 1634 to 2000.* Berkeley: University of California Press, 2004.

Dominion of Canada. Report of the Department of Immigration and Colonization 1934. Ottawa: Patenaude, 1934.

Dominion of Canada. Department of Immigration and Colonization for the Year Ended March 31, 1936, Report. Ottawa: Patenaude, 1937.

Dominion of Canada. Department of Immigration and Colonization for the Year Ended March 31, 1938, Report. Ottawa: Patenaude, 1939.

Draper, Paula Jean. "Fragmented Loyalties: Canadian Jewry, the King Government and The Refugee Dilemma," in Hillmer, Norman, Bohdan Kordan, and Lubomir Luciuk. *On Guard for Thee: War, Ethnicity and the Canadian State, 1939–45.* Ottawa: Canadian Committee for the History of the Second World War, 1988, 151–78.

Dreisziger, N.F. "The Rise of a Buraucracy for Multiculturalism: The Orgins of the Nationalities Branch," in Hillmer, Norman, Bohdan Kordan, and Lubomir Luciuk. *On Guard for Thee: War Ethnicity, and the Canadian State, 1939–45*. Ottawa: Canadian Committee for the History of the Second World War, 1988.

Dunkelman, David. *Dual Allegiance*. Toronto: Macmillan, 1976.

Einbinder, Esther. "An Exploratory Study of Attitudes Toward Jews in Toronto." MA thesis: University of Toronto, 1933.

Eisen, David. *Diary of a Medical Student*. Toronto: Canadian Jewish Congress, 1974.

Eisendrath, Maurice. *Can Faith Survive? The Thoughts and Afterthoughts of an American Rabbi*. New York: McGraw-Hill, 1964.

Elazar, Daniel J. *Community and Polity: The Organizational Dynamics of American Jewry*. Philadelphia: Jewish Publication Society, 1976.

– Harold M. Waller, and Yaakov Glicksman. "The Toronto Jewish Community Through Four Generations." In Elazar, Daniel J. and Harold M. Waller. *Maintaining Consensus: The Canadian Jewish Polity in the Postwar World*. London: Jerusalem Centre for Public Affairs, 1990, 153–78.

Feinberg, Abraham L. *Storm the Gates of Jericho*. Toronto: McClelland & Stewart, 1964.

Feingold, Henry L. *Zion in America*. New York: Hippocrene, 1974.

Figler, Bernard. *Lillian and Archie Freiman*. Foreword by Michael Garber. Montreal: Northern Press, 1962.

– *Sam Jacobs, Member of Parliament*. (Foreword by H. Carl Goldenberg). Gardenville: Harpell's Press, 1959.

– and David Rome. *Hannaniah Meir Caiserman: A Biography*. Montreal: Northern Printing, 1962.

Frager, Ruth. *Sweatshop Strife: Class, Ethnicity, and Gender in the Jewish Labour Movement of Toronto*. Toronto: University of Toronto Press, 1992.

Fraser, Derek. *The Evolution of the British Welfare State: A History of Social Policy Since the Industrial Revolution*. 2nd Edition. London: Macmillan, 1984.

Gans, Herbert. "The Orgins of a Jewish Community in the Suburbs." In Sklare, Marshall, (ed.). *The Jewish Community in America*. New York: Behrman House, 1974.

Gathercole, George C. "The City of Toronto in Depression and Recovery, 1929–39: A Study in Public Finance." MA thesis: Toronto, 1945.

Gilbert, Martin. *Atlas of the Holocaust*. Toronto: Lester, 1991.

Godfrey, Judith C., and Sheldon Godfrey. *Burn This Gossip: The True Story of George Benjamin of Belleville: Canada's First Jewish Member of Parliament*. Toronto: Duke and George Press, 1991.

- *Search Out the Land: The Jews and the Growth of Equality in British Colonial America, 1740–1867*. Montreal and Kingston: McGill-Queen's University Press, 1995.
Gordon, Milton. *Why They Give: American Jews and Their Philanthropies*. New York: Macmillan, 1976.
Goren, Arthur A. *New York Jews and the Quest for Community: The Kehilla Experiment, 1908–1922*. New York: Columbia, 1970.
Grusd, Edward E. *History of B'nai Brith in Eastern Canada*. Montreal: Apex Press, 1964.
Guttman, Alan. "The Nazi Olympics and the American Boycott Controversy." In Riordan, J. (ed.). *Sport and International Politics: The Impact of Fascism and Communism on Sport*. London: Routledge, 1998, 31–50.
Hart-Davis, Duff. *Hitler's Games: The 1936 Olympics*. London: Century, 1986.
Hawkins, Freda. *Canada and Immigration: Public Policy and Public Concern*. 2nd Edition. Montreal and Kingston: McGill-Queen's University Press, 1988.
Hawkins, Richard. "'Hitler's Bitterest Foe': Samuel Untermyer and the Boycott of Nazi Germany, 1933–1938," *American Jewish History* 93:1 (March 2007), 21–50.
Howe, Irving. *World of Our Fathers: The Journey of the East European Jews to America and the Life They Found and Made*. New York: Harcourt Brace Jovanovich, 1976.
Janowski, Oscar I. *Report of the Survey Commission by Salo W. Baron*. Foreword by Frank I. Weil. New York: Dial, 1948.
Jolliffe, Russell. "The History of the Childrens' Aid Society of Toronto, 1891–1947." MSW thesis: Toronto, 1952.
Kage, Joseph. *With Faith and Thanksgiving: The Story of Two Hundred Years of Jewish Immigration and Immigration Aid Effort in Canada*. Montreal: Eagle, 1962.
Kardonne, Rick. "Lecture Honours Christian Businessman," *Canadian Jewish News*, 1 December 1984, 21.
Karp, Abraham, J. *To Give Life: The UJA in the Shaping of the American Jewish Community*. New York: Schocken, 1981.
Karpf, Maurice E. *Jewish Community Organization in the United States*. New York: Bloch, 1938.
Katz, Jacob. *Tradition and Crisis: Jewish Society at the End of the Middle Ages*. New York: Schocken, 1971.
Kayfetz, Ben G. "On Community Relations in Ontario in the 1940s," *Canadian Jewish Studies/Études Juives Canadiennes* 2 (1994), 57–65.

- "Only Yesterday." Article presented at meeting of Toronto Jewish Historical Society, 1972 (In author's possession).
- "The Development of the Toronto Jewish Community," *Tradition*. 13 (summer 1983), 5–17.
- "The Toronto Jewish Press," *Canadian Jewish Historical Society Journal*. 7:1 (spring 1983), 50–2.

Kidd, Bruce. "Canadian Opposition to the 1936 Olympics in Germany," *Canadian Journal of Sport and Physical Education* 9 (December 1978), 20–40.
- "The Popular Front and the 1936 Olympics," *Canadian Journal of Sport and Physical Education* 11 (May 1980), 1–18.

Kirkconnell, Watson. *Canada, Europe and Hitler*. Toronto: Ottawa University Press, 1939.
- *Canadians All*. Toronto: University of Toronto Press, 1940.

Kordan, Hohdan and Lubomir Luciuk. "A Prescription for Nationbuilding: Ukrainian Canadians and the Canadian State, 1939–45." In Hillmer, Norman, Bohdan Kordan, and Lubomir Luciuk. *On Guard for Thee: War, Ethnicity, and the Canadian State, 1939–45*. Ottawa: Canadian Committee for the History of the Second World War, 1988, 82–100.

Lamberton, Ross. "The Dresden Story: Racism, Human Rights, and the Jewish Labour Committee of Canada." In MacDowell, Laurel Sefton, and Ian Radford. *Canadian Working Class History: Selected Readings. 3rd Edition*. Toronto: Canadian Scholars' Press, 2006, 331–60.

LaMonte, Edward Shannon. *Politics and Welfare in Birmingham, 1900–1975*. Tuscaloosa and London: University of Alabama Press, 1995.

Lappin, Ben. *Community Workers and the Social Work Tradition: Their Quest for a Role Examined in Israel and Canada*. Toronto: University of Toronto Press, 1971.
- *The Redeemed Children: The Story of the Rescue of War Orphans by the Jewish Community of Canada*. Toronto: University of Toronto Press, 1963.
- "Social Work Activism, the Reform Tradition, and the Influence of the Sixties," University of Toronto Faculty of Social Work. "Occasional Papers" #10. Toronto: Faculty of Social Work, 1978.
- *Stages in the Development of Community Organizational Work as a Social Work Method*. DSW dissertation: University of Toronto, 1965.
- "Toronto's Tombstones: An Old Cemetery Reveals Interesting History." *Shem Tov 20:1* (March 2004), 1–12.

Laqueur, Walter. *The Terrible Secret*. London: Weidenfeld and Nicholson, 1980.

Latimer, Elspeth Anne. "An Analysis of the Social Action Behaviour of the Canadian Association of Social Workers from its Organizational Beginnings to Modern Times." PhD dissertation, Toronto, 1972.

Lazin, Frederick A. "The Non-Centralized Model of American Jewish Organizations: A Test Case." *Jewish Social Studies* 44 (1982), 299–314.

Levendel, Lewis. *A Century of the Canadian Jewish Press.* Ottawa: Borealis Press, 1988.

Levitt, Cyril and Shaffir, William. *The Riot at Christie Pits.* Toronto: Lester & Orpen Dennys, 1987.

Lipinsky, Jack. "The Agony of Israel: Watson Kirkconnell and Canadian Jewry," *Journal of the Canadian Jewish Historical Society* 6:1 (1982), 57–72.

– "The Apprenticeship of an Executive Director: M.A. Solkin, A.J. Paull, and the Jewish Immigrant Aid Society of Canada." *Canadian Jewish Historical Society Journal* 9:2 (fall 1985), 67–81.

– "The Progressive Wedge: The Organizational Behaviour of Toronto Jewry, 1933–1948." PhD dissertation: University of Toronto, 2003.

– "Watson Kirkconnell: Ethnic Interpreter." Unpublished "2000" (MA) Paper for Professor Carl Berger, University of Toronto, 1979.

Lubove, Roy. *The Professional Altruist.* Cambridge: Harvard University Press, 1965.

Luftspring, Sammy (with Brian Swarbrick). *Call Me Sammy.* Scarbrough: Prentice-Hall, 1975.

Lurie, Harry L. *A Heritage Affirmed.* Philadelphia: Jewish Publication Society of America, 1961.

– "Character of Relationships of Jewish Agencies with Public or Non-Sectarian Agencies in the Field of Public Welfare." In Morris, Robert and Michael Freund (eds.). *Trends and Issues in Jewish Social Welfare in the United States, 1899–1952.* Philadelphia: Jewish Publication Society, 1968.

– "Developments in Jewish Community Organization," *Jewish Social Service Quarterly* 15:1 (September 1938), 34–41.

MacGregor, Agnes C. "The Department of Social Science, 1919–40." In MacGregor, Agnes, *Training for Social Work in the Department of Social Science of the University of Toronto.* Toronto: University of Toronto Press, 1940, 9–32.

Marrus, Michael R. *Mr. Sam: The Life and Times of Samuel Bronfman.* Toronto: Viking, 1991.

Martz, Fraidie. *Open Your Hearts: The Story of the Jewish War Orphans in Canada.* Montreal: Véhicule, 1996.

Masters, D.C. "Toronto vs. Montreal: The Struggle for Financial Supremacy." *Canadian Historical Review* 22 (June 1941), 133–46.

Mendelson, Alan. *Exiles from Nowhere: The Jews and the Canadian Elite*. Altona: Robin Brass Studio, 2008.

Moore, Deborah Dash. *B'nai Brith and the Challenge of Ethnic Leadership*. Albany: State University of New York Press, 1980.

Morton, W.L. *The Progressive Party in Canada*. Toronto: University of Toronto, 1950.

Nathanson, Deena. "A Social Profile of Peddlers in the Jewish Community of Toronto, 1891–1930," *Canadian Jewish Studies/Études Juives Canadiennes* 1 (1993), 27–40.

Neatby, H. Blair. *William Lyon Mackenzie King*. Volume 2. *The Lonely Heights, 1924–1932*. Toronto: University of Toronto Press, 1963.

– *William Lyon Mackenzie King*. Volume 3. *The Prism of Unity, 1932–1939*. Toronto: University of Toronto Press, 1976.

Nefsky, Marilyn F. "The Shadow of Evil: Nazism and Canadian Protestantism." In Davies, Alan (ed.). *Anti-Semitism in Canada: History and Interpretation*. Waterloo:Wilfrid Laurier University Press, 1992, 197–226.

Newman, Peter C. *The Bronfman Dynasty*. Toronto: McClelland & Stewart, 1979.

Odenkrantz, Louise C. *The Social Worker*. New York and London: Harper, 1929.

Oliver, Peter. *Unlikely Tory*. Toronto: Lester & Orpen Dennys, 1985.

Ostrower, Francie. *Why the Wealthy Give: The Culture of Elite Philanthropy*. Princeton: Princeton University Press, 1995.

Paris, Erna. *Jews: An Account of Their Experience in Canada*. Toronto: Macmillan, 1980.

Patrias, Carmela and Ruth A. Frager. "'This is our country, these are our rights': Minorities and the Origins of Ontario's Human Rights Campaigns." *Canadian Historical Review* 82:1 (March 2001), 1–35.

Phillips, Nathan. *Mayor of All the People*. Toronto: McClelland & Stewart, 1967.

Pfeifer, Mark Edward. "'Community', Adaption and the Vietnamese in Toronto." PhD dissertation: Toronto, 1999.

Raben, Harvey. "Bringing Order to Chaos: The Centralization of Jewish Education in Ontario." *Canadian Jewish Historical Society Journal* 10:1 (fall 1988), 34–45.

– "History of the Board of Jewish Education in Toronto: A Study of Autonomy and Control." EdD dissertation: Toronto, 1992.

Reitz, Jeffery G. and R. Breton. *The Illusion of Difference: Realities of Ethnicity in Canada and the United States.* Toronto: C.D. Howe Institute, 1994.

Rome, David. *Clouds in the Thirties: On Antisemitism in Canada.* 13 Volumes. Montreal: Canadian Jewish Congress, 1977–82.

Rooke, P.T. and R.L Schnell. *No Bleeding Heart: Charlotte Whitton, A Feminist on the Right.* Vancouver: University of British Columbia Press, 1987.

Rosenberg, Louis. *Canada's Jews: A Social and Economic Study of Jews in Canada in the 1930s.* Edited by Morton Weinfeld. Montreal and Kingston: McGill-Queen's University Press, 1993.

– "Jewish Mutual Benefit Friendly Societies in Toronto," 1945. Manuscript article in Louis Rosenberg Papers.

– "A Study of the Changes in Geographic Distribution of the Jewish Population in the Metropolitan Area of Toronto, 1851–1951." In *Canadian Jewish Population Studies* 3 (1954), 1–25.

Ross, Murray G. with Ben Lappin. *Community Organization: Theory, Principles, and Practice.* New York: Harper and Row, 1967.

Sachar, Howard M. *The Course of Modern Jewish History.* New York: Dell, 1958.

Samuel, Sigmund. *In Return: The Autobiography of Sigmund Samuel.* Toronto: University of Toronto Press, 1963.

Saunders, Leslie Howard. *An Orangeman in Public Life: The Memoirs of Leslie Howard Saunders.* Toronto: Britannia Printers, 1980.

Scharf, Fred. "Beatrice Street and the Pits Gang" in Sharp, Rosalie, Irving Abella, and Edwin Goodman. *Growing Up Jewish: Canadians Tell Their Own Stories.* Toronto: McClelland & Stewart, 1997, 91–99.

Scheinberg, Stephen J. "From Self-Help to National Advocacy: The Emergence of Community Activisim." In Klein, Ruth and Frank Dimant (eds.). *From Immigration to Integration: The Canadian Jewish Experience. A Millenium Edition.* Toronto: Malcolm Lester/Institute for International Affairs of B'nai Brith, 2001, 52–63.

Schick, Abel (ed.) *History of the B'nai Brith in Eastern Canada.* Montreal: Apex Press, 1964.

Schmidt, Alvin J. *Fraternal Organizations.* Westport: Greenwood, 1980.

Schottland, C.J. "Proceedings of the National Conference of Jewish Social Welfare Agencies. Washington DC, 28–31 May 1938." *Jewish Social Service Quarterly* 15:1 (September 1938), 38–44.

Seeley, Robert, Buford Junker, R. Wallace Jones, and N. C. Jenkins. *Community Chest: A Case Study in Philanthropy.* Oxford: Transaction Press, 1989.

- Alexander Sim, and E. W. Loosely. *Crestwood Heights: A Study of the Culture of Suburban Life.* Toronto: University of Toronto Press, 1956.
Shapiro, David H. *From Philanthropy to Activism: The Political Transformation of American Zionism in the Holocaust Years, 1933–1945.* Oxford: Pergamon, 1994.
Shapiro, Shmuel Myer. *The Rise of the Toronto Jewish Community.* Toronto: Now and Then Books, 2010.
- "The Rise of the Toronto Jewish Community: The Reminiscences of S.M. Shapiro," *Polyphony* 6:1 (spring/summer 1984), 59–64.
Sklare, Marshall. *Conservative Judaism: An American Religious Movement.* New York: Schocken, 1972.
Sohn, Herbert A. "Human Rights in Ontario: The Role of the Community." *Journal of the Canadian Jewish Historical Society* 4:2 (fall 1980), 100–16.
Speisman, Stephen A. "Anti-Semitism in Ontario: The Twentieth Century." In Davies, Alan (ed.). *Anti-Semitism in Canada: History and Interpretation.* Waterloo: Wilfrid Laurier University Press, 1992, 113–33.
- *The Jews of Toronto: A History to 1937.* Toronto: McClelland & Stewart, 1979.
- "The Jews of Toronto." PhD dissertation, Toronto, 1975.
Splane, Richard B. *Social Welfare in Ontario, 1791–1893.* Toronto: University of Toronto Press, 1965.
Srebrnik, Henry. "Red Star Over Birobidzhan: Canadian Jewish Communists and the 'Jewish Autonomous Region' in the Soviet Union," *Labour/Le Travail* 44, 1999: 129–47.
Strong, Margaret Kirkpatrick. *Public Welfare Administration in Canada.* Chicago: University of Chicago Press, 1930.
Tittle, Diana. *Rebuilding Cleveland: The Cleveland Foundation and Its Evolving Urban Strategy.* Columbus: Ohio State University Press, 1992.
Toronto Public Library. "Toronto: A Place of Meeting: 10,000 Years of Virtual History, 1791–1839" at http://ve.torontopubliclibrary.ca/TPM/sec2.html (15 July 2005).
Troper, Harold. "Canada and the Survivors of the Holocaust: The Crisis of the Displaced Persons" in *She'erit Hapletah, 1944–48 Rehabilitation and Political Struggle. Proceedings of the Sixth Yad Vashem Conference, Jerusalem, 1985.* Guttman, Yisrael and Avital Saf (eds.). Jerusalem: Yad Vashem, 1990.
- "Jews and Canadian Immigration Policy, 1900–1950." In Moses Rischin (ed.). *The Jews of North America.* Detroit: Wayne State University Press, 1987, 44–56.

- "New Horizons in a New Land: Jewish Immigration in Canada." In Klein, Ruth and Frank Dimant (eds.). *From Immigration to Integration: The Canadian Jewish Experience: A Millennium Edition.* Toronto: Malcolm Lester/Institute for International Affairs of B'nai Brith, 2001, 3–18.
Tulchinsky, Gerald. *Branching Out: The Transformation of the Canadian Jewish Community.* Toronto: Stoddart, 1998.
- *Canada's Jews: A People's Journey.* Toronto: University of Toronto Press, 2008.
- *Taking Root: The Orgins of the Canadian Jewish Community.* Toronto: Lester Publishing, 1993.
Ungerman, Irving. "Fighting My Way Up." In Sharp, Rosalie, Irving Abella, and Edwin Goodman. *Growing Up Jewish: Canadians Tell Their Own Stories.* Toronto: McClelland & Stewart, 1997, 119–25.
Wade, Jill. "Wartime Housing Limited, 1941–47: Canadian Housing Policy at the Crossroads," *Urban History Review* 15:1 (June 1986), 41–59.
Walker, James W. St. G. *"Race," Rights and Law in the Supreme Court of Canada.* Toronto: Osgoode Society for Canadian Legal History and Wilfrid Laurier Press, 1997.
Weinfeld, Morton. *Like Everyone Else ... but Different: The Paradoxical Success of Canadian Jews.* Toronto: McClelland & Stewart, 2001.
Wiebe, Robert H. *The Search for Order, 1877–1920.* Toronto: HarperCollins, 1967.
Willinsky, A.T. *A Doctor's Memoirs.* London: Macmillan, 1961.
Wyman, David S. *The Abandonment of the Jews: America and the Holocaust, 1941–1945.* New York: Pantheon, 1985.
- *Paper Walls: America and the Refugee Crisis, 1938–1941.* New York: Pantheon, 1985.
Young, William R. "Chauvinism and Canadianism: Canadian Ethnic Groups and the Failure of Wartime Information." In Hillmer, Norman, Bohdan Kordan, and Lubomir Luciuk. *On Guard for Thee: War, Ethnicity, and the Canadian State, 1939–1945.* Ottawa: Canadian Committee for the History of the Second World War, 1988.
- "Making the Truth Graphic: the Canadian Government's Home Front Information, Structure and Programmes during World War II." PhD dissertation, University of British Columbia, 1978.

Periodicals

Yiddisher Zhurnal (Toronto), 1933–48
Canadian Jewish Chronicle (Montreal), 1933–48
Kanada Adler (Montreal), 1933–34

Index

Actions Committee, 119–24
Allen, Gurston, 258
Allen, Jule J., 26, 50
Altschul, Harold, 171–3
American Jewish Committee, 29, 35, 113–14, 137
American Jewish Congress (AJC), 29, 49, 110–16
Anti-Nazi Consumer League, 133
Anti-Semitism, xxvii, xxx, 7–9, 31–49, 54–8, 77, 109–16, 120–4, 137, 145–6, 151, 176, 178, 182, 208, 219, 253, 274, 277
Aplin, Tom, 244, 250–1
Associated Jewish Charities, 25
Atkins, Dr John, 103

B'nai Brith, 8, 49, 110–15, 118–19, 134–7, 145, 182, 198, 247, 270
Belkin, Simon, 40
Bennett, A.B., 30, 37, 45–6, 48, 50, 54, 56–67, 89, 91, 129–38, 143, 148–51, 182–83, 196, 279
Bennett, W.B., 33, 89, 92
Bialystock, Franklin, 245
Blair, Frederick, C., 85, 88, 101, 180

Borochov School, 214, 216–17
Boycott Committee, 111, 117, 133
boycott, 16, 42, 49–50, 56, 110–13, 117, 123–5, 133–4, 138–9
Brickner, Rabbi Barnett, 63, 82, 155
Brodey, Dr. Abraham, 82, 85–107
Brown, Alexander, 118, 144, 314n99

Caiserman, Hannaniah Meir 30, 35–41, 44–8, 51–4, 56–8, 107–19, 123–39, 144–51, 175–82, 188, 195–6, 198, 253, 276
Canadian Committee for Jewish Refugees (CCJR), 185
Canadian Community Chest, 205
Canadian Fur Commission (CFC), 251
Canadian Jewish Chronicle, 36, 56, 236, 240
Canadian Jewish Committee for Refugees (CJCR)
Canadian Jewish Congress (CJC), xvi, 28, 30, 33, 35–6, 71, 78–9, 106–7, 109, 114–15, 122, 128, 135–6, 153, 168, 175–8, 187, 195, 270, 276, First Plenary (1933),

49–50, 54, 92, 110–11, 114–15, 126
Canadian Legion, 194
Canadian National Committee on Refugees (CNCR), 185
Canadian Olympic Committee, 141
Canadian Overseas Garment Commission (COGC), 141, 246, 250
Catzman, Fred, 45, 111, 272
Children's Aid Society of Toronto (CAS), 63, 70
Christie Pits Riot, 44, 121, 127
Cohen, Arthur, 50, 53, 166
Cohen, Oscar, 50, 116, 137, 149, 175–6, 179, 193, 195
Cohn, Abraham, 159, 161
Cohn, Martin, xx, xxvi, 62, 79, 107, 131, 143, 162, 169, 200, 210, 222, 275, 283
Communists, 34–5, 39, 47, 132, 134, 140–1, 143, 191, 193, 275, 281

De Sola, Clarence, 29–30
"Downtown" Jews, xxii–xxvii, 16–17, 22, 25, 29–30, 32, 38, 47, 50, 72, 89, 113, 115, 121, 127, 129, 144, 156, 167, 183, 231, 275
Dunkelman, David, 42, 50, 161, 171, 275

Eisendrath, Rabbi Maurice, 38, 40, 45–8, 50, 53–8, 112, 114–20, 122–4, 127, 129, 131–4, 136, 139, 141, 143, 146–7, 149, 183–4, 192–3, 275, 281, 294nn15, 16
Eitz Chaim Talmud Torah, 20, 155, 168, 170, 203, 217–18
Enkin, Max, 239, 242, 243, 251

Factor, Samuel, 45, 50
Fair Employment Practices Act (FEPA), 270, 272–4, 278
Family Welfare Bureau (FWB), 64–7, 69, 71–3, 75, 174, 182, 184
Farband (Federation of Polish Jews), 148, 173, 188–90
Federation of Jewish Philanthropies (FJP), 26–8, 34, 47, 59–78, 79, 89, 92, 103, 105, 106–7, 109, 126, 130, 131–2, 143, 144, 153, 159, 162, 165–6, 168, 169, 202, 203, 210, 213, 235, 280–2
Federman, Max, 251, 253
Feinberg, Rabbi Abraham, 272, 275
Finkleman, Professor, 272
Frankel, Egmont, 46, 47, 50, 53, 116, 118, 124, 127–32, 184
Freiman, Archie, 34, 81, 118, 127, 135, 170, 176, 186, 264, 265, 276, 293n9
Frost, Leslie, 273–4
Furriers' Project, 229, 237, 249, 250–3, 254, 255, 256–7, 260, 271

Gelber, Moses, 157, 167, 171, 334n115
Glass, John J., 37, 45, 50, 115, 124, 133, 143, 270
Godfrey, Samuel, 137–8, 160, 167–9, 171, 173, 195
Goel Tzedec Synagogue, 16–17, 19, 20, 22, 25, 26, 27, 28, 26, 27, 45, 49, 50, 59, 82, 92, 154, 218, 275
Goldstick, Morris, 37–8, 45, 50–1, 53–4, 56, 103, 116–17, 129, 133, 144

Gordon, Rabbi Jacob, 16, 154
Grand, Solomon, 228, 238, 242, 244, 248, 249, 253
Gutstadt, Richard ("Dick"), 112, 114–15, 134, 135

Hayes, Saul, 185, 195–9, 208, 209, 218, 220–2, 226, 228–39, 230–32, 237–8, 241, 242, 244–6, 248–9, 254–5, 257–60, 262–3, 266, 267, 271, 276, 277, 325n13, 334n117
Heaps, Abraham A., 81, 88
Hebrew National Association (Folks Farein), 29, 59, 65, 66, 96 167, 168, 184, 243, 244, 248
Henry, George S., 122–3
Hermant, Percy, 144, 171, 274
Holy Blossom Temple, 7, 8, 9, 10, 12, 13, 17, 18, 19–20, 22, 23, 25, 26, 27, 28, 34, 38, 43, 47, 49 50, 51, 59, 62, 63, 70, 74, 82, 114, 116, 144, 153, 166, 167, 168, 215–16, 218, 272, 273, 280, 281
Howe, Clarence D., 239, 242
Hutner, Florence, 174, 202, 246, 258, 271, 274

Immigration, 4, 6, 7, 12, 15, 18, 21, 22, 31, 33, 78, 79–108, 115, 130, 135, 164, 178–80, 181–5, 198, 209, 219–62, 271–6; see also Furriers' Project, Jewish Immigrant Aid Society (JIAS), Orphans' Project, Tailors' Project
International Ladies Garment Workers Union (ILGWU), 16, 39

Jacobs, Samuel W., 81, 83, 85, 88, 129, 181, 299n5

Jewish Children's Home (JCH) 69–71, 73–5, 77
Jewish Child Welfare Association (JCWA), 202
Jewish Educational Community Institute of Toronto (JECIT), 160
Jewish Family and Child Services (JFCS), 203, 209, 224–7, 231, 233, 236, 355, 256, 258, 261–2, 277
Jewish Family Welfare Bureau (JFWB), 75–6, 202, 224
Jewish Immigrant Aid Society (JIAS), 30, 31, 41, 79–108, 109, 126, 131, 168, 170, 171, 179, 180, 182, 184–5, 198, 208, 219, 220, 221–2, 223, 228, 229, 241–2, 243–4, 245, 246–7, 251, 253, 256–7, 261, 262, 264, 276, 282
Jewish Labour Committee (JLC), 188, 237, 239, 250, 271, 273, 277–8
Jewish National Workers School, 20, 218
Jewish Standard (newspaper), 50, 57, 116, 120, 149
Jewish Times (newspaper), 14, 19
Jewish Vocational Service (JVS), 226, 246, 251, 252, 260
Jewish Women's League, 49, 50, 110–11, 124
Joint Distribution Committee (JDC), 41, 88, 96, 130, 168, 186, 187, 189–90, 214, 254, 277
Joint Public Relations Committee (JPRC), 136, 143, 150, 162, 182, 192, 193, 270, 272, 273–4, 277–8
Junction Shul, xvii, 156

Kaplansky, Kalman, 271–2
Kesher shel Barzel Society, 8

King, William Lyon Mackenzie, 15, 83, 178, 219, 220
Kraicer, Manny, 198, 241
Kronick, Samuel, 222, 334n115

Labour Relations Act (1954), 274
Lappin, Ben, 64, 205, 235, 251, 252, 254–5, 257, 258, 259–60
Laskin, Professor Bora, 272
League for the Defense of Jewish Rights, 36, 47
Luftspring, Sammy, 141–3, 313n91, 92, 314n94

Macleod, Alistair, 270
Monson, Rabbi David, 191, 236
Morris Winchevsky School, 218
Mount Sinai Hospital, 65, 86, 92, 126, 145, 168, 170, 200–1, 203, 207, 215, 263, 268

Nordheimer, Abraham, 5, 6
Nordheimer, Joseph, 5, 6

Oelbaum, Joseph I., 272
Olympic boycott campaign (1936), 138–45
Organization for Rehabilitation through Training (ORT), 41, 130, 168
Orphans' Project, 221–37, 240, 245, 254, 260, 262, 277

Palevsky, Mary, 260
Palevsky Report, 260–3, 267
Paull, A.J., 88–108, 198
Phillips, Nathan, 50, 269, 274
Pierce, Sydney, 185
Posluns, Samuel, 238

Price, Rabbi Abraham, 217
Pullan, Elias, 37, 45, 50, 53

Rabinoff, George, 162–4, 166, 174
Racial Discrimination Act (1944), 270
Robinson, Benjamin, 90–108, 184, 221–2
Roger, Otto B., 119, 125, 127, 128–30, 133, 135–6, 138, 143–5, 148, 150
Rosenberg, Louis, 55, 57

Sachs, Rabbi Samuel, 36, 37, 48, 50, 51, 53, 54, 117, 131, 133, 281
Sadowski, Ben, 166–8, 169, 171, 173, 203, 248, 255–6, 263, 274, 334n115
Salsberg, Joseph B., 66, 193, 270
Salvation Army, 194, 205, 206
Scheuer, Edmond, 19, 26, 46–7
School of Social Work, University of Toronto, 62, 275
Shaar Hashomayim Congregation (Montreal), 35, 38
Shaarei Shomayim Synagogue (Toronto), 191, 216, 218
Shane, Bernard, 239, 240, 271
Shapiro, Samuel Meir, 35, 37, 45, 48, 50–1, 53, 56, 57, 92–3, 96, 103, 116, 129, 131, 133, 144, 184, 188
Shane, Bernard, 239, 240, 271
Siegal, Ida, 48, 133
Silcox, Claris, 185
Singer, Fred, 45, 50, 123
Singer, Joseph, 84, 85–6, 300n10
Solkin, Maurice, 96–108, 109, 179, 198, 221–2, 244–5
Speisman, Stephen A., 6, 13, 47, 70, 78, 127

steamship agents, 81–2, 84–5, 86, 88, 90–1, 93, 95, 96, 97, 99, 102, 103, 106, 179, 180, 219
Stern, Rabbi Harry, 38, 39

Tailors' Project, 237–50, 251, 252, 261, 271
Toronto Hebrew Free School (Brunswick Talmud Torah), 77–8, 96, 126, 145, 153–62, 168, 216, 218
Tulchinsky, Gerald, 33, 91

United Community Chest, 205, 210, 212, 278
United Jewish Refugee Agencies (UHRA), 221–3, 226, 228–9, 230, 241, 255–9, 262
United Jewish Refugee and War Relief Agencies (UJRWRA), 196–8, 209, 214
United Jewish Welfare Fund (UJWF) 105, 168–76, 177, 180, 182, 184, 186–8, 189–90, 192, 194–214, 215–19, 221–2, 224, 225, 229–30, 246, 247, 248, 251, 255, 257, 259, 260, 262, 263–7, 267–8
United Palestine Appeal (UPA), 168, 170, 176, 186–7, 215, 263–7, 275
University of Toronto, 28, 62–3, 66, 166, 225, 272
"Uptown" Jews, xxii–xxvii, 16, 73, 107, 115–16, 121–2, 156, 160, 167, 183, 208, 273, 275, 278, 282

Vise, Bernard, 160–2, 166, 171

Wilensky, Dora, 66, 69, 72–4, 76, 225–6, 227–8, 273

Yack, "Baby" (Benjamin Norman Yakubowitz), 141–4
Yeshivat Torat Chaim, see Rabbi Price
Yiddisher Zhurnal (newspaper), 26, 35, 37–8, 57, 73, 82, 85–6, 89, 92, 96, 97, 103, 116, 129, 147, 184, 189, 281

Zacks, Samuel J., 221, 222, 264–5, 274
Zionist Organization of Canada (ZOC) 37, 53, 117–18, 126, 127, 130, 135, 186, 190, 198, 264–8, 276, 282